THE **COMPLETE**
IDIOT'S
GUIDE® TO

The GED 5-Subject Crash Course

by Del Franz, Phyllis Dutwin, Richard Ku, Kathleen Peno, and Courtney Mayer

ALPHA

A member of Penguin Group (USA) Inc.

ALPHA BOOKS

Published by Penguin Group (USA) Inc.

Penguin Group (USA) Inc., 375 Hudson Street, New York, New York 10014, USA • Penguin Group (Canada), 90 Eglinton Avenue East, Suite 700, Toronto, Ontario M4P 2Y3, Canada (a division of Pearson Penguin Canada Inc.) • Penguin Books Ltd., 80 Strand, London WC2R 0RL, England • Penguin Ireland, 25 St. Stephen's Green, Dublin 2, Ireland (a division of Penguin Books Ltd.) • Penguin Group (Australia), 250 Camberwell Road, Camberwell, Victoria 3124, Australia (a division of Pearson Australia Group Pty. Ltd.) • Penguin Books India Pvt. Ltd., 11 Community Centre, Panchsheel Park, New Delhi—110 017, India • Penguin Group (NZ), 67 Apollo Drive, Rosedale, North Shore, Auckland 1311, New Zealand (a division of Pearson New Zealand Ltd.) • Penguin Books (South Africa) (Pty.) Ltd., 24 Sturdee Avenue, Rosebank, Johannesburg 2196, South Africa • Penguin Books Ltd., Registered Offices: 80 Strand, London WC2R 0RL, England

Copyright © 2012 by Del Franz, Phyllis Dutwin, Richard Ku, Kathleen Peno, and Courtney Mayer

International Standard Book Number: 978-1-61564-141-3
Library of Congress Catalog Card Number: 2011943382

14   13   12   8 7 6 5 4 3 2 1

Interpretation of the printing code: The rightmost number of the first series of numbers is the year of the book's printing; the rightmost number of the second series of numbers is the number of the book's printing. For example, a printing code of 12-1 shows that the first printing occurred in 2012.

Printed in the United States of America

Note: This publication contains the opinions and ideas of its authors. It is intended to provide helpful and informative material on the subject matter covered. It is sold with the understanding that the authors and publisher are not engaged in rendering professional services in the book. If the reader requires personal assistance or advice, a competent professional should be consulted.

The authors and publisher specifically disclaim any responsibility for any liability, loss, or risk, personal or otherwise, which is incurred as a consequence, directly or indirectly, of the use and application of any of the contents of this book.

Most Alpha books are available at special quantity discounts for bulk purchases for sales promotions, premiums, fund-raising, or educational use. Special books, or book excerpts, can also be created to fit specific needs. For details, write: Special Markets, Alpha Books, 375 Hudson Street, New York, NY 10014.

Publisher: *Marie Butler-Knight*

Associate Publisher: *Mike Sanders*

Executive Managing Editor: *Billy Fields*

Executive Acquisitions Editor: *Lori Cates Hand*

Development Editor: *Lynn Northrup*

Senior Production Editor: *Janette Lynn*

Copy Editor: *Amy Borrelli*

Cover Designer: *Kurt Owens*

Book Designers: *William Thomas, Rebecca Batchelor*

Indexer: *Brad Herriman*

Layout: *Ayanna Lacey*

Senior Proofreader: *Laura Caddell*

ALWAYS LEARNING   PEARSON

Contents

Introduction

Are you thinking about taking the GED Tests? Or have you already made that decision and are beginning to review and prepare for the tests? Or maybe you've already taken one or all of the GED Tests, but need a little help getting a passing score when you retake them? Whatever stage you are at now, this book will help you move forward and get to the next level so you can accomplish your educational goals.

Passing the GED Tests provides proof of achieving the level of education equivalent to a high school diploma. So if you missed out on getting a high school diploma for whatever reason, now's your chance to get one. This can be an important step to getting a better job, moving ahead in your career, or even getting further education beyond high school if you want. Getting a GED can also build your confidence and help you gain more respect from others.

So if you're on a path that leads towards passing the GED Tests, you've made a smart decision.

How This Book Can Help

If you've decided you need to review the knowledge and practice the skills you'll need to pass the GED Tests, you've made another smart decision. The tests are no easy walk in the park; only about two thirds of those with high school diplomas can pass them. This book provides a crash course for each of the five subject areas covered on the GED Tests. It reviews the skills you need to master. This book also provides realistic practice questions similar to the questions on the actual GED Tests. Review and practice will improve your chances of passing each of the GED Tests.

The Complete Idiot's Guide to the GED 5-Subject Crash Course starts at square one and moves forward in a simple, straightforward manner to help keep you from getting lost or confused along the way. The book is broken down into 33 chapters, making it easy to find what you're looking for, work through each chapter, plot your progress, and complete your preparation before test day. While this book is easy to use, it's focused on serious learning. It won't show you an easy way to try to "beat" the tests, but it will help you develop the knowledge and practice the skills you need to pass the GED Tests. Admittedly, we're a little biased, but choosing this book may be yet another smart decision that you've made.

How This Book Is Organized

The Complete Idiot's Guide to the GED 5-Subject Crash Course is designed to be flexible and adaptable to different needs. You can work through it from beginning to end, or you can prioritize and focus first on the areas where you feel less confident. Develop your own plan and use this book in the way that makes sense to you.

For ease of use, this book is divided into five parts:

Part 1, Language Arts: Writing, is divided into seven review chapters designed to help you develop the writing skills that will be tested on in the multiple-choice test, including identifying nouns, verbs, and other parts of a sentence; using parts of speech; using punctuation; and writing paragraphs.

Part 2, Social Studies, reviews five subject areas: U.S. history, U.S. government, economics, world history, and geography.

Part 3, Science, is drawn from life science, physical science (physics and chemistry), and earth and space science. The six review chapters cover these areas and provide a basic understanding of science and scientific inquiry.

Part 4, Language Arts: Reading, evaluates reading comprehension and interpretation skills. The five review chapters focus on different types of reading: nonfiction and fiction, including poetry, drama, and prose.

Part 5, Math, covers four major areas: number operations and number sense; measurement and geometry; data analysis, statistics, and probability; and algebra functions and patterns. It also includes a chapter on taking the Math Test.

Parts 1–5 each contain a final chapter that provides a half-length practice test containing questions that reflect those on the actual tests. Don't skip these chapters! They allow you to learn more about the types of questions you'll encounter and to practice test-taking strategies and pacing. They will also give you a sense of how well you are doing and whether or not you need further review and practice.

Extras

Throughout this book you'll find definitions, cautions, tips, and other good-to-know information set off in sidebars. There are four types of these, each providing something extra that you can really use:

DEFINITION

These sidebars clarify and define words, giving you a better understanding of important terms you may encounter on the GED Tests.

HEADS UP!

These sidebars provide cautions to help you steer clear of trouble when studying for and taking the GED Tests.

GOOD IDEA

These sidebars are tip-offs to proven strategies or actions you can take to do better on the tests.

IN THE KNOW

These sidebars provide key information that will help you understand the subject content and do better on the tests.

But Wait! There's More!

Have you logged on to idiotsguides.com lately? If you haven't, go there now! As a bonus to the book, we've provided realistic practice questions similar to the questions on the actual GED Tests. Review and practice will improve your chances of passing each of the GED Tests. You'll definitely want to check them out, all online at idiotsguides.com/gedcrashcourse.

Here you'll also find bonus chapters to enhance your understanding of the book. These chapters are dedicated to helping you do well on the GED essay. These chapters walk you through the steps of planning what you will write about; crafting an effective introduction, body, and conclusion; and proofreading and editing your work.

Point your browser to idiotsguides.com/gedcrashcourse, and enjoy!

Acknowledgments

Many people have helped and supported the authors in this project. We especially wish to thank the development editor, Lynn Northrup, for her constructive suggestions and careful editing of this book. In addition, the editorial team at Alpha Books has done an excellent job in resolving problems along the way and producing this book; our thanks to Lori Cates Hand, Janette Lynn, and Amy Borrelli. Finally, Richard Ku would like to thank his wife Doreen for her support and encouragement.

Trademarks

All terms mentioned in this book that are known to be or are suspected of being trademarks or service marks have been appropriately capitalized. Alpha Books and Penguin Group (USA) Inc. cannot attest to the accuracy of this information. Use of a term in this book should not be regarded as affecting the validity of any trademark or service mark.

Language Arts: Writing

Part

1

The seven review chapters in Part 1 cover the structure of sentences in English; the part of speech (e.g., nouns and verbs), with a particular focus on verb tense; common errors in using parts of speech; grammar and punctuation, including many of the errors often made in punctuation; and the correct way to write paragraphs.

The language arts practice test at the end of this part helps you use all you've learned. Most of the questions on the GED ask you to use writing, grammar, and language skills in practical ways. You are presented with a document (often a letter, memo, or email) and asked to find errors in grammar, punctuation, sentence construction, and meaning, and to choose the correct fix. The questions on this test are all multiple choice and provide you with the correct fix as one of the choices. This test will also ask you to restructure paragraphs for the clearest meaning, again through multiple choice.

Note: For help in planning and writing your GED essay, point your browser to idiotsguides.com/gedcrashcourse and review the four bonus chapters found there. They will take you step by step through the process of creating an effective and high-scoring essay.

The English Sentence Revealed

In This Chapter

- Overview of complete sentences, subject and verb, agreement between subject and verb, and avoiding fragments, run-on, and comma fault sentences
- GED-like questions to practice the skills you'll be tested on
- Answers and explanations for all the questions

Most of us have daily reasons to write, whether for work, for a course we're taking, or for our own personal reasons. Whatever your motive, you want to present your thoughts clearly and correctly. In fact, if you think of your writing as another way to present yourself to friends, family, and fellow workers, you'll want to use correct English.

In this chapter, you will learn many of the secrets of creating a complete thought. Your English sentences will function well if you remember a few basic rules about creating complete thoughts.

The Foundation of the English Sentence: Subject and Verb

Your reader might not find these two-word sentences interesting, but if you wrote them, you would, in fact, be correct:

1. Sara cooks.

2. Cars crash.

3. Stars shine.

The sentences, though short, are correct because they include the two basic elements: *subject* and *verb*.

	Subject	Verb
1.	Sara	cooks
2.	cars	crash
3.	stars	shine

DEFINITION

The **subject** of a sentence is the person, place, or thing doing or being something. The **verb** provides the action or being in the sentence.

To know if the sentence contains both a subject and a verb, ask yourself these questions:

What is happening in sentence 1? Cooking is happening. That is the action in the sentence. Who is doing the cooking? Sara is doing the cooking. She is the subject of the sentence.

When did the cooking, crashing, and shining happen—in the present or the past? All of these verbs are in the present tense. You can make simple changes to the verbs (cook, crash, shine) so that the actions took place in the past: cooked, crashed, shone.

Practice

For 1–3, practice identifying the subject (person, place, or thing) and the verb (action). They will be easier to identify if you find the action word first and then ask, "Who did it?" For example in sentence 1, what is the verb or action word? The action word is *won*. Who did it? The *team* did it—that is the subject.

1. Our team won.

2. A child fell.

3. The balloon burst.

For 4–6, punctuate the sentences correctly.

4. A complete sentence contains a subject and a verb

5. The child's mother exclaimed, "I won't argue with you about your bedtime"

6. Is it raining again

Answers

	Subject	Verb
1.	team	won
2.	child	fell
3.	balloon	burst

Of course, all sentences—no matter how simple—end with punctuation. The three sentences above all end with periods. If you write a question, of course, the sentence will end with a question mark. An exclamation point ends both a command and a strong statement. Here are some examples:

Question: How long have you been waiting?

Command: Cover your mouth when you cough!

Strong statement: Oh no! You're not leaving without me!

4. This is simply a statement of fact and requires only a period at the end.

5. The child's mother exclaimed, "I won't argue with you about your bedtime!" An exclamation point should follow the word *bedtime*. The fact that the mother exclaimed is a clue to the punctuation.

6. The sentence asks a question, so it needs a question mark.

IN THE KNOW

Punctuation has a specific place with quotation marks. Periods and commas always go inside quotation marks. Exclamation points follow the emphasized words. Read more about the rules of punctuation in later chapters.

What Makes the English Sentence a Complete Thought?

You may look at a group of words that contains the name of a person or thing and an action word. Still, it's not a complete sentence. For example:

Because the car stalled.

Car is the name of a thing and the subject. *Stalled* is an action word or verb. What happened to make this an incomplete thought? If you read the sentence aloud, you can hear that the thought is incomplete. You want to ask what happened when the car stalled. Why did it stall? The complete thought might be this:

> We rolled to the side of the road because the car stalled.

Which word in the original sentence makes the sentence incomplete? That word is *because*. It's important to see the difference between the two groups of words. The first is a common error called a *fragment*. Your writing will definitely be judged by your ability to write complete thoughts. Learn what to do and what to avoid!

 DEFINITION

A **fragment** is a sentence that is incomplete. The sentence cannot stand by itself.

Later in this chapter in the section, "Words That Make a Sentence Incomplete," you'll learn more about words such as *because*. For now, read the following sentences and complete the incomplete thoughts. Ask yourself: what's missing in the sentence, the subject or the verb?

Practice

1. A lost child.

2. Rainy to dry.

3. Picked up the apples.

Answers

There are several ways to complete each sentence. Here are some of the possibilities:

1. A lost child cried. (subject, *child*; verb, *cried*)

2. The day changed from rainy to dry. (subject, *day*; verb, *changed*)

3. The scouts picked up the apples. (subject, *scouts*; verb, *picked up*)

Avoid Run-On Sentences

Remember that too much of a good thing can be wrong as well. Sentences that go on and on without punctuation are a problem area for many people. Read this sentence:

> I left home very early I got to the beach early enough to get a good parking place it was less than a quarter mile from the ocean.

How many thoughts can you find in this sentence?

1. I left home very early 2. I got to the beach early enough to get a good parking place 3. it was less than a quarter mile from the ocean.

Obviously, there are three separate thoughts in the sentence, but they are strung together, one after the other. This is called a *run-on sentence*. Later in this section, you'll learn to build more interesting sentences with connecting words. For now, just add punctuation and capitalization to correct the run-on error:

> Because I left home very early, I got to the beach early enough to get a good parking place. The space was less than a quarter mile from the ocean.

or

> Because I left home very early, I got to the beach early enough to get a good parking place less than a quarter mile from the ocean.

 DEFINITION

A **run-on sentence** is an error in which two or more complete sentences (independent clauses) are strung together without proper punctuation.

Practice

Some of the following sentences are run-on sentences. Correct them with simple punctuation changes. You can insert a period between two complete thoughts. Or, you can use a comma and a connecting word such as *and* or *but*. Leave the correct sentences as they are. The first sentence is corrected for you.

1. My boss gave us our new schedules mine is worse than before. *Correction:* My boss gave us our new schedules, but mine is worse than before.

2. I thought I was signing up for half days, but I found out I was wrong.

3. There is a new pizza place in town we should go there for lunch someday.

4. I ran out of gas I won't be home in time for dinner.

Answers

2. Correct as is

3. There is a new pizza place in town. We should go there for lunch someday.

4. I ran out of gas, so I won't be home in time for dinner.

Comma Faults

This next sentence contains a *comma fault*. Can you explain why?

> Some computer-related injuries occur on the job, many are associated with overuse at home.

The sentence contains two complete thoughts. A comma cannot connect two complete thoughts. To correct the sentence, insert a comma and a connecting word, or separate the thoughts with a period:

> Some computer-related injuries occur on the job. Many are associated with overuse at home.

> Some computer-related injuries occur on the job, although many are associated with overuse at home.

DEFINITION

A **comma fault** occurs when you string complete thoughts together with commas. A complete thought needs to end in a period or be connected to another thought with a semicolon or comma plus connecting word.

Practice

Look for fragments, run-ons, and comma faults in paragraph 1. Insert punctuation or correct marks where needed.

Paragraph 1:

(A) Having many questions about health-care coverage and retirement funds as well. (B) Ask about continued benefits while you look for a job, any company that interviews you should be able to answer your questions, finding a job you'll be ready to pick up your protection.

In paragraph 2, rewrite fragments to make complete sentences. Look for comma faults and run-on sentences and separate them into complete thoughts.

Paragraph 2:

(A) There are many safety issues linked to children's clothing, flammability is a primary concern, that's why federal regulations were written. (B) The law says that sleepwear for children 9 months or older must be flame resistant or snug fitting that's because 300 child-burn injuries are treated in emergency rooms yearly.

For each question, decide which is the best way to write the underlined portion of paragraph 3.

Paragraph 3:

(A) At work, I learned that I had <u>a one-week vacation the only</u> condition was that I had to take it before August 1. (B) <u>When we bought airplane tickets</u> for Disneyland on a flight that leaves at 7:30 A.M. (C) <u>Having to set our alarm</u> for 4 A.M. in order to get to the airport in time. (D) <u>Rushing and making it through security just in time.</u> We collapsed into our seats once we were on the plane.

1. What correction should be made to the underlined portion of sentence A?

   (1) a one-week vacation that the only

   (2) a one-week vacation so the only

   (3) a one-week vacation. The only

   (4) a one-week vacation of which the only

   (5) a one-week vacation after which the only

2. What correction should be made to the underlined portion of sentence B?

    (1) Buying airplane tickets

    (2) Having bought airplane tickets

    (3) Since buying airplane tickets

    (4) We bought airplane tickets

    (5) Because of buying airplane tickets

3. What correction should be made to the underlined portion of sentence C?

    (1) We had to set our alarm

    (2) We were having to set our alarm

    (3) When we have to set our alarm

    (4) Since setting our alarm

    (5) While setting our alarm

4. What correction should be made to sentence D to make it complete?

    (1) While rushing and making it through security just in time.

    (2) Since rushing through security just in time.

    (3) After rushing and making it through security just in time.

    (4) Because we rushed, we were able to make it through security just in time.

    (5) Although rushing and making it through security just in time.

Answers

Paragraph 1:

Sentence A is a fragment. When a sentence begins with an *ing* verb *(Having)*, you need to be especially careful to complete the thought. What the writer meant here was this:

> If you lose your job, you'll have many questions about health-care coverage and retirement funds as well.

Sentence B is a comma fault. There are three thoughts all combined with commas. Create three separate and complete thoughts instead:

> Ask about continued benefits while you look for a job. Any company that interviews you should be able to answer your questions. When you finally find a job, you'll be ready to pick up your protection.

Here's the rewritten paragraph:

> If you lose your job, you'll have many questions about health-care coverage and retirement funds as well. Ask about continued benefits while you look for a job. Any company that interviews you should be able to answer your questions. When you finally find a job, you'll be ready to pick up your protection.

Paragraph 2:

Sentence A contains a comma fault. Correct it by changing the comma to a period:

> There are many safety issues linked to children's clothing.

Correct the run-on sentence with a comma and a connecting word *and*:

> Flammability is a primary concern, and that's why federal regulations were written.

Sentence B is a run-on sentence. Correct with a period and capital letter:

> The law says that sleepwear for children 9 months or older must be flame resistant or snug fitting. That's because 300 child-burn injuries are treated in emergency rooms yearly.

An even better sentence would be:

> Because 300 child-burn injuries are treated in emergency rooms yearly, the law says that sleepwear for children 9 months or older must be flame resistant or snug fitting.

Paragraph 3:

1. **(3)** As it stands in the paragraph, this is a run-on sentence. There are two complete ideas run together with no punctuation to show where one ends and the other one begins. The correct answer inserts a period between the two complete thoughts.

2. **(4)** The word *When* makes the sentence incomplete. Delete it, and the sentence has a clear subject *(We)* and verb *(bought)*.

3. **(1)** *Having* makes the sentence incomplete. Correct it by substituting *We had to*.

4. **(4)** The original sentence has no subject. The addition of a subject, *we*, makes it correct. None of the other answers solves that problem.

Words That Make a Sentence Incomplete

The words *when, before, because, since, as soon as, while, although,* and *as* are *conjunctions,* or connecting words. If you start a sentence with one of these words or phrases, be sure you complete the thought. For example:

Incomplete thought: When I last saw Jason. Complete thought: When I last saw Jason, we had a big disagreement.

Practice

Read the following examples of incomplete thoughts. How would you finish them? The first one is done for you.

1. Because I like that teacher so much. *Correction:* Because I like that teacher so much, I'm taking the other course she teaches.

2. Since our train left at noon

3. While you slept

4. Before my parents gave me an allowance

Answers

There are many ways to finish these sentences. Here are some of the possible ways. The important thing is to recognize that an introductory group of words or clause (for example, *when you go to work*) needs a completing thought.

2. Since our train left at noon, we brought lunch with us.

3. While you slept, I finished cleaning the basement.

4. Before my parents gave me an allowance, I had to promise to do chores.

Agreement Between Subject and Verb in Number

Among the most frequent errors in English is lack of agreement between subject and verb in number. Agreement between subject and verb in number simply means that if the subject you use is singular (one), the verb form must be singular as well. Here's an example:

> A cat chases its tail.

You know that the subject *(cat)* is singular because it does not end in *s*. This is where it gets tricky. We think of a word that ends in *s* as plural (more than one), but that is not true of a verb. A verb that ends in *s (chases)* is usually singular. See what happens when the plural subject requires a plural verb:

> Two cats chase their tails.

Cats indicates more than one cat. *Chase* is the plural form of the verb and agrees in number with *cats*.

Always be aware that subjects and verbs form their plurals differently. Is the following sentence correct? Before you answer, find the verb and then the subject.

> The nuts in the cupcake makes it so crunchy.

To decide if the subject and verb are in agreement, find the two of them first: verb *(makes)* and subject *(nuts,* plural).

If you still don't know if the verb is singular or plural, use the pronoun test. Substitute *they* for the plural subject *nuts:*

> They make it so crunchy.

You were correct not to add an *s* to the verb. It may not seem logical, but while a plural subject is spelled with an *s*, a plural verb is not spelled with an *s*.

What's the other problem you face when you choose the correct verb form in this sentence? The answer is that the subject and verb are separated by a phrase. You need to simplify the sentence in order to decide whether the verb should end in *s*. The verb form *makes* is incorrect in the following sentence:

> The nuts in the cupcake makes it so crunchy.

Which phrase would you delete in order to make this a more straightforward sentence? In other words, which words stand between the subject and verb? If you said *in the cupcake*, you are right! In order to choose the correct verb form, remove the interrupting phrase.

Practice

For 1–3, find the subject and verb in each sentence. Draw one line under the subject and two lines under the verb. Then, decide if subject and verb agree in number. Write Yes for agree and No for disagree.

1. Maia and Hector cook some delicious recipes.

2. At the senior center, volunteers helps with the activities.

3. Lemons grow in my backyard.

Now we'll add interrupting phrases to some of these sentences. For 4–6, find the verb, find the subject, and then decide if subject and verb agree.

4. Ben and Eden, and sometimes their mom, collects shells at the beach.

5. A desk and a chair, although big and heavy, fits nicely in that room.

6. The man with all the dogs walk through the park each evening.

Look for fragments, run-on sentences, and comma faults in 7–9. Correct the errors.

7. When a classroom is filled with students who have the freedom to express themselves for who they are and along with a great teacher tied in with a strong curriculum it allows us a chance to explore education deeper than ever before.

8. Diversity is a commitment to recognizing and appreciating the variety of characteristics that makes individuals unique, they represent the many ways we are different.

9. If I were to write a list of my philosophies as a teacher I would be sensitive to differences and I will understand that everybody is different and not everybody is as gifted with athleticism, but I would expect everyone to do their best.

10. Read the following paragraph to find errors in subject-verb agreement. One sentence is a fragment. Can you find it?

(A) When it comes to the classroom, there is two different aspects of diversity. (B) The first one deal with people who may have special needs, whether they are learning or physical disabilities. (C) Teachers who have a good understanding of these people's issues is sensitive to challenging problems. (D) These teachers helps make all students feel comfortable. (E) The second aspect of diversity in the classroom are all the different cultures, ethnicities, and sexual orientations we have. (F) It is important for children to admire and respect different cultures. (G) While also realizing that minority groups has been exposed to a large amount of unnecessary hostility.

Answers

	Subject	Verb	Agree?
1.	Maia and Hector	cook	Yes
2.	volunteers	helps	No

Plural *volunteers* needs a plural verb: *help*.

	Subject	Verb	Agree?
3.	Lemons	grow	Yes

4. Incorrect. The subject *(Ben and Eden)* is plural, so *collects* needs to take the plural form (no *s*), *collect*. *Correction:* Ben and Eden, and sometimes their mom, collect shells at the beach.

5. Incorrect. The subject *(A desk and a chair)* is plural, but the verb *(fits)* ends in *s*, which makes it singular. *Correction:* A desk and a chair, although big and heavy, fit nicely in that room.

6. Incorrect. The subject *(man)* is singular, but the verb *(walk)* is plural. *Correction:* The man with all the dogs walks through the park each evening.

7. The first paragraph is one long run-on sentence. Find the three major ideas and present each in its own sentence:

   There are ways we can explore education more deeply than ever before. We need classrooms in which students have the freedom to express themselves in their own distinctive voices. Along with that freedom, we need great teachers and a strong curriculum.

8. The second paragraph consists of one sentence with a comma fault. Two complete sentences were connected with a comma and no connecting word. Here is a possible correction:

   Diversity is a commitment to recognizing and appreciating the variety of characteristics that makes individuals unique. The various characteristics represent the many ways we are different.

9. In the third paragraph there is no division of ideas. With all ideas connected by *and*, it is one long run-on sentence. There are several ways to correct the paragraph. Here is one:

   If I were to write a list of my philosophies as a teacher I would first list sensitivity to differences. A teacher needs an understanding that not everybody is gifted in the same way. For example, not everybody is gifted athletically, but everyone can do his or her best.

10. (A) *Correction:* there *are* two different aspects

    Be careful of sentences that start with *there is/are* (avoid them if possible). The subject is hidden, so it's difficult to know whether the subject is singular or plural. In this sentence, the subject is *aspects*—a plural subject—so your verb needs to be plural, *are.*

    (B) *Correction:* The first one *deals*

    What is the verb? *Deal* is the verb, and it's plural. What is the subject? The subject is *one*, and it's singular. What needs to be changed? Add an *s* to *deal* to make it singular also.

    (C) *Correction:* Teachers who have a good understanding of these people's issues *are* sensitive

You may run into a problem when the subject and verb are far apart in the sentence. The verb is the singular *is*. The subject is the plural word, *teachers*. Change *is* to the plural form, *are*.

(D) *Correction:* These teachers *help*

Plural *teachers* needs a plural verb, *help*. Remember that plural verbs don't end in *s*.

(E) *Correction:* The second aspect *is*

The subject is singular, *aspect*. Change the plural verb, *are*, to the singular, *is*.

(F) is correct.

(G) This sentence has two errors. Error 1: The sentence begins with *While*, a word that makes the sentence an incomplete thought. It is a fragment. *Correction:* Add the fragment to the previous sentence:

It is important for children to admire and respect different cultures while also realizing that minority groups has been exposed to a large amount of unnecessary hostility.

Error 2: that minority groups has been

The subject *(groups)* and the verb *(has been)* don't agree. *Correction:* groups *have been* exposed

What Role Do Parts of Speech Play?

In This Chapter

- Overview of names and functions of English words
- GED-like questions to practice the skills you'll be tested on
- Answers and explanations for all the questions

A big part of writing effectively is understanding the various parts of speech and the role each plays in a sentence. In this chapter we look at the basics: nouns, pronouns, adjectives, adverbs, prepositions, and more.

English Words Have Both Name and Function

Did you know that every word in the English language has two names? Learning and understanding those names is the gateway to correct English usage.

If you've ever taken an English course or studied an English text, you probably know the term *part of speech*. Examples are noun, pronoun, and verb. These are names for words. However, as shown in the following table, each word also has a function name that tells what a word does in a sentence. Examples are subject, verb, and object.

It's much easier to grasp this idea if you see a sentence with names and functions noted:

Name

Pronoun	verb	article	adjective	noun
→	→	→	→	→
She	*mixed*	*the*	*cake*	*batter.*
→	→	→	→	→
Subject	verb desc.		desc. object	

Function

Part of Speech	Function	Examples
Noun, pronoun	Names a person, place, or thing	Leo, Captain Anderson, she, them, house
Verb	Provides the action or state of being	hit, crash, are, be
Adjective	Describes a noun	small, quiet, cold, busy
Adverb	Describes a verb or adjective	quietly, hardly, easily
Preposition	Introduces a relationship between a noun or pronoun and other words in a sentence	in, above, over, up
Conjunction	Joins words, phrases, and clauses	and, but, or, yet
Interjection	Expresses emotion	oh, hey, wow
Article	Points out a noun	the, a, an

Why do you need to understand that words have both names and functions? There is a very good reason: Correct English usage is based upon it. What if you confused the functions of words? Is there a problem, for example, if you replace the subject (noun) with the object (noun)?

Subject	object
→	→

Mateo hit the ball.

Subject   object

→   →

The ball hit Mateo.

Now, answer the question: Is there a problem if you replace the subject with the object word? Mateo says yes, because he was hit by the ball in the second sentence!

The most common error of this type occurs with pronouns. *I, you, he, she, it*, and *they* are correctly used as subjects. *Me, you, him, her, it*, and *them* are used as objects.

Nouns and pronouns may also function as objects in sentences. Instead of *performing* the action, as subjects usually do, objects *receive* the action and usually follow the verb. For example:

> He beat him at cards.

If *he* equals *Billy* and *him* equals *Mateo*, you could say *Billy beat Mateo at cards.* But here's a good question: Could you say *Mateo beat Billy at cards* and have the same meaning? No? Why?

Practice

One of the most common errors in English usage is the use of an object pronoun as the subject or a subject pronoun as the object. Find subject pronoun errors in these sentences and rewrite them correctly.

1. Me and Lee are best friends.

2. You and him share lockers, don't you?

3. The tickets were for Mickey and I. (Clue: Remove the word *Mickey* before you decide on the answer.)

Answers

1. Lee and I are best friends. *Lee and I* are the subject words. *I* is the subject pronoun. Good idea! Always put yourself second; put your friend Lee first.

2. You and he share lockers, don't you? *You* and *he* are subject pronouns.

3. The tickets were for Mickey and me. Did you use the clue? If you did, it was easy to choose the right answer: The tickets were for me. You would never say *for I*. In this sentence, the word *tickets* is the subject. *Me* is an object pronoun.

If this is still a mystery to you, keep reading for more about pronouns and their functions.

Nouns and Pronouns

As you read earlier in the chapter, nouns are the names of people, places, and things. People and places include names such as Boston, David, General Washington, and Grand Central Station. Things include pencils, computer, table, and TV.

There's one other kind of noun that's more difficult to recognize because it doesn't fall into the categories of people, or places, or things. You can't touch them or see them because they are abstract, not concrete. These are idea words or qualities, such as loyalty or determination.

GOOD IDEA

If you want to know if a word is a noun, place the word *a, an,* or *the* in front of the word; if it makes sense, it's a noun. For example: an idea, the weather, a rule, the curiosity.

Practice

Find the nouns in these sentences.

1. Send an email to confirm the party.

2. I'll buy invitations if I have time.

3. My resolution to eat more healthfully is going well so far.

Answers

1. email, party

2. invitations, time

3. resolution

You can place *a, an,* or *the* in front of any of these words; they are nouns.

Nouns and Verbs Agree in Number

In Chapter 3, you read about words being singular or plural. You need to understand how being a singular or plural noun or pronoun changes a sentence. Most nouns that end in *s* are plural, while verbs that end in *s* are singular. In a sentence, nouns and verbs must agree in number. For example:

The typical teenager loves talking to people.

Typical teenagers love talking to people.

teenager	loves
teenagers	love

What are some other ways of making a noun plural?

For words that end in *ch*, add *es:*

church	churches

Some words change their internal spelling:

child	children

Nouns that end in *y*, preceded by a consonant, usually change the *y* to *i* and add *es:*

candy	candies
city	cities

Nouns that end in *y*, preceded by a vowel, usually form the plural by adding *s:*

key	keys
boy	boys

Nouns that end in *f* or *fe* change those letters to *v* and add *es:*

life	lives
knife	knives

Practice

Find and correct any errors in the spelling of plural nouns.

1. We did endless searchs for the lost toys.

2. The people loved the senator but hated his policys.

3. After I took the cooking class, I bought a whole new set of knifes.

Answers

1. The correct spelling is *searches*. For words that end in *ch*, add *es*.

2. The correct spelling is *policies*. Nouns that end in *y*, preceded by a consonant, usually change the *y* to *i* and add *es*.

3. The correct spelling is *knives*. Nouns that end in *f* or *fe* change those letters to *v* and add *es*.

Verbs

Now we're ready to fill in the basic sentence pattern of noun and verb. You'll be able to recognize and write sentences in which subject and verb agree in number. In this exercise, start by finding the verb or action in each sentence. Then ask yourself, "Who or what did that?" Now you've found both the subject and the verb.

Practice

In each sentence, place a *v* over the verb and an *n* over the noun/subject.

1. Jackie carpools the neighborhood children to school.

2. My aunt and uncle live with us.

3. Dan cooks dinner each day.

Answers

1. Carpools (verb) Jackie (noun/subject)

2. Live (verb) aunt and uncle (plural noun/subject)

3. Cooks (verb) Dan (noun/subject)

Linking Verbs

A *linking verb*—sometimes called a *being verb* because it simply expresses a state of being—shows no action. This type of verb links the subject with a word that describes or equals a word that follows the verb. For example:

> The football team was tired after the overtime loss.

The linking verb *was* links *tired* to *team.*

> He is the president of our club.

The linking verb *is* links *He* to *president.*

The most common linking verbs are *am, are, is, was, were,* and *been.* Linking verbs also follow the rules regarding singular and plural forms: if the subject of the sentence is singular, the linking verb is singular. If the subject is plural, the linking verb is plural.

Practice

For 1–3, choose a singular or plural linking verb to complete each sentence. Notice that a pronoun stands in for a noun as subject in sentence 3.

1. Her two grandsons _____ five and eight years old.

2. Jack _____ my favorite dance partner last year.

3. I _____ sure that's my book; please return it.

For 4–6, correct the action or linking verb in each sentence.

4. You and Erin was the first to arrive.

5. The cake in my kitchen are my favorite.

6. My favorite of all flavors are chocolate.

Answers

1. Grandsons (noun/subject) *are* (linking verb)

2. Jack (noun/subject) *was* (linking verb)

3. I (pronoun/subject) *am* (linking verb)

4. The subject *(You and Erin)* is plural, so the sentence needs a plural linking verb *(were)*.

5. The subject *(cake)* is singular, so choose a singular verb *(is)*.

6. The subject *(favorite)* is singular, so choose a singular verb *(is)*.

HEADS UP!

Here's the real test of selecting correct verbs. Remember that subjects and verbs (both action and linking) must agree in number.

Adjectives and Adverbs

Adjectives and adverbs modify or describe other words. Adjectives describe nouns. Adverbs describe verbs, adjectives, and other adverbs. For example:

1. My *new* car is a *blue* Ford.

        adj.   adj.

2. The *huge* airplane took off *smoothly*.

      adj.   adv.

3. Running can be *extremely exhausting*.

          adv.   adj.

In sentence 1, *new* describes *car; blue* describes *Ford*. What does *Ford* do? It stands for or equals the subject, *car* (thanks to the linking verb *is*).

In sentence 2, *huge* describes *airplane*. *Smoothly* describes the verb and tells how the plane took off.

In sentence 3, *extremely* describes the adjective *exhausting*.

Adjectives and adverbs are easy to use correctly, except in a few special ways. What's wrong with the following sentences?

My error was seriouser than yours.

That dog is more beautifuler than mine.

To correct these sentences, add the word *more* when the adjective being compared has more than two syllables. Both *serious* and *beautiful* have more than two syllables:

> My error was more serious than yours.

> That dog is more beautiful than mine.

Adjectives can help us to compare two or more things or ideas. However, we need to add -*er* or -*est* to the end of the adjective to make the comparison among two or more things, people, or ideas. For example:

> Jan is tall. Her sister is taller. Mia is the tallest of all.

> **IN THE KNOW**
>
> Adverbs frequently end in -*ly,* so they're very easy to recognize. For example: If you clean the garage *willingly,* I'll double what I *usually* pay you. *Willingly* ends in –ly and is the adverb that describes the verb *clean.*

You recall that adverbs describe verbs (in addition to adjectives and other adverbs), and that is the case in these sentences:

> Get up *quickly* and eat breakfast *immediately.*

> The nurse wrapped the injury *neatly.*

> Format the computer document *correctly.*

Quickly describes the verb *get up*, and *immediately* describes *eat.*

Neatly describes the verb *wrapped.*

Correctly describes the verb *format.*

You can compare adverbs as well as adjectives. Once again, you need to be aware of the word's length. For example:

> One nurse wrapped the injury *neatly*, but the other nurse wrapped it *more neatly.* (Use *more neatly* instead of *neatlier.*)

Practice

Choose the correct form of the adjective or adverb in each sentence.

1. The (more slightly, more slightlier) faded wallpaper is on the north wall.

2. I dress (more simplier, more simply) than she does.

3. This is the most (efficient, efficientist) car we've ever owned.

Answers

1. slightly

2. simply

3. efficient

Conjunctions

To show relationships among thoughts, we use connecting words called conjunctions. Using connecting words adds meaning to sentences. Here are a few conjunctions that coordinate ideas: *for, and, nor, but, or, yet, so.* The acronym FANBOYS is a way to remember these words. This is how *coordinating conjunctions* work to show ideas that are equal in importance. Notice that the thoughts on each side of the comma and conjunction are both complete thoughts. Each could stand as a complete thought—a sentence:

I will bring the kayak, *and* you can bring the paddles.

The bus was very late, *so* Luis arrived tired and grumpy.

On the other hand, if you need to say that one idea is more important than the other, you use a *subordinating conjunction*, in which only one part of the sentence can stand alone as a complete thought:

You can help with dinner *if* you get back early.

Here are some subordinating conjunctions:

after	how	until
although	if	when
as if	in case	whenever
as though	in order that	where
assuming that	provided that	wherever
because	since	while
before	so that	why
even if	though	
even though	unless	

DEFINITION

Coordinating conjunctions join equals to each other: Miro ate all the pizza, *so* Juan finished the soda and dessert. **Subordinating conjunctions** join two ideas, but one is dependent upon the other: *Because* it was raining, we wore raincoats and carried an umbrella.

.Examples:

> We had water in our basement because it rained again.

Which part of this sentence can stand alone? The words before *because* form a sentence. The words *because it rained again* do not form a sentence. Do you recognize that kind of error? Yes, it's a fragment (see Chapter 1 for more about fragments).

> Since I'm ready to go, I'll warm up the car.

> Although we're early, we should leave.

Since and *Although* are the subordinating conjunctions.

Prepositions

Prepositions are small words that do a big job. They link words and phrases to each other. In effect, they act as adjectives and adverbs. Here is a partial list of common prepositions:

about	before	near
above	beside	of
after	between	on
against	for	over
along	from	under
among	in	up
around	into	with
at	like	

As you write a sentence, you may include an interrupting phrase that starts with a preposition. That's a good thing, because a preposition is a connecting word that shows a relationship between a noun and some other word in the sentence. However, the phrase that interrupts may cause you to choose an incorrect verb. This is how it happens:

> The chair and end table in the basement (is, are) from my aunt's house.

Let's figure out how this sentence might go wrong.

1. The preposition *in* shows the relationship between *the chair and end table* and *the basement.* That's correct.

2. The subject of the sentence is *chair and end table.* This is a plural subject.

3. The phrase *in the basement* separates the subject from the verb. The noun *basement* is singular, but it is not the subject of the sentence. Hopefully, it did not influence you to choose the singular verb *is.*

4. The correct choice is the word *are.*

Practice

In each sentence, find the prepositional phrase that comes between the subject and the verb. Underline the phrase. Choose the correct verb.

1. The oversized leather chair and ottoman in the attic (is, are) too big for this space.

2. One of the air conditioners (is, are) out for repair.

3. The slide with too many people at the top (are, is) going to collapse.

Answers

1. The correct answer is *are*, a plural verb. The plural verb agrees with *leather chair and ottoman*, the plural subject. Prepositional phrase is *in the attic*.

2. The correct answer is the single verb *is*, which agrees with the single subject, *one*. The prepositional phrase is *of the air conditioners*.

3. The correct answer is the singular verb *is*. The singular subject is *slide*. The prepositional phrases are *with too many people* and *at the top*.

Interjections

Interjections are words that show emotion. They frequently stand alone because they're not really related to any other words in the sentence:

Yea! I'm almost finished learning parts of speech and their functions!

Wow! That wasn't as bad as I thought it would be.

Ahh! I'm so glad you think so.

Other interjections include the following:

ahem	congratulations	gee whiz
boo	darn	phew
bravo	eek	

Practice

Underline the interjection in each sentence.

1. Yikes! I stepped on the dog's toes again!

2. Eek! I saw a mouse!

3. Phew! I thought I'd never finish, but I did!

Answers

1. _Yikes_ expresses surprise and concern.

2. _Eek_ expresses fear.

3. _Phew_ expresses relief.

Back to Verbs

In This Chapter

- Overview of verbs
- GED-like questions to practice the skills you'll be tested on
- Answers and explanations for all the questions

Verbs are key. If you understand how they work in a sentence, and, better yet, which form of a persnickety verb you should use, you're on your way to a grammatically accurate sentence that clearly conveys your meaning. Conversely, messing up the verb is one of the easiest mistakes you can make. Therefore, there are lots of verb errors that need to be spotted and corrected on the Language Arts: Writing Test. We've already reviewed what a verb is in Chapter 1. In this chapter, we'll return to verbs and make sure you understand all of their possibilities, with a particular focus on the forms of *to be*.

Remember, a verb provides the action or being in a sentence. Verbs don't describe, and they're not people, places, things, or ideas. They're the motor of the sentence!

Verb Tenses

Verbs change their form in sentences so that readers can understand what time the sentence tells about. Those changes in form are called *tenses*. The Language Arts: Writing Test includes many questions that require you to find and fix errors in *verb tense*.

Past, Present, and Future

There are three basic tenses: past, present, and future.

Past tense tells readers about something that happened in the past:

> Danielle *wrote* the letter last week.
>
> Maile *emailed* the complaint over a year ago.
>
> Sam *walked* home after the party.

Those things all happened before this present minute, so we use the past tense.

For things that are happening in the present, it's correct to use *present tense:*

> Danielle *writes* the letter.
>
> Maile *emails* the complaint right now.
>
> Sam *walks* while I read.

And for things we expect to happen in the future, we use *future tense:*

> Danielle *will write* the letter.
>
> Maile *will email* her complaint.
>
> Sam *will walk* after the party.

Notice that the future tense often includes a *helping verb*—that is, a linking verb that helps the main verb.

DEFINITION

Helping verbs help the main verb by making the tense more clear. Common helping verbs include *will, may, could, must, should, would, might,* and *can.*

A good tip for figuring out the correct verb tense, especially on a test like the GED, is to look at the rest of the sentence. Often, another verb in the sentence will tip you off to the tense needed. For example, in the following sentence, the first verb gives you a hint about the second's tense:

> We will leave after she asks.

It's clear that the second verb has to be either in the future or present tense. You can eliminate any other choices.

Practice

Choose the correct verb from those provided. Use cues from the other words in the sentence to help you figure them out.

1. Alice bikes/biked before winter came, but now it's too cold.

2. At the party tonight, she wears/will be wearing the necklace we gave her.

3. Threw/Throw the ball.

Answers

1. Biked (the sentence makes it clear that winter has arrived—no more biking!).

2. Will be wearing (because the sentence is referring to an event that will happen).

3. Throw (it's a command, so it's happening in the present).

Present Perfect, Past Perfect, and Future Perfect

Now verb tense gets a little more complicated. There are three other tenses that you should be able to spot on the Language Arts: Writing Test.

Present perfect tense is for when you're writing or speaking about a specific action or state of being that happened at an unspecified time before now. Present perfect can *never* be used with a specific time (or words that designate a specific time, such as yesterday, last week, on October 9th …). Here are a few examples of sentences in the present perfect tense:

I've heard that song so many times.

She has walked away from him before.

We have chosen to move.

Notice that present perfect tense always involves a helping verb!

Past perfect tense indicates something that happened *before* something else that happened in the past. Here, the examples might be less confusing than the explanation:

> He had moved to Miami before we went to college.

> Nigel had purchased that farm before Grandmother died.

> They had let the sled go before they realized there was a crash.

In the first example, he moved *before* we went to college—two events that happened in the past, put into their proper order. That's past perfect tense.

Future perfect tense expresses the idea that something will be completed before something else in the future. For example:

> By 2015, I will have completed my GED.

> When it's Christmastime again, I'll have mastered my fruitcake recipe.

> By next Tuesday, I will have broken up with him.

It might be difficult to believe, but there are actually more complicated verb tenses than these, and specific names for all of them—past perfect conditional, anyone?—but for the GED, and general usage, knowing these six will be more than sufficient.

Practice

Name the verb tense for each of the following sentences:

1. The dog had stopped barking by the time the police arrived.

2. My farm lies to the west of the highway.

3. Next year, we'll have completed our conversion to gas heat.

4. The taxi waited for you!

5. Nedra will go to the concert.

6. Gladys has asked that question 30 times already.

Answers

1. Past perfect

2. Present

3. Future perfect

4. Past

5. Future

6. Present perfect

Participles

Participles are verb forms that are used as adjectives. For example, in the sentence *The truck hit a parked car, parked* is an adjective, describing *car. Parked* is also a participle, because it's a verb. At one point, before being hit by a truck, the car was also parked.

Here are two other examples of participles in sentences:

> The hired caterer brought all of the food we ordered. (*Hired* is the participle, as it's the adjective form of *to hire,* modifying the noun *caterer.*) Many people say the written word is more powerful than the spoken word. (*Written* is the participle, as it's the adjective form of *to write,* modifying the noun *word.*)

Although you do not need to identify participles on the Language Arts: Writing Test, knowing the role of each word in a sentence is always helpful in understanding how the sentence works.

Transitive and Intransitive Verbs

Although you do not have to analyze grammar on the GED, it's useful to know what transitive and intransitive verbs are. Here's a simple explanation.

Transitive verbs show action and have a direct object:

> The chorus sang a song.

The subject *(the chorus)* completes an action *(sang)* of an object *(a song).*

Intransitive verbs show action but do not have a direct object:

> The chorus sang.

We don't know what they sang, so the verb is intransitive.

Irregular Verbs: Spelling and Tense

While many verbs follow the conventions of spelling—such as adding *–ed* to make them past tense or *-ing* to make them present tense—there are quite a few common verbs that do not follow these conventions at all. Look at the following table:

Verb	Past	Present	Future
to call	called	calling	will call
to bring	bringed	bringing	will bring

To call is a standard verb, and its past tense is *called*. But when we try the same construction with *to bring*, we see that something went wrong in the past tense. There's no *bringed* in the English language. This confusion over verbs has led to many mistakes in speaking and writing. To help you prepare for the GED, here's a handy chart to review:

Chart of Irregular Verbs

Verb	Past	Present	Future
to bring	brought	bringing	will bring
to choose	chose	choosing	will choose
to do	did	doing	will do
to come	came	comes	is coming

There are also words that are irregular *and* have two different forms of the past tense, depending on whether a helping verb is involved:

Verb	Past	Present	Future
to grow	grew, have grown	growing	will grow
to know	knew, have known	knowing	will know
to give	gave, have given	gives	will give

Verb	Past	Present	Future
to break	broke, have broken	breaking	will break
to drink	drank, have drunk	drinking	will drink
to eat	ate, have eaten	eating	will eat
to run	ran, have run	running	will run
to ring	rang, have rung	ringing	will ring
to ride	rode, have ridden	riding	will ride
to sing	sang, have sung	singing	will sing
to see	saw, have seen	seeing	will see
to speak	spoke, have spoken	speaking	will speak
to swim	swam, have swum	swimming	will swim
to throw	threw, have thrown	throwing	will throw
to wear	wore, have worn	wearing	will wear
to write	wrote, have written	writing	will write

Practice

Choose the correct form of the irregular verb. Look for the helping verb if you get confused.

1. Many wild animals have drunk/drank at the watering hole.
2. My uncle has grew/grown oranges for 10 years.
3. The chorus sang/sung songs at the concert.
4. The catcher threw/thrown the runner out at second.
5. She has swam/swum in the Olympic trials.

Answers

1. Drunk
2. Grown
3. Sang
4. Threw
5. Has swum

The Many Forms of *to Be*

There are quite a few forms of the verb *to be*, and none bear any real semblance to another. That's too bad, as *to be* is one of the English language's most used verbs. It is used to show a state of being. It will definitely appear multiple times on the GED, so make sure you are comfortable with it.

The Four Purposes of *Be* in a Sentence

The verb *to be* can take many forms in a sentence: *am, are, is, was, were, have been, will have been, will be,* or *had been*.

We'll take a closer look at these in the next section. *To be* takes two basic purposes in a sentence. First, *to be* can be, and most often is, a linking verb, as in the following examples:

>   I *am playing* the piano.

>   The dog *was running* through the water.

As a linking verb, the forms of *to be* provide support for the main verb.

Second, *to be* can stand on its own and simply state the existence of something:

>   I am, I said.

>   You are?

>   They will be.

Third, *to be* can act as a *subject complement*, which means it simply provides a link between the subject of a sentence and further information about the subject:

>   Diane *is* the boss.

>   The trucks *were* all Fords from the 1950s.

In the first example Diane is the subject, and the verb *is* acts as a subject complement to give us further information about her.

In the second example the trucks are the subject, and the verb *were* acts as a subject complement to fill us in on what type of trucks they were.

Fourth, *to be* can be an *adjective complement*. In this case, the verb provides a link between the subject and some kind of modifying adjectives:

> Reba *is* very successful.

This sentence gives us more information about Reba, using an adjective and an adverb.

For the GED, you will not need to differentiate between subject complements and adjective complements, but you do need to know how *to be* can work in a sentence, so that you can spot any errors. It's easy to get tripped up by the different forms of *to be*. Studying this section just before taking the GED will help keep you on the right path.

Present, Past, and Future of *to Be*

No matter how *to be* is used in a sentence, it will fall into one of the tenses and forms shown in the following table:

	Present	**Past**	**Future**
I	am	was	will be
You	are	were	will be
He/She/It	is	was	will be
They	are	were	will be

In some regions of the United States, it's common to change the usage of *to be*. For example, some people are used to saying "You was …" for the past tense instead of "You were …." Some people also say, "They was …" instead of "They were …." These regionalisms are technically incorrect, and you should be ready to fix them on the GED.

Be especially wary around questions. A sentence like "Was you the only person who joined the team that night?" might seem like it's correct. The same is true for "Was they ready for the test?" But both are wrong. Reverse the order of the words and you'll see why:

You was the only person …

They was ready …

HEADS UP!

You is always considered to be plural, even if you are writing about only one person. In other words, there is never a time when *you was* will be correct in formal English!

Problem Areas with *to Be*

To be is a vital verb, but it can also easily lead you into trouble. Let's look at a few problems to watch out for:

- There is no such word as *ain't*, at least not in formal English. If you're writing a song, a play, or quoting someone who speaks with this regionalism, go ahead and use *ain't*. Otherwise, don't use it on the GED, including in the essay section!

   Not only is *ain't* always wrong, but it often tends to turn up in sentences with double negatives, such as *We ain't never going to believe that guy.* Double negatives are always wrong, too! It's much simpler to write *We don't believe that guy.*

- Sometimes we use *to be* when it's not really necessary. When you're writing, it's worth taking a minute to review your words and see if you can take out any forms of *to be.* For example, if you look carefully at the sentence *Everyone who is willing to participate will get an A*, you'll notice that you don't need "who is." It can just read *Everyone willing to participate will get an A.*

   Another way *to be* is unnecessary is when an action verb could take its place. Action verbs are always more enticing to readers. For example, instead of writing *Beyonce was influential in my decision to become a singer*, you could write *Beyonce influenced my decision to become a singer.* That's much more direct!

Practice

Read the following paragraph and fix the *to be* usages if needed.

1. It were the only way to find out what had happened.

2. We were all in agreement.

3. All five of us will have taken part.

Answers

1. *It* is singular, but *were* is plural. Change *were* to *was*.

2. You could just write *We agreed*. The form of *to be* isn't needed.

3. No mistakes.

Agreement Between Subjects and Verbs

Making sure your subjects and verbs agree is of utmost importance if you want your writing to be clear and professional. When you're writing, it's easy to mismatch your verb and subject, and readers are quick to spot such mistakes. You need to be sure you understand the rules of subject and verb agreement! We've already covered making sure subjects and verbs agree in number in Chapter 1. In this section, we'll look at a few other tips for subject-verb agreement.

Special Forms of Several Linking Verbs

Linking verbs are a key area to pay attention to when looking for errors in verb usage. It's crucial that you remember which linking verbs are singular and which are plural. If your subject is singular, your linking verb must be as well, and the same is true for plural subjects and linking verbs. Just make sure they match. Singular linking verbs include *is*, *was*, *has*, and *does*. Plural linking verbs include *are*, *were*, *have*, and *do*.

Does Is Singular, But *Do* Is Plural

For example, *She has three sisters* is correct. (*She* is singular, and so is *has*.) *She do the dishes* is not correct. (*She* is singular, but *do* is the plural form of that verb.)

Watch Out for Phrases

A *prepositional phrase* is a series of words inserted into a sentence that begins with a preposition. It may modify the subject or verb, but it never contains the subject or verb.

Remember, on the Language Arts: Writing Test you will not need to diagram a sentence, so you do not need to be able to label a prepositional phrase. However, you do need to recognize when one is contained in a sentence so that you don't allow it to affect your verb choice.

IN THE KNOW

Common prepositions include *to, of, by, in, around, above, below, at, until, like,* and *for.* A prepositional phrase usually begins with a preposition and contains its object and any modifiers (adjectives or adverbs) of the object. For example, in the prepositional phrase *below the garage, below* is a preposition, and *the garage* is the object. In the phrase *in the city park,* the preposition is *in,* and the object is *park. City* modifies *park.*

For example, let's look at two sentences:

> One of the plates was/were smashed.

> The president, in addition to his staff members, is/are here.

Which form would we use?

The correct answers are, respectively, *was* and *is.* Why? Because although *plates* and *members* are plural, they are part of prepositional phrases: *of the plates* and *in addition to his staff members.* So they cannot be the subject. The true subjects of both sentences, *One* and *The president,* are both singular.

If you find this confusing, remember that a prepositional phrase can always be removed from a sentence, and the sentence will still be complete and make sense:

> One was smashed. (We may not know what exactly was smashed, but the sentence is still a sentence!)

> The president is here.

Matching Verbs with Compound Subjects

Sentences with compound subjects—in which the subject is more than one noun—should also put you on the alert. The question of whether to use a singular or plural verb comes down to how the compound subject is constructed. Here are two rules:

- A compound subject that contains the conjunction *and* is plural. Use a plural verb.

- With a compound subject that contains the conjunctions *or* or *nor*, match the verb to the subject nearest to it.

That's right! One of these rules is based on proximity! Still, it works. For example, look at this sentence:

> The orchestra and the singer is/are performing tonight.

We look to the conjunction, and see that it's *and*. The case is closed—the verb is plural, just like its compound subject: *The orchestra and the singer are performing tonight.*

Here's another example:

> George or the cowboys were/was the first choice.

We look to the conjunction, see that it's *or*, and know we must look to the subject closest to the verb. In this sentence, that's *the cowboys*, so *George or the cowboys were the first choice* is correct.

Verbs in Inverted Sentences

An *inverted sentence* is just a fancy name for a sentence in which the verb comes before the subject. For example:

> In the garden is a beautiful rose.

The typical way of writing that sentence is *A beautiful rose is in the garden*, but the inverted way is also correct. We just need to be sure we still match the verb and subject. What would you do for this sentence?

> Through the stadium stream/streams a thousand fans.

Not sure which to choose? Reorder the sentence:

> A thousand fans stream/streams through the stadium.

With the reordering, it's clear that the subject, *fans*, is plural, so the verb *stream* should be as well.

Verbs with *There*

Many English sentences use *there* where a subject is expected—but *there* isn't the subject, usually. Look farther along in the sentence, and you'll often see the subject. Yet, *there* must match the accompanying verb, so we need to figure out if it is singular or plural:

> There are/is all of my friends.

Here, the trick is to look ahead for the subject. In this sentence, it is *all* (*of my friends* is a prepositional phrase), and *all* is plural. So:

> There *are* all of my friends.

Practice

In the following paragraphs, spot and correct the errors in verb usage.

1. (A) Most of our films have been distributed. (B) We have been waiting for all of the contracts to be signed and returned. (C) Fortunately, there is no festivals we want to enter them in this year. (D) Festivals in New York, Chicago, and Berlin is of interest to us, however. (E) The film or prints of it has to be sent.

2. (A) There are several different routes to becoming a doctor. (B) Doesn't they all seem to be difficult? (C) More and more people are choosing to major in a field other than Pre-Med. (D) For example, Lenora do want to become a doctor, but she's majoring in Accounting so that she can work first. (E) An internship or volunteer work is her next step in getting more experience.

Answers

1. (A) Correct. Remember, ignore the prepositional phrase *of our films*, and look at the subject, which is the plural *Most*. (B) Correct. (C) *is* should be *are*. Take a look at the rest of the sentence to see whether *there* is plural or singular. Since it's tied to *festivals*, it is plural. (D) It's the same mistake: *is* should be *are*, because *festivals* is plural. Check and you'll see that *in New York, Chicago, or Berlin* is a prepositional phrase. (E) *Had* should be *have*. In this sentence, there is a compound subject joined by *or*. That means you look at the subject closest to the verb and match the verb to it. (And ignore the prepositional phrase, *of it*.)

2. (A) Correct. (B) *Doesn't* should be *Don't*. If you're not sure why, remember to change the question to a statement. (C) Correct (it has a compound subject which is joined by *and*, so the plural verb is correct). (D) *Lenora does*, not *Lenora do*. (E) Correct. It doesn't seem like it's correct, does it? But if you look at the sentence, it has a compound subject, joined by *or*. So we look to the subject closest to the verb, which is *volunteer work*, and see that it is singular, so a singular verb is used.

Parts of Speech Used and Abused

In This Chapter

- Overview of the correct way to use confusing parts of speech
- GED-like questions to practice the skills you'll be tested on
- Answers and explanations for all the questions

In this chapter, we'll review some of the grammatical rules that are most likely to cause you to slip up on the Language Arts: Writing Test. The bulk of this chapter will be spent on tricky pronouns, but we'll also take a look at adjectives, adverbs, and, especially, the comparison of adjectives, a very dicey area in the grammar neighborhood. Don't worry, though—by the end of this chapter, you'll be able to deploy the correct grammar rules that will help you ace the test!

Using the Correct Pronoun

A pronoun is simply a word used in place of a noun. There are three forms of all pronouns: the subject, object, and possessive forms. Nouns don't change, even if they're used differently in a sentence, but pronouns change depending on what role they take in the sentence. Let's begin by looking at all three.

Subject

Subject forms of pronouns are used as the subject in a sentence. They're not very difficult to remember, as they are words like *he*, *she*, *it*, and *they*. For example:

> Sue ran = she ran. *Sue* is the subject in the sentence, and *she* is the subject form of the pronoun.

The bike crashed = It crashed. *The bike* is the subject, and *it* is the subject form of the pronoun.

> **HEADS UP!**
>
> Don't confuse *pronouns* with *proper nouns*! Pronouns replace a noun, but proper nouns are the name given to a particular noun. For example, we can talk about a rock singer—that's a noun—or Bono, which would be a proper noun. The pronoun form, of course, would be *he, him,* or *his.*

The one usage that can trip you up with subject forms of pronouns is when they are used as predicate pronouns. A predicate pronoun is a pronoun that follows a linking verb and is linked by the verb to a subject. Remember, a *linking verb* shows a state of being. Here's an example:

The students were she and I.

In that sentence, *she* and *I* are the pronouns. They are used in the subject form because *were* is a linking verb.

Are you wondering why it wouldn't be *The students were her and me?* That's a common confusion. A simple tip is to flip the sentence's predicate and subject. You would end up with this:

She and I were the students.

But *Her and me were the students* doesn't sound right at all!

Object

The object of a sentence is the noun or pronoun receiving the action of the verb. In the sentence *Ted saw Dwight, Ted* is the subject and *Dwight* is the object, since he's the receiver of the action of seeing.

The usage of pronouns is instinctual here. We know what sounds right. If we change *Dwight* to the correct pronoun, we know we would write *Ted saw him,* not *Ted saw he* or *Ted saw his.*

The only exception to this rule is the wacky *you,* which is the same in both subject and object form: *You are going to the store; I saw you.*

By the way, one of the most common mistakes in the English language is trying to determine the difference between subject and object pronouns. Let's say you wanted to talk about your all-female book club and the trip you took. Do you say *We girls went on vacation* or *Us girls went on vacation?*

Neither one really sounds great, but the correct choice is best found by trying the pronoun alone in the sentence: *We went on vacation* or *Us went on vacation.* The first one, right? If you get confused, take out the extra parts of the sentence to focus on the word in question.

Possessive

Possessive forms of pronouns show ownership by the pronoun. They are *my, mine; our, ours; your, yours; his, her, hers, its;* and *their, theirs.*

Note that these don't use apostrophes. We'll go over the apostrophe and its usage in Chapter 6, but, for now, remember that the possessive form of *it,* which is *its,* has no apostrophe. Therefore, we write *The horse turned its head* because the head belongs to it (the horse).

IN THE KNOW

Only use *it's* with the apostrophe when you can substitute *it is* into the sentence and have it make sense.

Antecedents are the nouns replaced by the pronouns. For example, in the sentence *Mel came by today and brought his payment, Mel* is the antecedent, and *his* is the pronoun that replaces it.

Antecedents may seem obvious—and they are!—but they become more important when we're dealing with singular and plural nouns. Replace a singular noun, which deals with one thing, with a singular pronoun; replace a plural noun, which deals with more than one thing, with a plural pronoun. For example:

> The *actor* learned *his* lines.

> The *girls learned their harmonies.*

When you get confused about whether to use a singular or a plural pronoun, look to the antecedent.

Other Types of Pronouns

There are a few more particular kinds of pronouns to be aware of, and here's a quick review.

Compound personal pronouns are pronouns that have *–self* or *–selves* added to them for emphasis. For example:

> *We* always do the cooking *ourselves.*

Demonstrative pronouns are used to point out which persons or things are referred to. They are *this, that, these,* and *those.*

This and *these* refer to persons or things that are near. *That* and *those* refer to persons or things farther away:

> *That* is the lighthouse we could see from the house.

> *This* is my aunt.

Interrogative pronouns ask questions. They are *who, whose, whom, which,* and *what.*

Did you just panic at the thought of trying to decide between *who* and *whom?* Don't worry! The way to tell the difference is to remember that *who* is the subject form of the pronoun, while *whom* is the object form. So you'd write *Who is coming today?* and *Whom did Lori call?*

Indefinite pronouns do not refer to a particular person or people. That's why they're called indefinite—who they're referring to is not definite!

Singular indefinite pronouns include *anybody, anyone, anything, each, everybody, everyone, everything, neither, nobody, no one, somebody,* and *someone.*

When we use these words in a sentence, if we want to show their possession, we must use singular possessive pronouns, such as *his, her,* and *its.* For example:

> Everybody took his turn.

> Something left its tracks here.

When a singular pronoun must refer to both males and females, the English language defaults to the awkward *him or her.* So we would write:

> Someone left his or her skates.

There are also a few plural indefinite pronouns: *both, few, many,* and *several.* Use the plural form of the pronoun with them:

> Both watched their pets.

There are also four indefinite pronouns that are tricky enough to sometimes be singular and sometimes plural: *all, any, none,* and *some.*

In this sentence, *all* is singular:

> All of the cake was eaten.

And here, it's plural:

> All of the seats were empty.

Sure-Fire Pronoun Table Prevents Mistakes

Writers get in trouble using pronouns when they don't pay attention to (or don't know) which type of pronoun they should use: subject, object, or possessive. If you get confused, figure out what role in the sentence the pronoun plays, and then remember this handy table.

	Subject	**Object**	**Possessive**
Singular:	I	me	my, mine
	you	you	your, yours
	she, he, it	her, him, it	her, hers, his, its
Plural:	we	us	our, ours
	you	you	your, yours
	they	them	their, theirs

Practice

For each sentence, choose the correct pronoun.

1. We/Us and the book club had dinner.

2. The magician balanced him/himself on the pedestal.

3. Who/Whom made this CD?

4. Will somebody loan me his or her/their pocketknife?

5. All of the snakes shed its/their skin.

6. The spider spun its/it's delicate web.

Answers

1. We (take *and the book club* out, if needed)

2. Himself (to make it clear he balanced his own body)

3. Who (because it's used as the subject of the sentence)

4. His or her (even though it's awkward)

5. Their (in this usage, *all* refers to more than one)

6. Its (*it's* is only for *it is*, and *The spider spun it is delicate web* doesn't make sense)

Don't Confuse Adjectives and Adverbs

Adjectives and *adverbs* play such similar roles in sentences, it's easy to confuse them, since both help us describe what's around us. However, you can't just substitute one for the other, so it's a good idea to be clear on which is which before you take the Language Arts: Writing Test.

DEFINITION

Adjectives modify nouns. **Adverbs** modify verbs, adjectives, and other adverbs.

Adjectives

Adjectives help us describe what we've seen and heard, by *modifying* (that is, changing the meaning of another word by making it more precise) nouns. For example, the word *sky* is a noun. By adding adjectives, we can modify the meaning and make it more clear:

a *blue* sky	a *darkening* sky	a *rose-tinged* sky
a *low* sky	a *threatening* sky	a *damp* sky

Adverbs

Adverbs, on the other hand, modify much more than nouns. While adjectives describe, adverbs answer *how, when, where,* or *to what extent.* Adverbs can modify verbs, adjectives, and even other adverbs. Let's look at a few examples.

Adverbs modify verbs in the sentence *I walked:*

> I walked *slowly.*

> I walked *recently.*

> I walked *outside.*

Adverbs modify adjectives in the sentence: *It was a nice day.* (Did you notice that *nice* is an adjective, describing *day?*)

> It was a *fairly* nice day.

> It was a *surprisingly* nice day.

> It was a *very* nice day.

In all of these examples, the italicized words are adverbs modifying an adjective to tell readers more about what kind of nice day it was.

Adverbs can even modify other adverbs, as in the sentence *Andrew danced well.* Here, the first adverb is *well,* which describes how Andrew danced. If we add in more adverbs:

> Andrew danced *very* well.

> Andrew danced *really very* well.

The adverbs modify *well*, making it more clear just how well Andrew danced!

Many adverbs are formed by adding *–ly* to an adjective:

Adjective	Adverb
plain	plainly
brave	bravely
noisy	noisily
large	largely

And so on.

IN THE KNOW

There are only a few words in the English language that end in *–ly* but are not adverbs. *Lovely* and *lonely*, for example, are adjectives. However, you're usually pretty safe guessing that if a word ends in *–ly*, it's an adverb.

Good vs. *Well*

A pitfall in grammar and writing is not knowing when to use *good* and when to use *well*. It's actually quite simple: use *good* as an adjective and *well* as an adverb unless you're talking about someone's health. For example:

> He plays tennis well. (*Well* modifies the verb *plays*, so it's an adverb.)

> That book was good. (*Good* modifies the noun *book*.)

Practice

Choose the adjective or adverb form of the word to complete the sentence.

1. Our team won easy/easily.

2. Keisha plays the piano good/well.

3. John felt bad/badly about the accident.

Answers

1. Easily (use the adverb form, since you're describing the verb *won*)

2. Well (remember, *good* is only used as an adjective to modify nouns and pronouns; the adverb form is always *well*)

3. Badly (use the adverb form, since you're describing the verb *felt*)

Adjectives in Comparisons

Adjectives are useful in so many ways, especially in making comparisons. Yet the rules for making comparisons are not widely employed. Here's how to do it, and how to catch and fix errors in comparisons on the GED.

There are two forms of adjectives you'll need to know: *comparative* and *superlative*. The comparative form is used when you compare one thing or person with another. The superlative form is used when you compare a thing or person with more than one other of its kind.

Here's an example. If I want to compare the cleanliness of two rooms, I might write: *This room is cleaner than the living room. Cleaner* is the comparative form, which is correct because I'm comparing the room to only one other.

However, if I wanted to say that *This room is the cleanest in the house*, I'm correct in using the superlative form, *cleanest*, because I'm comparing the room to all of the other rooms in the house.

Making the Comparative Form

We form the comparative version of an adjective in one of two ways. For a short adjective (like *slow* or *clean*), we simply add *–er:*

Clean + -er = cleaner

Slow + -er = slower

Happy + -er = happier (note that the spelling changed, too!)

For longer adjectives, like *delicious* or *selfish*, we add the word *more* or *less* in front:

The food was more delicious than I remember.

Her uncle was less selfish than I remember.

IN THE KNOW

There are some adjectives—generally those that are one or two syllables long—that can be used in the comparative form by adding *–er* or using *more*. For example, *soft* can be *more soft* or *softer*. It's really the writer's preference.

Making the Superlative Form

Remember, the superlative form is only used when making a comparison between more than two things. Again, there are two ways to do this. For adjectives to which you added *–er* to make the comparative form, now add *–est* to make the superlative form. On the other hand, if you made the adjective into the comparative form by adding the word *more* before it, to make the superlative, you'll want to add *most* before it.

Here are a few examples:

Adjective	Comparative	Superlative
Full	fuller	fullest
Dim	dimmer	dimmest
Annoying	more annoying	most annoying
Courageous	more courageous	most courageous

Tips for Using Comparative and Superlative Forms

Remember to look for how many things or people are being compared. That will tell you which form to use:

> That kitten is the cutest of the two.

Sounds about right? Nope! You've only got two kittens, so the one can only be *cuter*, not the *cutest*.

Also, remember not to leave out the word *other* when you are comparing something with everything else of its kind. Therefore, we wouldn't write:

> That kitten is cuter than any animal.

That makes it seem like the kitten is not an animal! Instead, write:

> That kitten is cuter than any other animal.

Written that way, it's clear that the kitten is an animal, and that you're comparing it to one, other, unspecified animal.

Avoid using both *–er* and *more* or *–est* and *most* in the same sentence. *Wool is more harsher than cotton*, for example, is incorrect.

Finally, there are a few irregular comparisons. They don't follow the rules, so you'll just have to know them:

Adjective	Comparison	Superlative
good	better	best
well	better	best
bad	worse	worst
little	less or lesser	least
much	more	most
many	more	most
far	farther	farthest

Practice

Find the pronoun, adjective, and adverb faults in the paragraphs, and decide how to fix them.

1. (A) We guys were late for the meeting. (B) We were held up by a truck that had jackknifed, blocking it's lane of traffic. (C) Joel called the office, but the reception was poorer. (D) We ended up walking fast back to the nearest exit.

2. (A) Sam was feeling poorly. (B) His sister was ill, too, but Sam felt worst. (C) He wanted a new medicine and asked if the doctor would bring them. (D) Before too long, he was fastly asleep.

Answers

1. (A) The usage of *we guys* sounds a little off, but it's correct. (B) That's the wrong form of *its*. It doesn't need the apostrophe, since it's showing possession, not substituting for *it is*. (C) *Poorer* is incorrect, since there's no comparison in the sentence. (D) *Fast* is incorrect, since it is an adjective and it's being used to modify a verb, not a noun. The adverb form, by the way, would be *quickly*. By the way, *nearest* is okay, too, because the sentence compares that exit to all of the other exits in the world!

2. (A) It might sound like a regionalism, but *poorly* is correct in this sentence. (B) Sam is compared to only one other person, so we'd write *worse*, not *worst*. (C) Remember the antecedent rule: *a new medicine* is singular, so you should use *it*, not *them*. (D) *Fast*, not *fastly*, because *asleep* is an adjective. Don't overthink your answers!

Put Sentences Together Correctly

In This Chapter

- Overview of constructing sentences correctly
- GED-like questions to practice the skills you'll be tested on
- Answers and explanations for all the questions

In Chapter 1, you reviewed how a sentence in English works. Of course, many errors in sentences come from misusing the two main parts of a sentence, the subject and the verb. Take a look at Chapter 3 for more on those errors. In this chapter, you'll look more closely at some of the common errors in sentence construction. If you can spot these on the Language Arts: Writing Test, you'll be able to fix them—and that puts you closer to passing the test!

Sentence Fragments and Run-On Sentences

Sentence fragments and run-ons are most likely to occur when we write and read the way we speak—that is, for content's instead of clarity's sake. Remember, what sounds correct may not be correct in formal writing, and formal writing is what the GED is looking for.

Identifying and Fixing Sentence Fragments

As you recall, a *sentence fragment* is a group of words that does not form a complete sentence. Something is missing, either a subject or a verb. When you read a fragment, you don't feel like you have all of the information that the sentence could convey. Here are some examples of sentence fragments:

> When she called me.
>
> Bought a hamburger.
>
> Left earlier.
>
> Called his wife.

Notice that in all of these examples, we're left wondering about the rest of the information that should be provided. What happened when she called me? Who bought a hamburger? Left earlier than who? (Or, who left earlier?) Who called his wife? We just don't know.

Sometimes the subject is implicit, especially in sentences that contain commands directed at *you*. These are not fragments. For example:

> Go now!
>
> If it starts to rain, pack up.

Again, because the *you* is implicit, these are complete sentences.

To fix a sentence fragment, add the subject or the verb:

> I was out when she called me.
>
> Jason bought a hamburger.
>
> We left earlier.
>
> The boss called his wife.

HEADS UP!

Sentence fragments can and do appear in novels, plays, and conversation. If a character says, "What did he do next?" and another responds, "Called his wife," we understand that the subject is implicit (*He* called his wife). However, in the kind of formal, nonfiction writing the GED asks you to analyze, a sentence fragment is never okay.

Practice

Are the following sentences or fragments?

1. Snow and hail

2. In Yellowstone as autumn arrives

3. Three apples

4. Just before the end of the game, leave.

Answers

1. Fragment

2. Fragment

3. Fragment

4. Sentence (*leave* is the verb, and the sentence directs an implicit *you* to leave)

Identifying and Fixing Run-On Sentences

A *run-on sentence* contains two or more sentences, but is punctuated incorrectly as one sentence. It's important to note that a run-on sentence does not have to be very long to be a run-on, and that a sentence can be quite long but not run on, if it's punctuated correctly.

The most common error in run-on sentences is to place a comma where a period or other end punctuation should be. That's called a *comma splice*. For example:

Corey worked at the bar for a double shift, his co-worker Joyce was sick.

There are really two sentences there:

Corey worked at the bar for a double shift. His co-worker, Joyce, was sick.

There are four basic ways to fix a run-on sentence, particularly those with comma splices:

- Add punctuation that will create two or more new sentences, whether periods, exclamation points, or question marks.

- Insert a semicolon. (See Chapter 8 for more on using semicolons correctly.)

- Rework the sentence so that it has a conjunction used with a comma. (Remember, the main conjunctions are *and*, *or*, *nor*, and *but*. You can also use *yet* and *so* in many sentences that you want to change from a run-on.)

- Use a preposition to make one of the thoughts expressed in the run-on into a clause or phrase.

Let's look at an example and apply all of these ideas to it. Our run-on sentence is:

> Anthony played video games for 3 hours his boss called and yelled at him for being late.

Idea #1: Change the run-on to two or more independent sentences:

> Anthony played video games for 3 hours. His boss called and yelled at him for being late.

Idea #2: Add a semicolon:

> Anthony played video games for 3 hours; his boss called and yelled at him for being late.

Idea #3: Add a conjunction and a comma:

> Anthony played video games for 3 hours, and his boss called and yelled at him for being late.

Idea #4: Make one of the expressed thoughts into a clause or phrase:

> Because Anthony played video games for 3 hours, his boss called and yelled at him for being late.

As you can see, it is often the case that making one of the thoughts expressed into a phrase or clause makes for a more sophisticated sentence.

Practice

Take the following two run-ons and fix them in all four of the ways presented above.

1. We were at the beach for more than an hour we came in to get warm.

2. The airport was so crowded we were sure we would never clear security.

Answers

1. (a) We were at the beach for more than an hour. We came in to get warm.

   (b) We were at the beach for more than an hour; we came in to get warm.

   (c) We were at the beach for more than an hour, so we came in to get warm.

   (d) Since we'd been at the beach for more than hour, we came in to get warm.

2. (a) The airport was so crowded. We were sure we would never clear security.

   (b) The airport was so crowded; we were sure we would never clear security.

   (c) The airport was so crowded, and we were sure we would never clear security.

   (d) Because the airport was so crowded, we were sure we would never clear security.

IN THE KNOW

Remember that when you use a semicolon in a sentence, the first word after the semicolon is not capitalized unless it is a proper noun.

Fixing Other Run-On Problems

Another common mistake that leads to run-ons is when the writer believes that by adding a comma and a conjunction, the sentence can just go on forever. This looks like:

> I told my sister that we would be late, but she didn't seem to mind, so I just ended up spending a longer time shopping than I meant to, but it turns out that my sister really was annoyed, so by the time we got to the party, she was in a horrible mood.

Whoa! That's too much information for one sentence. Go back and break that up into several sentences with end punctuation. How do you know how much information you can pack into one sentence? In general, one conjunction (unless you are making a list) is about the limit. Here's how it might look:

> I told my sister that we would be late. She didn't seem to mind, so I just ended up spending a longer time shopping than I meant to. As it turned out, my sister really was annoyed. By the time we got to the party, she was in a horrible mood.

IN THE KNOW

Many famous authors were and are notorious for their extra-long sentences, including Henry James and Nathaniel Hawthorne, whose works appear regularly in high school curricula. Keep in mind that the GED won't present you with classic works like theirs, so you can feel confident in cutting down run-on sentences.

Parallel Construction

Parallel construction might be more accurately termed balanced construction. It's the idea that your sentences should be balanced, in verb tense and subject, when a comparison is being made. This doesn't just mean that verbs and their subjects should match (although that is important), but that slightly more complex constructions balance as well. Let's take a look at three of these ideas.

Balance Between Verb Tense and Subject

Take a look at this sentence:

> The closer to the edge Sheila walked, the further away Amanda moved.

It's a nicely balanced sentence, comparing what Sheila did (walk closer) and how Amanda responded (moved further way).

Now look at this example:

> The closer to the edge Sheila walked, Amanda moves away.

See the lack of balance in that sentence? The verb changed in the second part: *moved* became *moves* in the present tense. Since *walked* is in the past tense, the parallel verb should be, too.

You also want to balance sentences that begin with *The more* or *The less*. For example:

> The more he talked, the more I wanted to listen.

Or

> The less interested he looked, the less enthusiastic Bob was in talking to him.

Words That Go Together

Another way that parallel construction is important is with certain pairs of words. These go together:

- neither/nor
- either/or
- both/and
- whether/or
- not only/but also

For example, *Neither Hernandez nor Nikki was invited* is correct, but *Neither Hernandez or Nikki was invited* is not. *Not only did I pick cranberries, but I also baked a cranberry tart* sounds much more balanced than *Not only did I pick cranberries, and I will make a cranberry tart.*

HEADS UP!

Verb tense is always the most important source of balance in a sentence. Make sure your verb tenses match in parallel construction!

Parallelism in Sentence Construction

The GED likes to present you with a sentence like this:

> On our trip, we hiked into the Everglades, swam at the beach, and will be playing baseball.

See the problem? The last part of the list *(will be playing baseball)* of what *we* did on our trip is in a different verb tense than the rest of the sentence. Make sure that all verbs align by tense in a list:

> On our trip, we hiked into the Everglades, swam at the beach, and played baseball.

Practice

The following sentences may have errors. Spot and fix them!

1. The more my date babbled on, I wanted to go home.

2. Either James Taylor or Carly Simon wrote that song.

3. During the work week, Cyn orders lunch in, brings it from home, or eating out.

Answers

1. It's not a balanced sentence. It should read: *The more my date babbled on, the more I wanted to go home.*

2. No mistakes.

3. There's a mistake in parallelism, so it should read: During the work week, Cyn orders lunch in, brings it from home, or eats out.

Place Modifiers Correctly

A *modifier* is a catch-all term for any phrase or clause included in a sentence to modify or clarify its meaning in some way. For example, look at the sentence *Rinsing the dishes, I realized I was late for class.* The modifier in the sentence is *"Rinsing the dishes."* It tells readers more about what I was doing when I made the realization that I was late for class. Is it necessary? Nope. But modifiers make sentences more interesting.

The trick with modifiers is to place the modifier as close to possible to the word or words it is modifying. If you don't, you end up with sentences that are unclear, even comical:

> Making a call on her cell phone, the approaching mugger went unnoticed by Stephanie.

Was the mugger making a call on her cell phone? Probably not. These mistakes are called *dangling modifiers*. The Language Arts: Writing Test will likely throw at least one at you. You can fix the sentence by moving the parts:

The approaching mugger went unnoticed by Stephanie, who was making a call on her cell phone.

Or

Making a call on her cell phone, Stephanie did not notice the approaching mugger.

Here's another example:

Being completely empty, I was able to park easily.

You can see why this is confusing. Worded this way, the sentence leads readers to think that the subject, *I*, was completely empty. After some thought, readers can see that a parking lot is meant, but the sentence should be worded in a way that makes it immediately clear:

Because the lot was empty, I was able to park easily.

Sometimes modifiers are wrong simply because they interrupt the flow of a sentence. For example:

You will be, as the supervisor of the work team, the first person we call in a snow emergency.

It's much more clear to write:

As the supervisor of the work team, you will be the first person we call in a snow emergency.

IN THE KNOW

Keep in mind that a modifier is not automatically incorrect—it just must be placed properly in the sentence. The good news is that dangling modifiers are always easier to spot in others' writing than in your own—so you should be able to catch them on the Language Arts: Writing Test. The most famous example of a dangling modifier is Groucho Marx's quip, "This morning I shot an elephant in my pajamas. How he got into my pajamas, I'll never know." Remember Marx's example when you're fixing sentences on the GED!

Practice

Fix the following sentences so that they do not contain dangling modifiers.

1. Leaving before the sun rose, the trip was begun.

2. Mr. Shirley will, as acting principal, represent our school at the games.

3. Wearing a hat, the team didn't recognize Adele.

Answers

There are several ways to fix these sentences, but here are a few examples:

1. The trip began before the sun rose.

2. As acting principal, Mr. Shirley will represent our school at the games.

3. The team didn't recognize Adele, who was wearing a hat.

Punctuation Holds Sentences Together

In This Chapter

- Overview of punctuation
- GED-like questions to practice the skills you'll be tested on
- Answers and explanations for all the questions

Punctuation marks are the street signs on the highway of reading and writing. They exist to guide readers toward a correct understanding of what the written words are trying to convey. When you, the writer, know what you're doing with commas, quotation marks, or brackets, your reader has a smooth ride ahead. However, whenever punctuation is not properly used, mixed signals may lead the reader off the highway and into a confusing side road that slows reading down. An understanding of the rules of punctuation is a must for anyone who writes in any way.

In this chapter, you will learn or review the basic rules of punctuation, and practice spotting the same types of punctuation errors you will see on the Language Arts: Writing Test.

Correct Usage of End Marks

End marks do two things: they alert your reader that your sentence is over, and they indicate the tone of the sentence they end.

There are three types of end marks:

- The period
- The question mark
- The exclamation point

DEFINITION

End marks are the punctuation at the end of a sentence, signaling that the sentence has ended. The three types of end marks are the period, the question mark, and the exclamation point.

The period closes a declarative sentence, which makes a statement:

> The car is red.

A period can also end an imperative sentence, which requires or tells someone to do something:

> Please open the window.

The question mark goes at the end of an interrogative sentence, which asks a question:

> Has anyone seen my ferret?

HEADS UP!

Do not use a question mark with an indirect question, which is part of a statement that tells what someone has asked, without giving the exact words. For example:

Incorrect: Micah asked if anyone had seen his ferret?

Correct: Micah asked if anyone had seen his ferret.

The exclamation point is used at the end of an exclamatory sentence, which expresses strong feeling:

> That was a great game!

Exclamation points are also used after interjections or after any exclamatory expression:

> Oh boy!

Exclamation points also are used at the end of imperative sentences that express excitement or emotion:

> Close that window, now!

It's easy to get confused about whether to end an imperative sentence with an exclamation point or a period. When in doubt, consider whether the sentence is meant to convey *strong* feeling.

Practice

Choose the end mark for each of the following sentences.

1. Do you know the way to San Jose
2. That's the ferret he lost
3. Oh my goodness
4. Sue was asking everyone if they had seen the movie yet

Answers

1. ?
2. .
3. !
4. . (Remember, indirect questions do not end with question marks!)

The Many Purposes of the Comma

Think of commas as the breaths, or pauses, in a sentence, giving both you and your reader a quick moment to relax or blink your eyes before moving on to the rest of the statement. When you read the sentence to yourself, the moments where you naturally pause in your speaking are often where a comma should be used.

Here are the comma's major uses:

- To avoid confusion
- To indicate a series
- After introductory words
- With multiple adjectives

- With *interruptors*
- With names in direct address
- With *appositives*
- With quotations
- In compound sentences
- In dates, locations, addresses, and letter parts

DEFINITION

Interruptors are words or phrases that interrupt the flow of a sentence. The most common interruptor is when you add the name of the person you're speaking to in the middle of the sentence: *I asked him, Sam, but he said no.* **Appositives** are words placed immediately after other words to clarify meaning or define who or what is meant. (Interruptors and appositives are discussed in more detail later in the chapter.)

That list may look overwhelming, but most comma usage is instinctual and simple to understand. Let's take a closer look at the rules.

To Avoid Confusion

Use a comma to avoid confusion. For example:

>   After eating my grandma takes a nap.

It's made much more clear by the use of a well-placed comma:

>   After eating, my grandma takes a nap.

Whew! Grandma's okay!

To Indicate a Series

In a series, a comma should be used after every item except the last:

>   We ate, packed, and departed an hour later.

>   Sheila, Danielle, and Erica were the first to arrive.

>   It was getting cold, the wind picked up, and Yung began to worry about getting home safely.

After Introductory Words

Commas should be used after introductory words, such as in this sentence:

> Then, Shelby demanded a ride home.

Practice

Let's pause for some practice. Where should the commas go in these sentences?

1. It was the best sweetest most amazing gift ever.
2. Also I'm tired of waiting for you.
3. When we entered the room was empty.
4. It's nice to see a sweet old couple taking a walk together.

Answers

1. It was the best, sweetest, most amazing gift ever. (series of adjectives rule)
2. Further, I'm tired of waiting for you. (introductory word rule)
3. When we entered, the room was empty. (to avoid confusion)
4. No commas needed! (the adjectives are closely linked)

With Multiple Adjectives

Commas also should appear in lists of two or more adjectives, except before the last item in the list (remember, adjectives modify nouns):

> It was a great, big, wild party.

> I love how a bright, sunny, brisk day makes everything better.

Watch out, though! If two adjectives are used together to express a single idea of closely related thoughts, don't use a comma:

> The little old woman lived in a shoe.

> The big red truck thrilled the little boy.

With Interruptors

Commas are used with interruptors, which pop up in the middle of a sentence:

> This ferret, however, is not the one we lost.

> The true story, it seems, will never be known.

With Names in Direct Address

Commas also are used to set off nouns of direct address:

> Call me later, Steve.

> Did she ask you, Jane, if you would go?

With Appositives

Commas are also used with appositives, which are most often used in conversations about people. The comma should appear on either side of the appositive, unless it is at the end of a sentence:

> My teacher, Mr. Smith, is not returning to our school.

> Andrew, the boy in the flannel shirt, is my best friend.

Practice

Take a moment now to practice using the comma with appositives. Where should the commas go in these sentences?

1. Yes Justin is my brother.

2. Give me a kiss Sam.

3. She is the best person for the role I guess.

4. The minister Rev. Hale is late.

Answers

1. Yes, Justin is my brother. (introductory word rule)

2. Give me a kiss, Sam. (direct address rule)

3. She is the best person for the role, I guess. (interrupter rule)

4. The minister, Rev. Hale, is late. (appositive rule)

With Quotations

Commas should be used in quotations to set off the explanatory words of a direct quotation. The explanatory words tell you who is speaking. For example, consider the following sentence:

Amir said, "Let's get some ice cream."

Amir said are the explanatory words. We follow them with a comma to help set up the quotation better.

Explanatory words can come at the end of a quotation sentence, too, such as:

"I like the penguins best," said the girl.

In this case, the comma is placed after the last word of a sentence.

Explanatory words can also be placed in the middle of a sentence. This is called a divided quotation. A comma is used after the last word of the first part, and again after the last explanatory word:

"We can see the penguins," said her brother, "but then let's get ice cream."

We'll discuss quotation marks a bit more later in this chapter.

GOOD IDEA

Rules for commas can be confusing. Remember that you don't have to explain the rules for comma usage on the GED, you only have to be able to identify how they should be used in a sentence.

In Compound Sentences

Commas are also used in compound sentences, in which two or more simple sentences are joined together with a conjunction. Remember, conjunctions are *and, nor, but,* and *or.* For example, we can join together the two simple sentences *Sue got back from her trip* and *Now, Sue is sleeping* into:

> Sue got back from her trip, and now she's sleeping.

We insert a comma after the first simple sentence, and before the conjunction.

Shorter compound sentences that are joined with *and* do not need commas. *We were thirsty and we were tired* is an example.

In Dates, Locations, Addresses, and Letter Parts

Include commas in dates, locations, addresses, and letter parts. Commas go between the parts of a date (except between the month and date), between the name of a city or town and the name of its state or country, and between the parts of an address except between a street number and street name, and a state and a zip code. So we write:

> Dear friend,
>
> May 25, 2012
>
> 1231 Mitchell Dr., Des Moines, Iowa

Practice

Add commas where they are needed in the following sentences.

1. We were sad but we weren't very surprised.

2. I'm having trouble finding information for what happened on June 18 1889.

3. "If it rains" Joe said "we'll have to cancel."

4. I agreed and we left immediately.

Answers

1. We were sad, but we weren't very surprised. (compound sentence rule)

2. I'm having trouble finding information for what happened on June 18, 1889. (dates, locations, addresses, and letter parts rule)

3. "If it rains," Joe said, "we'll have to cancel." (divided quotation rule)

4. I agreed and we left immediately. (No change. This compound sentence isn't long enough for a comma.)

Semicolons and Colons

In contrast to the comma's many usages and rules, the semicolon and colon are much simpler. The semicolon looks like a period over a comma (;) while a colon looks like two dots, one on top of the other (:). On the GED, you only need to know one way the semicolon will be used, and that's to join the parts of a compound sentence together when no conjunction is used.

HEADS UP!

Remember, the conjunctions are *and, nor, but,* and *or.* If you see one of them, do not use a semicolon.

For example, look at this sentence:

Mother threw the frying pan away it was worn out.

Inserting a semicolon corrects the sentence and keeps it from being a run-on:

Mother threw the frying pan away; it was worn out.

Colons have three uses as far as the GED is concerned. They follow the greeting of a business letter:

Dear Sir or Madam:

To Whom It May Concern:

They separate numbers indicating hours and minutes:

11:11 A.M.

9:30 P.M.

And they are used to introduce a list of items:

I gave Michael a list of what he needed to bring: firewood, marshmallows, graham crackers, and chocolate.

 GOOD IDEA

The GED will often present a business letter or email and ask you to locate and fix any errors. Colon and semicolon errors are often included in those sections. Keep your eyes peeled for them!

Practice

Add semicolons and colons where they are needed in the following sentences.

1. I bought my aunt a new blouse it is red, her favorite color.

2. She liked it but she said it was too small.

3. When the store opens at 1000 A.M., Mother wants me to buy the following for our ski trip gloves, a hat, warm socks, a scarf, and snow boots.

Answers

1. I bought my aunt a new blouse; it is red, her favorite color.

2. Trick question! You need to add a comma, not a semicolon: She liked it, but she said it was too small.

3. When the store opens at 10:00 A.M., Mother wants me to buy the following for our ski trip: gloves, a hat, warm socks, a scarf, and snow boots.

Quotation Marks

Quotation marks may well be the most abused form of punctuation, but the rules for how to use them are actually quite simple. Just be sure you know them before you take the GED and you'll be fine.

Quotation marks enclose the exact words of a speaker or writer:

> "Now is the time," he yelled.

> "To be or not to be" is a famous quote from Shakespeare's *Hamlet.*

Quotation marks are only used for the exact words of another speaker or writer. Indirect quotations and paraphrases—when one is definitely not using the writer or speaker's exact words—do not need quotation marks:

> She asked if we were from around here.

Quotation Marks with Commas

We already know from looking at commas that the explanatory words around a quotation require commas, whether they are at the beginning, middle, or end of a sentence. Just remember that the explanatory words at the beginning of a sentence are followed by a comma outside the quotation marks, but the punctuation at the end of a sentence is usually placed inside the quotation marks:

> Her daughter responded, "I did well on the test."

When explanatory words arrive at the end of the sentence, the quoted words earlier in the sentence are followed by a comma inside the quotation marks:

> "I'll text you when I'm home," I said.

For divided quotations, the first part of a divided quotation is followed by a comma that is placed inside the quotation marks. Then, remember, the explanatory words get a comma *before* the second part of the quotation's marks. The punctuation at the end of the sentence is still included in the quotation marks:

> "Of course," he said, "you can go."

Practice

Add quotation marks where they are needed in the following sentences.

1. If you like, we will stay, she said.

2. Gina said, I will bring the sauce.

3. I guess I can go, said Rafael, but I want to bring something.

Answers

1. "If you like, we will stay," she said.

2. Gina said, "I will bring the sauce."

3. "I guess I can go," said Rafael, "but I want to bring something."

Quotation Marks with Question Marks and Exclamation Points

Don't be confused by the end punctuation in a quotation if it's a question mark or exclamation point. If they're a part of the original quotation, include them in the quotation marks:

Kim asked John, "Did you finish the dishes?"

"Look out!" Miguel shouted.

If not, place them outside the quotation marks and don't include a period:

Did Rachel say, "I'll meet you at 5"?

My boss said, "I'll give you a raise"!

Practice

Add quotation marks where they are needed in the following sentences.

1. The woman screamed, Stop that thief!

2. Would you ask her Which way is it to Edgeware Road?

3. Do you think Jim said That's my first choice.

Answers

1. The woman screamed, "Stop that thief!"

2. Would you ask her, "Which way is it to Edgeware Road?"

3. Do you think Jim said, "That's my first choice"?

Hyphens, Dashes, and Apostrophes

Hyphens, dashes, and apostrophes are not as complex as quotation marks. Let's review how to use them. The rules for dashes, in particular, have changed greatly over the last 10 years. For simplicity, we'll only focus on the usages that you might see on the Language Arts: Writing Test.

Hyphens

Hyphens shouldn't be confused with dashes. While dashes have a variety of usages *within sentences*, hyphens primarily function *within words*. Use a hyphen when separating the parts of a word at the end of a line (but only for words of two or more syllables). For example:

I get extra pay when I have to work at the office overtime.

Also, use hyphens in compound numbers from twenty-one to ninety-nine, and in fractions:

We found twenty-eight occurrences of the two-thirds rule.

Hyphens should also be used in compound nouns:

> commander-in-chief
>
> great-grandmother

There are also, occasionally, adjectives comprised of compound words, which need hyphens. These include words like up-to-date and four-cylinder.

Dashes

Dashes come in two forms: the en dash and the em dash. An en dash (–) is shorter (more like a hyphen) and an em dash (—) is longer. If you were typing, you'd hit the dash bar twice to make an em dash.

En dashes have two basic functions. One function is to indicate a range, whether pages, dates, or something else. So use an en dash for the following:

> Pages 81–90
>
> June 20–30
>
> October–December

The other function is in compound adjectives:

> The New York–Miami flight

Em dashes get around a bit more, with two basic usages. First, an em dash is used to provide further information:

> The company has established a broad market—the United States, Japan, Russia, and India.

Em dashes are also used to provide additional information that the author wants to emphasize (these are sometimes called "asides"):

> The plan we devised—both the product line and how to develop it—was met with overwhelming acclaim.

Practice

Insert the correct punctuation where it's needed.

1. She is thirty seven years old.

2. Threefifths of the people involved stockholders and company workers disagreed with the decision.

3. Review pages 15 30 in the workbook.

Answers

1. She is thirty-seven years old.

2. Three-fifths of the people involved—stockholders and company workers—disagreed with the decision.

3. Review pages 15–30 in the workbook.

Apostrophes

The apostrophe looks like a comma that's floating. This little mark has two basic usages. First, apostrophes show *possession* of a singular noun by adding an *s* and an apostrophe:

The bike belongs to the girl. It's the girl's bike.

That is the lunch Charles brought. It's Charles's lunch.

To form a possessive of a plural noun that ends in *s*, add only an apostrophe:

These are my friends' designs.

There are the countries' flags.

To form the possessive of a plural noun that does not end in *s*, add an apostrophe and an *s:*

The women's department is through that door.

I thought the mice's cage was larger than the hamsters'.

To form the possessive of a singular noun that ends in *s*, add an apostrophe:

> I found Travis' shoes by the door.

> We studied Jesus' teachings at church.

Possession means that a noun owns something, whether it's an object, quality, or idea.

Apostrophes are also used in contractions. The apostrophe simply replaces one or more omitted letters from the two words joined together to make the contraction. Here's a list of some common contractions:

- We're = We are
- She's = She is
- Here's = Here is
- I'd = I would
- We'll = We will
- They're = They are
- Can't = Cannot
- Won't = Will not
- Wasn't = Was not
- Wouldn't = Would not

Watch out, though, for *it's* and *its!* Remember the rule:

> *It's* (with an apostrophe) means *It is* or *It has.*

> *Its* (without an apostrophe) is the possessive of *It.*

For example: It's time for the bird to have its dinner.

Practice

Insert the apostrophes in the following sentences.

1. Its late. Are you done?

2. That wasnt what I expected.

3. The childrens gifts are hidden.

4. Watch out for its bite.

Answers

1. It's late. Are you done? (Remember, you can't substitute *It is* for that *Its*, so it needs an apostrophe.)

2. That wasn't what I expected.

3. The children's gifts are hidden.

4. Watch out for its bite. (No change needed, since you can't substitute *it is* or *it has* for the *its*.)

As an Aside: Parentheses and Brackets

Before our final review, let's take a look at parentheses and brackets. These forms of punctuation look very similar but have different purposes.

Parentheses ( ) are used to insert information that is not essential to the meaning of the sentence. There are many different types of nonessential information, but what's important to remember is that whatever's in the parentheses could be removed and the sentence would still make sense.

IN THE KNOW

Parentheses will never contain the subject, object, verb, or main idea of a sentence.

Here are a few examples of parentheses:

That woman (who is related to our host) is dressed oddly.

We spent over 20 hours (more or less) on the road.

Brackets, on the other hand, exist to add clarifying information. The most common use of brackets is when an author adds something to another writer's words in a quote in order to clarify the meaning. For example, if the author wanted to quote someone saying, "He was the best of the best," she might be concerned that her readers would not know who *he* was. So she would use brackets:

Jose was heard to say, "He [My uncle Rick] was the best of the best."

Notice the brackets stay inside the quotation marks and the comma placement is not affected.

Practice

Insert the parentheses or brackets in the following sentences.

1. If you ask me not that you did, it's too long a trip.
2. "She his mother prefers to walk," Dane said.

Answers

1. If you ask me (not that you did), it's too long a trip.
2. "She [his mother] prefers to walk," Dane said.

IN THE KNOW

It bears repeating: you need to be able to spot and fix the grammatical errors on the GED. You do *not* need to explain why the errors you spot are wrong!

The Rules of Capitalization

There are quite a few rules guiding capitalization, so for clarity's sake, we'll break them down into two categories: when to capitalize and when *not* to capitalize!

When to Capitalize

Sometimes capital letters are there to make reading easier. For example, they signal the beginning of a sentence, and the first and main words in a title: Tina loved reading *The Help*.

We also capitalize the following:

- Proper nouns: John, Paris, Sweden, Ohio, Congress

- Adjectives made from proper nouns: Parisian, Swedish, Congressional

- Initials and titles in a name: Rev. Mark A. Miller, Dr. M. J. Byre

- Titles of people and groups whose rank is very high, even without their proper name: the President of the United States, the Queen of England

- Family relationships when they are used as names: Hi, Mom! Is Dad home yet? Aunt Gladys is here!

- The pronoun I: She and I went outside.

- All words referring to God and religious scriptures: We read the Gospel of St. John from the Bible, and a passage from the Koran.

- Geographical names, whether continents, bodies of water, land forms, states, public areas, or roads: North America, Lake Erie, the Rocky Mountains, Pennsylvania, Mount Rushmore, Route 66

- Sections of the country: the American South, the Pacific Northwest

- Names of organizations and institutions: Windser Hospital, Starbucks, Inc.

- Proper adjectives derived from names of sections of the country: a Western painting

- Names of events, documents, and periods of time: World War II, the Magna Carta, the Middle Ages

- Months, days, and holidays: May, Sunday, Christmas

- Languages, races, nationalities, and religions: French language, African American, Irish linen, Lutheranism

- Ships, trains, airplanes, and automobiles: the Titanic, a Mustang

- Abbreviations and acronyms: B.C.E., A.M., SCUBA

- The first word of a letter or email and the first word of the closing: Dear Cynthia, Yours truly,

- The first word of a quotation: Shakespeare wrote, "To thine own self be true."

Don't Capitalize

Don't capitalize the following:

- Common nouns: woman, nation, government

- Titles that aren't very important: the PTA president

- Family relationships when they are not used as names (usually preceded by *a, the, my, your*, etc.): Say hello to your mom for me. I saw my dad at the gas station.

- Directions on the compass: We drove north through the rain and hail. I like to fly south for the winter.

- Words such as *church, college, school*, and *hospital* when not used in titles: Did you go to church? I left school at 16.

- School subjects (unless they are course names followed by a number, or a language): I studied math. She practiced for her Italian test. I like Astronomy 101 so far.

There! Now you've thoroughly reviewed punctuation. Let's take the rest of the chapter to practice using these punctuation rules as you may need to apply them on the GED. The practice paragraphs that follow specifically focus on punctuation errors.

Practice

Insert or correct the punctuation as needed in the following sentences.

1. (A) Sues car won't start. (B) She's frustrated that its happening again. (C) Her husband not a great mechanic himself couldn't get it to work either. (D) He tried turning over the engine, looking in the manual, putting the car into neutral and kicking the tires.

2. (A) We were the first to arrive at the park; and we were the last to leave. (B) While other people stayed for only a few minutes, we couldn't stop staring at the view, (C) "I've never seen anything like this", my wife said. (D) I couldnt help but agree.

Answers

1. (A) is missing an apostrophe: *Sue's* is possessive. (B) is also missing an apostrophe: *it's* stands in for "it is" so one is needed. (C) needs parentheses: Her husband (not a great mechanic himself) couldn't get …. (D) Remember the serial comma! It should appear in the sentence after "neutral": He tried turning over the engine, looking in the manual, putting the car into neutral, and kicking the tires.

2. (A) Either the semicolon or the "and" needs to come out. They serve the same purpose. (B) Watch that end punctuation! You need a period, not a comma. (C) The comma should go inside the quotation marks: "I've never seen anything like this," my wife said. (D) Put an apostrophe in "couldn't."

The Right Way to Write Paragraphs

In This Chapter

- Overview of organization in your essay, letter, or other document
- GED-like questions to practice the skills you'll be tested on
- Answers and explanations for all the questions

We're almost done reviewing what you'll need to know for the first part of the Language Arts: Writing Test. This chapter covers the last type of question that you'll need to be familiar with: restructuring paragraphs. As you know, the GED will present you with several passages in the form of essays, letters, emails, or other documents. The passages will be broken up into paragraphs in which each sentence is numbered. A series of questions, about 10 per passage, will ask you to fix grammatical errors.

Additionally, some of these questions may use language such as:

Which revision would improve the effectiveness of paragraph 1?

Then, the answer choices give you the option to replace certain sentences, move sentences, or remove sentences.

Here's an example, albeit with just one paragraph instead of an entire passage, and lacking any grammatical errors:

> (A) Growing to be about 44 inches tall, at maximum, they weigh between 60 and 90 pounds, making them 10 times the size of the eggs they protect. (B) Emperor penguins are renowned in the animal kingdom for being devoted parents. (C) While Emperor penguins usually eat fish and crustaceans, including shrimp and crabs, they eat nothing while raising their eggs. (D) In fact, male penguins may lose half their body weight when taking care of the egg, because they do not eat.

Which correction would improve the effectiveness of the paragraph?

(1) Remove sentence D.

(2) Move sentence B to the beginning of the paragraph.

(3) Move sentence A to the end of the paragraph.

(4) Replace sentence 1 with *Emperor penguins are also considered the most docile of the species.*

(5) Move sentence C to the end of the paragraph.

The correct answer is (2). You could make a case that sentence D is redundant when presented with sentence C, but removing or rewriting it is not one of the choices, so (2) is the correct answer.

As you can tell, with this type of question, your ability to organize your writing effectively is tested. In this chapter, we'll review several important skills you'll need to ace these questions.

Organize for Clarity

The goal with any passage, whether you're writing it (as in your essay) or just restructuring it (as in this section), is to keep your meaning clear. You don't want a reader to have to piece together what is being conveyed. The paragraph should flow in such a way that the meaning is easily apparent. To do that, your paragraphs need to be organized. In this section, you have all the puzzle pieces (the sentences); you just need to put the pieces together correctly (in an organized paragraph).

HEADS UP!

You can only fix the passages and sentences with the options available to you. You may see a much better solution, or a problem that is not addressed, in this part of the GED. However, your only options are the answer choices, so don't get caught up in something you really can't do anything about!

When looking for how your paragraph ought to be organized, consider the following options:

- Chronologically
- How to
- Persuasive

Let's look at each of these.

Chronologically

When a paragraph is ordered *chronologically*, it just means that the paragraph tells a story as it happened in time. In a clearly written paragraph, the events described will unspool as they occurred. Look at this example from an email written to make a complaint:

> The customer service representative was of no help. Before, I had asked at the front counter what I should do. They had sent me to the customer service rep. As I said, she was of no help. I should mention that I began this request for a refund at 9 A.M., as the store opened.

Typical chronology is not followed in this paragraph, making it very hard to figure out what has happened. Remember, in most cases, organize the sentences to follow chronologically. A well-organized paragraph would express the thoughts like this:

> At 9 A.M. today, I made a request for a refund at the store's front counter. I was then sent to the customer service desk, but the representative there was not able to help me, either.

How To

A *how to* paragraph is very similar to a chronological paragraph in that a clear order is easily apparent. In this type of paragraph, some sort of instruction is given, and the reader should be able to follow it without backtracking. That's why recipes don't read like this:

> Take the cake out of the oven, and let it cool. The frosting can now be made. The butter should have been removed from the refrigerator and allowed to soften by now.

Just like with a chronology, the paragraph needs to be ordered in a way that makes sense and is helpful to the reader. In this example, "The butter should be removed from the refrigerator and allowed to soften" should be the first sentence. Here's the fixed paragraph:

> The butter should be removed from the refrigerator and allowed to soften while the cake bakes. When the cake is done, remove it from the oven and allow it to cool. Then prepare the frosting.

GOOD IDEA

Look for words to alert you that a passage is chronological. Any phrase or word that indicates time is a hint, such as *yesterday, earlier, last night, previously, on Tuesday,* and so on. How to paragraphs have key words, too, including *next, last,* and *then.*

Persuasive

In a *persuasive* paragraph, the writer is trying to convince his or her readers of an opinion. The stated opinion is usually presented at the beginning or end of the paragraph and the reasons for the opinion stated around it. You should check to make sure the paragraph flows logically. Here's an example:

> Yarn is relatively inexpensive, and needles don't cost much, either. Knitting is a relaxing, and thrifty, hobby. While it can be complicated to learn, it provides hours of enjoyment after doing so. Further, many knitters report a feeling of relaxation and contentment after knitting for even just a few minutes. Scientific studies back up this anecdotal evidence, showing that the brain waves of people who are knitting are considerably more even than those who are merely sitting and thinking.

As the paragraph is written now, a reason is presented (yarn is relatively inexpensive), then the topic of the paragraph (knitting is a relaxing, and thrifty, hobby), and then further reasons. It's clear that the paragraph could be organized in a way that is less confusing for your reader.

Finding the Topic Sentence

The topic sentence in a paragraph is key. Being able to recognize one, and place it correctly within the paragraph, will greatly help you as a writer—and on this section of the GED.

A *topic sentence* states the main idea of a paragraph. It is often, but not always, the first sentence of a paragraph; it's also common to find it as the second or last sentence of a paragraph, depending on the structure employed. When a topic sentence appears at the beginning of a paragraph, the rest of the paragraph explains it. When a topic sentence appears at the end of a paragraph, it serves as a summary for what's come before.

The GED doesn't usually use the phrase "topic sentence," but often asks you to find and move it, nonetheless. They may put it this way: Which sentence would be most effective if inserted at the beginning/end of the paragraph?

While looking at the beginning and end of the paragraph is a good tip for finding the topic sentence, it's not foolproof. Remember that you're looking for the sentence that states the main idea of the paragraph. To do this, when you're looking at your choices, ask yourself these questions:

- What is the main idea of this paragraph?

- Which of these sentences best states that idea?

You can also help yourself by eliminating sentences. You can be fairly sure that if the sentence includes the words *for example* or *to illustrate*, it is not the topic sentence. Also, sentences that include *transitional words*—which connect ideas in the text to each other, such as *first, next,* or *last*—are not usually the topic sentence, whereas sentences that include transitional words such as *overall* or *in the main* might be the topic sentence. (Don't get your hopes up, though; the writers of the GED do not usually include transitional words that are so clearly tip-offs to the correct sentence order.)

DEFINITION

Transitional words connect ideas to each other, usually giving some information about how the ideas are related. They include *therefore, on the other hand,* and *similarly,* as well as words like *first, next, last,* and *finally.*

Practice

In the following two paragraphs, try to identify which sentence would be the best topic sentence. Remember that on the GED, you'll be asked which sentence would be most effective when inserted at the beginning or the end of the paragraph.

1. (A) Although almost always indoors, often staying in her room, Dickinson nonetheless was an avid correspondent. (B) She wrote to many friends and family members. (C) The popular image of the poet Emily Dickinson as an uncommunicative recluse is incorrect. (D) Many of her thousands of poems were dedicated and sent to one of her correspondents.

2. (A) Journalists are faced with a barrage of enticements to act unethically in order to nail the story. (B) Whereas once a certain decorum was in place, today all media outlets compete to break a major story, even if the subject matter is indelicate. (C) The 24-hour news cycle and rise of web journalism are the driving forces of this new climate.

Answers

1. The topic sentence is (C). It states the main idea and serves as an introduction for the rest of the information within the paragraph.

2. The topic sentence is (B). It states the main idea and leads into the other sentences.

Achieving Unity and Coherence in Your Writing

While unity and coherence are always important in your writing, within this section of the GED, they should be your guiding light. Much of the work of writing has been done for you, and you're given a passage in the form of an essay, letter, email, or other piece of writing. The trick then becomes that you must apply unity and coherence to the writing you've been given.

Unity

Unity means that every sentence in the paragraph relates to the main idea expressed in the topic sentence.

Take a look at this example:

(A) Blue is widely reported to be most peoples' favorite color in informal surveys. (B) Yet during scientific trials, photos that prominently feature green are most often chosen as "most soothing" or "most pleasing" by participants.

(C) Brown was not included in this experiment, because no one likes brown. (D) Therefore, the question becomes, which color is truly the country's favorite: green or blue?

Here, you can tell that (C) doesn't belong. It's tangentially tied to some of the information included in the paragraph, but doesn't relate to the topic sentence (D). Therefore, the unity of the paragraph is broken. Removing (C) would be an option in a question about improving the paragraph unity.

Coherence

Coherence occurs in a paragraph when all of the sentences are presented in a logical order. Earlier in this chapter we looked at some of the logical ways of organizing a paragraph. That's what coherence provides.

IN THE KNOW

A paragraph can be unified but lack coherence. That is, all of the sentences may relate to the topic of the paragraph, but they may not be in a logical order. However, it's essentially impossible for a paragraph to have coherence without unity. Just think about it!

While many of the paragraphs previously presented in this chapter lack coherence, here's an example of a paragraph that does flow coherently:

> The film *Titanic* was not only a box-office phenomenon, it also launched the careers of its stars. Neither Kate Winslet nor Leonardo DiCaprio was unknown in Hollywood, but neither had enjoyed instant recognition. Winslet was known for a sparkling turn in *Sense and Sensibility;* DiCaprio had won raves for a supporting role in *What's Eating Gilbert Grape.* After *Titanic,* both became household names.

See how the paragraph is coherent? It starts by stating a premise in the topic sentence—that *Titanic* launched the careers of its leading actors—and goes on to provide facts that back up the premise. That's a coherent paragraph.

The Ringer Sentence

Spotting the incoherence in a paragraph on the GED may be easier if you can think of it as finding "the ringer sentence." By this, we mean the sentence that, just like a "ringer" in sports, has come from elsewhere and stands out.

For example, take a look at this paragraph:

> (A) Hawaii is a beautiful place to visit. (B) While the flight from the continental United States is long, the relaxed pace of life that awaits travelers is well worth the inconvenience. (C) The 50th state offers beautiful beaches, top-notch surfing, delicious cuisine, and breathtaking scenery. (D) My grandmother hated to fly, though. (E) Many people who make the trip to Hawaii plan to return frequently, despite their jet lag.

See the ringer sentence? It's (D). What does the writer's grandmother have to do with Hawaii? Nothing, so that sentence destroys the paragraph's coherence.

Practice

Read the following email and then answer the questions, remembering what you reviewed so far.

> TO: All employees
>
> FROM: Stephan Swope, Director of Human Resources
>
> DATE: April 21, 2012
>
> RE: Dress code
>
> **Paragraph 1:** (A) What's most important is that shoes must be worn at all times. (B) After last week's factory floor incident, I wanted to take a few minutes to review the company dress code with you. (C) Coveralls are mandatory, and will be provided for those who do not have, or have lost, theirs. (D) Hairnets are suggested for those with hair longer than one inch.
>
> **Paragraph 2:** (A) A sturdy set of work boots are also suggested, although steel-toed boots are not mandatory. (B) We deeply regret the injury caused to one of our employees because dress code regulations were not followed. (C) Unfortunately, liquid does occasionally condense on the floor of the factory near the larger machines, which is why boots are suggested. (D) You know, my wife's father lost half of his arm because he wasn't cautious about loading

the machine correctly at the factory where he worked. (E) Unfortunately, I ask you to consider contributing to the fund set up for our co-worker's medical care, and please conform to the suggested dress code as stated above.

1. Which revision would improve the effectiveness of paragraph 1?

   (1) Removing sentence (D)

   (2) Moving sentence (D) to the beginning of the paragraph

   (3) Moving sentence (B) to the beginning of the paragraph

   (4) Removing sentence (A)

   (5) Moving sentence (A) to the end of the paragraph

2. In paragraph 2, which revision would improve the effectiveness of sentence (E): "Unfortunately, I ask you to consider contributing to the fund set up for our co-worker's medical care, and please conform to the suggested dress code as stated above."?

   (1) Change *Unfortunately* to *Additionally.*

   (2) Remove *and please conform to the suggested dress code as stated above.*

   (3) Remove the comma after *Unfortunately.*

   (4) Replace the comma after *medical care* with a semicolon.

   (5) Change *Unfortunately* to *In conclusion.*

3. In paragraph 2, which revision would improve the effectiveness of sentence (A)?

   (1) Move it to the end of paragraph 2.

   (2) Move it to the end of paragraph 1.

   (3) Remove the comma in the sentence.

   (4) Replace the comma in the sentence with a semicolon.

   (5) Move it to after sentence (B).

Answers

1. **(3)** This is the topic sentence, and needs to be moved to be effective in organizing the information contained within the paragraph.

2. **(1)** *Unfortunately* does not make sense in the sentence or paragraph; negative (or unfortunate) information is not being conveyed. Changing *Unfortunately* to *Additionally* makes much more sense.

3. **(2)** This sentence belongs at the end of paragraph 1. When it's moved there, both paragraphs 1 and 2 are more unified.

Language Arts: Writing Practice Test

Taking the practice test will help prepare you for the real test by providing examples of the types of information you need to demonstrate proficiency in and by helping you identify any areas that you need to go back and review. For the actual Language Arts: Writing Test, you will be assessed on your knowledge and usage of grammar. You will need to show proficiency in organization, sentence structure, usage, and mechanics. To demonstrate your understanding of organization (15 percent of your score) you will be asked to restructure parts of paragraphs to make them flow appropriately. For sentence structure (30 percent of your score), you will be asked to correct run-on sentences, comma splices, and lack of parallel construction. For usage (30 percent of your score), you will be asked to correct errors in subject-verb agreement, pronoun use, and verb tense. Finally, for mechanics (25 percent of your score), you will correct spelling, punctuation, and capitalization errors.

On the actual test, you will be presented with 50 questions and will have 75 minutes to complete them. For the practice test, you will be provided with one-half the number of questions or 25, and should allow yourself one-half the time allotment, or $37\frac{1}{2}$ minutes. Once you complete the test, check your answers against the answers and explanations provided after the test and look for any areas of weakness. Go back to the appropriate chapters to review those areas you need help with.

If, after taking the test provided here, you feel you need more practice and want to take another simulated test, there are several online sites that offer free GED practice tests. One site we recommend is PBS Literacy Link (http:litlink.ket.org). Keep in mind, though, that the actual GED Tests are paper-and-pencil tests like those in this book and cannot be taken on a computer.

Instructions

The Language Arts: Writing Test is designed to measure your understanding of grammar. Some questions are based on a short reading. Use the information provided to answer the question(s) that follow. You can refer to the reading as often as you want in answering the question(s).

You will have about $37\frac{1}{2}$ minutes to complete the 25 questions on this practice test. Work carefully, but don't spend too much time on any one question. If you are having trouble with a question, make the best guess you can and move on. Your score is based on the number of correct answers; there is no penalty for guessing.

When taking the practice test, try to simulate actual test conditions. Get a timing device of some sort and a couple of No. 2 pencils with good erasers. Go to a place where you won't be interrupted and follow test instructions. Start the timer after you've read the instructions and are ready to begin the first question.

Go on to the next page when you are ready to begin.

Questions 1–4 refer to the following letter.

Mr. Harry Stockwell, Manager Complaint Department

ABC Small Appliances

267 main Road

Wilmington, DE 11234

January 10, 2012

Dear mr. Stockwell,

(1) I visited ABC Appliance on November 20th and purchased a So toaster oven. (2) I was pleased for about a week with the way it cooked, toasted, and broiled food however in the second week, the broiler burst into flames. (3) Scorching my counter top. (4) I know you will want to replace the toaster oven we have to discuss replacing the counter top. (5) Please let me know when you are available to meet with me.

Thanks a lot.

Perry Webb

1. What correction should be made to sentence 2?

   I was pleased for about a week with the way it cooked, toasted, and broiled food however in the second week, the broiler burst into flames.

   (1) food; however,

   (2) broiled, food

   (3) week, with

   (4) pleased, for

   (5) second-week

2. What type of sentence is sentence 3?

   Scorching my counter top.

   (1) A correct sentence

   (2) A comma fault sentence

   (3) A fragment

   (4) A run-on sentence

   (5) A wordy sentence

3. Choose the best correction for the underlined part of sentence 4.

    <u>oven we</u>

    (1) oven. we

    (2) oven. You

    (3) oven, we

    (4) oven. We

    (5) oven. Your customers

4. What correction should be made to the inside address?

    267 main Road

    (1) Change 267 to 276

    (2) Change main to Main

    (3) Change Road to rd.

    (4) Change Road to road

    (5) No correction needed

For questions 5–8, select the answer that corrects the underlined portion of the sentence.

5. <u>Him and me</u> carpool to work every day.

    (1) Me and he

    (2) He and I

    (3) He and me

    (4) I and him

    (5) I and he

6. The pictures belonging to my aunt <u>is well known</u>.

    (1) are well known

    (2) all well known

    (3) is not well known

    (4) isn't well known

    (5) am not well known

7. <u>breaking too many dishes</u>.

   (1) Breaking too many dishes today

   (2) Breaking many dishes

   (3) I found myself

   (4) Too many dishes broken

   (5) Braking dishes too

8. Jim <u>is more better</u> at math than Harry.

   (1) is most better

   (2) is not most better

   (3) is mostest better

   (4) is not more better

   (5) is better

Questions 9–15 refer to the following passage.

(1) Have you ever had a problem working with a co-worker? (2) If you have you would not be alone. (3) Research shows that 80 percent of employees report conflicts at work that affect their ability to work well. (4) It's easy to see that being angry at a co-worker would sap your energy, it could keep you from using your time productively.

(5) What can you do to get passed the bad feelings—and get back to work? (6) This may surprise you, but you shouldn't expect the first move to come from the other person. (7) Instaed, look at yourself. (8) What might you do to improve the situation? (9) Think of it this way The only person you know for sure that you can change is *you!* (10) Find one small thing that you can change and do it. (11) For example, try to place yourself in their shoes and see the situation from their perspective. (12) This may help you understand where they are coming from. (13) You may have more in common than you think?

(14) Another strategy is to look for one good quality the co-worker possesses. (15) For example, maybe the employee is always the first to arrive at the office. (16) The point is that you need to respect everyone at work. (17) To do that look for their strengths and skills and concentrate on them instead of their weaknesses.

(18) Finally, schedule a meeting with the person you're having a problem with in fact invite her out to lunch so it's a friendly environment in which to talk to her. (19) The first rule to follow is to concentrate on the problem. (20) Do not attack the person. (21) For example, instead of saying your way of doing things bothers me say how can we come up with a better way to get this done.

9. What corrections should be made to sentence 2?

    If you have you would not be alone.

    (1) have,

    (2) had

    (3) haven't you wouldn't

    (4) have;

    (5) have.

10. What corrections should be made to sentence 4?

    It's easy to see that being angry at a co-worker would sap your energy, it could keep you from using your time productively.

    (1) energy, It

    (2) your energy; it

    (3) co-worker. Would

    (4) its easy

    (5) No correction necessary

11. What correction should you make to sentence 7?

    Instaed, look at yourself.

    (1) Instaed with no comma

    (2) Youself

    (3) Instead

    (4) Yourselves

    (5) No correction necessary

12. What change should you make to sentence 9?

Think of it this way The only person you know for sure that you can change is *you!*

(1) this way, The

(2) this way. the

(3) this way the

(4) this way, the

(5) this way: The

13. What should you correct in sentence 13?

You may have more in common than you think?

(1) More,

(2) You,

(3) You, ...

(4) think.

(5) No correction necessary

14. What change should you make to sentence 17?

To do that look for their strengths and skills and concentrate on them instead of their weaknesses.

(1) that,

(2) To do that. Look

(3) To do that; Look

(4) strenths

(5) consentrate

15. How should you change sentence 18?

Finally, schedule a meeting with the person you're having a problem with in fact invite her out to lunch so it's a friendly environment in which to talk to her.

(1) with; in fact,

(2) with in fact,

(3) Finally, schedule a meeting. With

(4) its

(5) No correction necessary

Questions 16–20 refer to the following passage.

Job Posting

The XYZ store is looking for sales associates for immediate hire. If you meet the minimum qualifications please forward your resume and a letter of application to J.D. Ducklemeyer at Suite, 2020 1400 Thirsty Street, Applegate MD 45545 by November 30, 2012.

Qualifications

(1) The perfect candidate will have previous sales experience in childrens clothing, televisions, small appliances, or pet supplies. (2) Experience in all of these areas are a plus but not necessary. (3) Additionally, candidates who speak a second language such as spanish or portuguese would be highly desirable. (4) A salary commensurate with experience will be negotiated with the successful candidate. (5) As well as benefits and employee discounts. (6) Bonuses will be offered to those meeting certain sales goals on a quarterly basis. (7) Must be outgoing and comfortable with a variety of products. (8) High school diploma or GED required.

16. What correction should be made to sentence 1?

    The perfect candidate will have previous sales experience in childrens clothing, televisions, small appliances, or pet supplies.

    (1) childrens'

    (2) children's

    (3) expereince

    (4) clotheing

    (5) No correction necessary

17. What change should be made to sentence 2?

    Experience in all of these areas are a plus but not necessary.

    (1) Experience in all these areas are a plus to you

    (2) Experience in all of them areas is a plus

    (3) Experience in all of these areas is a plus

    (4) Experience in all of these areas is a plus to you

    (5) No correction necessary

18. What correction should be made to sentence 3?

    Additionally, candidates who speak a second language such as spanish or portuguese would be highly desirable.

    (1) Language

    (2) Spanish or Portuguese

    (3) whom

    (4) candadates

    (5) desirible

19. Sentence 5 contains what kind of sentence error?

    As well as benefits and employee discounts.

    (1) Incorrect information

    (2) A run-on sentence

    (3) A comma fault sentence

    (4) A fragment

    (5) There is no sentence error

20. How should sentence 6 be rewritten?

    Bonuses will be offered to those meeting certain sales goals on a quarterly basis.

    (1) Meeting certain sales goals, bonuses will be offered to those.

    (2) Goals on a quarterly basis should be met for a bonus.

    (3) Those meeting certain sales goals on a quarterly basis will be offered bonuses.

    (4) Bonuses will be offered on a quarterly basis meeting certain sales goals.

    (5) Certain sales goals are met for bonuses on a quarterly basis.

Questions 21–25 refer to the following passage.

Product Recall

(1) If you are in possession of Super Chunky Extra Peanutty Brand peanut butter. (2) Sold in Vermont and Florida between the dates of August 10 and August 20, 2012, with a serial number of 22233223. (3) please remove it from your home immediately and return it to the store you purchased it from for a full refund.

(4) This peanut butter contains a substanse used in chicken feed and should not be consumed by humans (especially young children), dogs, or cows. (5) If previously consumed call your doctor right away for the antidote. (6) The Super Chunky Extra Peanutty Brand peanut butter company regrets any inconvenience this recall may cause.

21. What type of sentence is sentence 1?

    If you are in possession of Super Chunky Extra Peanutty Brand peanut butter.

    (1) A complete sentence

    (2) An unnecessary detail

    (3) A run-on sentence

    (4) A comma fault

    (5) A fragment

22. What addition should be made to sentence 1?

    If you are in possession of Super Chunky Extra Peanutty Brand peanut butter.

    (1) , return it to the store.

    (2) If you, our customers,

    (3) are in posession

    (4) Supper chuncky

    (5) No addition necessary

23. What addition should be made to sentence 2?

    Sold in Vermont and Florida between the dates of August 10 and August 20, 2012, with a serial number of 22233223.

    (1) Sold, in Vermont

    (2) The peanut butter was sold

    (3) sold in Vermont, and

    (4) dates, of August 10

    (5) with no serial number

24. What changes should be made to sentence 3?

please remove it from your home immediately and return it to the store you purchased it from for a full refund.

(1) Please remove it from your home immedialtely

(2) Please

(3) Please remove it from your home, immediately, and return it to the store

(4) Store

(5) for a Full Refund

25. Which word is misspelled in sentence 4?

This peanut butter contains a substanse used in chicken feed and should not be consumed by humans (especially young children), dogs, or cows.

(1) substanse

(2) chicken

(3) consumed

(4) especially

(5) children

Answers and Explanations

1. **(1)** Connect two sentences with a semicolon, a conjunction, and a comma: *food; however, ….*

2. **(3)** It is a fragment. One possible rewrite: *I was pleased for about a week with the way it cooked, toasted, and broiled food. However, in the second week, the broiler burst into flames, scorching my counter top.*

3. **(4)** This run-on sentence can be corrected by inserting a period after the first thought: *I know you will want to replace the toaster oven. We have to discuss replacing the counter top.*

4. **(2)** A street name is capitalized.

5. **(2)** You need subject pronouns here. The subject pronouns are *He and I.*

6. **(1)** The subject, *pictures,* is a plural noun that requires a plural verb, *are.*

7. **(3)** The sentence needs a subject, *I.*

8. **(5)** Do not use *more* with the comparative adjective.

9. **(1)** Use a comma after an introductory phrase.

10. **(2)** Connect two thoughts with a semicolon.

11. **(3)** Spell *instead* correctly.

12. **(5)** The colon indicates that a solution follows.

13. **(4)** The sentence doesn't ask a question; it's a statement.

14. **(1)** Insert a comma after the introductory phrase, *to do that.*

15. **(1)** This is a run-on sentence. The two complete thoughts need to be separated with a semicolon or period.

16. **(2)** Form the plural in this way.

17. **(3)** The subject, *experience,* is a singular noun and requires a singular verb, *is.*

18. **(2)** Names of foreign languages are capitalized.

19. **(4)** The sentence is a fragment. The fragment can be added to the previous sentence: *A salary commensurate with experience will be negotiated with the successful candidate, as well as benefits and employee discounts.*

20. **(3)** This is the best (and correct) rewriting of the sentence.

21. **(5)** Beware of sentences that start with *If.* Remember, *if this, then that.* Otherwise, the sentence remains a fragment.

22. **(1)** These words provide the missing action.

23. **(2)** The sentence needs a subject.

24. **(2)** Start a sentence with a capital letter.

25. **(1)** *Substance* is the correct spelling of the word.

Social Studies

Part

2

Each of the five review chapters in Part 2 provides an overview of one of the subject areas on the Social Studies Test along with GED-style practice questions. Chapter 9 focuses on U.S. history, on which 26 percent of the test questions are based. Chapter 10 discusses U.S. government and politics, which comprises 24 percent of the test. Chapter 11 reviews basic concepts of economics, which accounts for 20 percent of the test questions. Chapter 12 deals with world history (16 percent of the test questions), and Chapter 13 provides concepts of geography (14 percent of the test questions).

In Chapter 14 you can take a realistic social studies practice test (half the length of the actual test). On the test, a reading and/or visual item (graph, cartoon, map, photo, or table) is followed by questions. You won't need to memorize dates and facts; instead, you'll be tested on your skill in comprehending, interpreting, analyzing, or applying the information you are given.

U.S. History

In This Chapter

- Overviews of key periods and developments in U.S. history
- GED-like questions to practice the skills you'll be tested on
- Answers and explanations for all the questions

U.S. history comprises the largest number of questions on the Social Studies Test. You can expect 13 of the 50 questions to be based on U.S. history content.

You won't be required to memorize dates and facts to ace the test. Most of the facts you'll need to know will be given in the reading passages or the visuals (graphs, maps, tables, etc.) that are included with the test questions. However, you will need to have a good understanding of U.S. history in order to put the readings and visuals into their historical context and work through the questions quickly. The test focuses on your skills in understanding, analyzing, and applying the information presented to you.

This chapter provides overviews of important areas of U.S. history that will almost certainly be included in some way on the test. Following these overviews are GED-like questions that will help prepare you for the types of skill-based questions you will confront on the real test. Be sure to read the explanations for all those you missed or did not completely understand.

The Establishment of the United States

The Eastern Seaboard of North America was one of the last areas of the New World to be colonized by Europeans. The Spanish already controlled Mexico, Central America, and much of South America. The Portuguese had colonized Brazil, the

French had settled in Quebec, and British, French, Dutch, and Spanish had established sugar plantations throughout the West Indies. No obvious source of wealth was found along the Eastern Seaboard of North America. Many of the British colonies established along the North American coast in the 1600s were founded by people seeking, not wealth, but religious freedom; examples are the Puritans in New England, Quakers in Pennsylvania, and Catholics in Maryland. Of course, many early settlers also came for economic opportunity, a possibility that became more likely after a demand for tobacco, grown in Virginia, developed in Europe in the 1600s.

The British colonies along the Eastern Seaboard grew and prospered, but by the mid-1770s, many colonists wanted greater self-government and resented not having representation in the British Parliament. The Boston Tea Party (1774) is an example of American revolt against the distant British government. "No taxation without representation" became the American slogan, and tea with a tax imposed by the British Parliament was dumped into the Boston harbor. The government in Britain seemed remote and deaf to colonial views. Other disputes developed and skirmishes with British troops caused reactions that drove the sides farther apart. The result: in 1776 the 13 colonies united together for the purpose of gaining their independence from Britain.

The Declaration of Independence was written to justify the American rebellion; it was based on the ideas of French and British Enlightenment thinkers. Among the revolutionary ideas it contained was that governments derive their powers from the consent of the governed (rather than from the divine right of kings). It also stated the revolutionary idea that people have natural, God-given rights to life, liberty, and the pursuit of happiness. It went on to say that government's role is to protect these rights and, when it does not, the people have the right to rebel.

IN THE KNOW

Historians estimate that 15 to 20 percent of Americans remained loyal to Britain during the American Revolution. Sometimes families were divided. For example, William Franklin, son of Benjamin Franklin, remained loyal to Britain and never spoke to his father again. After the war, loyalists found themselves citizens of the new United States; some moved to England and Canada in order to remain British.

A rudimentary national government was formed—the Continental Congress—and George Washington formed a national army to fight the British. While at first the effort to defeat the army of what was then the world's most powerful nation seemed almost hopeless, the Americans enjoyed some advantages, such as popular support and familiarity with the land. Finally, with the support of the French military and assistance from other European nations with a score to settle with Britain, the Americans prevailed, the British army surrendered, and Britain granted independence to its colonies.

But it wasn't until almost 10 years later that the Americans established a unified nation and an effective national government. The U.S. Constitution that went into effect in 1789 was a bundle of political compromises among competing interests. One key compromise ended a bitter dispute between the larger, more populous states and the small ones. It established a bicameral legislature (Congress) in which all states large and small had equal representation in one house (the Senate), while representation in the other (the House of Representatives) was based on the state's population. To become law, a proposed bill had to be passed by both houses of Congress. Other difficult compromises had to be worked out between slave states (the six Southern states) and the states that had already outlawed slavery (the seven Northern states). Among these were an agreement not to limit the importation of African slaves for at least 20 years and to count slaves as three fifths of a person for purposes of taxation and representation. Another compromise agreed to by the supporters of the proposed Constitution (the Federalists) in order to gain the votes of states needed to ratify the document was an agreement to add a bill of rights specifically stating limitations on the power of government. As a result, shortly after ratification of the new constitution, 10 amendments were added which are today known as the Bill of Rights.

GOOD IDEA

You can expect that the Social Studies Test will have at least one question based on an excerpt from the Constitution or Declaration of Independence. Understanding these documents is doubly important since the documents are key parts of two subject areas covered on the test: U.S. history and U.S. government. Chapter 10 has more information about the Constitution and the government it established.

Practice: Establishment of the United States

Questions 1 and 2 refer to the following passage from the beginning of the Declaration of Independence.

> When in the course of human events it becomes necessary for one people to dissolve the political bands which have connected them with another ... a decent respect for the opinions of mankind requires that they should declare the causes which impel them to the separation.
>
> We hold these truths to be self-evident, that all men are created equal, that they are endowed by their Creator with certain unalienable Rights, that among these are Live, Liberty and the pursuit of Happiness. That to secure these rights, Governments are instituted among Men, deriving their just powers from the consent of the governed ....

1. The reason this passage was written was to:

   (1) make the case that people have God-given rights.

   (2) reform the British government.

   (3) state new theories developed by American philosophers on the nature of government.

   (4) justify the American position that they need to set up their own indepen-dent government.

   (5) end the British royalty and replace it with a government elected by the people.

2. The existence of slavery in the United States is inconsistent with which of the following ideas stated in the Declaration of Independence?

   (1) One reason for the existence of governments is to protect rights, including property rights.

   (2) The Americans and British need to go their separate ways.

   (3) All men are created equal and have a right to life, liberty, and the pursuit of happiness.

   (4) The government's powers are derived from the consent of the governed.

   (5) The British government has abused its power and not respected the rights of Americans.

Question 3 relates to the following political cartoon that was first published in 1754 and is attributed to Benjamin Franklin.

3. What opinion is the cartoonist expressing?

    (1) The large states can "go it alone" and do not need to join the United States.

    (2) Compromise is necessary if a Constitution is to be ratified.

    (3) Human beings need to stop acting like snakes if they are to succeed.

    (4) Transportation routes between the colonies need to be improved to better connect the colonies.

    (5) The colonies need to unite in order to maximize their power and stand up to Britain.

Answers: Establishment of the United States

1. **(4)** The first sentence states the purpose of the document: to explain why they are revolting and want to set up their own country. The document does state the belief in God-given rights (1), but this is only in the context of explaining why they are revolting. At this point they have clearly gone beyond simply trying to reform the British government (2) (5). The ideas contained in the Declaration of Independence (3) came from European theorists (chiefly John Locke), not Americans.

2. **(3)** The existence of slavery in the American colonies is completely inconsistent with the idea that all men are created equally and endowed with a right to liberty. The ideas that Americans and Brits should go their separate ways (2) and that the British government has abused its power (5) had little or nothing to do with slavery. Choices (1) and (4) do not directly contradict the existence of slavery; slave owners regarded owning slaves as a property right and the majority of the governed in slave states might support the existence of slavery.

3. **(5)** In this famous cartoon, Franklin was urging the colonies to unite. A snake cut up will not survive, but can be ferocious if it's all together. This included even the larger colonies (1) like New York (N.Y.), Pennsylvania (P), and Virginia (V). There is nothing in the cartoon to indicate Franklin was talking about how humans behave (3), trade routes (4), or the Constitution (2), which, by the way, wasn't written until 30 years later.

Growth of the United States

At the time of American independence, all states bordered the Atlantic Ocean and American settlement ended at the Appalachian Mountains only a couple hundred miles inland. Scarcely 65 years later (1848) the land of the United States stretched 2,500 miles across the continent to California and Oregon on the Pacific Ocean. Territory was added to the United States by purchases (the Louisiana Purchase from France and Florida from Spain), by military conquest (California and the Southwest from Mexico), and by boundary negotiations (Oregon Country south of the 49th parallel in an agreement with Britain). Texas was a unique case: Americans settled in Mexican-controlled Texas in great numbers, came to outnumber Mexicans living there, then fought for and gained their independence from Mexico, and finally joined the United States.

Large numbers of Native Americans were wiped out by diseases, mostly European diseases to which they had no built-up natural immunity. Remaining Indians were pushed westward, defeated militarily, and eventually forced onto unproductive reservations, where many more died from disease and starvation. The U.S. Army established bases throughout the West to subdue Native American people and make the land "safe" for settlement.

Most settlers moved westward in search of new farmland, but gold rushes in the California and the Rocky Mountains were also instrumental in pulling settlers to the western frontier. Settlers moved westward via canals (especially the Erie Canal), rivers (especially the Ohio, Mississippi, and Missouri), and rudimentary roads (the most famous is the Oregon Trail). As the nation developed industrially, railroads were built across the continent—the first transcontinental railroad was completed in 1867—and these became the primary means of westward settlement.

Westward movement was fueled partly by the arrival of thousands of new immigrants each year. Successive waves of immigrants came first from Britain, then Ireland and northern Europe, then southern Europe and Asia, and finally today, from Latin

America. As a result, the United States grew rapidly in population as well as land area. The United States is still a nation where most people are either immigrants themselves or can trace their family background to immigrant parents, grandparents, or great-grandparents.

HEADS UP!

Don't confuse immigrant with emigrant. An *immigrant* is a person who comes to a new country to live there, while an *emigrant* is a person who leaves a country to live in a different one. So each immigrant is also an emigrant; which word is used depends on the perspective of the speaker. A person moving from Italy to the United States would be an immigrant to Americans but an emigrant to Italians.

Although a nation of immigrants, many Americans have typically feared that later waves of immigration would change the character of the United States and threaten their dominance. For example, in the 1850s the Know Nothings, a secretive organization formed to oppose the immigration of Catholics, became one of the largest political parties in the United States, scoring victories in gubernatorial, congressional, and mayoral elections across the United States. From the mid-nineteenth century to the mid-twentieth century, Asian immigrants particularly faced anti-immigrant sentiment and many discriminatory laws. But immigrant energy, derived from a strong desire to work hard and create a better life for themselves and their children, has fueled American economic development and created one of the world's most dynamic economies.

Not only were the land area and population of the United States rapidly expanding, so was industry. As industry developed in the Northeast and Midwest, immigrants increasingly moved to impoverished ethnic enclaves in the cities, where they provided labor for factories, rather than settling on the Western frontier. By the end of the nineteenth century, the United States was the world's leading industrial power. But industrial strength and wealth had been achieved partly through the exploitation of labor. In the early twentieth century, in what is called the Progressive Era, government began to step in to protect worker rights, outlaw child labor, set minimum wages, limit working hours, establish safety regulations, and break up business monopolies. This economic system of capitalism with some government intervention and regulation defines the American economy today.

Practice: Growth of the United States

Question 1 refers to the following map.

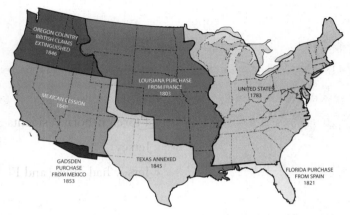

U.S. territorial acquisitions.

1. According to the map, from what country did the United States first acquire land for expansion?

   (1) France

   (2) Mexico

   (3) Spain

   (4) Britain

   (5) Texas

Questions 2 and 3 refer to data presented in the following table.

States with the Highest Percentages of Immigrants, 2009

State	Total Population	Foreign-Born Population
California	36.3 million	26.8%
New York	19.4 million	21.3%
New Jersey	8.7 million	19.7%
Nevada	2.6 million	18.7%
Florida	18.2 million	18.7%
Texas	23.8 million	15.8%

Source: U.S. Census Bureau

2. In which state(s) in 2009 were more than one out of five residents immigrants to the United States?

(1) California only

(2) California and New York

(3) California, New York, and New Jersey

(4) All of the states listed

(5) None of the states listed

3. Which states had a larger number of foreign-born residents than Nevada?

(1) California, New York, and New Jersey

(2) California, New York, and New Jersey had more, and Florida had the same number as Nevada

(3) Florida and Texas

(4) All of the other five states

(5) None of the other five states

Answers: Growth of the United States

1. **(1)** The earliest acquisition shown on the map was the 1803 Louisiana Purchase, which doubled the size of the original United States (1783 was the date of the Treaty of Paris, which officially granted American independence).

2. **(3)** Twenty percent is equivalent to one out of five. In three states immigrants comprised more than 20 percent of the population in 2009. A basic understanding of percent is important to understanding data presented on the Social Studies Test.

3. **(4)** This question is asking for numbers, not percentages. Numbers of foreign-born residents are not given on the table, but you don't really need to do any math to see that Nevada's foreign-born population is much smaller than any of the other states in this table. Doing the math, Nevada's 18.7 percent of 2.6 million (486,000) is much smaller than even Texas's 15.8 percent of 23.8 million (3,998,000).

The Civil War, Reconstruction, and the Civil Rights Movement

Sectional issues divided the United States for 4 decades before war broke out between the states in 1861. In the United States two conflicting social and economic systems were developing: an industrial, more egalitarian North (where slavery was illegal) and an agrarian, hierarchical South (where slavery formed a vital part of the plantation economy). Irresolvable conflicts arose over issues like whether slavery should be allowed to spread into Western territories, whether taxes on imports (tariffs) should be levied to help Northern manufacturers, whether runaway slaves who made it to the North had to be returned, etc. Compromises were hammered out in Congress. One example: from 1820 until 1850, states joined the Union in pairs (a slave state and a free state) so that there was always the same number of slave and free states and the Senate was equally divided between North and South. But anti-slavery sentiment was building in the North, and the South was feeling more vulnerable as the North became increasingly more populous, more industrial, and more technologically advanced than the South.

When the Republican Party, which wanted to stop the expansion of slavery to new territories, won the presidency with the election of Abraham Lincoln in 1860, 11 Southern states declared they were leaving the United States and setting up a new country, the Confederate States of America. Technically the issue over which the Civil War was fought was whether or not a state which had decided to join the United States could secede (leave the Union) if it later wanted to. The South argued in favor of state rights, while from the Northern perspective the states rights' issue was just a cover for the real issue dividing the North and South: slavery.

IN THE KNOW

Eleven states formed the Confederate States of America, also known as the Confederacy, or the South. Twenty-two states remained in the United States, also known as the Union, or the North. The Union included four "border states" (Missouri, Kentucky, Maryland, and Delaware) that continued to allow slavery but for various reasons did not leave the Union. The terms *North, South,* and *border states* are still used in discussing regional differences within the United States.

To be victorious, the South only had to keep the Union army out or inflict enough casualties to cause the North to give up and let the South go its own way. The South almost succeeded. For the North to be victorious, the Union army had to defeat and occupy the South. The North, which had an enormous advantage in manpower, industrial capacity, and transportation systems, accomplished that goal after 4 years of war. The Civil War was by far the United States' most deadly and destructive war; over a million Americans died, including 620,000 soldiers. The North succeeded because it destroyed not only the South's army but also its economy, which had provided food and supplies to the soldiers. At the end of the war, the South was in ruins.

The Civil War was followed by a period called Reconstruction, a period of reform imposed by the North on the South. The Thirteenth Amendment freed the slaves, the Fourteenth Amendment required state governments to treat all their citizens equally regardless of race, and the Fifteenth Amendment gave voting rights to former slaves. But with the election of Rutherford Hays as president in 1870, Reconstruction ended and control of the state governments of the South reverted to the same interests, classes, and race that controlled them before the Civil War. African Americans were effectively denied the right to vote by literacy tests and poll taxes. Races were segregated (separated) so that African Americans could not attend the same schools, ride in the same railroad cars, or eat at the same lunch counters as whites. In the end most African Americans were not in much better situations than before the war. As a result, a century-long migration of African Americans to Northern cities began.

About a hundred years after Reconstruction, a second reconstruction known as the civil rights movement occurred. This period of reconstruction differed in that it was led by African Americans, who in nonviolent protests demanded equal rights. Dr. Martin Luther King Jr. became the best known leader of the civil rights movement, which was characterized by peaceful protest marches and sit-ins that called attention to injustice and succeeded in bringing far-reaching change. Some of the key achievements of the civil rights movement are summarized as follows:

- **1948** President Truman desegregates the armed forces, allowing blacks and whites to serve in the same units.

- **1954** In *Brown v. the Board of Education of Topeka*, the Supreme Court rules that segregation of public schools by race is inherently unequal and thus unconstitutional under the Fourteenth Amendment.

- **1957** President Eisenhower orders federal troops to Arkansas to force the state government to allow African Americans to enroll at Little Rock's all-white Central High School.

- **1964** In *Loving v. Virginia*, the Supreme Court rules that states cannot prohibit interracial marriage.

- **1964** Congress passes the Civil Rights Act that ends racial segregation and discrimination in public accommodations like restaurants, stores, buses, and parks.

- **1964**   The Twenty-Second Amendment outlaws the poll tax (a tax on voting used to keep poor people, especially African Americans, from voting).

- **1965**   Congress passes the Voting Rights Act, which ends literacy tests and requires state governments to take action to encourage minorities to register and vote.

Practice: Civil War, Reconstruction, and the Civil Rights Movement

1. According to the previous list, milestones of the civil rights movement included all of the following types of governmental actions *except*

   (1) laws passed by state governments.

   (2) Supreme Court decisions.

   (3) a constitutional amendment.

   (4) laws passed by Congress.

   (5) presidential orders.

Question 2 refers to the following bar graph.

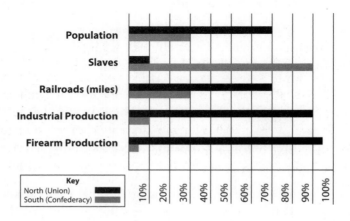

**Comparison of the North and the South
at the Beginning of the Civil War**

2. Which statement correctly describes information shown in the bar graph?

(1) At the beginning of the Civil War, the North and South each had about the same population.

(2) Having more slaves gave the South an advantage in the Civil War.

(3) At the beginning of the Civil War, the South had slaves and the North did not.

(4) At the beginning of the Civil War, nearly all firearms manufactured in the United States were produced in the North.

(5) The North's railroads were the key factor that helped it win the war.

Question 3 refers to the following passage, which contains excerpts from the 1858 Lincoln-Douglas debates between Abraham Lincoln and Stephen A. Douglas, both campaigning at the time to become a senator from Illinois in the U.S. Congress. Note that at this time the United States contained states and territories, which were areas under federal control on the Western frontier that did not yet have enough population for statehood.

Lincoln (a member of the Republican Party): "The Republican Party looks upon slavery as a moral, social, and political wrong …. [We] nevertheless have due regard for its actual existence among us and the difficulties of getting rid of it in any satisfactory way …. Yet having a due regard for these …, [we] insist that it should be treated as a wrong and one of the methods of treating it as a wrong is to make provision that is shall spread no further …. [I am in favor of] restricting the spread of [slavery] and not allowing it to go into territories where it has not already existed."

Douglas (a member of the Democratic Party): "Mr. Lincoln tries to avoid the main issue by attacking the truth of my proposition that our fathers made this government divided into free and slave states, recognizing the right of each state to decide all its local questions for itself [including whether or not to permit slavery]. I assert that this country can exist as they made it, divided into free and slave states, as long as any state chooses to retain slavery …. I assert that the people of a territory, as well as those of a state, have the right to decide for themselves whether slavery can or cannot exist in such territory."

3. Lincoln and Douglas would probably agree that

(1) slavery is wrong.

(2) states and new territories should decide for themselves whether or not they want to permit slavery.

(3) slavery should not be allowed to spread to new territories within the United States.

(4) nothing should be done to immediately end slavery in the states where it already exists and most people favor it.

(5) it would be easy to simply abolish slavery in the United States.

Answers: Civil War, Reconstruction, and the Civil Rights Movement

1. **(1)** Most state governments in the South strongly resisted the civil rights movement, and a number of Southern governors tried to block desegregation. All of the milestones were actions of the U.S. government, including the Supreme Court, the Congress, and the president as well as an amendment to the U.S. Constitution.

2. **(4)** The bar graph shows that at the beginning of the Civil War, 95 percent of firearms manufactured in the United States were produced in the North, making statement (4) correct. Statements (1) and (3) are contradicted by the information shown in the graph. Statement (2) correctly states that the South had more slaves, but there is no information in the graph to indicate this was an advantage for the South. In fact, slavery didn't help the South's war effort; slaves could not be relied upon to fight for the South and many ran away and joined the Union army. There is no information in the bar graph to indicate how important railroads were in causing the North's victory (5); in fact the North's advantage in railroads was just one of a number of advantages that helped it win the Civil War.

3. **(4)** Both Lincoln and Douglas would agree that nothing should be done to immediately end slavery in the states where it already exists. Statement (1) is Lincoln's position, but not that of Douglas, who believes it should exist as long as the people in a state want it. Statement (2) is Douglas's position, which contrasts with Lincoln's position in statement (3). Both Lincoln and Douglas would disagree with the statement that slavery can be easily ended.

The United States as a World Power

Until the twentieth century, the United States was absorbed with internal affairs such as westward expansion, economic growth, and the conflict between the North and South. The United States had only a small army, stayed out of foreign alliances, and did not get involved much in world affairs. In the twentieth century, however, this changed dramatically as the United States increased the size of its armed forces, became involved in wars around the world, established alliances, joined international organizations, and became a leader in world affairs.

As a result of a victory in a war with Spain (1898), the United States suddenly found itself an imperialistic power—a country with an empire containing distant lands and peoples. Americans took control of Puerto Rico (which it still controls) and the Philippines (a country it controlled until 1946).

These events changed Americans' view of themselves and their role in world affairs. Business interests began promoting American intervention in world affairs as a way of promoting U.S. economic interests around the world. Hawaii, an independent nation, was annexed by the United States (1898), and the United States took control of land in Panama (1903) for the building of the Panama Canal.

Then, in 1917, Americans, for the first time, entered a European war that did not directly involve the United States. Involvement was driven in part by commercial interests but also by an idealistic view that this war (called the "Great War" at the time but today known as World War I) would be "the war to end all wars," as President Woodrow Wilson described it. He envisioned American leadership in a new international order that included the League of Nations, an international organization whose purpose was to help peacefully resolve international disputes. In World War I American forces ended a military stalemate and brought victory to France, Britain, Russia, and Italy against Germany and Austria-Hungary, gaining international recognition of the United States as a world power. But Wilson's vision of a new global political order in which the United States would play an important role ended when American isolationists in the U.S. Senate blocked the United States from joining the League of Nations and playing a leadership role in world affairs.

Only 2 decades later, an even larger war had broken out in Europe and Asia between the Axis Powers (Germany, Italy, and Japan) and the Allied Powers (Britain, France, the Soviet Union or Russia, and China). The United States, which opposed the Nazism of Germany and the imperialism of Japan, supported the Allied Powers but did not actually join the war until Japan attacked the U.S. naval base at Pearl Harbor, Hawaii in 1941. World War II (1939–1946), the first truly global conflict, involved most of the world's nations and over 100 million troops. It brought death to over

70 million people and total destruction to large areas of Japan, Germany, Russia, China, and other countries. It also brought the Holocaust, an effort by the German Nazis to destroy the Jewish people; six million were systematically killed. Finally, the Allies achieved victory in 1945, first in Europe and a few months later in Asia after the United States used nuclear weapons against Japan.

After the war, peace did not result; instead, two of the victorious Allied Powers—the United States and the Soviet Union—immediately squared off against each other in the Cold War. Largely due to the threat of mutual nuclear annihilation, the Cold War (1946–1991) between the two nuclear superpowers did not actually involve direct fighting between American and Soviet troops. Instead, it was fought through a continuing series of "proxy wars" (national and regional wars in which the Soviet Union supported one side and the United States the other). The most significant of these wars were in China, Korea, Cuba, Vietnam, and Afghanistan. The Cold War also included direct confrontations between the United States and the Soviet Union (the Berlin airlift and the Cuban missile crisis) that stopped just short of direct warfare between the two nuclear superpowers. In the Cold War, the Soviet Union and its allies sought to expand throughout the world through its system of totalitarian government and communism, while the United States and its allies tried to contain communism and Soviet expansion while promoting the systems of democratic government and capitalism. The Cold War came to an end in 1991 when the Soviet Union collapsed under the weight of its own inefficient economy and government. The Soviet Union broke up into 15 separate countries, of which Russia is the largest one.

Since the 2001 terrorist attacks on the World Trade Center and the Pentagon, U.S. foreign policy has focused on a "war on terror" in which the enemy is not a foreign nation but small extremist terrorist groups operating on their own in the international arena. Today, the conduct of international affairs no longer involves only the governments of countries interacting with each other. There are many other actors wielding power on the international stage, including international terrorist groups; multinational corporations (global banks and companies); and international organizations such as the United Nations, the International Monetary Fund, the European Union, and NATO.

GOOD IDEA

Understanding World Wars I and II and the Cold War could be especially helpful on the GED, since both U.S. history and world history questions can focus on these events.

Practice: The United States as a World Power

Question 1 refers to the following map.

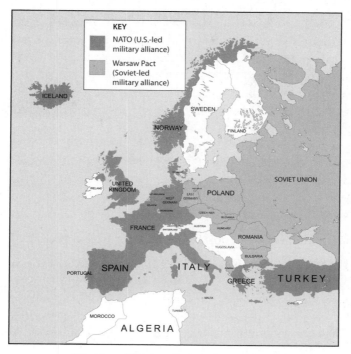

Division of Europe during the Cold War.

1. Which statement best summarizes the information shown on the map?

   (1) All the European nations along the border of the Soviet Union were allied with the Soviet Union.

   (2) Alliances such as NATO and the Warsaw Pact dangerously divide the world and encourage war.

   (3) During the Cold War most nations of Eastern Europe were allied with the Soviet Union, while most nations of Western Europe joined the United States in opposing the Soviet Union.

   (4) The Soviet Union controlled most of Europe while the United States had relatively little power there.

   (5) All Europe would be communist if the United States had not stood up to the Soviet Union.

Question 2 refers to the following bar graph.

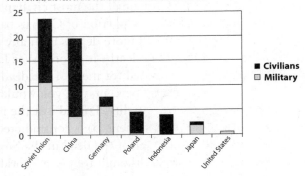

World War II Deaths
(in millions)

The chart below shows the six countries with the highest number of deaths in World War II. For comparison the United States has been added to the chart. Germany and Japan were Axis Powers; the rest of the countries shown were Allied Powers.

2. Which statement is supported by the information presented in the bar graph?

(1) Most of the dead in World War II were citizens of the Soviet Union.

(2) In World War II, the Soviet Union lost a higher percentage of its people than any other country.

(3) The overwhelming majority of Soviet deaths in World War II were civilians.

(4) More civilians were killed in China than in any other country.

(5) Germany and Japan, who lost World War II, had the highest numbers of military deaths in the war.

Answers: The United States as a World Power

1. **(3)** This statement correctly summarizes the information displayed on the map. Not all European nations along the Soviet border (1) aligned themselves with the Soviet Union (Finland, for example). There is no information on the map about whether alliances threaten the world or promote peace (2); more information would be needed to research this question. The Soviet Union, which itself makes up about half of Europe, did control more land area of

Europe (4), but there is no information on the map about the power of the United States in Europe. The United States in fact had considerable power in Europe due to many American military bases there, a strong U.S. navy presence, and a strong NATO alliance. Statement (5) is an opinion; there is no evidence on the map to support or reject this opinion.

2. **(4)** The bar graph shows that China had the most civilian deaths of any country in World War II. (The dark portion of China's bar on the graph is the biggest.) The Soviet Union had more deaths than any other country, but you cannot say that most of all the deaths in World War II were in the Soviet Union (1). No one country accounted for most of the dead. The map does not show percentages (2); to figure percentages, you would need to know the populations of each country. In actuality, Poland lost the highest percentage of its people in World War II. Statement (3) is contradicted by the graph, which shows about an equal number of the dead in the Soviet Union between civilians and military personnel. Although they lost World War II, Germany and Japan did not suffer nearly as many deaths as the Soviet Union and China, which were on the winning side.

U.S. Government

In This Chapter

- Overviews of key areas of U.S. politics and government
- GED-like questions to practice the skills you'll be tested on
- Answers and explanations for all the questions

U.S. government comprises the second-largest number of questions on the Social Studies Test. You can expect 12 of the 50 questions to be based on U.S. government content.

You won't be required to memorize facts like the names of government agencies, presidents, or Supreme Court decisions to ace the test. Most of the facts you'll need to know will be given to you in the reading passages or the visuals (graphs, maps, tables, etc.) that are included with the test questions. However, a good background in U.S. government and politics will help you understand the readings and work through the questions quickly. The test focuses on your skills in understanding, analyzing, and applying the information presented to you.

This chapter provides an overview of the fundamentals of U.S. government that will almost certainly be included in some way on the test. Following each overview of a key subject, you'll find GED-like questions that will help prepare you for the types of skill-based questions you will confront on the real test. Don't forget to read the explanations, not just for the questions you missed, but for all the questions and answer choices you did not completely understand.

The Framework of U.S. Government

One of the most basic ideas or principles of American government is the idea that government is limited to the powers that have been granted it by the people. This principle is known as *limited government* or *constitutionalism*. The U.S. Constitution defines what powers are granted to the U.S. government and sets up the framework of government.

Another fundamental principle of American government is *federalism*. Federalism is the coexistence of independent state and federal governments. State governments have their own constitutions that define and limit government. Under the U.S. Constitution, some powers are given to both state and national governments (taxation and public works, for example), while some powers are only given to the national government (printing money, controlling interstate commerce), and other powers have traditionally been reserved for the states (education). Increasingly, state and federal governments work together on all types of problems, from education to health care to transportation.

The U.S. Constitution sets up three separate, independent branches of government, summarized in the following table. This is called the *separation of powers*. Congress, the legislative branch, makes the laws. The president heads the executive branch, which carries out the laws. The Supreme Court and the federal court system make up the judicial branch, whose role is to settle disputes about the law. The executive branch includes most agencies (offices) of the federal government, from the Department of Defense to the Environmental Protection Agency to the Social Security Administration—all of which carry out laws passed by Congress. The agencies of the federal government—including the two million people who work there—are known as the federal bureaucracy.

The Branches of the U.S. Government

Legislative Branch	Executive Branch	Judicial Branch
Congress (the Senate and House of Representatives)	President and the federal bureaucracy	Supreme Court
Makes laws	Carries out laws	Settles disputes about the law

Contained within the Constitution is a *system of checks and balances*—another basic principle of American government. Although each branch of government operates independently, the Constitution provides ways each branch can block or "check" the other branches. For example, the president can check the power of Congress by vetoing proposed legislation passed by Congress. But Congress can check the president's power by overriding the president's veto by a two-thirds majority. Congress can also check the power of the president and the federal bureaucracy through its control of the federal budget. The Supreme Court can check Congress and the president by declaring a law or presidential order unconstitutional and thereby invalidating it. Congress can check the power of the Supreme Court by passing a new law using different language or proposing a constitutional amendment. The system of checks and balances prevents any one branch of government from becoming too powerful and dictatorial.

IN THE KNOW

While the Constitution sets up the framework of American government, much of the way our government operates is not in the Constitution but has developed over time through practice. For example, the idea that the Supreme Court can declare a law unconstitutional is not in the Constitution, but is today a widely accepted principle.

Following are the chief roles or powers of each of the three branches of the federal government:

The President ...

- Heads the executive branch (the federal bureaucracy).
- Commands the armed forces.
- Signs or vetoes laws (Congress can pass a law over the president's veto if it passes in both the Senate and House by a two-thirds majority).
- Conducts foreign policy.
- Nominates federal officials and Supreme Court justices.

Congress (the Senate and the House of Representatives) ...

- Makes laws.
- Determines the federal budget (how and for what purposes money will be spent by the federal government).
- Conducts investigations of the executive branch.
- Approves or disapproves the president's nominees for federal officials and Supreme Court justices (Senate).
- Ratifies (approves) treaties (Senate).

The Supreme Court ...

- Settles disputes about the meaning of federal laws.

- Interprets the Constitution, determining if laws passed by Congress or orders given by the president are constitutional.

Practice: The Framework of U.S. Government

Questions 1 and 2 refer to the previous lists.

1. Who has the most power in determining how much money the government spends on farm programs?

    (1) The president

    (2) Congress

    (3) The Senate

    (4) The federal bureaucracy

    (5) State governments

2. Which statement best describes the process by which Supreme Court justices are chosen?

    (1) They are selected by the president.

    (2) They are selected by the Senate but must be approved by the president.

    (3) They run for office and the people elect them.

    (4) They are selected by the president but must be approved by the Senate.

    (5) They are selected by the president but must be approved by the House of Representatives and the Senate.

Question 3 is based on the following reading.

What is a filibuster?

The filibuster refers to continuing debate endlessly to prevent a vote on a proposed law that is likely to pass. The rules of the House of Representatives do not allow a filibuster, but in the Senate a minority of the senators can block a vote on a proposed law that has majority support. Sixty percent of senators must vote to end debate (cloture) before a vote on the proposed law can be taken. Nowadays, the Senate usually moves on to other business until a sufficient number of senators can be convinced to support cloture rather than wasting time with endless debate.

3. The filibuster is an example of

   (1) federalism.

   (2) checks and balances.

   (3) limitations on the power of the majority.

   (4) separation of powers.

   (5) constitutionalism.

Answers: The Framework of U.S. Government

1. **(2)** Although the president (1) makes a budget request, it is Congress that writes the final budget and determines how much is spent on each federal program. The president can veto an appropriations bill (legislation that provides money to the federal government), but this would be risky and could result in the president getting a bill that is even less favorable to him or getting no bill at all (and thus no money to spend on federal programs). The Senate (3) can't act on its own; for an appropriations bill to pass, both the House and the Senate must approve it. The federal bureaucracy (4) and state governments (5) are directly affected by the federal budget and try to influence the result, but they are not the decision makers.

2. **(4)** The president selects Supreme Court justices but they must then be approved by a majority vote of the Senate, not the reverse (2). Choice (1) does not describe the whole process, and the House of Representatives plays no role in the process (5).

3. **(3)** The filibuster limits the power of the majority to take action. For a new law to pass, a supermajority (60 percent) is needed. The filibuster is a rule of the Senate and not part of the Constitution. Since filibustering is an action within one branch of government, checks and balances (2) and the separation of powers (4) are not involved. Filibustering is unrelated to federalism, which involves the division of power between state and federal governments (1).

Filibustering is also not related to the principle of constitutionalism (5), which is the idea that government is limited to the powers the people have granted it.

Elections and Political Parties

Democracy is rule by the majority; this is another fundamental principle of American government. However, this wasn't always the case. At the time the U.S. Constitution was written (1787), only white males who owned land could vote. By the time of the Civil War (1861), all white males—even those who did not own property—could vote. The Fifteenth Amendment (1870) extended the right to vote to African American males in all states. Women won the right to vote in all states with the passage of the Nineteenth Amendment (1920). The Twenty-Sixth Amendment lowered the minimum voting age to 18 (it had been 21 in most states). Thus, over the years, the right to vote has been broadened to allow voting by nearly all adults, establishing the principle of rule by the majority or democracy.

Democracy is characterized by elections. In indirect democracy, elections are held to elect representatives who then make the laws. In direct democracy, elections are held on laws themselves; if a majority approves a measure, it becomes a law. Both state and federal governments in the United States are characterized by representative government (indirect democracy). Some states, however, have provisions that allow votes by the people on laws themselves by referendum or initiative (direct democracy).

Political parties are not mentioned in the Constitution, but they play a vital role in the American political system. Political parties in the United States select the candidates and then try to get their candidates elected to office. The United States is characterized by a two-party system. Today the two parties are the Democratic Party (symbolized by a donkey) and the Republican Party (symbolized by an elephant). Many minor parties (often called "third" parties) also exist, but they seldom have enough support to get their candidates elected. An "independent" is a person who does not identify with any political party.

There are two basic types of elections in the United States. In the primary election each political party selects who its candidate will be. The primary election is followed by the general election, in which the final winner is chosen from the candidates who were victorious in the primary election.

IN THE KNOW

There is no requirement in the United States that people vote. In the last 30 years, voter turnout for presidential elections has ranged from 50 to 57 percent of eligible voters. Even fewer people, sometimes as low as 33 percent, vote for congressional candidates. Therefore, winning an election is often more about motivating your supporters to vote than about gaining the support of a majority of the people.

State legislators, state governors, and U.S. senators and representatives are all elected by votes of the people in general elections. The president, however, is not elected by the people, but by specially chosen persons called electors. When a presidential candidate wins the election in a state, a group of electors pledged to the winning candidate are chosen. The number of electors each state gets equals their number of senators and representatives in Congress. The electors then cast their votes for president a few weeks following the general election. If no candidate gets more than half of the electoral votes (for example, if there is a third candidate running who wins some states), then the president is selected by the House of Representatives, with each state getting one vote.

In this electoral system, the states with the most people get many electoral votes (California, for example, gets 55 votes) and the least populous states (Alaska, Delaware, Montana, North Dakota, South Dakota, Vermont, and Wyoming) get only 3. Each state's votes are cast as a block (exceptions: Maine and Nebraska). Thus, even if a candidate gets only one more individual's vote than his opponent, *all* the state's electoral votes go to the winning candidate. This winner-take-all system has the following effects:

- The electors sometimes select a president who did not get the most votes in the general election (as happened in 2000 when Al Gore won the popular vote but George W. Bush became president).

- Candidates focus on the big states; for example, only five states (California, Texas, New York, Florida, and Pennsylvania) account for 171 of the 270 electoral votes needed to win.

- Candidates focus on "swing" states where the election is close and the swing of a few votes could move the entire block of the state's electors from one candidate to another.

Practice: Elections and Political Parties

Question 1 refers to the following political cartoon.

Courtesy of William S. Wiist

1. What is the main point the cartoonist is making in this cartoon?

   (1) Politicians in both parties admire Abraham Lincoln.

   (2) Government officials will do anything for money.

   (3) Money plays too large a role in American elections.

   (4) Lincoln was able to provide real leadership and get both parties to support him.

   (5) Politicians are responsive to the people in their state or district.

Question 2 refers to the following map.

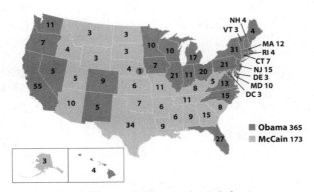

Electoral votes: 2008 presidential election.

2. Based on the information shown on the map, which one of the following statements is correct?

(1) Smaller states have no say in selecting a president.

(2) In awarding electoral votes to states, population is not important.

(3) The states with the smallest population get only one electoral vote.

(4) The number of electoral votes each state gets is based on how big the state is in land area.

(5) In the presidential electoral system, virtually all states cast their electoral votes as a block for the same candidate.

Answers: Elections and Political Parties

1. **(3)** The main idea of this cartoon is that money plays too important a role in American elections. The donkey (symbol of the Democratic Party) and the elephant (symbol of the Republican Party) are both bowing down in homage, not to President Lincoln, but to the money his image appears on. The cartoon does not show government officials, but political parties, so statement (2) is not the best answer. The cartoon does not say anything about Lincoln (1 and 4) or how responsive politicians are to the people they represent (5).

2. **(5)** The map shows how virtually all states cast their electoral votes as a block for the candidate who wins in each state. The only exceptions are Maine and Nebraska, which sometimes divide their small block of votes; in these two states electoral votes are awarded on the basis of which candidate won in each congressional district of the state. Choice (1) is incorrect because small states do have a say in selecting a president and occasionally the swing of one small state to the other side changes the election (this last happened in 2000). In fact, small states actually have a larger share of the electoral vote than their population would warrant since the minimum is three votes, making choice (3) incorrect. Population is the primary basis on which electoral votes are allocated to states (2), not land area (4). In fact, the largest state in land area (Alaska) gets only three electoral votes.

Interest Groups and the Political Process

Interest groups are a key part of the American political process. In fact, a common way of viewing the American political system is one in which competing interests struggle to determine public policy. The view that good government comes out of the compromises made by a multitude of competing interests is called *pluralism*.

Interest groups are groups of voters organized in support of a particular set of political goals. Unlike political parties, they do not field candidates for office, but they often endorse and raise money for candidates who support their political goals. Examples of interest groups are farmers, environmentalists, or petroleum companies; all of these have common interests and want to see certain types of laws passed. Interest groups may represent large groups like retired people (AARP) or automobile owners (AAA), or small special-interest groups like the oil companies (Petroleum Institute).

There are hundreds of interest groups in the United States; the most powerful are the ones with lots of members or lots of money (for contributions to election campaigns). Interest groups not only try to get candidates who support their goals elected, they also try to influence officials after they are in office. They try to influence both the law-making process of Congress and the administration of the law by the federal bureaucracy. This is called *lobbying*. Lobbying includes providing information favorable to their cause, mobilizing members to speak out and contact lawmakers, promising support (or opposition) in the next election, and conducting media campaigns to sway public opinion.

Political Parties and Interest Groups Compared

	Political Parties	Interest Groups
Number	Two important parties	Hundreds of important interest groups
Goal	Get their candidates elected	Advance their political agenda
Focus	Elections	Policy making
Role in elections	Select candidates and help their candidates win by raising money and providing other types of support	Endorse individual candidates (usually from both parties) and raise money for their campaigns

	Political Parties	Interest Groups
Role in government	None—once elected, officials act on their own, not on behalf of the party	Influence congressmen and federal officials in making laws and formulating policies

Practice: Interest Groups and the Political Process

1. Both interest groups and political parties are likely to

   (1) raise money for candidates running for office.

   (2) try to get all the candidates from one political party elected.

   (3) try to influence policy-making process of the federal government.

   (4) recruit candidates to run for office.

   (5) make compromises with opponents.

2. Which statement correctly contrasts political parties and interest groups?

   (1) Interest groups are not involved in elections, while political parties are.

   (2) Political parties need money and members to be effective, but interest groups do not.

   (3) There are many powerful interest groups but only two main political parties.

   (4) Political parties usually work with other political parties, while interest groups do not.

   (5) Interest groups do not have a formal organizational structure, while political parties are highly organized at federal, state, and local levels.

Answers: Interest Groups and the Political Process

1. **(1)** Both political parties and interest groups raise money for candidates running for office. Political parties try to get all their candidates elected (2) but interest groups only help candidates (from either party) that support their political goals. Only interest groups try to influence the policy-making process of the federal government (3) and make compromises with opponents (5). Only political parties take an active role in recruiting candidates to run for office (4).

2. **(3)** There are hundreds of powerful interest groups (automakers, environmentalists, anti-abortion groups, gun dealers, teachers, automobile owners, airline pilots, veterans, truck drivers, retired people, dairy farmers, and coal mine owners, to name just a few) but just two important parties in the United States. Both political parties and interest groups get involved in elections (1); interest groups endorse and raise money for candidates. Both interest groups and political parties need money and members to be effective (2). Political parties do not work with other parties—they run against them—but interest groups often work with other interest groups when their interests overlap (4). Both interest groups and political parties need to be well organized at federal, state, and local levels to maximize their effect (5).

Constitutional Rights

Another key idea in understanding American government is the concept of individual rights. Shortly after the Constitution went into effect, 10 amendments called the Bill of Rights were added to the Constitution to specifically list limitations on the power of government and thereby establish individual rights. Later, the Fourteenth Amendment was interpreted by the Supreme Court to expand these limitations on the power of government to state governments as well as Congress and the federal government.

The basic rights necessary to an effective democratic government are stated in the First Amendment to the U.S. Constitution. The text of this amendment prohibits the government from limiting freedom of speech, freedom of the press, freedom to peacefully protest, and freedom of religion. This last one involves two separate prohibitions: the government cannot make a "law respecting the establishment of a religion" or a law "prohibiting the free exercise" of religion. The prohibition of government establishment of a religion, which has been interpreted as prohibiting government-sponsored prayer in public schools and the display of religious symbols by the government, has been the most controversial part of this amendment.

Other rights contained in the Bill of Rights include the prohibition on "cruel and unusual punishment," guarantees on the right to a fair trial, and freedom from unreasonable searches and seizures of persons or property. Recently, the Supreme Court has interpreted the Second Amendment to guarantee a right to gun ownership. The Ninth Amendment states that an individual's rights are not limited to those specifically stated in the Constitution, and the Supreme Court has recognized rights implied in the Constitution, such as the right to privacy.

Often the extent of individual rights is subject to interpretation. What, for example, is "cruel and unusual" punishment? What exactly are "unreasonable" searches and seizures? And how far does the right of privacy go—does it include a woman's right to terminate a pregnancy? The Supreme Court must answer these questions through the individual cases appealed to the Court. Its decisions in these areas are often controversial.

Often, too, individual rights may conflict. For example, when a parent's religious belief not to seek medical treatment for a child could cause the child's death, does the parent's right to the free exercise of religion win out over the child's right to life? Here, too, the courts must answer these questions through the individual cases they hear.

GOOD IDEA

You won't need to know what each amendment of the Bill of Rights does. But the Social Studies Test will have an excerpt from the U.S. Constitution, Bill of Rights, or Declaration of Independence that you will have to read, interpret, and answer questions about. It's a good idea to read and try to understand the first few paragraphs of the Constitution and Declaration of Independence and the entire Bill of Rights so you have some familiarity with them before the test.

Practice: Constitutional Rights

Questions 1 and 2 refer to the following text of the Sixth Amendment.

Amendment VI

"In all criminal prosecutions, the accused shall enjoy the right to a speedy and public trial by an impartial jury ... and to be informed of the nature and cause of the accusation, to be confronted with the witnesses against him, to have compulsory process for obtaining witnesses in his favor, and to have the assistance of counsel for his defense."

1. Which right is granted by the Sixth Amendment to persons accused of a crime?

    (1) The right not to be tried twice for the same crime.

    (2) The right not to answer questions in court or in a police interrogation.

    (3) The right to a lawyer.

    (4) The right to be released on bail.

    (5) The right not to appear in court.

2. Which statement best summarizes the Sixth Amendment?

(1) The Sixth Amendment is part of the Bill of Rights.

(2) The Sixth Amendment lists various rights of citizens.

(3) The Sixth Amendment lists *all* the rights of persons accused of a crime.

(4) The Sixth Amendment lists rights of persons accused of a crime.

(5) The Sixth Amendment makes it too easy for criminals to get off free because of the rights it gives them.

Answers: Constitutional Rights

1. **(3)** The last phrase of the Sixth Amendment grants a person accused of a crime the right to a lawyer ("counsel for his defense"). Choices (1) and (2) are also constitutional rights of accused persons, but these rights are not contained in the Sixth Amendment; they appear in the Fifth Amendment. Choice (4) is also a general right of the accused (provided there is no evidence to suggest the person accused might flee); this right is contained in the Eighth Amendment. There is no right that allows accused persons to avoid appearing in court (5).

2. **(4)** The Sixth Amendment does list rights of persons accused of a crime. Choice (3) is virtually the same except the word *all* has been added. Be careful and don't jump to conclusions! The Sixth Amendment does not have *all* of the rights of persons accused of a crime; other rights of the accused are in the Fifth and Eighth Amendments. Choice (1) is a correct statement but not a summary of the amendment. Choice (2) is not as descriptive or as specific as the correct answer, which better summarizes the amendment. Choice (5) is not a summary of the amendment but an opinion about the effect of the amendment.

Economics

In This Chapter

- Overviews of important concepts in economics
- GED-like questions to practice the skills you'll be tested on
- Answers and explanations for all the questions

Economics accounts for 20 percent of the questions on the Social Studies Test. You can expect 10 of the 50 questions to be based on graphs, charts, and reading passages about economics.

Similar to the other subject areas of the Social Studies Test, you won't be required to memorize facts and formulas or know the definitions of technical terms in order to do well on the questions on economics. Facts and definitions will be given in the reading passages, graphs, and charts that are included with the test questions. The test focuses on your skills in understanding, analyzing, and applying the information presented to you.

Don't let economics scare you. Even if you've never had an economics class or think you know nothing about it, you probably won't have too much trouble understanding the basic economics presented on the GED. However, an understanding of key economic concepts will be helpful. Understanding these concepts will familiarize you with how economists think and help you in analyzing and interpreting the economics content on the test.

This chapter focuses on basic concepts of economics. The concepts will probably seem fairly simple—they're based on common sense—but it's in the application of these concepts that you'll likely be challenged. The GED-like practice questions in this chapter will help you prepare for the types of skill-based questions you will confront on the real test.

Basic Concepts of Economics

Economics is the study of the *production* and *consumption* of goods and services. *Goods* are products, from milk to automobiles. *Services* are also products, but intangible ones, like a haircut, a hotel stay, a checking account, or police protection. People are consumers of goods and services and, in their roles at work, produce goods and services.

Economic systems arise because of *scarcity*—the supplies of goods and services are limited. If something is not scarce, like air, it is not bought and sold, and therefore not part of our economy. The price of a good or service is determined by how scarce it is—the *supply*—and by how many people want it—the *demand*. Prices fluctuate based on supply and demand. For example, if half of Florida's orange crop is destroyed by frost (the supply decreases), the price of orange juice will go up. With that price increase, consumption will decline until supply and demand are back in balance. What would happen to the price of juice if the supply increases due to importation of orange juice from Brazil? The price of orange juice will fall until the cheap price encourages more people to drink juice and supply and demand are back in balance. Perhaps the most basic concept of economics is the relationship between supply and demand: the price of a product tends to move toward the price at which the supply equals the demand.

HEADS UP!

The law of supply and demand is a commonsense concept. But people often get tripped up when applying the concept to actual circumstances. Keep in mind the following:

- The price of a good or service will tend to go *up* if demand is greater than supply.
- The price of a good or service will tend to go *down* if supply is greater than demand.

Currency (money) was invented in ancient civilizations to facilitate trade. *Money economies* have pretty much replaced *barter economies*, in which people trade goods and services directly. The value of money is determined by how many goods and services it can buy. If prices, in general, are going up, *inflation* is occurring and the currency is losing value. This happens when people have money to spend but the supply of goods and services is limited. If prices are generally going down, *deflation* is occurring. This happens when consumers don't have a lot of money while unsold goods and services are plentiful.

GDP (Gross Domestic Product) is a measure of the monetary value of all the goods and services produced by a country in a year. It measures the size of a nation's economy. However, if GDP is not adjusted for inflation, it is difficult to compare GDP from one year to another. A rising GDP could mean more goods and services are being produced, or it could just mean prices are going up. Thus, economists use the concept of *real GDP* to adjust for price changes (inflation or deflation), allowing them to compare the size of the economy from one year to another year and determine economic growth or decline. To do this, economists use *constant dollars;* they pick a year (for example, 2010) and measure each years' production of goods and services in 2010 dollars. In other words, they use the prices of goods and services in 2010 to measure production in all years.

DEFINITION

Economists use the term **real GDP** to indicate that inflation/deflation have been adjusted for. They talk about real growth, real incomes, and real costs. To arrive at real amounts, they measure prices in constant dollars whose value does not change over the years. If a chart or graph says "in 2000 dollars" you know the amounts for all years are being measured using 2000 prices and that the figures are "real."

A decline of real GDP for at least 6 months is defined as a *recession.* In a recession, consumer spending, investment, business profits, and production all decline while unemployment rises. A *depression* is a more severe and sustained drop in GDP that usually involves deflation and financial crisis due to the failure of banks and other financial institutions.

In the United States, privately owned businesses produce most of the nation's goods and services. Businesses can be structured in different formats; the most common of these are individual proprietorships (single owner), partnerships (two or more joint owners), and corporations. In a partnership, the owners make decisions jointly and share in the profits. Corporations have many owners; each owner's share of ownership is determined by the amount of the company's stock owned. Stockholders elect the company's directors, who manage the company and distribute profits back to the stockholders based on the amount of stock each owns.

Businesses have both inputs (factors of production) and outputs (goods or services). The *factors of production* are divided into three groups: raw materials, labor, and capital. *Raw materials* (iron ore, unrefined petroleum, soil, water, etc.) and *labor* (workers) are self-explanatory. *Capital* refers to any item used to produce other goods or services; this includes a bank's computers, a car manufacturer's robot welders, and a farmer's tractor. All three factors of production are necessary to produce goods and services.

Practice: Basic Concepts of Economics

Question 1 refers to the following graph.

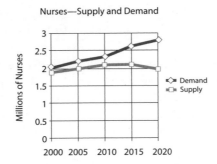

Nurses—Supply and Demand

1. Which statement best states what can be predicted to happen to the wages of nurses and why?

   (1) Wages will decline because the supply of nurses is growing.

   (2) Wages will rise because demand for nurses is growing.

   (3) Wages will rise because the demand for nurses exceeds the supply of nurses.

   (4) Wages will rise because the supply of nurses is growing.

   (5) Wages for nurses will not change much since hospitals can't afford to pay more to nurses.

Question 2 refers to the following graph.

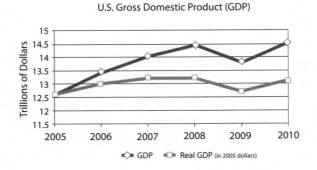

U.S. Gross Domestic Product (GDP)

2. Which statement best explains how unadjusted GDP could grow between 2007 and 2008 while real GDP was not growing?

   (1) Deflation was occurring with prices dropping.

   (2) Supply and demand were out of balance.

   (3) Unadjusted GDP increases when production of goods and services increases.

   (4) A recession was beginning.

   (5) The increase in unadjusted GDP was due to price increases, not increases in production.

Answers: Basic Concepts of Economics

1. **(3)** The concept of supply and demand applies to wages as well as products. Wages for nurses will tend to keep rising until supply equals demand. Regarding statement (1), an increase in supply would produce a decline in wages only if supply rises above demand. Statement (2) states only part of the reason wages will rise. In order to predict wages, projections for both supply and demand are needed. A growing demand for nurses won't necessarily lead to wage increases; that will happen only if demand exceeds supply. Wages are rising (4), but that is not because supply is rising; a rising supply of nurses would tend to bring wages down. Statement (5) doesn't relate to supply and demand and therefore isn't a basis on which predictions can be made on wages. Hospitals that cannot afford to pay nurses competitive rates won't have nurses, and therefore would have to close or make some kind of alternative arrangement in which nurses weren't needed.

2. **(5)** In this graph, the real GDP line shows the total value of goods and services produced for all years using 2005 prices. Thus, the real GDP line only measures production changes, while unadjusted GDP measures changes in both prices and production together. Since we know that production (real GDP) was flat between 2007 and 2008, we know that the increase in unadjusted GDP was entirely due to inflation. A period of price increases is inflation, not deflation (1). The concept of GDP has little to do with the concept of supply and demand (2). Statement (3) is only a half-truth, since unadjusted GDP measures both changes in production and prices together. A recession could be beginning (4), but that doesn't explain the difference between real GDP and unadjusted GDP.

Economic Systems

Different countries have different economic systems; in fact, each country's system is at least a little different from any other country's. The chief difference is in the role the government plays in the economy.

In pure *capitalism*, the government plays only a minimal role. It does not own factories, control prices, or regulate business. Businesses are privately owned and the owners (capitalists) are free to operate how they want. But even in pure capitalism, the government still plays a vital economic role in printing money, settling disputes, enforcing contracts, protecting property, setting standards of weights and measures, etc. Another term for a capitalistic economic system is a *free enterprise system.* The term *market economy* is also used, since prices and production are determined by free markets (supply and demand) rather than by the government.

On the other side of the spectrum is pure *socialism*, in which the government controls the economy. Under socialism, the means of production (mines, factories, land, businesses, etc.) are owned by the people as a whole through their government. The government decides what to produce and sets the prices at which products will be sold. Communism is a form of socialism in which a dictatorial government makes economic decisions and all private enterprise is suppressed. Under democratic socialism, there is more freedom, but the elected government sill owns and runs at least the largest mines, factories, and businesses.

Since the fall of the Soviet Union, nearly all countries have some form of market economy, where prices, wages, and production are largely determined by free markets (supply and demand) rather than the government. However, even in the United States, which prides itself on its free-enterprise system, the government often gets involved rather than letting privately owned businesses determine all economic decisions. An example of this is minimum-wage laws in which the federal and state governments set minimum wages, rather than allowing businesses to pay what they want. Today, nearly all countries, including the United States, have mixed economies, with a degree of government involvement and control somewhere between pure socialism and pure capitalism.

Practice: Economic Systems

1. Which statement correctly compares capitalism and socialism?

   (1) In both economic systems, the government plays a role in the successful operation of the system.

   (2) In both economic systems, the law of supply and demand determines prices.

   (3) In both economic systems, business enterprises are owned by private citizens who are motivated by profits.

   (4) Both economic systems allow wealth to accumulate in the hands of a few individuals.

   (5) In both economic systems, the government performs essentially the same role.

Questions 2 and 3 refer to the following reading passage.

Socialism was in decline even before the breakup of the Soviet Union in 1992 brought an end to its government-run economy. Well before that event, China, the world's most populous socialist country, started economic reforms that broke up communal farms and encouraged free enterprise. And after the free-market economies of four "Asian Tigers" (Korea, Taiwan, Thailand, and Singapore, Hong Kong) demonstrated "miracle" economic growth (1960–90), most of the developing world started emulating them rather than socialist models. Even Western European countries have backed away from socialism and returned many government-run industries to private ownership. Today, only a handful of countries remain deeply committed to socialism and opposed to capitalism.

But should socialism die? If you value economic growth, capitalism wins hands down. But if you value an equitable distribution of wealth, the revival of a more socialistic approach with more government involvement may be a better alternative.

The situation in which the rich get richer and the poor remain poor now characterizes most market economies, from Russia to India to the United States. In the United States, the median family income level was in decline for years even before the real estate bubble burst and recession set in. Workers in the United States are getting lower wages, less job security, longer hours, and less health coverage than before. Allowing the economy to operate without government controls serves the rich but not the majority of the people. At some point, the government should step into the economic system to make sure the benefits flow not just to business owners but to the workers as well.

2. Which statement best summarizes the author's argument?

   (1) Socialism should replace capitalism so that wealth is more equitably distributed.

   (2) Capitalism is better than socialism since it is better at generating economic growth.

   (3) Capitalism is good for economic growth, but the government should intervene to make sure wealth is distributed fairly.

   (4) Both capitalism and socialism should be replaced with a better system.

   (5) Some countries should continue to be socialistic so socialism doesn't die out.

3. Which statement is a fact the author uses to support her argument?

   (1) Socialism is in decline.

   (2) The government-controlled economy of the Soviet Union was a failure and collapsed.

   (3) Capitalism is an efficient system for economic growth.

   (4) The average American worker's salary and benefits are declining, while the rich get richer.

   (5) The gap between rich and poor in the United States is narrowing.

Answers: Economic Systems

1. **(1)** In both systems the government plays an important role. Under capitalism, the government builds infrastructure like roads, prints money, protects private property, establishes courts to settle disputes and enforce contracts, etc. Furthermore, even the most extreme proponents of capitalism usually agree that some services, like police protection, are best provided by the government rather than private enterprise. Under socialism, the government gets even more involved in the economy by owning businesses, setting prices, and making production decisions. Free markets governed by the law of supply

and demand (2), business enterprises owned by private citizens (3), and the accumulation of wealth in the hands of a few people (4) are all characteristic of capitalism, but not socialism. While government plays a role in both systems, it is not the same role (5). The government is much more involved in economic decisions under socialism.

2. **(3)** Questions 2–4 require you to analyze an argument. The best summary of the position the author is taking is choice (3). Statement (1) goes further than the author, who says only that the government should intervene to regulate a capitalistic system so that the wealth doesn't disproportionately go to the rich. Statements (2), (4), and (5) do not accurately reflect the argument the author is making.

3. **(4)** The author uses the fact that the average American worker's salary and benefits are declining while the rich get richer to make her case that the government should intervene to make sure that workers get their fair share of the wealth. The facts in (1) and (2) provide background information but are basically unrelated to the author's position on the role of government. The author agrees with statement (3), but this statement isn't used to support her main argument that government should intervene in the economy. The author says the gap between rich and poor is widening, not narrowing (5), and uses this fact to support her argument.

U.S. Economic Goals and Policies

The two most important goals of the U.S. government regarding the economy are promoting economic growth and controlling inflation. However, these two goals are often contradictory: Promoting growth usually increases inflation and reigning in inflation usually slows economic growth. Generally, the government must decide what the priority is at any given time. To accomplish its economic objectives, the government can use fiscal policy and/or monetary policy.

Fiscal policy refers to government's actions on taxation and spending. To promote economic growth, the government can do the following:

- **Decrease taxes.** Decreasing taxes has the effect of increasing individual incomes, allowing people to buy more products, thus encouraging business profits and expansion, increasing employment, and growing the economy.

- **Increase government spending.** Under this option, the government spends more to purchase products like weapons systems and roads or provide services like small business loans and medical care for the poor. Increasing government spending has the same effect of encouraging business profits and expansion, increasing employment, and growing the economy.

However, either decreasing taxes or increasing government spending has the negative effects of encouraging inflation and increasing the budget deficit. The *federal deficit* is the gap between what the government gets in taxes and fees and what it spends. The deficit must be covered by borrowing. The fact that the federal government often runs a deficit has increased the national debt to over 10 trillion dollars today (excluding debt one branch of the U.S. government owes another branch) or about 68 percent of the GDP. Economists are in disagreement over the long-term effects of an ongoing federal deficit.

On the other hand, if the government's main economic goal is to control inflation or reduce the deficit, the government can decrease government spending or increase taxes. However, these steps have the negative effect of slowing economic growth.

Monetary policy refers to the ways the government can influence the supply of money and interest rates. An easy-money policy is one that promotes low interest rates that encourage lending. The result is an increase in the supply of money in play in the economy. An easy-money policy promotes economic growth, but also encourages inflation and a decline in the value of the dollar. On the other hand, a tight-money policy promotes high interest rates that discourage borrowing, thus reducing the supply of money and slowing economic growth. A tight-money policy slows inflation and increases the value of the dollar.

In the U.S. economy, the money supply is influenced by the Federal Reserve Bank (often called "the Fed"), an independent government agency not directly under the control of either Congress or the president. Its Board of Governors can move interest rates upward by charging banks more to borrow money from the U.S. government. In 2011 the Federal Reserve Bank was following an easy-money policy with very low interest rates to try to encourage economic growth.

In today's global economy, an increase in the value of the Chinese currency, a loan default by a Western European government, the collapse of a bank in Japan, or a drop in wages in India would all directly affect the U.S. economy. Global economic interdependence means that events far beyond a nation's borders (and generally beyond its control) often influence a nation's potential for economic growth. The power of individual national governments to control their own economies through both fiscal and monetary policies has become more limited.

IN THE KNOW

In economics any action always has both positive and negative effects. For example, lowering interest rates encourages investment and results in economic growth, but low interest rates also lead to inflation and a decline in the value of the dollar. Even a decline in the value of the dollar has both positive and negative effects: a lower dollar means imports become more expensive for Americans, but it also means that U.S. exports increase and spur economic growth (with a lower dollar American products become cheaper for other countries to buy). Policymakers must always make guesses as to whether positive effects will outweigh negative effects for any proposed action.

Practice: U.S. Economic Goals and Policies

Questions 1 and 2 refer to the following pie charts and reading.

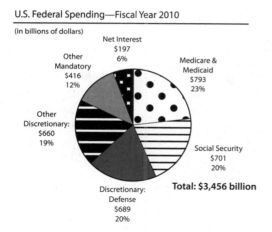

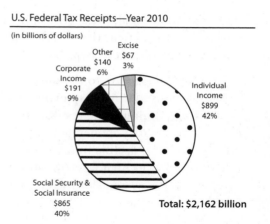

The *federal budget* is a complicated document thousands of pages in length. It includes interest payments on the national debt, mandatory spending, and discretionary spending. *Mandatory spending* is spending required by law, including Social Security, Medicare, and veterans benefits. After both interest on the national debt and mandatory spending are paid, everything left is called *discretionary spending*. Discretionary spending includes spending on defense, education, transportation, homeland security, welfare programs, disaster relief, national parks, agricultural subsidies, etc. The programs that will receive funding and the amount they will receive each year is determined by Congress.

1. About how much was the federal deficit in fiscal year 2010?

    (1) $1,294 billion

    (2) $2,162 billion

    (3) $3,456 billion

    (4) $5,618 billion

    (5) Can't be determined from the information given.

2. According to the first pie chart, about what percentage of the federal budget involves discretionary spending?

    (1) 19%

    (2) 20%

    (3) 39%

    (4) 45%

    (5) 62%

3. If Social Security payments were increased without any change in taxes or in other federal spending, which one of the following would be expected as a result?

    (1) Unemployment would increase.

    (2) Prices would move downward.

    (3) Production would increase and the economy would grow.

    (4) Consumer spending would drop.

    (5) The federal deficit would decline.

Answers: U.S. Economic Goals and Policies

1. **(1)** To compute the federal deficit, you subtract the amount of money the federal government takes in ($2,162 billion) from the amount it spends ($3,256 billion). The federal deficit for fiscal year 2010 was $1,294 billion, or about $1.3 trillion.

2. **(3)** Discretionary spending is what is left after interest on the national debt and mandatory spending is taken out. Programs like Social Security and Medicare involve mandatory spending, since these payments to individuals are required by law. Using the pie chart, you would add defense spending and other discretionary spending to get 39%.

3. **(3)** Increasing social security payments would give more money to seniors and other Social Security recipients. This would increase consumer spending, which would have the effect of encouraging businesses to hire more people to produce more goods and services to meet the increased demand. This would increase production and the economy would grow. Thus, choices (1) and (4) are incorrect. The increased consumer spending would increase the demand for goods and services and push prices upward rather than downward (2). Increasing government spending without increasing taxes would have the effect of increasing the federal deficit (5). But note that this increase would be offset in part by the increased taxes the government would get from the growth in business profits and from the income taxes generated by higher employment levels.

World History

In This Chapter

- Overviews of some important developments in world history
- GED-like questions to practice the skills you'll be tested on
- Answers and explanations for all the questions

World history accounts for 14 percent of the questions on the Social Studies Test. You can expect 7 of the 50 questions to be based on world history content.

Similar to the other subjects covered on the Social Studies Test, you won't be required to memorize any dates or facts to ace the questions on world history. Most of the facts you'll need to know will be given in the reading passages or the visuals (graphs, maps, tables, etc.) that are included with the test questions. The test focuses on your skills in understanding, analyzing, and applying the information presented to you. However, a good understanding of world history will be useful in putting the readings and visuals into their historical context and working through the questions quickly.

The subject area of world history is broad; it covers developments around the world since the beginning of history. It is impossible to provide even a sketchy review of all of the subjects that might appear on the Social Studies Test. Instead, this chapter summarizes a few key developments in world history. Following this are GED-like questions that will help prepare you for the types of skill-based questions you will confront on the real test.

Classical Civilizations

A classical *civilization* is one that endures for a long period of time, develops new social and political institutions, and has a lasting influence on the world. In this section are brief summaries of five classical civilizations that have changed the world.

DEFINITION

Civilization refers to a society with a relatively high level of cultural and technological development. World history is the study of the rise and fall of civilizations.

Western Civilization (Classical Greece and Rome)

Ancient Greek civilization is regarded as the beginning of western civilization. Greece was divided into many city-states (small countries around a single city) that never united to form a unified country. The most influential city-state was Athens. In the classical period (750–400 B.C.), the Greeks (especially the Athenians) valued the individual and had a high regard for the potential of individuals to learn, achieve, and govern themselves. The Greeks sought to develop the person's mind and body; even Greek gods looked like humans and had human personalities. Thus, western civilization places a high value on the worth and freedom of the individual.

The Romans adopted Greek ideas, including the worth of the individual, and built one of the largest and most influential of the world's civilizations. They established their control over Italy about 300 B.C. and expanded until their empire stretched from Egypt to Britain and included all the lands around the Mediterranean Sea. The Romans brought security and the rule of law that resulted in prosperity across the region. Their roads and sea routes carried trade, and many cities thrived. It was in the Roman Empire that Christianity was born; it spread rapidly and eventually became the official religion of the empire.

The western part of the Roman Empire collapsed as barbarian tribes from the north and east invaded. The fall of Rome (476 A.D.) brought a collapse of security and order, bringing an end to most trade. This was the beginning of the Middle Ages, also called the Dark Ages. However, the eastern part of the Roman Empire survived another thousand years. As Western Europe emerged from the Middle Ages centuries after the fall of Rome, people looked back to classical Greece and Rome for inspiration. This was the Renaissance (French for "rebirth") of western civilization.

The institutions and culture of classical Greece and Rome have deeply influenced not only the culture and institutions of Europe, but also, through the global spread of European culture, the entire modern world. The Greek and Latin (Roman) languages form the basis for many European languages, including English. Our alphabet is the Roman alphabet. The civilization of ancient Greece and Rome has influenced our beliefs, political system, sports (including the Olympics), art, and architecture. Our legal system, science, mathematics, and medicine all have foundations in ancient Greece and Rome.

IN THE KNOW

B.C. and A.D. are used in our system of dating events in history. Since there is no set year at which history began, years in history must be dated forwards and backwards from some arbitrary point in time. That point for Westerners was the birth of Jesus, and this system of numbering years is now used worldwide. B.C. means Before Christ and A.D. is an abbreviation for Anno Domini, a Latin term referring to the birth of Jesus. Today B.C.E. (Before the Current Era) and C.E. (Current Era) are often used for a more religion-neutral designation of years, although the birth of Jesus is still the point in time used as the basis for numbering years.

Chinese Civilization

China was one of the earliest centers of human civilization. Chinese culture developed around the idea of faithfulness to family and society, taught by China's most influential philosopher, Confucius. The first Chinese empire was established in 221 B.C., bringing under its control a large area of current-day China and completing the Great Wall of China to protect China's northern frontier from invasion by barbarian tribes. For the next 2,000 years, the Chinese system of government remained basically the same. It is defined by the dynasties (royal families) that ruled China as emperors under what was believed to be a mandate from Heaven.

Under the Han Dynasty (206 B.C.–220 A.D.), China achieved an advanced civilization, rivaling the achievements, wealth, and power of the Roman Empire, which existed at roughly the same time. In fact, trade routes were opened up that connected China and the Roman Empire, bringing silk to Europe and warhorses to China. An efficient government was created for the Chinese Empire; officials were hired on the basis of merit using an objective written test. Trade and commerce flourished and a money economy was established. Advancements were made in science and mathematics, including the use of negative numbers. Paper was invented and scholars established the currently used system of Chinese characters for writing.

During this period China created institutions and a culture that have had a lasting influence on China and neighboring Korea, Japan, and the countries of Southeast Asia. To this day, Chinese written characters are call Han characters, and the majority ethnic group of China is called the Han Chinese. Later dynasties borrowed from or built upon the achievements of the Han Dynasty. Although China was conquered several times by less civilized outsiders from the north and west, the invaders were usually quickly absorbed into Chinese culture and civilization.

Civilization of India

India was also an early center of civilization. It is known as the birthplace of both Hinduism, the oldest of the religions of our world today, and, later, Buddhism. Through Indian trade, Hinduism and then Buddhism spread from India to Southeast Asia. Buddhism also spread to China, Korea, and Japan.

India was first united under a single empire in the third century B.C., but for most of Indian history, India has been divided among a number of smaller states ruled by princes. During the Gupta Empire (320–535 A.D.), much of present-day India and Pakistan were again united. The peace and prosperity created under the Gupta Empire produced a golden age of Indian art, literature, science, and mathematics. During this time, the codes of law that defined the caste system were created. This system defined four castes (priests, warriors, peasants and artisans, and slaves or "untouchables"); people were born into castes and could not change their status.

One of the most influential achievements of the Gupta Empire was its mathematics, including the invention of the decimal system and the number zero. This system spread from India to the Arab Empire in the Middle East, and from there to Europe. Today it is used worldwide. In India, the influence of the Gupta Empire today is seen in its art, religions, and the caste system, which, although outlawed, continues to influence modern society.

Arab Civilization

Shortly after the death of Mohammed, the founder of Islam, in 632 A.D., Arab armies swept out of Arabia, quickly conquering the area from Egypt to Persia (Iran). In this area they established the religion of Islam as well as Arab language and culture. By 711 A.D., this empire had expanded across North Africa and conquered Spain, further spreading Arab religion and culture. In the east, Muslim armies swept into northern India, bringing Islam to the Indian subcontinent, from where it spread to Southeast Asia (Malaysia and Indonesia).

Following this expansion came what is known as the Islamic Golden Age under the Arab Abbasid Dynasty (750–1258 A.D.). The Arabs learned the art of papermaking from China, and they brought the Gupta decimal numerical system from India. In the great cities of the empire—Baghdad, Damascus, Cairo, and Cordova, Spain— science and mathematics flourished along with trade and commerce. From here, new ideas in math and science—including the art of making paper and books—spread to medieval Europe. The influence of the Arab empire is seen today in the wide extent of Arab language and culture, which is the dominant language and culture in the area from Morocco to Iraq. Its legacy is also seen in the spread of Islam to this area and beyond.

Mayan Civilization

One of the earliest advanced civilizations in the Americas was the Mayan civilization, whose classical period began around 250 A.D. It was centered in Guatemala and the Yucatan Peninsula of Mexico. It is believed to have been a collection of city-states rather than a centralized empire. The Maya developed trade routes and invented a system of writing. Their study of astronomy was more advanced than any other classical civilization, and they created a highly accurate calendar. The Maya built great religious-political centers, but are not believed to have built large cities.

Mayan civilization collapsed about 900 A.D. for unknown reasons, but its influence can be seen in later civilizations in the region. However, the Spanish, who conquered Mexico and Central America in the 1500s, tried to eradicate the indigenous (native) civilizations. During hundreds of years of colonial rule, they imposed the Spanish language, culture, and religion. Thus, today, the influence of the classical Mayan civilization is not as obvious as the other civilizations discussed in this chapter. However, some traditions and beliefs of Mayan civilization have survived in Mexico and Central America and, in some of the less modernized areas of this region, the Mayan language is still the spoken language.

Practice: Classical Civilizations

Question 1 refers to the previous sections on classical civilizations.

1. What was one way the civilizations of classical China and classical Greece and Rome differed from each other?

   (1) Greeks and Romans built great cities, but the Chinese did not.

   (2) Chinese civilization was threatened by less civilized warlike tribes from the north, but Greece and Rome were not.

   (3) Greece and Rome made trade among different regions an important part of their civilization, but China did not.

   (4) Greece and Rome built great stone structures (aqueducts, bridges, and temples), but the Chinese did not.

   (5) They had different ideas about the role of the individual in society.

2. Identify the influences of classical civilizations in this photo taken in Times Square in 2011.

   (1) The high-rise architecture was influenced by the towering jungle temples of the Mayan civilization and the decimal numeric system is from the Greek and Roman civilization.

   (2) The decimal numeric system shown on the sign is from the Chinese Empire of India and the alphabet is from the Roman Empire.

   (3) The alphabet shown on the sign is from Greek civilization and the decimal numeric system is from Chinese civilization.

   (4) The decimal numeric system shown on the sign is from the Gupta Empire and the alphabet from the Roman Empire.

   (5) The decimal numeric system shown on the sign is from the Arab Empire and the high-rise architecture is from the Chinese Empire.

Refer to the following world map to answer question 3.

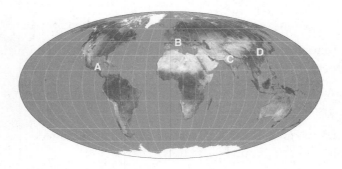

3. Identify the correct location of classical civilizations on the world map.

   (1) A is the Gupta Empire, B is the Roman Empire, and D is China.

   (2) B is the Arab Empire, C is the Gupta Empire, and D is China.

   (3) A is the Mayan civilization, B is the Roman Empire, and D is China.

   (4) A is the Mayan civilization, C is the Arab Empire, and D is the Gupta Empire.

   (5) B is the Roman Empire, C is China, and D is the Gupta Empire.

Answers: Classical Civilizations

1. **(5)** In classical western civilization (Greece and Rome), a high value was accorded the individual, while in classical China faithfulness to family and society were valued more. Both classical China and classical Greece and Rome built large cities (1) and conducted trade among different regions (3). Both the Roman Empire and the Chinese Empire were threatened by invasion from barbarian tribes to the north (2). China built the Great Wall to keep them out and, for the same purpose, Rome established garrisons along border rivers (Rhine and Danube) as well as a wall across Britain. Both civilizations built great structures of stone (4); the Great Wall of China remains the world's largest stone structure.

2. **(4)** The alphabet is the Roman (Latin) alphabet and the decimal numeric system was invented by mathematicians in the Gupta Empire of India.

3. **(3)** Mayan civilization was based in Guatemala and Mexico (A), the Roman Empire extended around the Mediterranean Sea (B), and the Chinese Empire, of course, was in China (D). Only answer (3) places these in the correct locations. The Gupta Empire was in India (C). The Arab Empire was centered in the Middle East (approximately midway between B and C).

The Global Expansion of Europe

The period from the late 1400s to the middle of the twentieth century was characterized by the spread of western civilization from Europe to all parts of the world. European civilization expanded through trade, *colonization*, and conquest.

DEFINITION

Colonization is the establishment of new settlements (colonies) in a distant land. During the Age of Discovery, European countries established colonies in the new lands they discovered, such as the 13 British colonies that eventually became the United States. The colonies were under the control of the colonizing country (mother country).

Age of Discovery

At the end of the Middle Ages, trade and commerce reappeared in Europe as governments became stronger and better able to guarantee security. As Europe began to prosper, there was a growing demand for products from the Far East, including silk, spices, porcelain, and tea. The Italian city of Venice became wealthy by controlling the final Mediterranean portion of a long overland route across Asia to China, but this route was slow, dangerous, and unreliable. The emerging European nations began looking for an alternative sea route to India, China, and the Indies (today's Indonesia). Thus began the Age of Discovery.

During this period the European nations discovered and colonized "new" lands previously unknown to them, such as North and South America. Europeans also discovered new sea trade routes that allowed them to establish and dominate world trade. For the first time, the world's continents—and economies—were linked by maritime trade. Making this possible were new European scientific advancements in navigation, the construction of better ships, and improvements in European firearms. While the Chinese invented gunpowder (which they used for fireworks), it was the Europeans who developed guns and cannon.

Portugal, one of the first modern nation-states in Europe, led the way. After discovering the sea route from Europe around Africa to Asia, this small European nation on the Atlantic Ocean was able to dominate trade on the Indian Ocean nearly halfway around the world for more than 100 years.

Spain, another of the first modern nations to emerge in Europe, took a bold move to counter Portugal by sending an expedition to reach the Far East by sailing not east but west around the world. When Christopher Columbus reached the Caribbean Islands in 1492, he thought he had reached the Indies. However, before long, Europeans realized Columbus had instead discovered a new continent, which they called the New World. After conquering the New World empires of the Aztecs and the Inca, Spain appropriated vast quantities of gold and silver, making it the wealthiest and most powerful country in the world.

In the 1500s, Spain and Portugal divided the world in half, each taking one side for expansion and thus avoiding war. However, in the 1600s Britain, France, and the Netherlands also began overseas expansions, bringing an almost continuous state of war, especially between archrivals Britain and France. Britain and France began by establishing colonies in the Caribbean and North America, but later extended their empires around the world.

Changes in the New World

In the 1600s, another source of wealth from overseas colonies developed: the production of crops that couldn't be grown in Europe. Sugar, especially, was in great demand in Europe; it replaced honey as the common sweetener, and rum was also widely consumed. To produce sugar cane, Britain, France, and the Netherlands took control of various Caribbean islands, while Portugal focused on Brazil.

To provide the labor needed for the sugar-plantation economy, Western Europeans (and their American colonists) forcibly took large numbers of people from West Africa and transported them to the New World as slaves. Slavery also provided workers for tobacco, rice, and cotton plantations. The legacy of slavery includes human suffering, civil wars, and racial tensions. Today the descendants of slaves throughout the Americas still have less economic and political power than the descendants of slave owners.

The British colonies in North America rebelled against British rule in 1776, the first modern successful rebellion of colonies against their mother country to obtain independence. This inspired Latin American colonies to revolt against Spain. By 1830, most of North and South America was composed of independent nations. However, these rebellions were carried out not by Native Americans but by the descendants of European settlers. Even after independence, the nations of the Americas remained examples of the spread of European civilization and culture.

Age of Imperialism

During the Age of *Imperialism* (from the mid 1800s until the mid 1900s), European culture and civilization continued to expand around the world. But instead of colonizing newly discovered lands, Europeans focused on conquering the peoples of Africa and Asia.

DEFINITION

Imperialism involves extending the power of one nation over the land and people of another nation. During the Age of Imperialism, European nations sought to conquer other peoples to form great empires. Some nineteenth-century European empires (such as Russia and Austria-Hungary) controlled neighboring peoples; others (such as Britain and France) extended their empires to include lands around the world.

In spite of the colonial rebellions in the Americas, the European expansion continued, but with the attention shifted to Asia. The British conquered India, the French Southeast Asia (Indochina), and the Dutch the East Indies (Indonesia). Russia, Britain, France, and Germany carved out spheres of influence in China; the Chinese emperor stayed on the throne but had little power. Finally, in the last half of the 1800s, Europe divided up Africa, with Britain and France getting the largest shares but with huge tracts of land also going to Italy, Germany, Portugal, and even tiny Belgium.

After World War II, with Europe in ruins, the worldwide empires of European nations finally began to crumble. India, the largest and most populous of the European colonies, gained independence from Britain (1947) after a nonviolent struggle led by Mahatma Gandhi. In most colonies, independence came fairly peaceably, but in some countries (for example, Vietnam, Algeria, and Angola) independence was won only after long, brutal wars against the ruling European country. By 1960, Europe had lost all its major colonies in Asia and by 1975 Africa was also free from European rule. As a result, the number of nations in the world increased from about 50 in 1945 to about 165 in 1975. Today, only a few small colonies remain; most of these have chosen this status in free elections.

As a result of the global expansion of Europe from the Age of Discovery to the Age of Imperialism, the influence of western civilization has spread around the world. Europe brought modern technology, government, and education systems to the rest of the world. On the other hand, European expansion subjugated native peoples—killing or enslaving many of them. But, paradoxically, it also brought the western ideals of democracy and the rights of individuals. Hundreds of revolutions—some to gain independence and others to simply gain a more democratic government—have been inspired by these western ideals, beginning with the American Revolution in 1776 and continuing today with the 2011 "Arab Spring" in the Middle East and North Africa.

Practice: The Global Expansion of Europe

Question 1 refers to the following map.

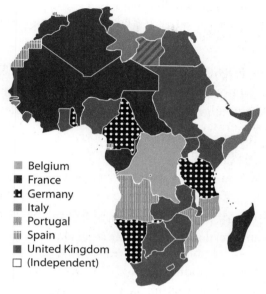

Belgium
France
Germany
Italy
Portugal
Spain
United Kingdom
(Independent)

European Empires in Africa, 1914.

1. What statement best summarizes the information shown on this map?

   (1) European domination of Africa was immoral because it violated the principle of self-determination.

   (2) Europeans took African lands to gain access to the slaves they needed in the New World.

   (3) Britain and France got more than their fair share of Africa.

   (4) Belgium controlled the Congo, an area 90 times Belgium's size.

   (5) European countries divided up nearly all of Africa and made these regions colonies in their empires.

Question 2 refers to the previous map of Africa and the following text of a United Nations treaty (1966) signed by nearly all the world's nations.

> "All people have the right to self-determination. By virtue of that right, they freely determine their political status."

> —International Covenant on Civil and Political Rights

2. Applying the principle of self-determination, what would happen in Africa?

   (1) The people of each European nation would vote to determine whether or not they wanted to give independence to their colonies in Africa.

   (2) The people of each empire (the mother country and the colonies) would vote to determine whether or not the colonies should be granted independence.

   (3) The people of Africa would vote to choose their status—whether or not they wanted to remain a colony or become an independent country.

   (4) The United Nations would vote to decide what the status of African colonies should be.

   (5) The people of Africa would vote on whether or not they wanted to become members of the United Nations.

Answers: The Global Expansion of Europe

1. **(5)** The map shows the facts of how the Europeans divided up Africa. Since only facts are presented, you can eliminate (1) and (3), which contain value judgments about morality and fairness. Nothing on the map makes any reference to slavery (2). In fact, by 1914 the slave trade and slavery had ended; Brazil was the last country to free its slaves (1888). Statement (4) is a true statement, but it refers to only one fact and is not a summary of the whole.

2. **(3)** Self-determination is the right of a people to determine their own future and not have it imposed by a foreign country or people. Statement (3) is what actually happened in most African colonies after World War II. All African colonies chose independence rather than remaining a colony in a European empire. Since 1975 the map of Africa has shown only independent countries. In most cases, independence was granted peaceably, but in a few cases (for example, Algeria and Angola) it was achieved only after a long war with the European country controlling it.

Geography

In This Chapter

- Overviews of some important concepts in geography
- GED-like questions to practice the skills you'll be tested on
- Answers and explanations for all the questions

Geography accounts for 16 percent of the questions on the Social Studies Test. You can expect 8 of the 50 questions to be based on maps and other geography content.

Similar to the other subjects covered on the Social Studies Test, you won't be required to memorize any facts or identify specific places on a map to ace the questions on geography. Most of the facts you'll need to know will be given in the reading passages or the visuals (maps, photos, graphs, etc.) that are included with the test questions. The test focuses on your skills in understanding, analyzing, and applying the information presented to you. However, a good background in geography will be useful in understanding the maps and reading passages, as well as helping you work through the questions quickly.

You have already practiced a basic skill of geography—interpreting maps—in Chapters 9, 10, and 12. But keep in mind that the subject area of geography covers more than maps. Geography includes topics such as climates, regions, oceans, and the interaction of humans with their environment. Included in this chapter are GED-like geography questions that will help prepare you for the types of skill-based questions you will confront on the real test.

Basic Concepts of Geography

Physical geography involves the study of physical features of the world, like glaciers, oceans, rivers, and landmasses. It includes the study of natural systems like climates and ocean currents. Physical geography focuses on the natural environment of earth, rather than the cultural or "built environment" of human geography.

Human geography is the study of human interaction with the environment. Topics of human geography include population, economic development, land usage, urbanization, agricultural development, and cultural change. Human geography overlaps with other social sciences, while physical geography overlaps with the natural sciences; however, in the study of geography, the emphasis is on the spatial dimension.

A central concept of geography is *location*. A standard system of identifying location on earth has been developed using latitude and longitude. Latitude is based on imaginary east-west parallel lines wrapping around the earth parallel to the equator. Longitude refers to imaginary north-south lines that intersect at the north and south poles. The equator, a line around the earth equidistant from the north and south poles, is latitude 0°. The prime meridian is longitude 0°, an arbitrary line drawn through the site near London of what was once one of the world's leading observatories. Longitudinal lines are numbered in degrees east and west from the prime meridian.

Another central concept of geography is *region*. Identifying, defining, and understanding regions is basic to both physical and human geography. Physical geography focuses on natural regions (for example, the Amazon Basin, the Gobi Desert, or the continent of Australia), while human geography looks at man-made regions. These can be well-defined regions with marked borders, like the country of Spain, or regions that are not well demarcated, like the French-speaking region of Belgium. They can be functional regions, like the regional management structure of a large corporation or the different interrelated systems of a metropolitan area. They can even be perceptual regions with only vague borders, like the Bible Belt or an ethnic neighborhood in a city.

Maps are a common tool used by geographers to provide information. Maps can show physical features and/or man-made features. Maps usually include a scale that relates the size of the map to the size of the actual area shown on the map. The scale can be depicted as an equation (1 inch = 100 miles) or a ratio (1:100,000). Most maps also include a key or legend that explains the markings on the map. However, one problem with maps, especially those showing a large region or the entire world, is distortion.

Any projection of the curved surface of earth onto a flat map is not entirely accurate. A number of different methods of projecting the curved surface of earth onto a flat map have been developed by geographers.

GOOD IDEA

While you won't have to locate places like Nebraska or Paris on a map, you may be required to recognize the continents. While the question won't focus on simply naming continents, this knowledge may be a basic requirement to interpreting information on a map. It's also a good idea to at least know on which continents major countries like India, Brazil, China, Australia, and Canada are located.

Practice: Basic Concepts of Geography

Question 1 refers to the following two world maps.

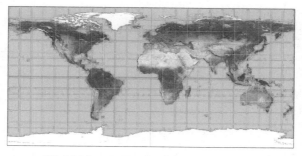

World Map A: Equirectangular Projection.

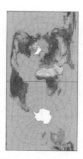

World Map B: Cassini Projection.

1. Which statement correctly describes the two maps?

   (1) Map A shows an accurate view of the world while Map B distorts reality.

   (2) Map B shows an accurate view of the world while Map A distorts reality.

   (3) Map A would be of greater use for a pilot trying to fly from Alaska to Europe than Map B.

   (4) Both maps distort the size, shape, and location of the continents.

   (5) Map B provides a less accurate view of the shape of Antarctica than Map A.

Refer to the following table to answer question 2.

The World's Largest Deserts*

Desert	Location	Size (square miles)	Selected Facts
Antarctic	The continent of Antarctica	5.4 million	With average annual precipitation of only 2–8 inches, Antarctica is the world's driest continent but, paradoxically, it contains most of the world's supply of fresh water.
Sahara	Northern Africa	3.3 million	Most of the Sahara, where the world's hottest temperature has been recorded, gets less than 1 inch of rainfall annually, but its Nile River Valley is lush and green year-round.

Desert	Location	Size (square miles)	Selected Facts
Arabian	Arabian Peninsula	900,000	Although the Arabian Desert is one of the hottest and driest areas of the planet, oases (sites naturally supplied with underground water) make it an important producer of dates.
Gobi	China and Mongolia	500,000	Most precipitation takes the form of snowfall in the Gobi Desert, where temperatures can drop to -40°F in winter.
Kalahari	Southern Africa	300,000	Although it only gets 3 to 7.5 inches of rainfall annually, areas of the Kalahari support an abundance of desert plants and wildlife.

Deserts are areas of earth that get less than 10 inches of annual precipitation (rain, snow, hail).

2. Which statement provides the best general conclusion that can be made from the table as a whole?

(1) Deserts are always sparsely populated areas.

(2) Deserts around the world look about the same.

(3) Most of the world's deserts are in Africa.

(4) Not all deserts have the same climate.

(5) South America doesn't have any deserts.

Answers: Basic Concepts of Geography

1. **(4)** Any projection of the world's curved surface onto a flat map distorts the size and shape of the continents. In this case, the amount of distortion on the two maps happens to be the same since both use the same method of projection. The only difference is that the Equirectangular Projection is centered on the equator (which runs horizontally across the center of the map), while the Cassini Projection centers on the prime meridian (which runs vertically through the center of the map). Both are equally accurate and correct, even though Map A looks more like the world maps we are used to. Since the earth is a ball in space, there is no fixed up or down or direction it must be put in. The Equirectangular Projection shows the area around the equator more accurately but distorts the polar regions, while the Cassini Projection does the opposite. Thus, Map B would be of greater use for a pilot flying across the polar region (3) and also provides a better view of Antarctica (5).

2. **(4)** You can conclude from the table that not all deserts have the same climate; in fact, the difference in climate between Antarctica, the coldest continent, and the Sahara, where the world's hottest temperatures have been recorded, is stunning. This contrast makes statement (2) incorrect. The table does not have information on population density, so it would not be logical to draw the conclusion that deserts are sparsely populated (1) based on this table. In fact, some areas of deserts, like the Nile River Valley, are among the most densely populated areas of the world. The table has information about five deserts (two of which are in Africa), but not about *most* of the world's deserts (3), so it is impossible to make conclusions about most deserts from this table. Similarly, the fact the table has no information about deserts in South America (5) does not mean they do not exist; they are simply not among the five largest deserts.

HEADS UP!

Be careful whenever a question asks for the "best" answer or conclusion. This is a dead giveaway that you will need to read all answer choices and use the process of elimination to compare choices. Throw out all the "worse" choices until you have only the "best" left.

World Population

The study of population is an important branch of human geography called *demography*. One important topic in this field is population growth. Demographers study population statistics (along with economic development, government policies, societal norms, and cultural values) to understand population growth and predict what will happen in individual cities, countries, and the planet as a whole. This topic is one of many geography topics that could appear on the test.

In 1800, the world's population was 1 billion, by 1927 it had reached 2 billion, by 1974 it was 4 billion, and in 2011 it reached 7 billion. This increase has been caused—not by an increase in birth rates (which have actually declined during this period)—but by a marked decrease in death rates, especially infant mortality rates. In the early 1800s, British scholar Thomas Robert Malthus posited that human population would grow faster than technology can increase earth's carrying capacity (the number of people earth can support on a sustainable basis). Whether this will ultimately prove true and lead to overpopulation of earth—along with economic and environmental disaster—remains an unanswered question.

There is a direct relationship between economic development and fertility rates (the number of children, on the average, a woman has during her lifetime). As nations develop economically, generally their fertility rates decline. The reasons for this include decreased infant mortality, greater economic security, and a better educated public. Countries with rapidly developing economies have seen large declines in fertility rates in recent years. For example, in Brazil, where the standard of living has risen significantly, the fertility rate declined from 6.2 in 1950 to 2.2 in 2000.

In some of the world's advanced industrial economies, fertility rates are now below the replacement level (the level needed for zero population growth). As a result, the populations of Japan, Russia, and Germany are declining. Due to falling fertility rates, Western Europe, Japan, and, to a lesser degree, the United States face a new and different kind of population problem: a large aging population that must be supported by a decreasing number of younger workers.

In the United States the fertility rate (2.2 children per woman) is near the replacement level, but population growth continues due to emigration from other countries. In any given period, a nation's population growth can be expressed as follows:

Population Growth = Births − Deaths + Immigrants - Emigrants

Along with population growth, geographers study *population density*. Seventy-five percent of the world's population lives on only 5 percent of the earth's surface. Most of the growth in the world's population is occurring in places where people are already thickly settled. Large cities, especially those in Asia, Africa, and Latin America, are getting much larger as a result of both natural population growth and migration from rural areas. The planet's human settlement pattern in the twenty-first century will be characterized by a growing number of densely populated cities, many with more than 10, or even 20, million people.

DEFINITION

Population density (the average number of people per square mile or square kilometer) is used to describe how thickly settled a region is. Singapore, a small island nation in Southeast Asia, has a population density of 16,444 people per square mile, while Mongolia, composed mostly of the Gobi Desert, has a population density of only 4.4 people per square mile.

Practice: World Population

Questions 1 and 2 refer to the following line graphs.

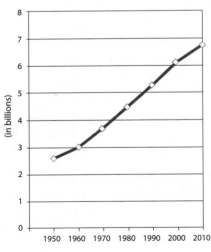

World Population

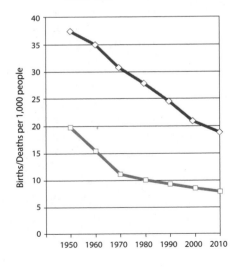

Global Birth and Death Rates

1. Which one of the following trends is *not* consistent with the information shown on the graphs?

   (1) World population is increasing.

   (2) The global birth rate is falling.

   (3) The global death rate is falling.

   (4) The global birth rate is higher than the global death rate.

   (5) World population is increasing at a faster rate today than it was 20 years ago.

2. What is the best explanation of the cause of the rapid growth in the world's population even though the birth rate is falling?

   (1) Both a falling death and a falling birth rate have the effect of causing the world's population to grow.

   (2) As long as the birth rate is above zero, the world's population will grow.

   (3) Seventy-five percent of the world's people live on 5 percent of the earth's surface.

   (4) A birth rate higher than the death rate causes world population to grow.

   (5) Immigration can cause the population of a country to grow even though its birth rate is low.

Questions 3 and 4 refer to the following passage.

Population Density and the Rise of Early Civilizations

For civilization to arise, a certain population density needed to be reached. Roaming tribes of hunters and gatherers or even scattered agricultural villages did not have the critical mass necessary to develop an advanced civilization. That critical mass was achieved through irrigation.

The agricultural surplus produced by the irrigation of crops made population growth possible and allowed many workers to specialize in jobs other than growing food. Cities came into existence, filled with craftsmen, merchants and traders, construction workers, religious and governmental officials, etc.

In the valley of the Tigris and Euphrates, the Sumerians are usually credited with creating the earliest civilization about 5,000 years ago. Besides extensive irrigation systems, they developed the first system of writing, the earliest cities, the calendar (on which ours today is based), and the first written code of law. Other locations where the development of irrigation led to the rise of early civilizations were the Nile River Valley in Egypt, the Yellow River in China, and the Indus River Valley in Pakistan.

3. Which statement best states the main idea of the passage?

   (1) Early civilizations developed along rivers, which served as a source of irrigation water and a highway for trade.

   (2) The rise of civilization about 5,000 years ago is a relatively recent event in the time span of human existence.

   (3) Early civilizations developed in the valley of the Tigris and Euphrates and in the valleys of the Nile, Indus, and Yellow rivers.

   (4) The birth of agriculture led to the development of civilization.

   (5) Irrigation produced the population growth and population density needed for civilization to develop.

4. An implication is something not stated that can be reasonably concluded from what is stated. The author of the passage implies that

   (1) the development of irrigation systems is related to the development of civilizations.

   (2) the rivers along which early civilization developed provided the source of water for irrigation systems.

   (3) irrigation produced the population density needed for civilization to develop.

   (4) the Sumerians were the first to develop civilization because they had two rivers in their valley (the Tigris and Euphrates).

   (5) an agricultural surplus allows some people to do jobs other than raising food.

Answers: World Population

1. **(5)** There is no evidence in the graphs that world population is growing at a faster rate today than 20 years ago. The growth rate has not changed much since 1960. If anything, the growth rate has started to level off a bit. All other answer choices state trends shown in the graphs.

2. **(4)** World population growth is caused by the fact that the world's birth rate is higher than its death rate. Be careful with questions that ask for a cause. Just because the birth rate is falling while population is increasing doesn't mean there is a causal relationship between the two trends. A falling birth rate has the effect of reducing population growth, making choice (1) incorrect. In this case, that downward pressure on population growth is offset by a falling death rate, which is keeping the gap between the birth rate and the death rate about the same. It is impossible for a birth rate near zero (meaning there are almost no births) to produce population growth unless, somehow, death has been eliminated (2). Statement (3) is a correct factual statement, but one that does not explain at all why the world's population is increasing. Immigration (5) plays a role in an individual country's population growth rate, but not in the global growth rate because there is no immigration from outer space to planet earth.

3. **(5)** The last statement best describes the main idea of the passage. You can eliminate (1) and (2) because these introduce new ideas (the time span of human existence and trade) not covered in the passage. Statement (3) is true but simply restates examples from the last paragraph and misses the main point—the relationship between irrigation, population density, and civilization. While it is true that the birth of agriculture (4) was a prerequisite to the development of irrigation and thus was also an important step in the rise of civilization, this passage doesn't mention that.

4. **(2)** All these early civilizations with irrigation systems probably didn't just happen to arise alongside rivers. The rivers, the author implies, were the source of water for the irrigation system of each civilization. Since an implication is something not stated, eliminate all the statements that *are* explicitly stated in the passage. This includes (1), (3), and (5), which were explicitly stated in different wording. Statement (4) doesn't seem to be something that the author is implying since there's no development of—or apparent reason for—the idea that two rivers are better than one.

Social Studies Practice Test

Taking a practice test is the most important part of your test preparation plan. The practice test in this chapter allows you to review the content and skills you'll be tested on, become more familiar with the type of questions you'll encounter, and most important, practice test-taking strategies, including pacing. Taking a practice test will also help you build confidence and control stress.

No matter how much you've studied and reviewed, you can expect that some of the content presented on the Social Studies Test will be new to you. Thus, some of the questions on this practice test are based on new content rather than the material you've reviewed in the five preceding chapters. Don't worry—most of what you need to know to answer each question is given. You only need to demonstrate your ability to work with the information using the skills you've been practicing.

The actual Social Studies Test contains 50 questions and requires 70 minutes. The practice test contains 25 questions for which you should give yourself 35 minutes to complete. Although this practice test is only half the length of the actual test, it contains the same mix of question types, subject areas, and skills tested that you will encounter on the real test.

If, after taking the test provided here, you feel you need more practice and want to take another simulated test, there are several online sites that offer free GED practice tests. One site we recommend is PBS Literacy Link (http:litlink.ket.org), which has two half-length free practice Social Studies Tests. Keep in mind, though, that the actual GED Tests are paper-and-pencil tests like those in this book and cannot be taken on a computer.

Instructions

The Social Studies Test is designed to measure your understanding of general social studies skills and concepts. Each question is based on a short reading or on a map, table, cartoon, graph, or photo. Use the information provided to answer the question(s) that follow. You can refer to the information as often as you want in answering the question(s).

You will have 35 minutes to complete the 25 questions on this practice test. Work carefully, but don't spend too much time on any one question. If you are having trouble with a question, make the best guess you can and move on. Your score is based on the number of correct answers; there is no penalty for guessing.

When taking the practice test, try to simulate actual test conditions. Get a timing device of some sort and a couple of No. 2 pencils with good erasers. Go to a place where you won't be interrupted and follow test instructions. Start the timer after you've read the instructions and are ready to begin the first question.

Go on to the next page when you are ready to begin.

Question 1 refers to the following passage.

The development of trade was an important factor that helped advance and spread early civilizations. Besides providing products a region may not have access to itself, trade allows regions to specialize in products they can produce best, thus increasing overall production.

Minoan civilization, centered in Crete, was the earliest civilization based on trade rather than agriculture. Unlike other early civilizations, the Minoans did not have an agricultural surplus produced by irrigation. Instead, Minoan cities were supported by trade conducted by ships that carried cargos on the Mediterranean Sea.

1. The author of the passage above implies that

   (1) Minoans developed wine making rather than the production of food crops.

   (2) Trade allows countries to specialize in the products they can produce best.

   (3) Minoans did not eat as well as other early civilizations.

   (4) Trade allows countries to obtain products they would not otherwise have access to.

   (5) Minoans obtained at least some of their food from trade rather than growing it all themselves.

Questions 2 and 3 refer to the following political cartoon.

Courtesy of William S. Wiist

2. What assumption is the cartoonist making?

   (1) Readers already know the elephant stands for the president and the donkey for Congress.

   (2) Readers already know the elephant stands for the Republican Party and the donkey for the Democratic Party.

   (3) Readers already know the economy is sinking.

   (4) Readers already know the human hand stands for the economy.

   (5) Readers already know the water stands for the Potomac River.

3. What is the main point the cartoonist is trying to make?

   (1) Republicans and Democrats are working together to help the economy.

   (2) Elections determine which party—Democrats or Republicans—decides how to rescue the economy.

   (3) Republicans and Democrats are fighting with each other for political advantage rather than working together to help the economy.

   (4) The political process in a democracy is at its best when the two parties keep each other in check.

   (5) A third party should arise to save the economy while the Democrats and Republicans bicker.

Question 4 refers to the following passage from the U.S. Declaration of Independence.

> We, therefore, the Representatives of the United States of America, in General Congress Assembled, appealing to the Supreme Judge of the world for the rectitude of our intentions, do, in the Name, and by Authority of the good People of these Colonies, solemnly publish and declare that these United Colonies are, and of Right ought to be Free and Independent States ....

4. Based on this passage, what value did the authors of the Declaration share?

    (1) A desire to maintain peace

    (2) A belief in inalienable rights

    (3) A belief in Christianity

    (4) A belief in national self-determination

    (5) A desire to be loyal to authority

Question 5 refers to the following paragraph.

> According to the economic law of supply and demand, prices fluctuate based on supply and demand. The price of a good or service will go up if demand is greater than supply. Or, if supply is greater than demand, the price will go down.

5. According to the economics of supply and demand, what is most likely to happen if the Brazilian soybean crop is one of the best ever?

    (1) The demand for soybeans will fall in Brazil.

    (2) Brazilian farmers will earn more money.

    (3) Brazilian farmers will earn less money.

    (4) The price of soybeans will go down in Brazil.

    (5) Demand for soybeans will grow as the world's population grows.

Question 6 refers to the following photo.

A Roman temple built 1,800 years ago in Heliopolis, a city located in Asia a short distance inland from the eastern shore of the Mediterranean Sea (present-day Lebanon).

6. Which statement can be rejected using evidence in the photo?

   (1) Romans were master builders of great public buildings.

   (2) The Romans only built great buildings in and around their capital of Rome.

   (3) Roman influence and control spread to all the lands around the Mediterranean Sea.

   (4) The Romans honored their gods by building large temples.

   (5) Heliopolis was an important religious center in Roman times.

Question 7 refers to the following graph.

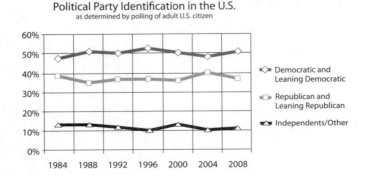

7. Which conclusion is supported by information presented in the graph?

   (1) Most independents usually vote for Republican candidates, giving Democrats and Republicans about an equal chance of winning.

   (2) The breakdown of Americans who identify with each political party did not change much between 1984 and 2008.

   (3) Independents comprise less than 10 percent of American voters.

   (4) The Democratic Party is about the same size as the Republican Party.

   (5) The U.S. political system is characterized by three main parties.

Questions 8 and 9 refer to the following paragraph and table.

It is difficult to compare how well off the people in one country are compared to the people in another. One simple way of making a rough comparison is by using GDP per capita. GDP (Gross Domestic Product) is the value of all the goods and services produced in a country in 1 year. However, GDP, by itself, doesn't tell us how well off individuals in a country are because some countries have large populations and others do not. Per capita GDP takes the GDP and divides it by the number of people in the country to arrive at an average GDP per person.

GDPs of Selected Countries, 2010

Country	GDP (in Trillions of US$)	Rank	GDP per Capita (in US$)	Rank
United States	14.5	1	46,860	10
China	5.9	2	4,382	91
Germany	3.2	4	40,274	19
Brazil	2.1	7	10,816	54
India	1.6	9	1,371	133
Russia	1.5	11	10,856	57
Australia	1.2	13	55,672	7
Mexico	1.0	14	9,522	61
Switzerland	.5	19	67,779	4
Norway	.4	25	84,144	2

8. In which countries shown in the chart are the people better off economically on the average than Americans?

(1) China

(2) Norway

(3) Norway and Switzerland

(4) Norway, Switzerland, and Australia

(5) No countries, the United States is highest

9. What is the best explanation why India has the world's ninth-biggest economy but ranks so low in how well off its people are?

(1) India's people are not well educated.

(2) India has a lot of people.

(3) Wages are very low in India.

(4) Workers put in long hours without overtime pay.

(5) The table doesn't give this information.

Questions 10 and 11 refer to the following passage.

Napoleon, emperor of France (1804–1814), and Hitler, dictator of Germany (1934–1945), both led their countries in wartime to conquer nearly all of Europe. But neither was able to end British naval dominance or completely defeat the Russian army. Both Hitler and Napoleon made the mistake of invading Russia. Although they won victories and reached or occupied Moscow, both lost most of their armies due to the vicious fighting and Russian winter. Napoleon was finally defeated in 1815 and exiled to a remote Atlantic island where he died. Hitler committed suicide in 1945 as the Russian army entered Berlin.

Napoleon is honored in France and regarded everywhere as one of the world's great political and military leaders, but Hitler is almost universally associated with absolute evil. Hitler is known for the Holocaust, the mass murder of 11 to 14 million people, including two thirds of Europe's Jews as well as large numbers of Poles, political opponents, homosexuals, and others. Napoleon, on the other hand, is honored both for his military genius and for helping lead Europe into the modern age. He freed serfs, spread the idea of national-ism, and established a fair, written code of law (the Napoleonic Code), which still forms the basic law for about a quarter of the world's nations.

10. What major contrast between Hitler and Napoleon is made in the passage?

    (1) One succeeded in conquering Europe, while the other did not.

    (2) One was a dictator, the other an emperor.

    (3) One is regarded as a hero, the other as one of the world's most evil villains.

    (4) One committed suicide and the other died of natural causes.

    (5) One was able to defeat the British navy, the other was not.

11. According to the reading, what was a major cause of both Napoleon's and Hitler's eventual downfalls?

    (1) Neither Hitler nor Napoleon was well educated.

    (2) They were both excellent military strategists.

    (3) Both Hitler and Napoleon wanted to end British naval dominance.

    (4) Both Hitler and Napoleon had absolute power in their countries.

    (5) Both Hitler and Napoleon decided to invade Russia.

Questions 12 and 13 refer to the following paragraph and map.

Presidents in the United States are not chosen directly by a vote of the people but by an electoral vote system. The number of electoral votes each state gets to cast is equal to the total number of representatives and senators it is allocated in Congress. The more populous states get more electoral votes since the number of representatives a state has in the House of Representatives depends on the state's population. Generally, a state's electoral votes all go to the candidate who wins the popular vote in that state. If a candidate wins more than half of the electoral vote, that candidate becomes president. If no candidate gets a majority of the electoral votes, the president is chosen by the House of Representatives.

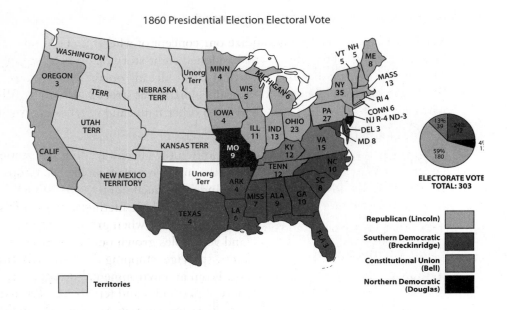

1860 Presidential Election Electoral Vote

12. Which factor best explains why Lincoln won the presidency in 1860?

(1) Lincoln carried more than half of the 33 states.

(2) More than half the people voted for Lincoln.

(3) Lincoln won a majority of the electoral vote.

(4) Lincoln carried the Northern states that stayed in the Union.

(5) The states that didn't vote for Lincoln weren't united and divided their electoral votes among three other candidates.

13. Which of the following states an assumption that can be accurately made based on the information presented above?

(1) Both states and territories participated in presidential elections.

(2) According to the most recent official U.S. census of the day, more people lived in Vermont than in California.

(3) Many states split their electoral votes to represent the voting pattern in their state.

(4) The Civil War could have been avoided if the Southern states had been given more electoral votes.

(5) The West was the key to Abraham Lincoln's victory.

Questions 14 and 15 refer to the following passage.

Vertical farming could revolutionize our concept of where food should be grown. Soon a farm inside an abandoned eight-story office building in Manchester, England, will join vertical farms already operating in Kyoto, Seoul, Chicago, and Seattle. The produce market at street level will be filled with lettuce, tomatoes, strawberries, and other fruits and vegetables grown year-round on the floors above.

While organic farming strives to take agriculture backward in time, vertical farming attempts to adapt farming to the modern urbanized world. Crops are grown in a nutrient-rich solution under artificial lighting in a sealed environment that requires no pesticides. Using these methods, vertical farming produces six times the yield as the same crops when grown outdoors. Furthermore, while half of fruits and vegetables grown outdoors are never eaten (due to droughts, floods, insects, spoilage, shipping damage, etc.), there is no such loss with vertical farming. From an environmental perspective, vertical farming ends the toxic runoff of pesticides and fertilizers, eliminates transportation costs and pollution, reduces pressure on world water supplies, and slows deforestation. Increasingly, vertical farming is being viewed as part of the solution for feeding the planet's growing population.

14. Which statement best states the main point of the passage?

(1) An alternative is needed to organic farming, which takes agriculture backward in time.

(2) Vertical farming causes less harm to the environment than our current system of growing fruits and vegetables.

(3) Vertical farming provides fresher fruits and vegetables to urban residents than organic farming.

(4) Vertical farming can efficiently provide fresh fruits and vegetables to urban residents while reducing damage to the environment.

(5) Traditional farming in outdoor fields should be cut back or stopped.

15. Which of the following is an effect of vertical farming?

    (1) Increased use of pesticides

    (2) Fresher fruits and vegetables year-round in cities

    (3) Increased transportation costs

    (4) Lower yields than when food is grown using natural sunlight

    (5) Increased water pollution

Question 16 refers to the following table.

Education and Participation in Presidential Elections

School Years Completed	Percentage of Voting Age Population Reporting That They Voted		
	2000	2004	2008
8 years or less	26.8	23.6	23.4
Some high school but no diploma	33.6	34.6	33.7
High school graduate or GED	49.4	52.4	50.9
Some college or associate's degree	60.3	66.1	65.0
College bachelor's or advanced degree	72.0	74.2	73.3

16. What conclusion can clearly be drawn from the data in the table?

    (1) The more education a person has, the more likely the person will vote in a U.S. presidential election.

    (2) Most voters in U.S. presidential elections have some college or a college degree.

    (3) There are more people with college degrees voting in U.S. presidential elections than people with only high school (or GED) diplomas voting.

    (4) People that have more education are smarter and better able to get involved in democratic government.

    (5) People with less education shouldn't vote because they are less likely to understand the candidates and issues.

Questions 17 and 18 refer to the following map.

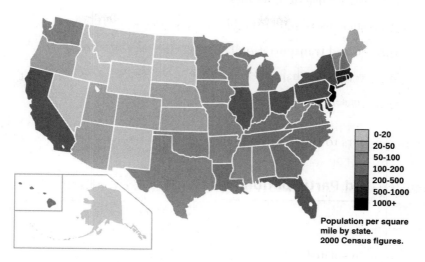

U.S. Population Density.

17. Based on the information in the map, which statement most accurately compares the Western states with the Eastern states?

(1) The states with the largest populations are in the East while the states with the smallest populations are in the West.

(2) The Western states generally have a lower population density than the Eastern states.

(3) States that cover a large area have lower population densities than states that cover only a small area.

(4) Western states are generally larger in territory and have larger populations than the Eastern states.

(5) Except for California, the Western states have higher population densities than the Eastern states.

18. What is the best explanation why Texas ranks second in population, but 25 states have a higher population density?

    (1) Many people in Texas are illegal aliens and not counted in the census.

    (2) Many people in Texas have moved there from other states.

    (3) Texas is one of the largest states in land area.

    (4) Texas's cities are spread out without a high population density.

    (5) Population density is lower in farming states than in urbanized states.

Questions 19 and 20 refer to the following paragraph.

Following the Supreme Court's ruling in *Brown v. Board of Education* (1954), 96 congressmen from the South signed the following declaration:

> We regard the decision of the Supreme Court in the school cases as clear abuse of judicial power. It climaxes a trend in the Federal judiciary undertaking to legislate, in derogation of the authority of Congress, and to encroach upon the reserved rights of the states and the people. The original Constitution does not mention education. Neither does the Fourteenth Amendment nor any other amendment. The debates preceding the submission of the Fourteenth Amendment clearly show that there was no intent that it should affect the systems of education maintained by the states.

19. Which statement correctly states the main point of the argument made by the 96 congressmen?

    (1) The racial integration of schools is not required by the Constitution.

    (2) States should disobey the Supreme Court decision because it violates the Constitution.

    (3) The Fourteenth Amendment should be repealed.

    (4) The federal government does not have the power to get involved in education, which is a matter that the Constitution leaves to the states.

    (5) State governments should not encroach on the authority of Congress to make laws regarding education.

20. Applying this argument to today's issues, which one of the following measures would this argument support?

    (1) Increasing federal loans to college students

    (2) Reduction of the federal deficit

    (3) Passage of a law by Congress to reform the health care delivery system of the United States

    (4) Strengthening federal laws regarding pollution

    (5) The elimination of the federal Department of Education

Questions 21 and 22 refer to the following passage and graph.

Imports are goods and services purchased from other countries, and exports are goods and services sold to other countries. Together imports and exports constitute international trade. The balance of trade shows the net effect of imports and exports on a country's economy.

Balance of Trade = Exports – Imports (computed for a one-year period)

If the balance of trade is favorable (a positive number), a country has balance of trade surplus. If the balance of trade is unfavorable (a negative number), the country has a balance of trade deficit. A country with a balance of trade surplus accumulates foreign currency, which it can keep in reserve, loan to other countries, or invest in other countries. A country with a balance of trade deficit must usually borrow money from other countries to finance its deficit.

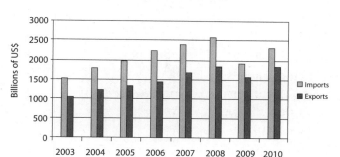

U.S. International Trade, 2003-2010

21. Which statement is best supported by the evidence in the graph?

    (1) The United States had a balance of trade surplus in all years shown in the bar graph.

    (2) With the recession in 2009, the U.S. balance of trade deficit increased.

    (3) U.S. international trade increased every year between 2003 and 2010.

    (4) For the time period shown in the graph, the balance of trade deficit was the smallest in 2009.

    (5) Imports and exports were in balance in 2003.

22. Adding together all countries' imports and all countries' exports, which statement best describes the global balance of trade?

    (1) The global balance of trade is always 0 (neither a surplus nor a deficit).

    (2) The global balance of trade is the total value of all countries' imports and exports added together.

    (3) There would generally be a global balance of trade deficit.

    (4) There would generally be a global balance of trade surplus.

    (5) The global balance of trade cannot be determined.

Questions 23 and 24 refer to the following political cartoon published in 1778 by a British newspaper during the American Revolution.

THE HORSE AMERICA, throwing his Master.

23. In the cartoon, who or what does the rider of the horse stand for?

    (1) The 13 colonies in rebellion against the British king

    (2) George Washington

    (3) The British government

    (4) The Americans as a whole

    (5) The Continental Congress

24. Which of the following is a statement of fact rather than an opinion or value judgment?

    (1) America is like an unruly horse that doesn't obey its master and needs to be disciplined.

    (2) The British army found it difficult to subdue the American colonies and end the rebellion.

    (3) The British government should have given the colonies more freedom.

    (4) The American colonies were rebelling against an unjust British government that denied them their rights.

    (5) King George V was not a good ruler.

Question 25 refers to the following passage from Article I of the U.S. Constitution.

Section 1: All legislative powers herein granted shall be vested in a Congress of the United States, which shall consist of a Senate and House of Representatives.

Section 2: The House of Representatives shall be composed of member chosen every second year by the people of the several States ....

Section 3: The Senate of the United States shall be composed of two Senators from each state, chosen by the legislature thereof for six years ....

25. Which statement is not consistent with Article I of the U.S. Constitution?

    (1) Representatives and senators are to be chosen by the people of each state.

    (2) Representatives are elected for 2 years and senators for 6 years.

    (3) There are to be two senators from each state.

    (4) Law-making authority is given to Congress.

    (5) There are to be two chambers of Congress.

Answers and Explanations

1. **(5)** Something implied is something not specifically stated but strongly suggested by what the author does state. Since the author says Minoan civilization was based on trade rather than agriculture, the implication is that at least some of their food was obtained through trade. The author doesn't imply anything about wine making (1) since it was a subject not addressed in the passage. Statements (2) and (4) were specifically stated by the author rather than implied. The author doesn't seem to be suggesting that the Minoans didn't eat well (3); in fact, because of their trade they may have had access to more different types of foods than other early civilizations.

2. **(2)** The cartoonist assumes that readers know that the elephant and donkey stand for the Democratic and Republican parties. The parties are pulling in opposite directions rather than working together (1). The cartoonist explains statements (3) and (4) in the cartoon rather than assuming readers already know this. The water does not stand for any particular body of water (5).

3. **(3)** Choice (3) states the cartoonist's position. Choices (1) and (4) state viewpoints contrary to the cartoonist's opinion. The cartoon doesn't contain anything about a third party (5) or elections (2).

4. **(4)** A value is a deeply held belief that forms part of the basis for a person's views and outlook. All the authors shared and were motivated by a strong belief in national self-determination, the idea that a people have the right to determine their own system of government rather than having it imposed by an outside power. By signing the Declaration of Independence, the authors knew they were disloyal to the established authority (5) and taking an action that would lead to war, not peace (1). In this passage there is nothing about Christianity (3) or inalienable rights (2).

5. **(4)** The supply of soybeans increases (while demand stays the same) so the price goes down. Then, at the lower price, there will be *increased* demand for soybeans (1). There is not enough information to determine if Brazilian farmers will earn more (2) or less (3) money. That depends on how much the price falls. Statement (5) is true, but not a result of the size of the Brazilian soybean crop.

6. **(2)** The temple in Asia shown in the photo provides evidence that the Romans built great buildings well beyond Rome, so statement (2) can be rejected. The temple in the photo provides evidence that helps to support all the other statements.

7. **(2)** The graph provides supporting evidence for the statement that the breakdown of Americans by political party did not change much. The graph doesn't give any information about how independents voted in any of these years (1). The Democratic and Republican parties are competitive despite the larger numbers of Democrats because the groups that tend to identify with the Democratic Party are also groups that tend to have lower-than-average voter turnout. Independents comprise 10 to 13 percent of the American public (3) and the Democratic Party is larger than the Republican Party (4). The United States is characterized by a two-party system (5); independents are people who do not identify with either of these two parties.

8. **(4)** According to the data, per capita GDP is higher in Norway, Switzerland, and Australia than in the United States.

9. **(2)** India produces a large number of goods and services (GDP), but with nearly a billion people, the average amount of goods and services per person (per capita GDP) is relatively small. Wages (3) have no influence on GDP, which only measures the value of goods and services produced. People who work long hours (4) and people with a good education (1) tend to produce more goods and services, thereby increasing GDP, but these factors play no role in explaining the gap between the ranking of India's GDP and the ranking of its per capita GDP.

10. **(3)** The reading paints a vivid contrast between how Hitler and Napoleon are regarded today. Both succeeded in conquering most of Europe (1) and neither succeeded in conquering Britain (5). It is true that Hitler was a dictator and Napoleon an emperor (2), but there is little difference between these titles so this is actually as much a similarity as a contrast. Hitler committed suicide, but the reading doesn't provide enough information to make the contrast stated in choice (4). Some believe Napoleon had stomach cancer, but others think he was poisoned or took his own life. Regardless, this isn't a major contrast made in the reading.

11. **(5)** The armies of both Napoleon and Hitler were severely weakened in their invasions of Russia, contributing to their eventual defeats. The reading doesn't give information about their education (1). Being good military strategists (2) was a cause of their conquests of most of Europe, not a cause of their downfalls. Both wanted to end British military superiority (and failed to achieve this goal), but trying to end British naval dominance (3) wasn't a direct cause of their downfalls. Both had absolute power (4), but this power did not directly contribute to their downfalls; both also enjoyed widespread popular support during most of their rule.

12. **(3)** A person becomes president by getting a majority of the electoral votes. The pie chart shows that Lincoln did this. He won just over half the states (1), but this doesn't make someone the president. You can become president by winning the most populous states without carrying most the states. The map and pie chart does not have information about the number of people who voted for Lincoln (2); in fact, only about 40 percent voted for Lincoln. The country didn't split up until after Lincoln was elected, so the breakup of the Union didn't affect the election (4). The fact that the opposition to Lincoln was not united had little effect on the election because, even combining all the other candidates' electoral votes, they would come up short and Lincoln would still be elected (5).

13. **(2)** Based on the information on the map, Vermont (VT) had five electoral votes and California (CA) had only four. Therefore, we can assume that Vermont had more people at the time of the most recent official census. From the information given, we can assume that the territories did *not* participate in the presidential election (1) since they had no electoral votes allocated to them. From the map, we can assume that states rarely split their electoral votes (3); only New Jersey did so in 1860. We can't jump to the conclusion that the Civil War could have been avoided if the South had had more electoral votes (more people); there is not nearly enough information to make such an assumption (4). The West, with only seven electoral votes, was not an important factor (5) in the election; Lincoln would have still easily won if he had not carried the West.

14. **(4)** Statement (4) provides a good summary of the entire passage. You can immediately eliminate (1) and (5) since they don't mention vertical farming, which is the subject of this passage. The passage is not about traditional farming (5) or finding an alternative to organic farming (1). Statement (2) makes a point not brought up until near the end of the last paragraph, so this choice can also be eliminated. Statement (3) makes a comparison not even made in the passage.

15. **(2)** Vertical farming would result in fresher fruits and vegetables in cities year-round. Vertical farming, compared to traditional farming, would have the effects of decreasing the use of pesticides (1), decreasing transportation costs (3), increasing yields (4), and reducing water pollution (5).

16. **(1)** The table shows that people with more education are more likely to vote. We can't make any comparisons involving numbers of people voting in each group (2 and 3) since the table doesn't give these numbers. For example,

26.8 percent of the people with only an eighth-grade education voted in 2000, not 26.8 percent of the people who voted had an eighth grade education. Statements (4) and (5) involve opinions not supported by the data.

17. **(2)** In general, the map shows that Western states have lower population densities than Eastern states. The map only has information about population densities, not populations. Therefore, the map contains no evidence that most populous states are in the East (1) or West (4). In fact, the states with the largest populations—California and Texas—are in the West, but most of the other more populous states are in the East. Statement (3) is not always true; California is a large state but also has one of the highest population densities. Furthermore, statement (3) makes no comparison between Eastern and Western states as required by the question. Western states generally have lower, not higher, population densities than Eastern states (5).

18. **(3)** The reason that Texas has a large population but a low population density is simply that Texas is a large state in land area. Illegal aliens (1) and where people came from (2) have nothing to do with population density. Statements (4) and (5) are true statements in general but do not completely explain why Texas is one of the most populous states but has a relatively low population density.

19. **(4)** Their argument is a states-rights one that holds that the federal government has no authority to get involved in education. Although *Brown v. the Board of Education* required public school integration, the 96 congressmen avoid arguing the case for or against racial integration (1) much as Southerners during the Civil War period tried to make states rights, rather than slavery, the issue. The congressmen do not go so far as to say states should disobey the Supreme Court decision (2) or that the Fourteenth Amendment should be repealed (3). The congressmen are making the argument that the federal government should not encroach on the power of state governments, rather than vice versa (5).

20. **(5)** This question requires you to apply the argument the Southern congressmen made in 1954 to today's issues. Since they argue the federal government should not be involved in education, they would have to support the elimination of the federal Department of Education. Their argument would also support the elimination of federal loans for college (1). Since they argue the case for states rights, they would probably take the position the federal government should not be involved in health care (3) or pollution control (4) since these areas are also ones not mentioned in the Constitution. Based on

their 1954 statement, we don't know how these congressmen would feel about the federal deficit (2) because the states-rights argument doesn't apply to the federal deficit and the Constitution clearly gives the federal government the power to borrow money.

21. **(4)** According to the graph, there was a balance of trade deficit in all years, making choices (1) and (5) incorrect. The gap between imports and exports was smallest in 2009, making choice (4) correct and choice (2) incorrect. International trade is the sum of imports and exports. In general, international trade increased during the time period shown in the graph, but in 2009 it decreased, making choice (3) incorrect.

22. **(1)** This question requires you to apply the concept of balance of trade to the global economy. Since one country's exports become another country's imports, imports and exports are always in balance when considered on a global scale. The only way the global balance of trade would not be 0 is if there were imports or exports to/from another planet. The world's total international trade is described in choice (2), but don't confuse this with the balance of trade.

23. **(3)** The American colonies (the horse) were rebelling to try to throw off their master, which was the British government.

24. **(2)** It is a factual statement that the British found it difficult to end the American rebellion. Words such as *should* (3), *unjust* (4), and *good* (5) imply value judgments or opinions. Statement (1) is also an opinion or value judgment regarding what should be done, rather than a statement of fact.

25. **(1)** According to the Constitution, senators were to be chosen by the state legislatures, not the people of each state. This was changed in 1913 with the passage of the Sixteenth Amendment. All the other choices correctly restate provisions of Article I of the U.S. Constitution.

Science

The six review chapters in Part 3 give you overviews of broad subject areas that are likely to be included on the Science Test. Each overview is followed by GED-like questions to give you practice with the types of skills you'll be required to use on the real test. The practice test in Chapter 21 allows you to test your understanding of what you have learned.

The Science Test is divided into three areas of study: life science (45 percent), physical science (35 percent), and earth and space science (20 percent). Because life science encompasses almost half of the test, you should concentrate the most time on studying that area. Approximately 25 percent of the test questions include a passage, chart, or graph for you to read or interpret. The other 75 percent of the test are stand-alone questions.

What Is Science?

In This Chapter

- Overviews of key areas of science, including the scientific method, data analysis, and classification
- GED-like questions to practice the skills you'll be tested on
- Answers and explanations for all the questions

Science is not only a list of facts and figures, but a way of looking at and interpreting the world around you. Scientists take the information they have and put it into precise and understandable language. For the Science Test you will need to know what method scientists use when testing and how they reach scientific conclusions—that is the basis of science.

This chapter will help you understand scientific method, data collection, and how organisms are grouped and classified. With this background you will be able to design experiments, read graphs and charts, and understand the history of science and the scientific method.

Scientific Method and Inquiry

The scientific method is a way of asking questions about a problem, testing the questions, recording data, and forming a conclusion. Good scientific method practice also involves repeating the experiment many times to make sure the information is correct.

The scientific method involves six steps:

1. **Observation.** Determine what problem you are trying to solve.

2. **Research.** Do background research about the problem.

3. **Hypothesis.** Make an educated guess of what you think will solve the problem.

4. **Experiment.** Perform an experiment to test your hypothesis (your educated guess).

5. **Analysis.** Use the information from the experiment to draw conclusions.

6. **Conclusions.** Report your results and decide if your hypothesis was correct.

The scientific method enables scientists to form theories and test those theories. On the Science Test you may be asked to read a passage about a lab that was completed and be asked questions about the lab. Make sure you know the six parts of the scientific method and can draw conclusions from the experiment that was performed and the data that was collected.

Two other very important parts of an experiment are the control and the variable. A *control* is the part of the experiment that is "normal" and is not being tested. The *variable* is the part of the experiment that is being manipulated and tested. There are two types of variables: dependent and independent variables. The independent variable is the part of the experiment that the scientist is manipulating, or the part he is changing. The dependent variable is the response to the independent variable—in other words, the effect or what happened to the independent variable.

For example, let's say that a scientist is studying the amount of light that a particular plant can take before the plant dies. If this plant is normally found outside in the sun, then the control plant in this experiment would need to be outside in the sun. The experimenter could then put other plants in various amounts of light (the variable) and record the results.

An experiment can never have more than one thing being tested at a time. In the experiment with the plant and the amount of light that it can take, the scientist must leave all other conditions the same. For example, she must water all the plants the same amount, give all the plants the same type of soil, etc. Then, the scientist can get accurate results.

If instead the scientist had taken one plant and left it outside in the sun where it got rain and good soil and took the other plants inside, didn't water them and left them in only rocks, this would be a bad experiment. The scientist might draw the conclusion that all plants taken inside die, when in reality the plants could have died due to lack of water, and not because they were taken inside. The only type of valid science experiment is when only one thing is being tested at a time.

Practice: Scientific Method and Inquiry

1. A scientist is conducting an experiment on how mice react to different temperatures. The scientist first makes an educated guess as to what he thinks will happen when the mice are subjected to various levels of heat and cold. What part of the scientific method is the scientist performing when he makes this educated guess?

    (1) The hypothesis

    (2) The control

    (3) The variable

    (4) Data collection

    (5) The conclusion

Answer: Scientific Method and Inquiry

1. **(1)** A hypothesis is an educated guess. The scientist is making a guess to what he thinks will happen. A control (2) is the part of the experiment that is "normal" and is not being tested. The variable (3) is the part of the experiment that is being manipulated and tested. Data collection (4) is when the scientist collects information such as height, days, and so on, in an experiment. The conclusion (5) is when the scientist sums up the experiment after he has finished it.

Science and Technology

Scientists are always searching to find answers to questions. They are curious about the world around them, and by performing experiments and testing hypothesis they have changed the way we look at our world.

Let's now take a look at the history of science. We will focus on the major events that have changed the field of science, and the people who have made those changes.

Beginning in the fifteenth century, following the Dark Ages, is the period of time known as the Renaissance, or rebirth. This was a time where many people began to question the thinking of the times. For example, Copernicus said the earth revolved around the sun. This was contradictory to early thinking that the sun revolved around the earth.

Galileo, another important scientist, invented the pendulum clock and the telescope. He used the telescope to prove Copernicus's *theory* that the earth revolved around the sun. Galileo also observed the moon through his telescope.

Following the Renaissance was the Enlightenment or Age of Reason. During this period Isaac Newton observed the *law* of gravity and helped to usher in the scientific revolution.

DEFINITION

A **theory** is something that has been shown to be true in many experiments but is unproven. A theory is valid as long as there is no evidence to dispute it. For example, the Theory of Plate Tectonics explains how the land masses on our planet went from one super continent, Pangea, to the seven continents we have today. A **law,** on the other hand, is something that has never been proven false. For example, the Law of Gravity has never been proven false and is therefore made a law.

The modern age followed the Enlightenment. People like Charles Darwin (who proposed the theory of evolution by natural selection), Watson and Crick (who discovered the structure of DNA), and Albert Einstein (who made huge strides in our understanding of physics with his theory of relativity) are notable scientists during the modern age. The following table lists 10 of the most notable scientists in history.

Important Scientists in History

Scientist	Contribution
Niels Bohr	Investigated atomic structure
Marie Curie	Discovered radiation
Charles Darwin	Proposed the theory of evolution
Albert Einstein	Proposed the theory of relativity
Galileo Galilei	Observed space as an astronomer

Scientist	Contribution
Gregor Mendel	Studied inheritance
Dmitri Mendeleev	Developed the periodic table of elements
Isaac Newton	Described the laws of motion/gravity
Louis Pasteur	Made breakthroughs in microbiology
Anton Van Leeuwenhoek	Invented the microscope

Practice: History of Science and Technology

1. Isaac Newton is a famous scientist who lived from 1642 to 1727. Newton was a physicist, mathematician, astronomer, philosopher, chemist, and theologian. One of the most important contributions that Newton made to science is known as Newton's three laws of motion. The first law states that every object in motion stays in motion. The second law states that force of an object equals its mass times its acceleration. The third law states that for every action there is an equal and opposite reaction.

   Which of the following would be the best title for this information?

   (1) "The History of Science"

   (2) "Physics Explained"

   (3) "Isaac Newton's Three Laws of Motion"

   (4) "The Life and Times of Isaac Newton"

   (5) "The Great Philosopher, Isaac Newton"

Answer: History of Science and Technology

1. **(3)** "Isaac Newton's Three Laws of Motion" summarizes what the entire article is about. "The History of Science" (1) is much too broad; a single article cannot include the entire history of science. "Physics Explained" (2) is not what the article is about, even though Newton was a physicist. "The Life and Times of Isaac Newton" (4) is partially correct, but we only read about one small part of Newton's life. "The Great Philosopher, Isaac Newton" (5) is incorrect because the article doesn't mention philosophy other than stating briefly that Newton was a philosopher.

Analyzing Data

Once information from an experiment has been gathered, it must be put into a clear and concise format. Information in science is known as *data*, and data is shown in a *data table* (also known as a chart) or in a graph—sometimes both are used. Often this data is in the form of numbers and is gathered from an experiment. Let's look further at different types of graphs and data tables.

Assume an experiment has been completed on the effects of a particular toxin, an herbicide, on a group of pesky yard weeds. The scientist is trying to find the dose of this toxin (let's call it toxin A) that it takes to successfully kill the weeds without harming the yard or the animals and microorganisms that live in the soil.

The experimenter sprays one weed with two squirts of toxin A, a second weed with four squirts of toxin A, and a third weed with six squirts of toxin A. The fourth weed is not sprayed with any toxin A and is the control. After 2 days, the experimenter comes back to count the number of dead leaves on each plant. Plant one has three dead leaves, plant two has eight dead leaves, and plant three has twenty dead leaves. Plant four, the control, has no dead leaves.

One way this information could be displayed is in a data table. Here is an example of a good data table for this experiment.

The Effects of Toxin A on Yard Plants

Number of Squirts of Toxin A	Number of Dead Leaves
2	3
4	8
6	20

By putting this information that the scientist gathered into a chart, a person can quickly and easily evaluate the experiment and the results.

Another way the information could be displayed is in a graph. There are many types of graphs, but the three most used in science are bar and line graphs, and pie charts.

A bar graph is used to compare one thing to another. A line graph is generally used to display change over time. A pie chart is another way to show comparisons, often of percentages.

Below are examples of a bar chart, line chart, and pie chart, respectively.

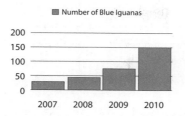

The number of blue iguanas between 2007–2010.

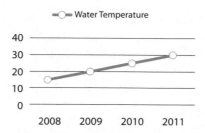

Water temperature of a lake from 2008–2011.

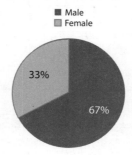

The percentage of males vs. females in the teaching profession.

 GOOD IDEA

Notice that all three graphs include a title. This is very important! Always include a descriptive title on any graph you make. A title gives the reader an overview of what is shown in the graph.

Now it's your turn to practice. Use the information in the earlier data table ("The Effects of Toxin A on Yard Plants") to make a graph using the following blank grid.

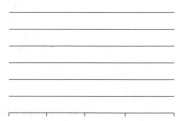

So which graph would you choose to display the data from this experiment? I would use a line graph, like this:

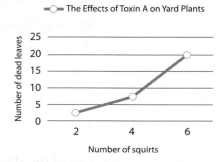

Practice: Analyzing Data

Questions 1 and 2 refer to the following graph.

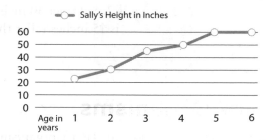

1. During which age did Sally grow the most in height?

   (1) Age 1–2

   (2) Age 2–3

   (3) Age 3–4

   (4) Age 4–5

   (5) Age 5–6

2. If Claire is 45 inches tall when she is 2 years old, what does the graph tell you about Claire in relation to Sally?

   (1) Claire is shorter at age 2 than Sally was at age 2.

   (2) Claire will be taller than Sally when Claire is 5.

   (3) Sally will catch up and end up taller than Claire.

   (4) Claire is 15 inches taller than Sally at age 2.

   (5) Claire is very tall for her age.

Answers: Analyzing Data

1. **(2)** Age 2–3 represents the steepest part of the graph. The other ages are less steep, indicating that Sally did not grow as tall.

2. **(4)** To solve this problem you would need to plot Claire's growth during year 2 on the graph. Claire is 45 inches tall when she is 2 and Sally is, according to the graph, 30 inches tall when she is 2. Subtract 30 inches from 45 inches and you come to the answer that Claire is 15 inches taller than Sally when they are 2 years old.

Classification of Organisms

Another important aspect in science is how to classify organisms. Organisms are grouped together by a system of increasing similarity. For example, a moon jellyfish and a human are clearly different, but both would fall into the kingdom animalia. However, that is where the similarities would stop. Likewise, a dog and a wolf are both in the kingdom animalia, but they are alike in many other ways. Both the dog and the wolf have backbones, both are mammals, and both are carnivores.

Kingdom is the broadest classification an organism can get. In the following example, the kingdom of both humans and moon jellyfish is animalia. Phylum is the next classification and is less broad. For example, both dogs and wolves have backbones and are in the phylum chordate, but a jellyfish does not have a backbone so it is not in this phylum. The classification continues to get more and more specific, with class, order, family, genus, and, finally, species—the most specific classification you can give an organism.

In the past, organisms were classified according to their physical characteristics. Today, with our modern techniques of mapping out DNA, using genetics has become an even more precise way of classifying organisms.

The first person to devise a system to classify organisms was Carolus Linnaeus, a Swedish doctor who published a book entitled *Systema Naturae*, where he described his system of classification. This is still the system we use today.

There are five kingdoms: animal, plant, fungi, protist, and moneran. The kingdoms are then further split into phylum, class, order, family, genus, and species.

The study of classification is known as *taxonomy*. Each time you move down a step on the taxonomy scale the organisms are more similar. Let's look at the examples of the human compared to the moon jellyfish and a dog compared to a wolf.

Comparison of Humans and Moon Jellyfish

Category	Human	Moon Jellyfish
Kingdom	Animalia	Animalia
Phylum	Chordata	Cnidaria
Class	Mammalia	Scyphozoa
Order	Primate	Semaestomeae
Family	Hominidae	Ulmaridae
Genus	*Homo*	*Aurelia*
Species	*Sapiens*	*Aurita*

As you can see, the similarities between the moon jellyfish and humans do not go below the kingdom category. Now let's look at two animals that are more similar, the dog and the wolf.

Category	Dog	Wolf
Kingdom	Animalia	Animalia
Phylum	Chordata	Chordata
Class	Mammalia	Mammalia
Order	Carnivora	Carnivora
Family	Canidae	Canidae
Genus	*Canis*	*Canis*
Species	*Familiaris*	*Lupis*

As you can see, the wolf and dog are the same until the last category, species. Of course, the characteristics of a dog and a wolf are much closer than a human to a moon jellyfish!

Now, I'm sure you are asking yourself if you will need to know the taxonomy for a moon jellyfish on the Science Test, and the answer is no. However, understanding how scientists classify organisms is important. A good way to remember the classification system is: King Phillip Cried Out For Good Soup—Kingdom, Phylum, Class, Order, Family, Genus, Species.

IN THE KNOW

All organisms are given a Latin genus and species name and these names are always italicized. This system of using Latin names is used by scientists around the world, no matter what language they speak.

Practice: Classification of Organisms

1. Which of the following is the most specific way to classify an organism?

    (1) Kingdom

    (2) Phylum

    (3) Class

    (4) Genus

    (5) Species

Answer: Classification of Organisms

1. **(5)** Species is the most specific classification you can give an organism. Kingdom (1) is the broadest classification, followed by phylum (2), class (3), and genus (4).

Health and Environment

In This Chapter

- Overviews of key areas of environmental science, including the major biogeochemical cycles, ecology, energy, risks, and the human population
- GED-like questions to practice the skills you'll be tested on
- Answers and explanations for all the questions

Environmental science, also called ecology, is very important in the world today, and therefore you should be familiar with the basics. Environmental science includes many other subjects and sciences such as chemistry, biology, sociology, economics, geology, and physics. When you study environmental science, you look at the relationships between what is happening in our natural world and what the human impacts have on earth.

In this chapter we will look at the various biogeochemical cycles that are constantly changing our planet, organisms that live on our planet and their role in nature, how energy is transferred, hazards and risks we must face, and how the size of the human population has been growing exponentially.

Biogeochemical Cycles

In nature, chemicals cycle. This means that they either change form, like a solid to a liquid, or change composition. There are five cycles that you should be familiar with that might be covered on the Science Test.

The Water Cycle

Water is found in nature in three forms: solid, liquid, and gas. Because water is important to life on earth, it is important to know how water cycles. As you can see from the following figure, water can be found in oceans, underground, in the atmosphere, and on the land.

As you can also see in the following figure, water can move from oceans to atmosphere, from atmosphere to land, from land to ocean, from land to atmosphere, and more. The water cycle explains how water can move around the earth in many forms.

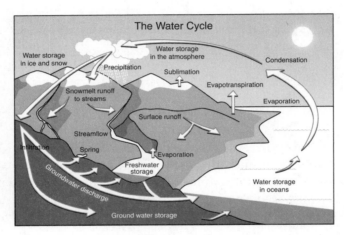

The water cycle.

There are many vocabulary terms that you should be familiar with to properly understand the water cycle:

- *Evaporation* is the conversion of liquid water into water vapor. This is how clouds form.

- When the water molecules in the air come together, they grow and get larger. At some point they are too large to remain in the atmosphere, and then they fall to the earth. This is precipitation—water vapor condensing and falling to the ground in the form of rain, snow, sleet, or hail.

- *Evapotranspiration*, similar to evaporation but involving plants, occurs when leaves lose water and the water becomes a vapor.

- *Groundwater* is water that has seeped into the soil and rocks and is stored underground. An underground water storage is known as an aquifer.

- *Surface water* is water stored above ground in lakes, rivers, and streams.

- *Condensation* occurs when water vapor collects, condenses, and forms droplets.

- *Sublimation* is the conversion of water from a solid phase directly to a gaseous phase.

- *Infiltration* is water soaking into the soil.

- *Surface runoff* is the runoff of water, usually from rain, into rivers, lakes, streams, and ponds.

IN THE KNOW

The water cycle is also called the hydrologic cycle. If the Science Test uses that term, you'll know they are talking about the water cycle.

The Nitrogen Cycle

In the nitrogen cycle, shown in the following figure, plants take nitrogen from land and water and turn it into a form that they can use. Nitrogen is a plant nutrient; without it most plants cannot survive. Plants are unable to take nitrogen directly from the soil, so they depend on bacteria to convert the nitrogen into a form that the plant can use.

There are many vocabulary terms that you should be familiar with to properly understand the nitrogen cycle:

- *Nitrogen fixation* occurs when bacteria convert nitrogen from the atmosphere or the soil into ammonia.

- *Nitrification* is the conversion of the ammonia into nitrites and then nitrates.

- *Assimilation* describes the nitrates converting into things the plant needs, such as proteins, DNA, and amino acids.

- *Ammonification* is the formation of ammonia due to an organism dying or excreting waste.

- *Denitrification* is the release of nitrates back into the air as nitrogen gas.

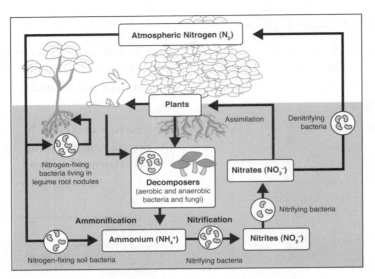

The nitrogen cycle.

The Carbon Cycle

Think about each time you breathe in and out. As you breathe in, you take in oxygen; when you breathe out, you release carbon in the form of carbon dioxide. Then, plants take in this carbon dioxide and release oxygen. The carbon cycle, shown in the following figure, is important because without it we would not be able to have life on earth.

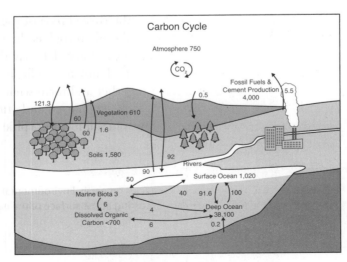

The carbon cycle.

The Phosphorous Cycle

Phosphorus is an essential nutrient for plants and animals. It is a part of DNA molecules, of molecules that store energy, and of fats of cell membranes. Phosphorus is also a building block of certain parts of the human and animal body, such as the bones, muscles, and teeth.

In the following figure, you can see that phosphorus is taken in by plants. Then, when an animal eats the plant, it obtains the phosphorus from the plant. When the animal dies or excretes waste, phosphorus is returned back to the environment. Phosphorus cycles on both land and water.

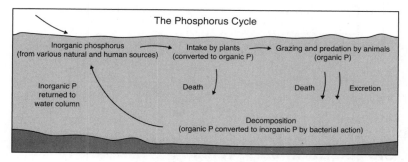

The phosphorus cycle.

The Rock Cycle

Igneous, sedimentary, and metamorphic are the three kinds of rock. An example of rocks cycling would be if a volcano erupts and molten rock is thrown out onto the earth. When this rock cools it is an igneous rock. Then, let's say the same rock ends up in a river and the water slowly breaks the rock down into little pieces; these small rock particles might end up getting glued together and form what is known as a sedimentary rock. Now let's say this same rock gets buried and after millions of years gets squeezed due to heat and pressure; it becomes a metamorphic rock.

IN THE KNOW

The rock cycle is the slowest of all the cycles on earth. Environmental science looks mainly at the rock cycle that is occurring at the surface of the earth.

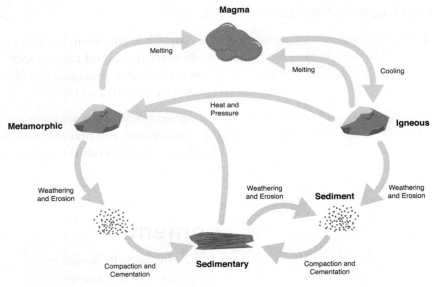

The rock cycle.

Practice: Biogeochemical Cycles

1. Which of the following best describes evaporation?

   (1) Rain falling to the earth's surface

   (2) The sun heating the earth

   (3) Water running off into lakes, rivers, and streams

   (4) Water seeping into underground aquifers

   (5) Water changing from a liquid to a gas

2. What type of rock forms when a rock is weathered, eroded, transported, and deposited somewhere else?

   (1) Sedimentary rock

   (2) Metamorphic rock

   (3) Igneous rock

   (4) Crystals

   (5) Minerals

Answers: Biogeochemical Cycles

1. **(5)** Evaporation is best described as water changing from a liquid to a gas. This occurs during the water cycle as water in a liquid form evaporates into the atmosphere into a gas. Statement (1) describes precipitation, (2) is what drives the water cycle, (3) describes surface runoff, and (4) is infiltration.

2. **(1)** Sedimentary rock is formed by sediment being deposited at the earth's surface. Metamorphic rock (2) is formed by heat and pressure. Igneous rock (3) is from magma that cools. Crystals (4) and minerals (5) are not types of rocks, but are found in rocks.

Ecology and the Environment

When you study the interaction between the living and the nonliving world, you must look at both the biotic and abiotic components of that ecosystem.

Plants take the sun's energy and convert it to food. *Herbivores* eat the plants, and *carnivores* eat the herbivores (or sometimes other carnivores). Some of the sun's energy is converted to heat and is therefore unusable, so as you move through the ecosystems there is less and less energy available at each level.

DEFINITION

Herbivores are animals that are adapted to eat plants. **Carnivores** are animals that eat other animals. Both herbivores and carnivores must obtain their energy from something else, unlike a plant that can make its own energy.

Organisms

A living organism is known as *biotic*. Examples of biotic organisms are animals, plants, and microorganisms. Something nonliving is *abiotic*. Examples of abiotic things are rocks, air, and chemicals.

Producers

Producers make their own food. They do this by using the sun's energy during the process known as photosynthesis. Primary producers are things like plants and algae.

A *consumer* cannot make its own food, and therefore must consume either animals or plants to gain energy. Primary consumers would be herbivores (for example, deer) that eat plants. A secondary consumer is an animal that eats the animal that ate the plant. For example, if a mountain lion eats the deer that ate the plant, the mountain lion is the secondary consumer.

Decomposers

Decomposers break down dead or dying things and help to recycle their matter and energy back into the environment. Without decomposers, animals and plants would die and never be broken down into nutrients needed in the soil. Examples of decomposers are bacteria and fungi.

Practice: Ecology and the Environment

1. Which of the following is an example of a secondary consumer?

    (1) Sunflower

    (2) Deer

    (3) Bacteria

    (4) Wolf

    (5) Fungi

Answer: Ecology and the Environment

1. **(4)** A wolf is a secondary consumer because wolves eat animals that eat plants; for example, a wolf eats a deer. A sunflower (1) is a producer, deer (2) are primary consumers, and both bacteria (3) and fungi (5) are decomposers.

Energy Transfer: Food Chains and Webs

Let's look at how energy is moved around the environment. A simple diagram of energy movement is called a *food chain*. A food chain shows how the calories move. If a grasshopper eats grass and a bird eats the grasshopper, you could show this transfer in a food chain.

For this example, the food chain would be:

grass → grasshopper → bird

Notice how the arrow points from the food source to the animal eating it. Since the grasshopper eats the grass, the arrow shows the energy from the grass going into the grasshopper.

Food Webs

However, a food chain is usually too simple of a diagram. For example, what if a snake also eats the grasshopper? In nature, there are many food chains going on at the same time. A *food web* is a way to show a more complex system.

An example of a food web would be:

        bird
        ↑

grass → grasshopper → snake

Now, a true food web will be even more complex than this one. Here is a picture of a food web in nature. As you can see, there are many interactions occurring in the picture. We see a bird eating a snake but the same bird is also eating the rabbit. This is more real life because there are often many different food choices an animal could have.

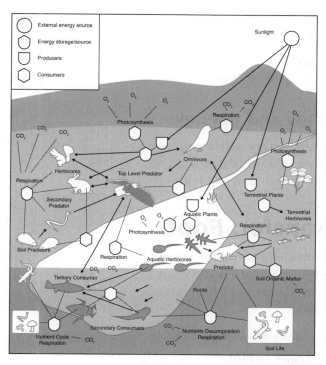

Food web.

Energy Pyramids

An *energy pyramid* shows the transfer of energy as it moves up the food chain. According to the First Law of Thermodynamics, energy cannot be created nor destroyed. However, energy can be converted to heat (the Second Law of Thermodynamics). When the grasshopper eats the grass, it uses the calories that it ate to do what grasshoppers do … jump, reproduce, etc. These actions used up some of the energy and transferred that energy into heat. The 10 percent rule explains this. If the grass offered the grasshopper 100 calories and the grasshopper used that energy, we generally say that the grasshopper used 90 percent and stored 10 percent. Now, when the bird eats the grasshopper, it only gets the stored energy, the 10 percent that was not used. So the bird only gets 10 of the calories that came from the grass.

An example of this energy pyramid would look like this:

grass →   grasshopper → bird

100 calories   10 calories

Practice: Food Chains and Webs

1. Which of the following statements is correct?

   (1) As energy moves through the environment, it is lost.

   (2) When energy moves through a food chain, approximately 10 percent is transferred to the next level of the chain.

   (3) Energy is stored in a food chain as heat.

   (4) When drawing a food chain, you should draw the arrow going from the animal to the plant.

   (5) The First Law of Thermodynamics states that energy is converted to heat.

Answer: Food Chains and Webs

1. **(2)** According to the 10 percent rule, 90 percent of energy is used by the animal and 10 percent moves to the next level. (1) is incorrect because energy cannot be created or destroyed. (3) is incorrect because energy is stored as living material, not heat. (4) is incorrect because you would draw the arrow going from the plant to the animal. (5) is incorrect because it is the definition of the Second Law of Thermodynamics.

Toxicology: Environmental Hazards and Risks

Toxicology is the study of the adverse effects of chemical, physical, or biological agents on people, animals, and the environment. To evaluate a risk, you first need to identify the hazard and the exposure. Then you can decide if the risk is worth it. Some risks are real while others are perceived. For example, many people are afraid to fly and would rather drive; however, it is actually much more likely in the United States to die in a traffic accident than it is in an airplane accident.

Types of Hazards

An environmental hazard is something in our environment that can potentially cause harm. There are three major types of hazards:

- **Biological.** A biological hazard would be from a bacterium, virus, insect, plant, animal, or another human. In history we have had times when biological hazards have been extremely deadly. The bubonic plague is one example, as well as HIV/AIDS.

- **Chemical.** A chemical hazard is from a substance that causes harm to people. There are a variety of chemicals that we are exposed to each day—pesticides, household chemicals, and pollution, for example.

- **Physical.** A physical hazard would be extreme heat, cold, noise, and UV light. Some physical hazards are weather related, such as tornadoes, hurricanes, and floods.

Acute vs. Chronic Diseases

You should also be familiar with acute versus chronic diseases. An *acute disease* rapidly attacks and affects the body. Some examples of acute diseases would be SARS (severe acute respiratory syndrome) and influenza (flu). A *chronic disease* is one that persists over a long time and slowly impairs a person. Some examples of chronic diseases are asthma, cancer, diabetes, and HIV/AIDS.

Practice: Toxicology

1. Air pollution coming from a coal-burning power plant would be an example of which of the following hazards?

   (1) Biological

   (2) Chemical

   (3) Physical

   (4) Seismic

   (5) Health

Answer: Toxicology

1. **(2)** Air pollution is an example of a chemical hazard because it comes from a substance that harms people. Biological hazards (1) would come from something such as a bacteria. A physical hazard (3) would come from something such as a tornado. A seismic hazard (4) is a type of physical hazard. A health hazard (5) is a broad term that can include all of the other types of hazards.

Population Growth

The human population is growing exponentially. This means that the population is growing at a faster and faster rate every year. The growth of the human population, when graphed, looks like the letter J. It took thousands of years before the population began to grow exponentially.

For much of history there were fewer than a billion people on the earth. Today, there are almost 7 billion people. The main reason for such a fast growth rate was the Industrial Revolution and modern medicine. As agriculture and sanitation improved, better living conditions caused death rates to fall. Modern medicine has also slowed death rates around the world. However, as death rates have decreased, birth rates continue to remain high in many countries, leading to the exponential growth of the human population.

Practice: Population Growth

Use the following graph to answer questions 1 and 2.

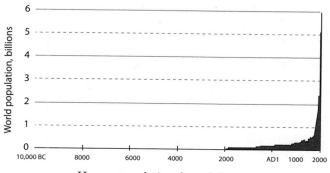

Human population through history.

1. According to the graph, approximately how many people were living in year 1000 B.C.?

   (1) 1 million

   (2) 5 million

   (3) 250 million

   (4) 4 billion

   (5) 7 billion

2. The shape of this graph is an example of what type of growth?

   (1) Linear

   (2) Exponential

   (3) Logistic

   (4) Inverse

   (5) Directly proportional

Answers: Population Growth

1. **(3)** You need to look at the graph and go across to the 1000 B.C. on the bottom (X axis). Then, take your pencil and go straight up to where the black, shaded portion stops. Now, go straight across to the left to where the line hits the Y axis. Read the graph and you find the answer is approximately 250 million.

2. **(2)** This graph is an example of exponential growth. Anytime you graph exponential growth, the graph will look like a letter J. Linear growth (1) will be a straight line. Logistic growth (3) will be shaped like an S. Inverse (4) is not a type of graph, but means that two things are opposite. Directly proportional (5) is also not a type of graph; it means *related to*.

Plants, Animals, and Human Body Systems

In This Chapter

- Overviews of key areas of biology, including cells, genetics, evolution, and the human body
- GED-like questions to practice the skills you'll be tested on
- Answers and explanations for all the questions

In this chapter we will look at biology, the study of living things. We will start by looking at the cell, the smallest unit of life. The Science Test might ask you to know the parts of a cell and the function of each of those parts. Cells make up tissues and tissues make up organs, so we will then move into the different organ systems found in the human body.

Another important part in the study of biology is how traits are passed from one generation to another—the study of genetics. Finally, we will focus on evolution. Evolution is change over time, or how the species alive on the planet today have changed over millions of years. Any student who is strong in the study of science will have a good knowledge of the basic study of biology.

Plant and Animal Cells

The smallest unit of life is a cell. There are single-celled organisms and multicelled organisms. Cells control the exchange of food and waste for an organism. Cells were first discovered in 1665 by Robert Hooke, a monk who looked at cork cells under a microscope.

Cells are made up of many parts, each part with a special purpose. It is important to know the parts and functions of a typical plant or animal cell.

The Structures of a Typical Cell

The structures (organelles) of a typical cell include the following.

Cell membrane—a protective wall found on the outside of the cell. The cell membrane controls what comes into and out of a cell. Both animal and plant cells have a cell membrane.

Cell wall—found in plant cells. The cell wall helps to support the plant.

Chloroplast—found only in plant cells. Chloroplasts contain chlorophyll that plants need to photosynthesize.

Chromosomes—house the genetic material of the animal or plant. The chromosomes contain the DNA that is the genetic code for the organism.

Cytoplasm—found outside the nucleus. The cytoplasm is where all the plant and animal organelles are found.

Endoplasmic reticulum—the cell's highway system. The ER transports substances around the cell. Both animal and plant cells can have ER.

Golgi apparatus—helps package the proteins and lipids for the cell. The apparatus are found in both animal and plant cells.

Lysosomes—help break down the waste materials of a cell.

Mitochondrion—help the cell to obtain energy from food. Both animal and plant cells have mitochondria.

Nucleus—the brain of the cell, containing the genetic material of a cell. Both animal and plant cells have a nucleus.

Ribosomes—help the animal or plant make protein.

Vacuoles—large sacs in plant cells that are filled with water to help support the plant. Most animal cells do not have vacuoles.

IN THE KNOW

You should be familiar with both the diagram of plant and animal cells as well as the function of each organelle. The Science Test will ask you questions regarding both the names and functions of cells.

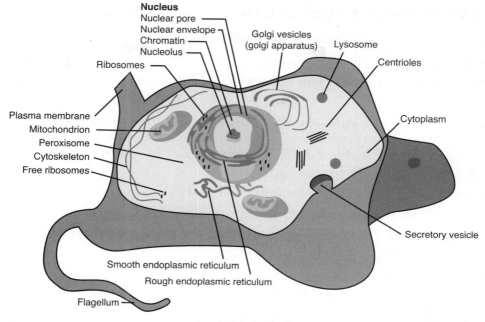

A typical animal cell.

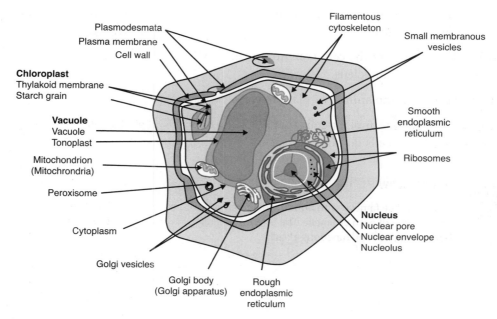

A typical plant cell.

Cellular Respiration

Cellular respiration is the process that cells use to take in oxygen to break down sugar and release energy. The formula for cellular respiration is:

glucose + oxygen → carbon dioxide + water + energy.

Just as you need food, air, and water to stay alive, cells also need these things to stay alive because cells are part of you. A cell cannot eat, breathe, or get rid of its waste like you and I do, so it must use its cell organelles to accomplish this and stay alive. This process is cellular respiration.

Practice: Plant and Animal Cells

1. Which of the following is the smallest unit of life?

(1) Cell

(2) Tissue

(3) Organ

(4) Organ system

(5) Body

2. You are looking through a microscope at a cell. You see that the cell is square in shape, has large saclike structures inside, and contains green objects throughout. What type of cell are you observing?

(1) Bacteria

(2) Fungi

(3) Plant

(4) Animal

(5) You would need more information to answer this question

Answers: Plant and Animal Cells

1. **(1)** The cell is the smallest unit of life. The other answers are all structures that contain cells.

2. **(3)** You are looking at a plant cell. You know this because of the presence of the "green" objects and the fact that the cell is square in shape. Both of these are characteristics of plant cells.

Human Body Systems

The human body has 12 systems. These are shown in the following table, along with the organs and function of each system. Each system has a way of keeping the body in homeostasis, or balance. One system can affect another system, and all systems work together in our bodies.

Human Body Systems

System	Body Organs	Function
Integumentary	Skin	Protection
Muscular	Muscles, connective tissue	Movement
Skeletal	Bones, joints	Support, movement
Digestive	Stomach, intestines, liver, gall bladder, esophagus, mouth, colon	Digestion
Endocrine	Glands	Hormone regulation
Immune	White blood cells	Fight disease
Lymphatic	Lymph nodes, blood	Clean the blood
Nervous	Brain, spinal cord, nerves	Sends information
Reproductive	Ovaries, testes, uterus, penis	Reproduction
Circulatory	Heart, blood, veins, arteries	Moves blood through the body
Respiratory	Lungs, bronchi, trachea, alveoli	Helps the exchange of carbon dioxide with incoming air
Excretory	Kidneys, ureter, bladder, urethra	Filters waste from the blood

The human body has a system of increasing complexity. Cells make up tissues, tissues make up organs, organs make up organ systems, and organ systems make up the human body.

Practice: Human Body Systems

1. You go to the doctor complaining of difficulty breathing and shortness of breath. What body system is the doctor going to investigate?

   (1) Circulatory

   (2) Respiratory

   (3) Integumentary

   (4) Digestive

   (5) Muscular

Answer: Human Body Systems

1. **(2)** The respiratory system includes your lungs and involves oxygen exchange. Circulatory systems (1) involve the blood and heart, integumentary (3) is your skin, digestive (4) is how your food is broken down, and muscular (5) is your muscles and how you move.

Genetics, Mitosis, and Meiosis

Genetics is the branch of biology that deals with heredity. You probably look like your mother, father, or a mixture of both. These characteristics that you inherited from your parents are known as *traits*. The study of how these traits are passed down from parent to offspring is genetics.

Mendel's Genetic Experiment

Gregor Mendel, a monk who lived during the mid–19th century, did many of the first experiments to try to figure out how traits are passed from parent to child. He experimented on pea plants, breeding the plants with one characteristic—say, short—with another plant that had a different characteristic—say, tall. The thinking of the day was that the offspring would "blend" and the plant would end up being medium in height, somewhere between the two parents. Mendel proved that this was incorrect.

In one of his experiments, Mendel took a tall pea plant (TT) and crossed it with a short pea plant (tt). Mendel used capital letters to show *dominant traits* and lowercase letters to show *recessive traits*. The traits that are seen (like hair color) are called phenotypes, and the actual genes, like TT or tt, are called genotypes. Tall pea plants were dominant, meaning that this characteristic is what will be seen (phenotype).

DEFINITION

A **dominant trait** is a trait that is "expressed" or seen. A **recessive trait** is a trait that is hidden. However, if two recessive traits are inherited, the trait will be expressed.

In the first generation of baby pea plants, all the plants were tall, but the genotype for each plant was Tt. This is because one parent plant gave a T and the other gave a t. Each parent will give one gene to the baby, and since the tall plant had two TT, it could only give a T; likewise, the short plant only had one t to give.

Now these pea plant babies were crossed to create the second generation, or the grandchildren. Since both plants are now Tt, when crossed they can give either a T or a t to the baby. It is like a flip of a coin. Mendel showed that this second generation had three tall plants and one short plant, and the genotypes were TT, Tt, Tt, and tt. In other words, if both plants gave a T, the baby would be TT (tall), if one gave a T and the other gave a t, the babies would be Tt (tall, but carrying the short gene), and if both parents gave a t, the baby would be tt (short).

Looking at Mendel's experiment, we can see that the offspring were not medium in height; he found that three of the offspring were tall and one was short. This is because the offspring will always have the dominant characteristic (T) unless both parents give the recessive characteristic (t).

Mitosis and Meiosis or Cell Division

Mitosis is how cells reproduce themselves. Mitosis is important to all living things because it is how the nucleus divides to make two identical cells, *diploid cells*. The following figure shows how mitosis occurs.

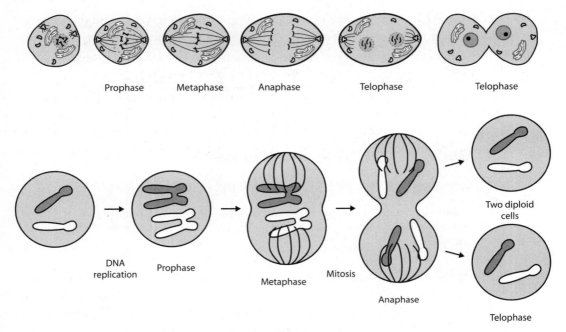

The stages of mitosis.

There are four stages of mitosis:

- During **prophase,** the genetic material inside the nucleus duplicates to form two identical chromatids, identical parts of a chromosome, and the nuclear membranes disappear.

- During **metaphase,** the chromosomes line up in the center of the cell and spindle fibers, structures that help to separate the chromosomes, attach to them. A chromosome contains all the genetic information that is passed from one generation to another.

- During **anaphase,** the chromatids separate and are pulled to the opposite sides of the cell by the spindle fibers.

- During **telophase,** the cell becomes two new cells with identical genetic information in each.

Meiosis is similar to mitosis, but involves sex cells. Again, we have four stages—prophase, metaphase, anaphase, and telophase—but during prophase the two identical chromosome pairs line up and separate. One set of chromosomes goes to one side of the cell and the other goes to the other side. This results in two cells, *haploid cells,* each with half the number of chromosomes as the parent.

> **DEFINITION**
>
> A **haploid cell** contains half the number of chromosomes as the parent, while a **diploid cell** contains a full set of 46 chromosomes, 23 from Mom and 23 from Dad. So when your mother's sex cells went through meiosis, she gave you a haploid cell, as did your father. Once these cells joined, it formed a diploid cell that became you!

Practice: Genetics, Mitosis, and Meiosis

1. What is the phase of cell division when the chromosomes line up in the middle of the cell?

    (1) Interphase

    (2) Prophase

    (3) Metaphase

    (4) Anaphase

    (5) Telophase

Answer: Genetics, Mitosis, and Meiosis

1. **(3)** Metaphase is the stage when the chromosomes line up in the center of the cell and spindle fibers attach to them. During interphase (1), the cell is not yet dividing. During prophase (2), the genetic material inside the nucleus duplicates to form two identical chromatids, and the nuclear membranes disappear. During anaphase (4), the chromatids separate and are pulled to the opposite sides of the cell by the spindle fibers. During telophase (5), the cell becomes two new cells with identical genetic information in each.

Evolution

In 1859, Charles Darwin published *On the Origin of Species*, in which he explained his theory of evolution. *Evolution* is how organisms change over time. Darwin proposed that all organisms alive today came from a single, common ancestor. He stated that through time these organisms gradually changed to the species we have today.

The basis of Darwin's theory is known as *natural selection*. According to natural selection, organisms with characteristics that help them to survive will live and produce offspring, while those organisms with characteristics that do not help them survive will not produce offspring and will die sooner. This is also known as survival of the fittest.

An example of natural selection would be insects that are resistant to insecticides. If a certain insecticide is applied to a crop and 90 percent of the insects are killed but 10 percent survive because they have a characteristic that allowed them to be immune to the pesticide, these insects will reproduce and pass the pesticide immunity on to their offspring. Over time, if these new insects with the pesticide immunity are isolated from other insects of the same species that did not come into contact with the pesticide (and therefore did not need this pesticide immunity), the pesticide-immune insects could become a separate species from the original insects. This is known as *speciation*.

Evidence of evolution can be found in the fossil record and in the genetic code of organisms. Scientists look at both of these to try to find how organisms on the earth became as diverse as they are today. When a scientist finds a fossil he can take a small amount of the remains, look at the genetic code that is specific to that organism, and send it to the lab to find out how old it is. This is a process known as *carbon or radioactive dating*. Once the age of the fossil is determined, the scientist can add it to the information he already has to try to see how organisms have changed over time.

Practice: Evolution

Up until the Industrial Revolution, the peppered moth was mainly white with black spots. As London's air became thick with soot from factories, the once-white trees that the moths used to live on became blacker. Birds were now able to spot and eat the moths that were white on the black trees. However, some moths had more black spots than others, making them harder to spot by the birds than their whiter relatives. These moths survived and passed the genetic trait of being darker to their offspring.

1. The previous passage describes what theory?

   (1) Theory of relativity

   (2) Theory of plate tectonics

   (3) Theory of homologous structures

   (4) Theory of natural selection

   (5) Big bang theory

Answer: Evolution

1. **(4)** The moths that were darker had a better chance to survive because they could hide from the birds. The theory of natural selection explains how organisms adapt to their environment to better survive. The theory of relativity (1) is about gravity, and the theory of plate tectonics (2) is how the earth is made of plates that move. The theory of homologous structures (3) is not a theory but the concept of two similar structures in different animals, and the big bang theory (5) is the theory of how the earth was formed.

Chemistry

In This Chapter

- Overviews of key areas of chemistry, including chemical formulas and reactions, density, pH, and compounds/mixtures
- GED-like questions to practice the skills you'll be tested on
- Answers and explanations for all the questions

Chemistry is the study of atomic matter. All matter is made up of atoms, and chemistry studies atoms and how they bond and react. On the Science Test you will need to understand the basics of chemistry; there are often questions on the test to see if you understand pH, acids, and bases. You also should be familiar with how atoms bond and what makes up the periodic table. Finally, make sure you can balance chemical equations—this is an important part of chemistry!

Chemistry Basics

Let's begin by discussing the basics of chemistry.

Matter, Atoms, Molecules

Matter is anything that has mass and takes up space. Examples of matter include paper, water, air, soil—and you. *Mass* is a measure of the amount of matter an object has. Do not confuse mass and weight. *Weight* includes the gravity, but mass does not. The basic building block of matter is the *atom*. An atom contains *protons*, *neutrons*, and *electrons*.

> **DEFINITION**
>
> A **proton** is a particle with a positive charge, a **neutron** is a particle that does not have a charge, and an **electron** is a particle with a negative charge.

A *molecule* is a particle that contains more than one atom. For example, the oxygen you breathe is O_2, which is a molecule, and so is carbon dioxide, CO_2.

Periodic Table

The periodic table of elements was arranged by Russian chemist and inventor Dmitri Mendeleev in the late 1800s. Mendeleev was looking for patterns within the elements. He organized the elements by increasing atomic mass. Because not all elements had been discovered at this point, he left some parts of the periodic table blank.

The periodic table is arranged by column and by row. All elements in a column are called groups or families and they all have similar characteristics. For example, all elements in column one have one electron in their outer shell, and they all are extremely reactive. All elements in a row have the same number of outer rings. For example, in row 1, both hydrogen and helium have one outer ring. In row 2, lithium, beryllium, and so forth have two outer rings, and so on.

Group →	1	2	3	4	5	6	7	8	9	10	11	12	13	14	15	16	17	18
↓ Period																		
1	1 H																	2 He
2	3 Li	4 Be											5 B	6 C	7 N	8 O	9 F	10 Ne
3	11 Na	12 Mg											13 Al	14 Si	15 P	16 S	17 Cl	18 Ar
4	19 K	20 Ca	21 Sc	22 Ti	23 V	24 Cr	25 Mn	26 Fe	27 Co	28 Ni	29 Cu	30 Zn	31 Ga	32 Ge	33 As	34 Se	35 Br	36 Kr
5	37 Rb	38 Cr	39 Y	40 Zr	41 Nb	42 Mo	43 Tc	44 Ru	45 Rh	46 Pd	47 Ag	48 Cd	49 In	50 Sn	51 Sb	52 Te	53 I	54 Xe
6	55 Cs	56 Ba		72 Hf	73 Ta	74 W	75 Re	76 Os	77 Ir	78 Pt	79 Au	80 Hg	81 Tl	82 Pb	83 Bi	84 Po	85 At	86 Rn
7	87 Fr	88 Ra		104 Rf	105 Db	106 Sg	107 Bh	108 Hs	109 Mt	110 Ds	111 Rg	112 Cn	113 Uut	114 Uuq	115 Uup	116 Uuh	117 Uus	118 Uuo

Lanthanides	57 La	58 Ce	59 Pr	60 Nd	61 Pm	62 Sm	63 Eu	64 Gd	65 Tb	66 Dy	67 Ho	68 Er	69 Tm	70 Yb	71 Lu
Actinides	89 Ac	90 Th	91 Pa	92 U	93 Np	94 Pu	95 Am	96 Cm	97 Bk	98 Cf	99 Es	100 Fm	101 Md	102 No	103 Lr

The periodic table of elements.

The periodic table is also grouped by metal, metalloids, and nonmetals. The nonmetals are on the right of the periodic table; the metals make up the majority of the periodic table; and the metalloids, elements that can behave like a metal or a nonmetal, are in the middle.

Chemical Reactions/Bonding

Each element on the periodic table has electron shells or rings. Protons and neutrons are found in the nucleus of the atom, and surrounding the nucleus are the electron rings.

In the following figure you see the element manganese. It has four rings around it, which are the electrons in each energy level. The first ring can hold two electrons, the second ring can hold eight, and so on. As you can see, in manganese, the first ring is full, as are the second and third rings. It is the number of electrons in the outer ring that determines the chemical's properties—in this case, two.

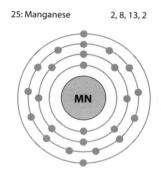

25: Manganese   2, 8, 13, 2

An atom with its electron rings.

A chemical reaction occurs when the atoms of one substance react together to form a new substance. For example, when two hydrogen atoms and one oxygen atom combine, a water molecule is formed.

An element is most stable if it has a full set of electrons in the outer ring. The first ring can hold two electrons, and the second and third rings can hold eight electrons. If an element does not have a full outer ring, the element will interact, or join together, with another element to try to fill the outer ring.

Covalent bonds are bonds where the elements share electrons. Once the elements form a covalent bond, the element is more stable. In the following figure you can see how the molecule methane contains one carbon atom and four hydrogen atoms that share electrons. The molecule is more stable now because the outer electron ring is full, with eight electrons. Before, each hydrogen atom needed another electron, and the carbon atom needed four more electrons for the outer ring to be full.

Methane

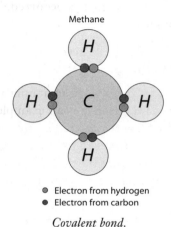

• Electron from hydrogen
• Electron from carbon

Covalent bond.

In an *ionic bond*, electrons are transferred from one element to the other. You can see how in this bond the element on the left is transferring its electron to the element on the right.

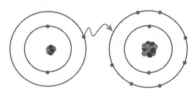

Ionic bond.

An *endothermic reaction* is when heat energy is absorbed. During an endothermic reaction, the temperature of the substance will decrease. An example of an endothermic reaction would be an ice cube melting. An *exothermic reaction* releases heat energy. During an exothermic reaction, the temperature of the substance will increase. An example of an exothermic reaction would be freezing water into an ice cube.

Physical and Chemical Changes

A *physical change* occurs when you change the physical properties of a substance. If a piece of ice melts and turns into water, a physical change has occurred. A *chemical change* occurs when you change one substance into a new substance. If I take a piece of wood and burn it, a chemical change has occurred, because I no longer have a piece of wood; I now have ashes.

Practice: Chemistry Basics

1. A coach takes a cold pack, pops the container inside, and immediately the pack becomes cold. This reaction is an example of what type of reaction?

   (1) Endothermic

   (2) Exothermic

   (3) Subjective

   (4) Heat of vaporization

   (5) Covalent bond

Use the periodic table shown earlier in the chapter to answer questions 2 and 3.

2. Which of the following elements is nonmetal?

   (1) Sodium (Na)

   (2) Iron (Fe)

   (3) Carbon (C)

   (4) Aluminum (Al)

   (5) Uranium (U)

3. Which of the following elements has one electron in its outer shell?

   (1) Sodium (Na)

   (2) Iron (Fe)

   (3) Carbon (C)

   (4) Aluminum (Al)

   (5) Uranium (U)

Answers: Chemistry Basics

1. **(1)** Endothermic reactions cause something to become cold, while exothermic reactions (2) cause something to become hot. Subjective (3) is not a reaction, heat of vaporization (4) is when water becomes a gas, and a covalent bond (5) is when two elements share electrons.

2. **(3)** Nonmetals are found to the right of the periodic table. Carbon is the only element in the list found to the right. Sodium (1), iron (2), aluminum (4), and uranium (5) are all metals.

3. **(1)** Column 1 elements have one electron in their outer ring. Sodium (Na) is found in column 1. None of the other elements are found in column 1.

Interactions of Matter

Let's now discuss the interactions of matter.

Acids and Bases

The *pH* of a substance is a measure of the amount of H+ (hydrogen) ions found in it. The pH is measured on the pH scale from 0 to 14. If a substance has a pH of 7, it is considered *neutral*. A neutral substance is a combination of an acid and a base, or lacks both. If a substance has a pH below 7, it is considered an *acid*. An acid has more H+ ions. Acids range from a pH of 0 to 7. The lower the pH, the more acidic the substance; the closer the pH is to 7, the weaker the acid is. A *base* is a substance with a pH greater than 7; bases have more OH- (hydroxide) ions. A base becomes stronger, or more basic, as you move up the pH scale, so a base with a pH of 14 is an extremely strong base and one of just above 7 is a weak base.

A pH of 4 is ten times more basic than a pH of 3, and similarly a pH of 9 is ten times more basic than a pH of 8. Each time you move up (more basic), or down (more acidic), you multiply by 10.

HEADS UP!

Many people are confused when it comes to the strength of a substance. We have been taught that acids are very strong, and so we assume that they may be stronger and more dangerous than a base. This is incorrect; a base of 14 is extremely dangerous and just as strong as an acid can be. Either end of the pH scale can cause burns, react with other substances, and cause a lot of damage to anything it comes into contact with.

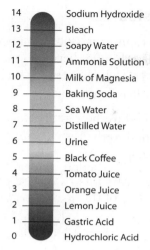

14	Sodium Hydroxide
13	Bleach
12	Soapy Water
11	Ammonia Solution
10	Milk of Magnesia
9	Baking Soda
8	Sea Water
7	Distilled Water
6	Urine
5	Black Coffee
4	Tomato Juice
3	Orange Juice
2	Lemon Juice
1	Gastric Acid
0	Hydrochloric Acid

The pH scale.

Mixtures and Compounds

If I take some sugar and dissolve the sugar in a glass of tea, I have just made a *mixture*. A mixture is two or more substances that can be separated back out. The water in the tea could be boiled out, leaving the sugar behind. A *compound*, in contrast, occurs when two or more atoms combine, like sodium and chloride combining to make salt.

Practice: Interactions of Matter

Refer to the figure of the pH scale above to answer the following question.

1. What is the pH of baking soda?

   (1) 1

   (2) 5

   (3) 7

   (4) 9

   (5) 13

Answer: Interactions of Matter

1. **(4)** The pH of baking soda is 9. It is found between sea water (pH of 8) and milk of magnesia (pH 10). 1 (1) is gastric acid, 5 (2) is black coffee, 7 (3) is distilled water, and 13 (5) is bleach.

Balancing Equations

If you need to describe a chemical reaction, you can do so with a chemical equation. One of the things you will be asked to do on the Science Test is balance a chemical equation. An equation must be balanced to show the change that occurs when two or more substances are converted into new substances. It is a simplified way to explain a chemical reaction. For example, you might be given an unbalanced equation like the following and asked to balance it:

$$OH + H_2SO_4 \rightarrow Na_2SO_4 + H_2O$$

Start by writing down each element with the number of atoms there are of each, as shown in the following table. In the previous reaction, you can see that some of the elements have a small number written next to them and some of the elements do not. Look at NaOH, you can see that there is one atom of Na, one atom of O, and one atom of H. Now, if you notice, there are no small (subscript) numbers written next to the Na, the O, or the H. When there is no number, there is only one atom; there will not be a subscript 1 next to the element. However, the next molecule is H_2SO_4. The subscript numbers mean there are two hydrogens, one sulfur, and four oxygens. You need to count up the total number of each element and write it next to the element's name. The arrow separates the chemical reaction to before the reaction on the left and after the reaction on the right.

Element	# Atoms Before Reaction	# Atoms After Reaction
Na	1	2
O	5	5
H	3	2
S	1	1

Next, we need to make the two sides balanced, or equal. We need first to add an Na atom to the left side. To do this, put only numbers in front of the molecule, like this:

$$2NaOH + H_2SO_4 \rightarrow Na_2SO_4 + H_2O$$

However, this didn't only change the Na, it also changed the number of Os and the number of Hs. So we need to redo our table.

Element	# Atoms Before Reaction	# Atoms After Reaction
Na	2	2
O	6	5
H	4	2
S	1	1

We fixed the Na, but now we caused the number of Os, which were balanced before, to not be balanced any longer. So we have to fix this by adding an O to the right side:

$$2NaOH + H_2SO_4 \rightarrow Na_2SO_4 + 2H_2O$$

Again, we must redo our table due to our new changes because now not only did we change the number of oxygen atoms, we also changed the number of hydrogen atoms as well.

Element	# Atoms Before Reaction	# Atoms After Reaction
Na	2	2
O	6	6
H	4	4
S	1	1

Now each side has the same number of atoms and is balanced.

Practice: Balancing Equations

1. Which of the following equations is balanced?

    (1) $2Mg + O_2 \rightarrow 2MgO$

    (2) $2Mg + 2O_2 \rightarrow 2MgO$

    (3) $Mg + 2O_2 \rightarrow 2MgO$

    (4) $Mg + O_2 \rightarrow MgO$

    (5) $Mg + O_2 \rightarrow 2MgO$

Answer: Balancing Equations

1. **(1)** This equation is balanced because there are 2 Mgs on the left side, and 2 Mgs on the right side. There are also 2 Os on the left side and 2 Os on the right side.

Properties of Matter

Let's now discuss the properties of matter.

Density

Density is the mass per unit volume of a material. You can calculate the density of a material by dividing the material's mass by its volume. For example, if a marble has a mass of 5 grams and a volume of 1 cm³, the density is 5g/cm³.

Consider if you took a wood block and a marble and put them in a glass of water. The wood would float and the marble would sink. This is because the marble is denser than the water and the wood is less dense than the water.

Solvents and Solutes

If a spoonful of sugar is dissolved into water, a solute and a solvent are being used. The sugar is the *solute* and the water is the *solvent*.

DEFINITION

A **solute** is the substance being dissolved. A **solvent** is the substance doing the dissolving.

Temperature can affect the rate at which a substance dissolves. If you want to dissolve more sugar, faster, you can heat the water up. Other things you can do to affect the rate of dissolution are stirring the mixture and changing the size of the solute. If you ground the sugar up into a fine powder, it would dissolve faster than a sugar cube would.

Gases

Gases do not have a definite volume or shape. They fill the size of their container and will continue to spread out until they are equally distributed. Gases have specific characteristics with which you need to be familiar:

- As temperature increases, pressure increases. This occurs because as the temperature rises, the molecules of gas begin to move faster in the same amount of space. This causes the pressure to increase.

- If the volume of a gas is decreased, pressure increases. This occurs because if you take the same amount of gas and squeeze it into a smaller area, the molecules move faster, which again causes the pressure to increase.

- As temperature increases, gases expand. This occurs because as you heat a gas, the distance between the particles expands.

Practice: Properties of Matter

1. If the volume of a gas decreases, the pressure does what?

   (1) Increases

   (2) Increases then decreases

   (3) Decreases

   (4) Decreases then increases

   (5) Remains the same

Answer: Properties of Matter

1. **(1)** The pressure increases because if you take the same amount of gas and squeeze it into a smaller area, the molecules move faster, which causes the pressure to increase. The other choices are incorrect because pressure can only increase if volume decreases.

Physics

Chapter 19

In This Chapter

- Overviews of key areas of physics, including force, energy, waves, simple machines, and electricity
- GED-like questions to practice the skills you'll be tested on
- Answers and explanations for all the questions

Physics is the study of the matter, motion, and the interactions of objects and energy. In this chapter we will analyze motion, how forces affect matter, waves and energy, and how machines make work easier.

The Science Test will cover Newton's three laws of motion and the different types of simple machines, as well as forces at work on different objects. Practice working different motion problems so you are familiar with these types of questions.

Physics Problems

Let's discuss different motion problems.

Force and Motion

A course in physics will cover *force* (a push or pull acting on an object) and *motion* (a change in the position of an object with respect to time). Other terms that you will need to be familiar with include the following:

- **Velocity:** Speed in a given direction
- **Momentum:** The property that a moving object has because of its mass and velocity
- **Work:** The force times the distance

You will need to be able to solve the problems given in a word problem. The formulas you should know are:

- velocity (m ÷ s) = distance (m) ÷ time (s)
- momentum (kg × m/s) = mass (kg) × velocity (m/s)
- force (N) = mass (kg) × acceleration (m/s/s)
- work (N × m) = force (N) × distance (m)

A typical force problem will look something like this:

> A 10 kg block is dropped from a building and is accelerating at 10 m/s/s. What force is acting on the block?

To solve this problem, you will take the mass (10 kg) and multiply it by the acceleration (10 m/s/s). So, 10 kg × 10 m/s/s = 100 kg × m/s/s (kg × m/s/s is also known as a Newton).

A typical velocity problem will look something like this:

> A car traveled 300 meters in 20 seconds. What is the velocity of the car?

To solve this problem you need to use this formula: velocity = distance ÷ time. So, 300 m × 20 s = 6,000 m/s.

Newton's Laws

Isaac Newton is known as the father of physics. Newton's three laws, which are the foundation of modern physics, changed our understanding of the universe because they show the relationship between the forces acting on an object and the motion due to these forces.

- Newton's first law states that an object in motion stays in motion, and an object at rest stays at rest, unless acted upon by an unbalanced force. For example, if you kicked a ball in space, the ball would continue moving forever. However, on earth, the force of gravity acts on the ball to slow it down.

- Newton's second law states that force = mass × acceleration. For example, because a bus has a much bigger mass than a car, even if the two vehicles are moving at the same speed, the bus will require more force to move than the car.

- Newton's third law states that for every action force, there exists an equal and opposite reaction force. For example, an ax strikes a tree. The ax exerts a force to cut the tree. The tree exerts the same force to stop the ax.

IN THE KNOW

Isaac Newton built the first light telescope, using mirrors rather than lenses. Known as the Newtonian reflector telescope, it is still in use today.

Power

Power is the rate at which work is done. The formula for power is work ÷ time. Remember, the formula for work is force × distance.

A typical power problem will look something like this:

> A 10 N force is applied to an object for 10 seconds. This moves the object 5 meters during the 10 seconds. Calculate the power used to move the object.

You can solve this problem in two steps. First you need to solve for work. So take the 10 N force and multiply it by the 5 meter distance to get a work of 50 N × m. Then, solve for power by taking the work of 50 N × m and dividing it by the time of 10 seconds. So the power is 5 watts.

Practice: Physics Problems

1. A 20 kg object is dropped from the top of a building and is accelerating at 5 m/s/s. What is the force acting on the object?

   (1) 20 kg × m/s/s

   (2) 15 kg × m/s/s

   (3) 25 kg × m/s/s

   (4) 100 kg × m/s/s

   (5) 1,000 kg × m/s/s

2. Which of the following is the best example of Newton's first law of motion?

   (1) A car accelerates as it goes down a hill.

   (2) A book in a car moves forward and slides off the seat as the car quickly stops.

   (3) Salt on a road helps the car to gain friction and move forward.

   (4) You push a car forward on the road after it runs out of gas.

   (5) A person on skates pushes against a wall, and as he does he moves backward, away from the wall.

Answers: Physics Problems

1. **(4)** Using the formula force = mass × acceleration, we can plug in the information to solve this problem. So 20 kg × 5 m/s/s = 100 kg × m/s/s.

2. **(2)** Newton's first law of motion states that an object in motion stays in motion. The example states that there is a book on the seat of a car and as the car quickly stops the book flies forward and slides off the seat. The book was in motion because the car was in motion, so when the car stops, the book continues to move in the direction it was moving. (1) is an example of a velocity question, and (3), (4), and (5) are all examples of Newton's third law.

Energy and Work

Energy is the capacity to do work. We will look at kinetic and potential energy. We will then see how this energy can be used to move an object using simple machines.

Kinetic and Potential Energy

Kinetic energy is energy in motion. *Potential energy* is stored energy. A boulder sitting at the top of a hill has a great deal of potential energy due to its place at the top of the hill. Think about the amount of damage this boulder could do if it began falling. Once the boulder begins rolling down the hill, it has energy in motion, or kinetic energy.

Simple Machines

There are six different simple machines: lever, pulley, wedge, inclined plane, screw, and wheel and axle. A person can use one of the machines to help lessen the amount of force he or she has to apply.

Picture a seesaw. This is an example of a *lever*. A seesaw has a long board suspended on a fulcrum, or pivot point. Levers help to lower the workload and make it easier to lift objects. The position of the fulcrum determines the amount of force needed to lift the object.

The following illustration shows two masses, one 100 kg and the other 5 kg. The fulcrum is not in the middle of the lever, but rather closer to the 100 kg mass because it is so much greater than the 5 kg mass. If instead both masses were equal, the fulcrum would be in the middle. The position of the fulcrum matters because the closer the fulcrum is to the mass, the easier it is to lift the object.

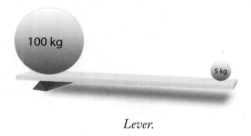

Lever.

A *pulley* is a system of ropes and a wheel that hoists an object upward. This changes the direction of the movement. For example, if you needed to lift a refrigerator up a flight of stairs, you would have a hard time pushing the heavy appliance by hand. However, if you put a pulley at the top of the stairs and connect the rope to the refrigerator, you could pull on the rope and lift the refrigerator up the stairs. Using multiple pulleys together lessens the force needed but increases the distance, because the amount of rope you will need to lift the refrigerator is greater than the distance the refrigerator needs to be lifted.

In the following illustration, a simple pulley has a 100 N mass on the end. As you can see, it will take a 100 N force to pick up this mass with a pulley. This pulley doesn't make the force you need to pick up the mass less, but rather changes the direction of the force.

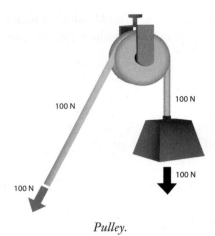

Pulley.

A *wedge* is a triangular-shaped object that can be used to drive two things apart. An example would be an ax. You can split wood with an ax because of its shape. In the following illustration, you see a wedge splitting a piece of wood in half. The wedge is the triangular-shaped object in the middle.

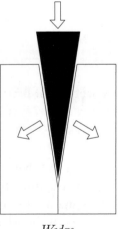

Wedge.

An *inclined plane* is like a ramp. It helps by reducing the amount of force needed to lift an object. By doing the work on the object over a greater distance, less force is used. For example, if you need to get your refrigerator into the back of a moving van, you could use an inclined plane to push the refrigerator up the ramp and into the van.

In the next illustration, you see a triangular-shaped inclined plane with a mass resting on it. By using the inclined plane, you reduce the force needed, but must move the object a greater distance.

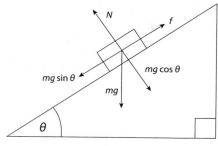

Inclined plane.

A *screw* is an inclined plane wrapped around a shaft, as shown in the next illustration. Again, the force is decreased but the distance is increased. An obvious example is just a hardware screw you would use at home to hold things together. In order to move the screw a few inches, you have to turn the handle around many times; you lessen the force but increase the distance.

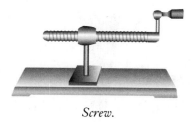

Screw.

A *wheel and axle* is a wheel attached to a rod that spins. A doorknob is a good example of a wheel and axle. Again, this lessens the force by increasing the distance. The next illustration shows a wheel and axle being used to raise a bucket. In order to raise the bucket up a few feet, you will have to turn the wheel many times, so again you lessen the force but increase the distance.

Wheel and axle.

Practice: Energy and Work

1. Which of the following would be the best simple machine to use if you wanted to lift a refrigerator to the top of a two-floor building?

(1) Screw

(2) Wedge

(3) Wheel and axle

(4) Lever

(5) Pulley

Answer: Energy and Work

1. **(5)** A pulley would be the best choice in this example because a pulley is a system of ropes and a wheel that helps to hoist an object upward. A pulley would be your best bet to lift a refrigerator to the top of a two-floor building.

Waves, Electricity, and Mass

In the next section, we will be looking at the different types of waves, learn to understand electricity, and find out how and why matter cannot be created or destroyed.

Waves

A *wave* is an oscillation that travels from one place to another. Waves can move in the form of water, light, sound, and microwaves, to name a few. Waves are a traveling form of energy and an important concept in physics.

Any wave that travels through matter is a mechanical wave. There are two types of mechanical waves:

- A *transverse* wave moves back and forth at right angles to the way the wave is moving, like a wave in the ocean. Picture if you took a jump rope and, holding one end, shook it up and down. You would be making a transverse wave.

- A *compressional* wave moves forward and backward in the same direction that the wave is moving. If you were to pull back on a spring and let it go you would be making a compressional wave. An example of a compressional wave is a sound wave.

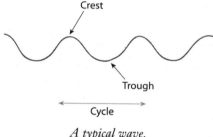

A typical wave.

One cycle of a wave is shown with the crest, the highest point, and the trough, the lowest point.

In this illustration, the *crest* of a wave is the highest point of a transverse wave and the *trough* of a wave is the lowest point. The *wavelength* is the distance between the crest (or trough) of one wave and the crest (or trough) of another. *Frequency* is the number of wavelengths that pass a point in a second. Frequency is measured in hertz (Hz).

Calculating wave speed is something you might be asked to do on the Science Test. The formula for frequency is frequency = wave speed ÷ wavelength.

An example problem might look like this:

> If the speed of a wave is 10 m/s and it has a frequency of 5 Hz, what is the wavelength?

First, we must move the equation around; instead of speed = wavelength × frequency, we have to isolate the wavelength in order to solve this. So since we need to solve for wavelength, we must move frequency to the other side of the = sign. Now, wavelength = speed ÷ frequency. 10 m/s divided by 5 waves per second equals 2 m per wave.

Electricity

Electricity is the flow of electric current through a wire or a motor. Electric current comes from the flow of electrons and is invisible. Electric current can do work like turn a motor or turn on a light. An *electric circuit* is the path where the electricity travels. For example, if you turn on a light switch, the electric circuit is the path the electricity travels from the switch to the light bulb.

Current (I) carries power and is measured in *amperes* (amps). *Resistance* (R) is the ability to resist current and is measured in *ohms*. *Voltage* (V), the difference in energy that is carried by charges in a circuit, is measured in *volts*. To solve for voltage, you would use the formula $V = I \times R$.

Matter has electric charge because atoms are made of electrons, protons, and neutrons. Electrons have a negative charge, while protons have a positive charge. Like charges (+ +) repel one another and unlike charges (- +) attract one another. The force that is around the charged particle is the *electric field*. As a distance between particles increases, the strength of the electric field decreases, and vice versa.

IN THE KNOW

If you have ever touched a doorknob or light switch and received a small shock, you have experienced static electricity. This occurs when there is a buildup of electrons on one of the two objects, you or the doorknob. The shock you feel was the electric current as it moves the excess electrons from you to the doorknob.

Conservation of Mass

Mass cannot be created or destroyed; however, it can change forms. Think of a boiling pot of water. If you leave the pot on the stove for hours, when you come back all the water will be gone. This is an example of conservation of mass. Actually, the water is not gone; instead, it was vaporized and is now in the form of steam.

Another example is burning a log in a fireplace. When the log burns, it seems as if it is disappearing. However, the log turned into ash, smoke, and gas that escaped as the log burned. The mass is not destroyed; it has just been changed to a different form. The law of conservation of mass states that mass cannot be created or destroyed, although it may be rearranged.

Practice: Waves, Electricity, and Mass

1. If I take a Slinky, stretch it out, and then push it forward so that the wave that is produced moves forward and backward along the length of the Slinky and in the same direction that the wave travels, what type of wave have I produced?

   (1) Compressional wave

   (2) Plane wave

   (3) Standing wave

   (4) Transverse wave

   (5) Wavelength

Answer: Waves, Electricity, and Mass

1. **(1)** A compressional wave is a wave that moves forward and backward in the same direction the wave is moving. As you pull the Slinky back and let it go, the wave will travel down the length of the Slinky. If you push a Slinky forward, you are demonstrating a compressional wave. There is no such thing as a plane wave (2), and a standing wave (3) is when two waves travel toward each other and interfere with one another. A transverse wave (4) moves back and forth at a right angle to the direction of a wave, similar to a wave in the ocean. So as the wave moves in one direction, say forward and backward, the transverse wave will move in the opposite direction, right to left. Wavelength (5) is the distance between one point of a wave to the next point on the next wave.

Earth and Space Science

In This Chapter

- Overviews of key areas of earth science, including plate tectonics, geologic time, and the earth's oceans
- GED-like questions to practice the skills you'll be tested on
- Answers and explanations for all the questions

This chapter discusses both the land and the oceans. We will discuss the theories of how the earth was made and what it is made of. Earth science is also known as geoscience and includes four major areas: geology, meteorology, oceanography, and astronomy. Geology is the study of the earth, meteorology is the study of the atmosphere, oceanography is the study of the oceans, and astronomy is the study of space or the universe.

The Science Test will quiz you over the layers of the earth, how the plates move, and what the earth looked like millions of years ago. The test will also cover the atmosphere, including weather and climate as well as the layers of the atmosphere.

Plate Tectonics

Our planet is constantly changing. During this very slow process, mountains are being formed, ocean crust is melting, volcanoes are adding new rock, and earthquakes are shifting the earth. These processes as a whole are called *plate tectonics*. A plate is a single piece of earth crust, either land or ocean. For example, Australia would be a single piece of earth crust. Another name for the earth's crust is the *lithosphere*. There are many different plates on our earth, known as tectonic plates; the largest is the Pacific plate, but there is also the African plate, the Antarctic plate, and others.

DEFINITION

Lithosphere is another name for the crust, the solid portion of our earth.

There are three ways in which plates interact:

- A *divergent plate boundary* occurs when two plates are moving apart. A divergent plate exists in the middle of the Atlantic Ocean that is moving apart like a conveyer belt. The plates spread apart and magma (molten rock) rises and fills in the gap. So the newest crust is right on the boundary and older crust is found as you move outward from the boundary. This is known as *seafloor spreading*.

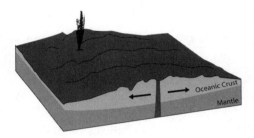

In this figure of a divergent plate boundary, you see the arrows pointing away from one another.

- A *convergent plate boundary* occurs when two plates are moving together. An example is an ocean plate is sliding under a land plate. Convergent plate boundaries offset the activity of divergent plate boundaries, keeping the earth the same size. The earth doesn't get larger; instead, somewhere else plates are coming together, or converging. Volcanoes are oftentimes associated with this type of boundary.

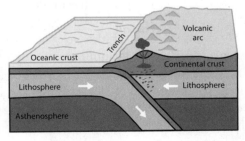

In this figure, you can see that the ocean crust is sliding underneath the continental or land crust. This is a convergent plate boundary.

- In a *transform plate boundary*, the plates are sliding next to each other. Transform boundaries can occur on land or ocean crust. Because the plate boundaries are not smooth, they do not slide evenly—instead, they get stuck. Eventually, the stress builds to a point where the plates slip past, releasing a lot of energy in the process. This slow buildup and sudden release of energy causes earthquakes.

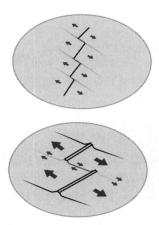

In this figure, the plates are sliding next to one another.
This is a transform plate boundary.

Practice: Plate Tectonics

1. The theory of plate tectonics states that

   (1) Earth's core is divided into plates that move.

   (2) Earth's mantle is divided into plates that move.

   (3) Earth's crust is divided into plates that move.

   (4) The crust of the earth is liquid.

   (5) The center layer of the core is liquid.

2. What is the name of the process when one plate is being forced below another plate?

(1) Divergent

(2) Convergent

(3) Transform

(4) Conduction

(5) Fragmentation

Answers: Plate Tectonics

1. **(3)** The plates are in constant motion according to the theory of plate tectonics.

2. **(2)** Convergent plates are plates that are coming together. If one plate is being forced beneath another, it is because the two plates are moving toward one another. Divergent plates (1) move apart from one another, while transform plates (3) slide next to each other. Conduction (4) and fragmentation (5) are not types of plate tectonic processes.

Geologic Time

The earth we see today is different from what it looked like millions of years ago. Today we have seven continents: North America, South America, Asia, Europe, Antarctica, Australia, and Africa. However, millions of years ago the planet had one large land mass known as Pangea.

Slowly, due to plate tectonic movements, this large land mass started to spread apart until the continents made their way to where they are today. In a few million more years, the continents will be in different places.

We have already discussed plate boundaries, but what is the driving force behind the movement of the plates? The answer is *convection currents*. Convection currents found in the mantle cause the ocean plates to spread outward. Just as warm air rises, so does molten magma. As the magma rises, it carries the plates along with it.

DEFINITION

Convection currents are currents that cause the plates to move. The extreme heat of molten rock causes it to rise up in the earth's mantle and spread out, moving the plates. As the magma rises, it cools, and sinks again. This is a continuous motion that slowly moves the earth's plates.

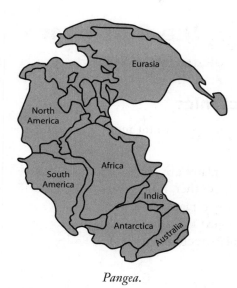

Pangea.

Practice: Geologic Time

1. When two plates move apart from one another and new crust is formed, it is known as what geologic plate boundary?

   (1) Divergent

   (2) Convergent

   (3) Transform

   (4) Pangea

   (5) Lithosphere

Answer: Geologic Time

1. **(1)** A divergent boundary is two plates moving apart. In a convergent boundary (2), plates move toward one another. Transform plates (3) slide next to one
   another. Pangea (4) is the one huge plate that existed on the earth millions of
   years ago. The lithosphere (5) is another name for the earth's crust.

Composition of the Earth and Atmosphere

In the next section we will study what the earth and the atmosphere are made of.
Knowing the layers of the earth and the first two layers of the atmosphere will be
important for your success on the Science Test.

The Layers of the Earth

The earth is composed of the core, the mantle, and the crust. The atmosphere contains the troposphere, stratosphere, mesosphere, thermosphere, and exosphere (space).

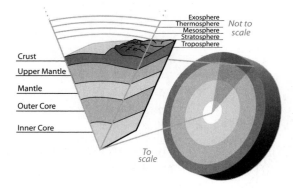

Earth's layers.

The *core* is the earth's center, mainly made up of nickel and iron. The core has a
center layer that is solid and an outer layer that is liquid.

The *mantle* is found between the core and the crust and is made up of silicon, iron,
magnesium, aluminum, and oxygen. The mantle is semi-liquid.

The *crust*, the outermost layer, is made up of silicon, oxygen, aluminum, iron, calcium, sodium, potassium, and magnesium. The crust is solid and is where all life exists.

IN THE KNOW

Earthquakes are measured with a device known as a seismograph. A seismograph detects the earth's movement and records it as zigzag lines on paper. The stronger the movement, the larger the markings will be on the paper. The strength of an earthquake is measured on the Richter scale.

The atmosphere has five layers; however, you will most likely be responsible to know only about the first two layers. You live in the *troposphere*. The troposphere is made up of 78 percent nitrogen, 21 percent oxygen, and other trace gasses. Three quarters of the mass of all the layers is in this first layer, where all of earth's weather occurs.

Moving outward, we reach the *stratosphere*. The stratosphere is extremely important to life on earth because it contains the ozone layer, which absorbs 99 percent of the ultraviolet light from the sun. Without the ozone layer, life on earth would not be possible.

Weather and Climate

Weather is the state of the atmosphere at a specific place and time. If it is raining outside, that is weather. Climate is the average weather that occurs over many years. So just because it is raining outside, it doesn't mean that the climate in that area is rainy.

There are also different types of air masses that can occur. In a *cold front*, cold air wedges its way under warmer air. Because warmer air is less dense, it will rise up on top of the colder air. A cold front typically will have a line of showers or a severe storm associated with it as the front moves through the area. A *warm front* occurs when warm air pushes its way beneath colder air. Typically, a warm front produces a long period of light rain. An *occluded front* is made up of two cold air masses pushing warm air between them, with the warmer air rising on top. Typically, an occluded front produces a lot of rain as the two fronts collide.

Practice: Composition of the Earth and Atmosphere

1. The center layer of the earth, which is made up mainly of nickel and iron, is known as the

    (1) Core.

    (2) Mantle.

    (3) Crust.

    (4) Thermosphere.

    (5) Mesosphere.

Answer: Composition of the Earth and Atmosphere

1. **(1)** The center layer of the earth is known as the core and is composed of iron and nickel. It has two layers, the inner core, which is solid, and the outer core, which is liquid.

Oceans

Seventy-one percent of our planet is covered with ocean. Oceans contain many different ecosystems, are important in regulating our climate, and house tens of thousands of life forms.

The uppermost layer of the ocean is known as the *euphotic zone*. The sun's rays can penetrate the water here; organisms like algae can grow, and therefore this zone is where most life exists. There are many different ecosystems found in the euphotic zone.

The coral reefs are the most diverse of all the ocean ecosystems. Corals are tiny animals that build reefs, providing shelter and food for many ocean creatures. Reefs are also important in protecting the shoreline from erosion. Reefs are found in warm, tropical waters which are shallow enough for sunlight to reach them. One big problem is coral bleaching, which causes the corals to die and look white because all that is left is their white exoskeleton.

Another extremely biodiverse and important ocean ecosystem is the kelp forest. While corals are found in warm, tropical waters, kelp is usually found in colder waters. Kelp forests provide food and shelter for many species.

Sea grass beds are another ocean ecosystem that provides food for many animals. There are many different species of sea grasses, but all are salt tolerant.

The middle layer of the ocean is the *bathyal zone*, a dimly lit zone under lots of pressure from the layers above it and containing little oxygen, and therefore less life than the euphotic zone.

The bottom layer of the ocean is the *abyssal zone*. It is completely dark and there are few life forms there due to the lack of oxygen and the extreme amounts of pressure.

The *benthic zone* is the ocean floor. This can be at the edge of the ocean right next to the beach where you walk, or the bottom of the deepest ocean. Many animals that bury themselves in the sand live in the benthic zone.

Practice: Oceans

1. Which ocean zone is the area of the ocean that contains lots of oxygen, and therefore lots of animal and plant life?

    (1) Euphotic

    (2) Bathyal

    (3) Abyssal

    (4) Benthic

    (5) Littoral

2. Approximately what percentage of the earth is covered with oceans?

    (1) 50%

    (2) 60%

    (3) 70%

    (4) 80%

    (5) 90%

Answers: Oceans

1. **(1)** The euphotic zone is the area of light, and therefore lots of photosynthetic activity makes oxygen. The bathyal zone (2) is dimly lit without much oxygen. The abyssal zone (3) is completely dark with hardly any oxygen. The benthic zone (4) is the floor of the ocean. This answer is not correct because we do not know if this is right at the shore, which would have a lot of oxygen, or at the deepest part of the ocean, with little to no oxygen. The littoral zone (5) is the layer of a lake, not the ocean.

2. **(3)** Seventy-one percent of the earth is covered with ocean; therefore, 70% is the best answer.

Science Practice Test

The Science Test will consist of 50 multiple-choice questions to see if you understand what you have learned in Chapters 15–20 of this book. You will have 80 minutes to complete the 50 questions. The practice test in this chapter is half the length of the actual Science Test, so plan on spending no more than 40 minutes to answer these 25 questions.

If, after taking the test provided here, you feel you need more practice and want to take another simulated test, there are several online sites that offer free GED practice tests. One site we recommend is PBS Literacy Link (http:litlink.ket.org). Keep in mind, though, that the actual GED Tests are paper-and-pencil tests like those in this book and cannot be taken on a computer.

Instructions

The Science Test is designed to measure your understanding of general science skills and concepts. You will have questions for which you will read a short paragraph and answer questions about what you read. You will also have graphs, data tables, and pictures that you will need to answer questions about. Use the information provided to answer the question(s) that follow. You can refer to the information as often as you want in answering the question(s).

You will have 40 minutes to complete the 25 questions on this practice test. Work carefully, but don't spend too much time on any one question. If you are having trouble with a question, make the best guess you can and move on. Don't skip any questions. Your score is based on the number of correct answers; there is no penalty for guessing.

When taking the practice test, try to simulate actual test conditions. Use a timing device of some sort and a couple of No. 2 pencils with good erasers. Take the test in a place where you won't be interrupted and follow test instructions. Start the timer after you've read the instructions and are ready to begin the first question.

Go on to the next page when you are ready to begin.

Questions 1 and 2 refer to the following information.

A student performs a lab in which he measures plant growth each day for a week. He takes one plant and puts it in a dark closet, he takes another plant and puts it in a room with one window, and he takes the last plant and puts it outside. He wants to see if the amount of light will affect the plant growth. This is the information that the student recorded.

	Plant in Dark	Plant in Window	Plant Outside
Day 1	10 cm	10 cm	10 cm
Day 2	10 cm	11 cm	12 cm
Day 3	10 cm	12 cm	15 cm
Day 4	10 cm	13 cm	18 cm
Day 5	10 cm	14 cm	21 cm

1. According to this information, what conclusion can the student draw?

   (1) The amount of light does not affect plant growth.

   (2) Plants grown in the dark die.

   (3) Plants grown in a window grow more than plants grown in the dark.

   (4) Plants grown outside require more water than plants grown in the dark.

   (5) Plants grown outside are more likely to get infected with insects.

2. Which of the following would be the best hypothesis for this experiment?

   (1) Plants grown in the dark do not increase in height.

   (2) Plants are called autotrophs.

   (3) Insects eat plants grown outside.

   (4) Plants need water to grow.

   (5) Plants will weigh more if they are grown outside.

Questions 3 and 4 refer to the following graph.

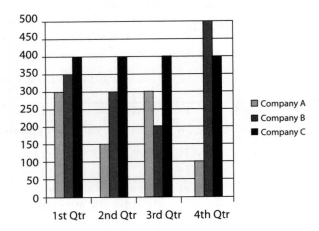

3. Which company had the most stable growth of the four quarters?

   (1) Company A

   (2) Company B

   (3) Company C

   (4) Companies A and B

   (5) Companies B and C

4. Which company had the most growth in the fourth quarter?

   (1) Company A

   (2) Company B

   (3) Company C

   (4) Companies A and B

   (5) Companies B and C

Questions 5 and 6 refer to the following information.

Carbon cycles through the environment quickly. Every time you exhale, you have taken carbon that was in your body and put it into the atmosphere. Plants take the carbon out of the atmosphere and convert it to glucose. Carbon is also found in the ground in many rock formations.

5. What is the main point in this paragraph?

   (1) Carbon is an important part of your body.

   (2) Oceans contain carbon.

   (3) Carbon is found in rocks.

   (4) Carbon can be found in many places in the environment.

   (5) Carbon is something humans do not need.

6. According to the paragraph, what can you tell about carbon?

   (1) Plants convert carbon to glucose.

   (2) Rock formations do not contain carbon.

   (3) You take in carbon to your body from the atmosphere.

   (4) Carbon is a slow cycle.

   (5) Carbon is important to the human body.

Refer to the following food chain to answer questions 7 and 8.

   Grass → Grasshopper → Bird

7. Which of the following can you conclude from this food chain?

   (1) Birds eat grass.

   (2) Grasshoppers eat birds.

   (3) Grasshoppers eat flies.

   (4) Birds eat mice.

   (5) Birds eat grasshoppers.

8. If the grass has 1,000 calories, according to the 10 percent rule, how many calories will the bird have to offer from the 1,000 calories of grass?

   (1) 1

   (2) 10

   (3) 100

   (4) 1,000

   (5) 10,000

9. Chloroplasts are organelles found in plant cells and contain chlorophyll that plants need to photosynthesize. What is another organelle found only in plant cells?

    (1) Chromosomes

    (2) Cell wall

    (3) Cell membrane

    (4) Lysosomes

    (5) Nucleus

10. Which of the following systems is responsible for support and movement of the human body?

    (1) Integumentary

    (2) Muscular

    (3) Skeletal

    (4) Digestive

    (5) Cardiovascular

11. Gregor Mendel experimented with pea plants and discovered how traits are passed from one generation to another. In Mendel's experiment, he crossed a tall pea plant (TT) with a short pea plant (tt). Which of the following would be the correct phenotype of this cross?

    (1) TT, TT, TT, TT

    (2) tt, tt, tt, tt

    (3) Tt, TT, tt, Tt

    (4) Tt, Tt, Tt, Tt

    (5) TT, TT, tt, tt

12. Which of the following is the correct order of mitosis?

    (1) Prophase, metaphase, anaphase, telophase

    (2) Telophase, anaphase, metaphase, prophase

    (3) Telophase, metaphase, anaphase, prophase

    (4) Metaphase, anaphase, prophase, telophase

    (5) Prophase, anaphase, metaphase, telophase

Use the periodic table to answer questions 13 and 14.

Group→ Period↓	1	2	3	4	5	6	7	8	9	10	11	12	13	14	15	16	17	18
1	1 H																	2 He
2	3 Li	4 Be											5 B	6 C	7 N	8 O	9 F	10 Ne
3	11 Na	12 Mg											13 Al	14 Si	15 P	16 S	17 Cl	18 Ar
4	19 K	20 Ca	21 Sc	22 Ti	23 V	24 Cr	25 Mn	26 Fe	27 Co	28 Ni	29 Cu	30 Zn	31 Ga	32 Ge	33 As	34 Se	35 Br	36 Kr
5	37 Rb	38 Cr	39 Y	40 Zr	41 Nb	42 Mo	43 Tc	44 Ru	45 Rh	46 Pd	47 Ag	48 Cd	49 In	50 Sn	51 Sb	52 Te	53 I	54 Xe
6	55 Cs	56 Ba		72 Hf	73 Ta	74 W	75 Re	76 Os	77 Ir	78 Pt	79 Au	80 Hg	81 Tl	82 Pb	83 Bi	84 Po	85 At	86 Rn
7	87 Fr	88 Ra		104 Rf	105 Db	106 Sg	107 Bh	108 Hs	109 Mt	110 Ds	111 Rg	112 Cn	113 Uut	114 Uuq	115 Uup	116 Uuh	117 Uus	118 Uuo

Lanthanides	57 La	58 Ce	59 Pr	60 Nd	61 Pm	62 Sm	63 Eu	64 Gd	65 Tb	66 Dy	67 Ho	68 Er	69 Tm	70 Yb	71 Lu
Actinides	89 Ac	90 Th	91 Pa	92 U	93 Np	94 Pu	95 Am	96 Cm	97 Bk	98 Cf	99 Es	100 Fm	101 Md	102 No	103 Lr

13. What type of element is iron?

    (1) Metal

    (2) Nonmetal

    (3) Metalloid

    (4) Gas

    (5) Liquid

14. Which of the following elements are found in the same family or group?

    (1) Calcium and helium

    (2) Lithium and chromium

    (3) Beryllium and sulfur

    (4) Fluorine and chlorine

    (5) Silicon and phosphorus

15. An athlete gets hurt on the football field and the trainer brings the athlete a cold pack. Before he places the cold pack on the athlete's leg, he takes the pack and breaks the vial inside. Instantly, the pack gets cold. This is an example of what type of reaction?

    (1) Endothermic

    (2) Exothermic

    (3) Physical change

    (4) pH change

    (5) Heat of vaporization

16. Ammonia has a pH of approximately 11, whereas urine has a pH of approximately 6. How many more times acidic is urine than ammonia?

    (1) 5 times

    (2) 6 times

    (3) 1,000 times

    (4) 100,000 times

    (5) 1 million times

17. Which of the following equations is properly balanced?

    (1) $2NaOH + H_2SO_4 \rightarrow Na_2SO_4 + H_2O$

    (2) $2NaOH + 2H_2SO_4 \rightarrow Na_2SO_4 + 3H_2O$

    (3) $2NaOH + H_2SO_4 \rightarrow Na_2SO_4 + 2H_2O$

    (4) $NaOH + H_2SO_4 \rightarrow Na_2SO_4 + H_2O$

    (5) $2NaOH + H_2SO_4 \rightarrow 2Na_2SO_4 + 2H_2O$

Use the formula force (N) = mass (kg) × acceleration (m/s/s) to solve the following problem.

18. A 1,000 kg box is dropped from a bridge and is accelerating at 10 m/s/s. What force is acting on the box?

    (1) 10 N

    (2) 100 N

    (3) 1,000 N

    (4) 10,000 N

    (5) 100,000 N

19. A car rolling down a hill has a lot of what type of energy?

    (1) Potential

    (2) Kinetic

    (3) Endothermic

    (4) Exothermic

    (5) Stored

20. A wheelchair ramp is an example of what type of simple machine?

    (1) Pulley

    (2) Wheel and axle

    (3) Inclined plane

    (4) Lever

    (5) Screw

21. The waves in the ocean go up and down as the wave moves toward the beach. What type of wave is this?

    (1) Transverse wave

    (2) Compressional wave

    (3) Microwave

    (4) Sound wave

    (5) Wavelength

22. The ring of fire is a circle around the Pacific plate, where many volcanoes are found. The volcanoes are found there because of what type of plate boundary?

    (1) Oceanic

    (2) Divergent

    (3) Convergent

    (4) Transform

    (5) Continental

23. The part of the earth where all life is found is known as what?

    (1) Crust

    (2) Upper mantle

    (3) Mantle

    (4) Outer core

    (5) Inner core

24. You go on a fishing trip off the coast of Costa Rica. After a day of fishing, you decide to write an article in the local paper about the fishing trip. You describe the ocean layer where you were fishing as what?

    (1) Euphotic zone

    (2) Bathyal zone

    (3) Abyssal zone

    (4) Benthic zone

    (5) Lithospheric zone

25. Today we have seven continents: North America, South America, Asia, Europe, Antarctica, Australia, and Africa. However, millions of years ago we had only one large land mass. What was the name of the large land mass that existed on the earth millions of years ago?

    (1) Euroafrica

    (2) Pangea

    (3) Geologica

    (4) Convergence

    (5) Mesosphere

Answers and Explanations

1. **(3)** The only answer that can be directly made from the data table is that plants grown in a window grow more than plants grown in the dark. This is because the plant in the window went from 10 cm to 14 cm over the 5 days.

2. **(1)** This is the correct answer because a hypothesis is an educated guess about an experiment. The experiment is about plants and how much they grow in the dark, in a window, and outside. Therefore, the only hypothesis that can be right must have something to do with the experiment; in this case plants grown in the dark do not increase in height.

3. **(3)** Company C is correct because company C's growth stayed at 400 during all four quarters; therefore, it is the company with the most stable (not changing) growth.

4. **(2)** Company B grew to 500, which was much greater than either company A or C.

5. **(4)** Carbon can be found in many places in the environment. The paragraph is telling all the places that carbon can be found—in your body, in plants, and in rocks. This is the only statement that can be concluded from the paragraph.

6. **(1)** Plants convert carbon to glucose. The paragraph clearly states that plants take the carbon out of the atmosphere and convert it to glucose.

7. **(5)** A food chain always has arrows pointing from the food item to the animal that eats it. When we look at this food chain, we see that the arrow is pointing from the grasshopper to the bird; therefore, birds eat grasshoppers.

8. **(2)** Every step up on the food chain has a decrease of 90 percent; only 10 percent goes up to the next level. If the grass has 1,000 calories, then the grasshopper would have 100 calories, so the bird now has 10 calories left from the original 1,000 calories of grass.

9. **(2)** The organelles that a plant has that an animal cell does not have are chloroplasts, chlorophyll, and a cell wall.

10. **(3)** The skeletal system is your system of bones and joints. Bones and joints are responsible for supporting and helping to move your body.

11. **(4)** Tt, Tt, Tt, Tt. When a tall (TT) plant is crossed with a short (tt) plant, the resulting offspring will all be tall but will be carriers of the short gene. This is because the tall plant only has a T to donate and the short plant only has a t to donate. Each offspring will get one from each parent, so since the tall one gives the T and the short one gives the t, the offspring will all be Tt.

12. **(1)** The orders of mitosis are best memorized by PMAT: prophase, metaphase, anaphase, telophase.

13. **(1)** Iron is on the left side of the diagonal line, which is where all the metals are found. The nonmetals are found on the right side of this line. Any element that touches the line is a metalloid.

14. **(4)** A family or group on the periodic table are all found in the same column. If we look we can see that fluorine is found right above chlorine in the same column and therefore in the same family or group.

15. **(1)** During an endothermic reaction, the temperature of the substance drops, or gets colder. The trainer used an ice pack and when he broke the vial he caused an endothermic reaction.

16. **(4)** Each time you move up the pH scale, you multiply the value by 10. So in this case, going from 6 to 11 is 5 steps up the scale—from 6 to 7, from 7 to 8, and so on. Therefore, we need 5 zeros, or 100,000.

17. **(3)** $2NaOH + H_2SO_4 \rightarrow Na_2SO_4 + 2H_2O$. We need to see how many atoms of each element are on the right side and how many are on the left. In this answer, there are 2 Na's on each side, 6 O's, 4 H's, and 1 S; therefore, it is balanced.

18. **(4)** To solve this, you take the 1,000 kg box and multiply it by the acceleration of 10 m/s/s to get 10,000 N (or kg × m/s/s).

19. **(2)** Kinetic energy is energy in motion. If the car is rolling down the hill, it has energy in motion.

20. **(3)** An inclined plane is a ramp that lessens the force by doing the work on the object over a greater distance, thus less force.

21. **(1)** A transverse wave is a wave that moves back and forth at right angles to the way the wave is moving. An ocean wave moves up and down at a right angle to the direction the wave is moving (toward the beach).

22. **(3)** Convergent plates are when two plates are moving together, often forming volcanoes. This is because the one plate is sliding underneath the other plate, melting, and rising to the surface.

23. **(1)** The crust is the outermost layer of the earth and where all life exists.

24. **(1)** The euphotic zone is the uppermost layer of the ocean where the sun's rays can penetrate. This is where most life forms are found.

25. **(2)** The large land mass that existed millions of years ago is Pangea. Since that time the plates have moved apart, forming the seven continents we have today.

Language Arts: Reading

Undoubtedly, you're already using most of the skills required for the Language Arts: Reading Test. However, you probably need to sharpen those skills as they apply to the four reading areas on the test. The five review chapters in Part 4 help you improve your skills as you read nonfiction, prose fiction, poetry, and drama. The chapters focus on getting meaning from a passage; practicing essential comprehension skills, including reading for the main idea, details, and inferences; and using context clues to determine the meanings of unknown words. Part 4 ends with a practice test so you can test your understanding of what you've learned.

The Language Arts: Reading Test does not test you on your knowledge of literature. Instead, it tests your ability to understand and analyze what you read. Importantly, each passage is preceded by a "purpose question" which focuses your thinking and prepares you for the passage's central meaning.

So Many Kinds of Reading, So Little Time

In This Chapter

- Overview of steps that prepare you for reading with good comprehension and faster speed
- GED-like questions to practice the skills you'll be tested on
- Answers and explanations for all the questions

All of us have something important in common. We all need to read. You may read at work—directions, announcements, job manuals, and more. Or, you may be in school where reading in different subject areas is a daily necessity. If you're really lucky, you have time to read for pleasure—stories, current information, biographies, and much more. All of your daily reading is good background experience for future learning or for test taking—including the GED Tests.

In this chapter, you will begin to harness all of your reading skills. You need to know that your life experiences have left you with many more skills than you thought you had. The question is this: how do you put your skills to work?

Even though you may not have realized it at the time, one of the first skills you learned as a new reader was to connect the new information to your own experiences. First, your teacher led you to talk about the subject. He or she knew that connecting to things in your life, and especially making an emotional connection, would help you to understand and remember what you read. Then your teacher led you to answer questions about the reading, to look at pictures, headings, subtitles, and, finally, to read the material. This was known as surveying the reading material—an active way to prepare for reading or studying at any age.

Obviously, you won't need to use all of these steps, that is, discussion, connection to your experience, answering questions, looking at pictures, etc., all of the time. If you're reading a three-paragraph GED passage, you'll use the first three steps. We'll show you how in the following section.

Secrets of the Elite Reader

You know that great athletes would never start a game or event without a warm-up. You just expect to see the team or individual players warming up before the beginning of the inning, quarter, or set. Why is that the case? Athletes know that a warm-up prevents injuries and ensures a better performance. Learn that lesson and you will be a reading star!

What do we mean by a reading warm-up? It can be as simple as looking at the title of the story or article and asking yourself, "Do I know anything about moon rocks? Where did I see one? Have I already read something about them?" All of these questions start your mind in the right direction—thinking about the subject at hand!

In his book *Effective Study, Fourth edition* (Harper and Row, 1970), Francis P. Robinson explains how the SQ3R Method can help you become a more efficient and faster reader. There are five steps:

1. **S Survey the material.** Glance at topic headings. Skim the sections and read the final summary paragraph if there is one. Just take a minute or so to do this.

2. **Q Question.** Ask yourself what you know about the subject. What information can you bring to the reading? What do you want to get out of it?

3. **R1 Read.** Read the article, asking yourself what the main idea of the article is.

4. **R2 Recite.** When you need to remember the content for some reason, try to recite the main points of the article.

5. **R3 Review.** If you're studying for a test, review the material at different times in order to keep it in your memory. It's interesting that even the Language Arts: Reading Test observes this good advice in the following way: Each reading passage starts with a question followed by a title. This is a format that encourages you to exercise your brain. Once your brain is awakened, you're ready for the paragraphs or the lines of poetry that follow. Let's see how it works with a portion of a poem by the American poet, Edgar Allan Poe (1809–1849).

What painful memory does the bird revive in the speaker?

"The Raven"

Once upon a midnight dreary, while I pondered, weak and weary,
Over many a quaint and curious volume of forgotten lore,
While I nodded, nearly napping, suddenly there came a tapping,
As of some one gently rapping, rapping at my chamber door.
" 'Tis some visitor," I muttered, "tapping at my chamber door—
Only this, and nothing more."

Ah, distinctly I remember it was in the bleak December,
And each separate dying ember wrought its ghost upon the floor.
Eagerly I wished the morrow;—vainly I had tried to borrow
From my books surcease of sorrow—sorrow for the lost Lenore—
For the rare and radiant maiden whom the angels name Lenore—

Nameless here for evermore.

And the silken sad uncertain rustling of each purple curtain
Thrilled me—filled me with fantastic terrors never felt before;
So that now, to still the beating of my heart, I stood repeating
" 'Tis some visitor entreating entrance at my chamber door—
Some late visitor entreating entrance at my chamber door;—

This it is, and nothing more."

Presently my soul grew stronger; hesitating then no longer,
"Sir," said I, "or Madam, truly your forgiveness I implore;
But the fact is I was napping, and so gently you came rapping,
And so faintly you came tapping, tapping at my chamber door,
That I scarce was sure I heard you"—here I opened wide the door;—

Darkness there, and nothing more.

Deep into that darkness peering, long I stood there wondering, fearing,
Doubting, dreaming dreams no mortal ever dared to dream before;
But the silence was unbroken, and the darkness gave no token,
And the only word there spoken was the whispered word, "Lenore!"
This I whispered, and an echo murmured back the word, "Lenore!"

Merely this, and nothing more.

Practice

1. On this dreary night, the speaker hears the raven tapping and

   (1) regrets the unnecessary hours spent studying.

   (2) mourns the loss of his pet bird.

   (3) opens the door to a flock of birds.

   (4) relives his sorrow for the lost Lenore.

   (5) continues to sleep soundly.

2. How does the poet use vocabulary to accentuate the speaker's sadness? Which words emphasize his dark feelings?

   (1) midnight dreary, darkness there, weak and weary

   (2) chamber door, rare, maiden

   (3) some visitor, I was napping, radiant

   (4) entrance, distinctly, hesitating

   (5) quaint, lore, token

Answers

1. **(4)** In the second stanza, the speaker says he's been looking for "surcease [an end to] of sorrow—sorrow for the lost Lenore." There is no mention of being joyous or unforgiving or any of the other choices.

2. **(1)** All these words call up sad pictures in your mind. All of the other vocabulary in (2) through (5) might be used in happy, ordinary situations.

Engage Your Brain in a Prereading Workout

Here's a simple warm-up secret of good readers: When you know something—anything—about what you are about to read, you are definitely more interested in it. And if you are more interested in what you're reading, what will happen? You will pay much closer attention to it and you will achieve much greater understanding—and faster, too. On the other hand, if you approach reading blankly, you will reach the end of a page and say, "What did I just read?" Such frustration!

Now would be the time to ask, "Exactly how do I do a reading warm-up?" Believe it or not, you probably learned how to do this early in your school career. Your teacher may not have explained it as such, but reading warm-ups were the order of the day in the early grades. No matter how old you are now, the way to accomplish the warm-up is to quickly look at the paragraph, page, or chapter. Is there a title—or titles—to read? What do you already know about the topic? Is there any visual clue to the topic or meaning of the material? Some readings, for example, include maps, charts, graphs, or photographs. If the passage is long, there may be subheadings. They are probably very important to your understanding of the material. Take a fast look at each element to see how it fits into the topic.

You are probably wondering how you fit the reading warm-up into a closely timed test. The answer is that it takes very little time—sometimes a matter of seconds—to go through the first two steps of the survey. And the payoff may be huge! Not only will your comprehension improve, but also the pace of your reading; your speed will definitely improve.

A good example of a visual clue was mentioned earlier in this chapter. On the Language Arts: Reading Test, each reading starts with a question. If you really think about the question and—importantly—attempt to answer it, you will start the wheels turning in your brain. Before reading "The Raven," for example, you knew what to look for. The introductory question gave you something to find—a painful memory. You will seek the answer to the question throughout your reading. In other words, you've begun the process of comprehension. You asked yourself, "What do I already know about the topic?" Inevitably, either the passage or your own experience will answer that question. Just try to jump-start the process by warming up with the question.

 GOOD IDEA

Did you know that titles often supply the answer to questions about the topic or main idea of a passage? If a title in your ordinary reading is not a question, turn it into one. Then, keep looking for the answer to the question as you read.

Before the space shuttle *Endeavor* returned to earth, many articles appeared in magazines and newspapers. The following is a sample of information written.

Where Are We in Space?

On May 29, 2011, the space shuttle *Endeavor* crew said a last goodbye to the astronauts on the International Space Station and began their journey earthbound. Although another crew will stay on the space station, *Endeavor* made its final trip. On this final mission, *Endeavor*'s crew installed equipment that will allow the ISS to send huge amounts of data to earth. Researchers around the world will gather the information and analyze it. Scientists have NASA's last crewed flight to look forward to when the space shuttle *Atlantis* is launched.

Practice

1. A main idea in this paragraph is that the International Space Station

    (1) will continue to send information to earth even though the *Endeavor* crew has left.

    (2) has never had anyone on board to fix equipment or install equipment.

    (3) has requested that *Atlantis* not launch.

    (4) is uninhabited; no people reside there.

    (5) has nothing more to contribute to space science.

Answer

1. **(1)** An important idea in the paragraph is that, although *Endeavor* made its final trip, the crew of the ISS prepared the space station to do much more work in the future. The only choice that makes this statement is (1).

Learn to Read More in Less Time

If you're trying to increase your reading speed, take heart; there is no lack of information out there. Speed reading books abound; internet help is plentiful. The question is, which speed-reading tips will work for you?

As you read the next passage, look for an answer to the question posed in the title. You will easily find the main idea. Also, be alert for details that support the main idea. See if you can gauge the author's opinion on ways to improve reading speed.

IN THE KNOW

There is no such thing as one appropriate reading speed—fast or slow. Reading speed is dictated by what you are reading—the subject matter, the vocabulary, and what you need to get out of it.

Which Speed Reading Tips Work?

To increase your reading speed, you first have to analyze your problem. Slow reading happens for different reasons, depending upon your particular habits. For example, do you form every word with your lips as you read silently? If you do, you're losing considerable reading speed. Experts will advise you to choose from these solutions:

- Place one or more fingers on your lips—a subtle reminder not to form the words. If you feel your lips forming the words, stop doing it.

- Put a small piece of tape on your lips—not so subtle—and when you remove it, it hurts!

What if your lips don't move? Instead, you subvocalize—you hear each word in your head as you read silently. Solutions to resolve this bad habit are very creative:

- Count from 1 to 100 out loud as you read silently.

- Play music—preferably loudly.

- Surround yourself with white noise.

All of this is meant to drown out the words in your head, thereby discouraging subvocalization.

These tips may help you, and that's great. What if they don't? Then you can do what really works, but you'll find that this way requires patience and adherence to the rules. It's very simple: you just decide to read faster. Don't close this book and run away! Believe it or not, there's logic in those words. This is what you do:

- Choose something to read. Be sure the reading is something that really interests you.

- Make sure it is easy reading material. You do not want to be challenged by difficult subject matter as you improve your reading speed. The words should be easy for you; the subject matter should be easy to grasp.

- As you read down the page, force your eyes to read phrases, not single words. When you start this process, you will miss some words along the way, but you'll still understand the text. Just keep practicing in this way.

- Move your fingers down the center of the page. Don't let them go back over anything. In fact, if you are a hard-core repeater, place a 3x5 card above the line you're reading so you can't see the earlier text. Again, move the card down the center of the page.

If you follow these tips, you can't help but increase your reading speed.

Practice

1. A main idea in this passage is that slow reading may result from

   (1) your need for new glasses.

   (2) reading in phrases.

   (3) poor reading habits.

   (4) reading down the center of the page.

   (5) using a 3x5 card to hide the previous text.

2. The writer provides details on how to improve your speed; for example,

   (1) always say the words under your breath, not out loud.

   (2) always sing along to the music on the radio or TV.

   (3) wear really sticky tape on your lips.

   (4) clap your hands to the rhythm of the sentences.

   (5) force yourself to read phrases in easy reading material.

Answers

1. **(3)** The entire article is about breaking poor habits, for example, subvocalization, and substituting good ones, such as forcing yourself to read phrases.

2. **(5)** A very important detail on how to improve your speed of reading came late in the passage: using easy reading material, force yourself to read phrases. Choice (5) is correct.

Comprehension and Speed Apply to All Kinds of Reading

Improving your comprehension and rate of reading will help you to tackle all the various kinds of reading available to you—even the reading categories found on the Language Arts: Reading Test.

In this chapter, you've read a poem, an article on space, and a textlike article on reading speed. Ahead is a magazine article. After that you will read a workplace document—and all to show that reading skills exist in every kind of reading you do. Sharpen those skills and apply them everywhere! In a magazine you may see an article on fitness.

How Do You Plan for Fitness?

So often we make promises to ourselves to "get fit." Why do we fail? To begin, you need to answer a question: what does fitness mean to you, and how can you actually accomplish it? For many of us, fitness involves weight loss, and we want it now! However, we're more likely to accomplish it if we set manageable goals to be accomplished over a reasonable period of time.

Start by specifically stating your fitness goals. For example, you may want to lower your blood pressure and lose weight. You need to state your goal (a reasonable one!) before you start. For example: I want to lose 5 pounds in 6 months and lower my blood pressure to acceptable levels. That is clearly different from saying that you want to lose weight. Five pounds are doable; an unstated amount may be *daunting*. Just that small weight loss may lead to lower blood pressure. Take your blood pressure reading frequently to track your progress.

Practice

1. The main idea of this passage is that

   (1) fitness goals need to be stated specifically.

   (2) 5 pounds is all you can lose in a year.

   (3) most people have high blood pressure even if they are not overweight.

   (4) we meet our goals, whether stated or unstated.

   (5) immediate weight loss is always possible.

2. You can infer (conclude from reasoning) from the passage that the word *daunting* found in paragraph 2 means

   (1) easily accomplished.

   (2) too much weight loss.

   (3) impossible.

   (4) overwhelming.

   (5) rejected.

Answers

1. **(1)** The main idea is stated in the last sentence of the first paragraph and in the first sentence of the second paragraph.

2. **(4)** In the same sentence, you are told that a 5-pound loss (the amount in your goal statement) can be accomplished, but an unstated amount is the opposite: daunting, or discouraging, even frightening.

Use Comprehension Skills in a Workplace Document

Read the following document regarding smoking in the workplace.

There are many versions of nonsmoking rules and policies. The one that follows is a small portion of the U.K. version, but you can find one as well for every state—and even town—in the United States. Skim through the document to find out why the policy is widely implemented and whom it affects. Look for a section on how smokers are given consideration and help.

What Is Our Workplace Smoking Policy?

Draft Workplace Smoking Policy

Smoking Policy for: (company name)

Effective from: (date)

Introduction

Secondhand smoke—breathing in other people's tobacco smoke—has now been shown to cause lung cancer, heart disease, and many other illnesses in nonsmokers.

Section 2 (2) (e) of the Health and Safety at Work Etc. Act 1974 places a duty on employers to provide a working environment for employees that is "safe, without risk to health, and adequate as regards facilities and arrangements for their welfare at work."

The Health Act 2006 requires workplaces to be smoke free by the end of May 2007. Smoking rooms will no longer be allowed.

The employer acknowledges that breathing other people's tobacco smoke is both a public hazard and a welfare issue. Therefore, the following policy has been adopted concerning smoking in (name of organization).

General Principles

This smoking policy seeks to guarantee nonsmokers the right to work in air free of tobacco smoke, while taking account of the health needs of those who smoke.

All premises will be designated smoke free from (date).

Smoking will only be permitted at designated smoking area outside the buildings.

Smoking while on duty will only be allowed during official break periods.

Common Areas

Smoking is not permitted in the following areas:

Lifts	Toilets
Corridors	Reception areas
Stairways	Entrances
Canteen	Car parks
Restrooms	Other areas
Meeting rooms	Work areas

Smoking is not permitted in any work area. This applies to all offices and work areas, whether occupied by one person, or shared by two or more. Anyone who wishes to smoke must do so during official break periods and only in designated areas.

Smoking Areas

Designated smoking areas are provided at (location).

Unions/Health and Safety Representative

This policy has been devised in full consultation with all of those employees who are concerned with health and safety in this workplace. It enjoys the support of the relevant representatives.

Informing Staff of the Policy

The employer has informed staff 90 days in advance and will provide all members of staff with a copy of this policy upon their request.

Visitors and Temporary Staff

Visitors and temporary staff are expected to abide by the terms of this policy.

The following arrangements have been made for informing them of its existence:

Adequate signage

Receptionist/person greeting will inform the person of the policy

To be reinforced via the invitation letter or email if required

Recruitment Procedures

Job advertisements, job descriptions, and interviews will include reference to this policy. On their appointment, all new staff members will be given a copy of this policy.

Help for Those Who Smoke

This policy recognizes that secondhand smoke adversely affects the health of all employees. It is not concerned with whether anyone smokes, but where they smoke, and the effect this will have on nonsmoking colleagues.

However, it is recognized that the smoking policy will impact on smokers' working lives.

In an effort to help individuals adjust to this change, the following help is being provided:

Time off (up to x number of hours) to attend any courses that will help smokers to quit.

Smoking cessation support provided by Surrey Stop Smoking Service, which runs regular stop smoking groups and can offer one-to-one support. For more information, call (phone number).

Enforcement of This Policy

Breaches of this policy will be subject to normal disciplinary procedures.

Implementation, Monitoring, and Review

Responsibility for implementing and monitoring this policy rests with senior managers.

Twelve weeks' notice will be given of the introduction of this policy.

Monitoring this policy will be carried out at 3, 6, and 12 months.

Trade unions and health and safety representatives will be consulted over the results of the monitoring and review.

Changes to the Policy

Twelve weeks' notice will be given of any changes made to the policy. Trade unions and health and safety representatives will be consulted in good time about any proposed changes.

Policy dated _____.

Practice

1. According to the document, the overriding reason for a smoking ban in the workplace is to

   (1) have the pleasure of telling people what they can and cannot do.

   (2) stop absolutely everyone from smoking.

   (3) spend more money on health care.

   (4) provide a safe and healthful environment for all who work there.

   (5) conduct business in exactly the same way everyone else does.

2. An important detail in this document says that second-hand smoke is

   (1) your second cigarette of the day.

   (2) the smoke that children only breathe in from others.

   (3) the smoke that other people—not you—breathe in.

   (4) smoke produced by the company's operations.

   (5) the smoke you breathe in from other people's tobacco smoke.

Answers

1. **(4)** All other answers are incorrect details.

2. **(5)** None of the other statements can be found as correct details in the reading.

Nonfiction: Reading That's All Around Us

In This Chapter

- Overview of nonfiction reading, including biographies, autobiographies, factual articles and books, legal documents, and workplace documents
- GED-like questions to practice the skills you'll be tested on
- Answers and explanations for all the questions

You may think of yourself as an infrequent reader, but almost no day will go by without your reading nonfiction, which is writing based on facts, such as you find in biographies or histories. We all read nonfiction daily when we look at information as simple as a bus schedule or a TV listing, a map, a restaurant menu, or a workplace document. Just think about it. You may decide to take a day off from reading—until you …

- Need last night's score of your favorite football team (Go, Patriots!).
- Want the TV listings for the day.
- Want to check the daily recipe in the newspaper.
- Decide to read a magazine article on physical fitness.
- Try to understand the language in the warranty you received with a new appliance.

Look for the Main Idea and Details as You Read

Every kind of reading requires skills. When you practice certain skills, you'll find that you need to use those skills again and again. For example, all reading requires that you read for the main idea and important details. There's not much point to reading an article on fitness, for example, if you don't glean the main idea from the time spent.

The question is, how do you find the main idea in a magazine or newspaper article? The answer starts with what you've already learned in Chapter 22. That is, before you read you need to warm up your brain. You can do the warm-up by looking through the entire magazine article first. Look at the title of the article and ask yourself what it means to you, what you already know about it. Now read the first paragraph or introduction as well as the last paragraph or summary. At this point, you'll have a better idea of what the article is about.

It also helps to read the first and last sentences of paragraphs. You'll find that main ideas are often placed first or last. The sentence that holds the main idea is called the *topic sentence*. If the main idea (or topic sentence) comes first, the rest of the paragraph adds details to support the main idea. If the main idea comes last, the supporting details appear first and then are summarized in the main idea (or topic) sentence. Supporting details give you information that backs up the main idea. It's helpful to turn the title of the article around and form a question. Then, actually give yourself the task of finding the answer to the question as you read. For example, make a question out of this title:

Happy Families Have Certain Characteristics

How can you turn this into a question that leads you to the main idea and details? Try the following:

What characteristics do happy families have?

Look for the main idea and supporting details as you read the following passage.

What Characteristics Do Happy Families Have?

If you read 10 articles written by experts in family happiness, at least five of them will contain this quote from a famous book, *Anna Karenina*, by Tolstoy:

"All happy families are alike; each unhappy family is unhappy in its own way."

What does that mean? Perhaps there are *discernible* [visible or noticeable] patterns in happy families. If so, what defining features make up the pattern? The experts seem to agree on at least five characteristics. Here are five that appear over and over again.

Communication

Happy families seem to enjoy talking to each other. Although it's difficult for today's busy families to enforce a rule about having dinner together every night, it is one of the ways that families gather to talk. Not all of the conversation may be about happy moments in the family's life. Parents may want to ask what happened that day that was happy, but just as important about something that was unhappy or disappointing. Then, at least, there is the possibility of getting the conversation and the path to solutions going. One good rule: you can keep conversations going if you stay away from questions that require only one-word answers. Stay away from, "How was school today?" The answer is undoubtedly going to be, "Fine" or "OK." If your question is, "What was the worst (or best) thing that happened in school today?", you are likely to start a conversation.

Activities for Mom and Dad

A mom and dad or single parent should try to maintain few activities that they love. Kids don't want to give up soccer or baseball, so why should parents give up everything they love? Parents should plan for an activity that provides exercise as well as fun. Fun activities away from work at home or on the job make for happier parents. Happy parents are likely to bring home a smile and positive outlook. When parents spend time with each other, laughing and having fun, their smiles become contagious and soon appear on their kids' faces.

A Few Good Rules

Happy families do have rules by which they live. Many say that the simpler they keep the rules, the better. For example, one family chose to follow a broad rule, such as showing respect for everyone in their circle. Their circle includes children, parents, grandparents, friends, and teachers. However, this family's rule included the children showing respect for each other. You don't need very many rules if the guiding rule is respect for each other.

Commitment

Happy families are committed to each other in good times and in difficult times. Happy families tend to pull inward to rally around an adult or child in trouble. This is simply putting the family first. It is also a commitment to help each individual in the family become all that he or she can be. To accomplish this, a parent or child may have to give up an immediate desire in order to help the family member who needs special help or attention.

Practice

1. Which answer best states the main idea of this passage?

   (1) Only parents can make a family happy, healthy, and committed to each other.

   (2) Happy families have certain characteristics in common, such as enjoying each other and being committed to the family.

   (3) Only families who have many strict rules are happy.

   (4) Happy families don't need any rules; good behavior comes naturally.

   (5) Happy families are extremely outgoing at all times.

2. In the paragraph under "Commitment," which of these sentences carries the main idea?

   (1) This is simply putting the family first.

   (2) It is also a commitment to help each individual in the family become all that he or she can be.

   (3) Happy families are committed to each other in good times and in difficult times.

   (4) A parent or child may have to give up an immediate desire.

   (5) A family member needs special attention.

3. In the paragraph under "A Few Good Rules," which of the following statements is a main idea you can infer from reading all of the details?

(1) Happy families seem to allow for Mom and Dad to do fun activities together as a couple or alone.

(2) Without the children, no activities are fun.

(3) Emergencies always stand in the way of parents' activities.

(4) Kids always want to give up soccer or baseball, so why shouldn't parents give up everything they love?

(5) Kids never want to leave the house unless they absolutely have to, so Mom and Dad shouldn't, either.

Answers

1. **(2)** This answer is reflected in the title as well. Answers (1), (3), (4), and (5) are all incorrect details and opposite to what the passage states.

2. **(3)** Answers (1), (2), (4), and (5) state only a small portion of the main idea.

3. **(1)** Answer (2) is the opposite of the paragraph's main idea. Answer (3) is incorrect because it is an exaggeration. Answers (4) and (5) are incorrect details.

IN THE KNOW

Occasionally a writer does not include a main idea or topic sentence in a paragraph. As a reader, being able to infer the main idea is a useful skill. You need to figure out the main idea by "adding up" all the clues in the paragraph.

Reading Autobiographies and Biographies

An author's attitude or viewpoint about a subject will almost certainly influence how he or she writes about it. For example, suppose an author holds higher regard for classical music than for rock and roll. It's likely he or she might say more positive things about classical music. What clues can you look for to identify the author's viewpoint? Consider the author's vocabulary, the details the author chooses to reveal, and the author's own background.

In the following biography of Bill Gates, you'll learn some important details about his life, his education, and his personality. Look for the sentences in which the author reveals his viewpoint of Gates' achievements.

Bill Gates and the History of Great Inventions

Many times in history, there have been men and women who profited from new inventions. In the late 1800s and early 1900s, new inventions turned up regularly. The typewriter, the telephone, and the internal combustion engine gave forward thinking businessmen reasons to cheer. Alexander Graham Bell (telephone), Thomas Edison (the incandescent light bulb), Andrew Carnegie (innovations in the steel industry), to name just a few, saw the opportunities that important discoveries provided. These people were made enormously wealthy by the discoveries of the industrial age.

Bill Gates, chairman and CEO of Microsoft, along with a few good friends, followed that model. Just remember, though, that when Bill Gates was born in 1955, no one owned a personal computer. Yet, after being introduced to computers, he understood that everyone would want and need a personal computer. Yes, there were the massive computers in government offices and huge computers owned by businesses. However, you could not buy and carry one of these home.

As a youngster, Bill Gates was fun loving and attention seeking, so much so that his parents transferred him to a very demanding school. Here he excelled in reading, math, and science. Doing well in this difficult school got him positive attention. While Gates was at Lakeside School, a Seattle computer company offered to provide computer time for the students. The school purchased a teletype terminal for students to use. Bill Gates became totally absorbed with what a computer could do. At 13 years old, Gates began programming computers. He spent much of his free time working on the terminal. Some of that time was spent writing a tic-tac-toe program in BASIC computer language. The program allowed users to play against the computer.

While in Seattle schools, using an existing computer, Gates honed his programming skills and developed his new ideas. Years later, the eventual result was Microsoft, the most successful software company in the world.

At Lakeside School, Bill met Paul Allen, who was 2 years older. Both boys had such enthusiasm for the computer that they became great friends. However, they were two very different people. Allen was more reserved and shy. Bill was energetic and at times aggressive. Nonetheless, the two spent much of their free time together working on programs. Later, Gates left Harvard University to form Microsoft with Paul Allen.

Practice

1. The author's opening paragraph leads the reader to view Bill Gates as

    (1) a rowdy but brilliant school boy.

    (2) one of the most successful businessmen in American history.

    (3) a great inventor, but terrible businessman.

    (4) the inventor of the telephone and telegraph.

    (5) someone who would never reach his goals.

2. You can infer that Bill Gates was very intelligent, but he

    (1) only excelled in math.

    (2) was not willing to learn a new skill.

    (3) clearly enjoyed recess more than class.

    (4) disliked all of his classmates at the new school.

    (5) needed the right school environment to build on his intelligence.

Answers

1. **(2)** By starting the article with information about American tycoons, the author places Gates in their company. All other answers are incorrect details.

2. **(5)** Answer (1) is not an inference; it's a stated detail. Answers (2) and (4) are incorrect details. There is no proof for answer (3).

Recognizing the Author's Style and Tone

The author's style is the way he or she writes—the choice of words, the length of sentences, the level of vocabulary. Style is the way the writer chooses to talk to his or her audience.

The author's tone is revealed in his or her attitude toward the subject. Tone is based on the purpose of the writing and the audience. Tone may be matter-of-fact, critical, friendly, serious, calm, humorous, and many other things.

You will find another example of an author's viewpoint in a book called *Unplug your Kids* by David Dutwin, PhD (Adams Media, 2009). This is an excellent how-to book on raising children in the digital age. Interestingly, the book does not propose taking all television and other media away from children completely. It does show the reader how to work around all that is available. The book is organized around the stages in a child's life, from baby to college bound. In the next section is an excerpt from the book. Can you apply anything here to your life or your household? Also, how would you describe the author's tone?

Applying the Ideas You've Read to a New Situation

If you want to apply the ideas you've read in a passage, you first need to make sure you understand the main idea and the details in the passage. Then apply that information to a new situation that's presented to you.

> What Is a Parent to Do?
>
> Strategies to Maintain a Healthy Electronic Household for Your 0- to 3-Year-Old
>
> Do you need help? I can answer that in two simple questions. Does your child have a television in his or her room? Does he or she watch it more than one hour a day? If the answer is yes to either of these, you ought to reconsider your child's media habits.
>
> It's not easy. Why do people fail to reduce their child's television time, despite best intentions? In short, because they do not have a replacement. If one abruptly turns off the television on a child, what's going to happen? Likely, a lot of screaming. That is because when it comes to children, the most important lesson is distraction! If you have something other than the television at the ready, you will find the transition away from television easier.

So here is your homework for the weekend. When your child is napping or you find some other free time, spend an hour setting up fast "distraction attractions" for your child. These are objects and activities that are likely to divert your child's attention for a half hour or more. Then, when you find yourself putting your child in front of a TV, try one of these alternative approaches.

Distraction Attractions

Ye old kitchen. Take old kitchen objects and place them somewhere easily accessible. As is often the case, such objects are novel and interesting to a child under the age of 3. When needed, pull one out. You'll be amazed how much time they will spend with just an old plastic spatula and an empty cereal box!

The old toy bin. Many families have too many toys. Between hand-me-downs and holiday gifts, many households have literally hundreds of toys, big and small. When you find your child intensely interested in a toy, allow him to play with it for a few days, then put it away for a month just as his interest starts to wane. Then, at that critical moment, say when you are trying to make dinner and your child is hugging your leg and you are ready to turn on the TV, bring out that long-lost toy … The activity center. Do you have an activity center for your children? That is, a place where they can color, paint, use chalk, and the like? Every household needs one. Use this center strategically to minimize television use. For example, say your child starts each day watching television and you want to break the habit. Simply set up a craft for the following morning before you go to bed. For example, cover the activity center with paper and leave out crayons or markers.

… When your child is screaming for something and you are busy doing 10 other things—well, that is the worst moment for you to try to think of something for your child to do and then find the time to set it up. Get in the habit of preplanning these things. Look, your child is going to cry and scream tomorrow … most kids 0 to 3 seem to with pretty regular frequency … get ready before you are in need.

… The key here is to keep it basic. … You need help when you have things to do. Pay bills. Make dinner. Have a conversation with your best friend. … Dress for work. These are the times of the day when interaction is simply impossible. We tend to allow our children to use television when we have no time. The trick is to have these readymade activities that a) take little of your time to set up and b) are quite likely to hold a toddler's attention for a good 15 minutes to a half hour.

So get to it. Get that television out of the [child's] bedroom. Turn off the television when no one is watching, and turn off the adult programming … (news, sitcoms …) when the child is in the room …. And prepare a few simple activities and "toys" for easy access in times of need. The research does not indicate that being a good parent requires you to totally remove television from your child's life. You are just trying to minimize it to a half hour a day—occasionally, an hour. Less is probably better …

From Unplug Your Kids by David Dutwin, PhD, © 2009 by David Dutwin, PhD
Used by permission of Adams Media, an F&W Media, Inc. Co. All rights reserved.

Practice

1. According to the passage, if you are the baby-sitter for a 3-year-old and a 5-year-old and both scream when you turn off the TV during the day, consider doing this:

    (1) Make a note of their bad behavior and give it to their parents.

    (2) Give them both an extra treat when they scream.

    (3) Teach them a new game even if you're not sure they'll like it.

    (4) Prepare a game you know they love ahead of time.

    (5) Let them scream, no matter how long it takes.

2. Which of the following words would you say describe the author's tone?

    (1) dramatic and heavy

    (2) critical and demanding

    (3) theatrical

    (4) agitated

    (5) calm and helpful

3. A main idea of the passage is that

(1) parents need to keep children and television away from each other at all times.

(2) *Teletubbies* is the worst program for 3-year-olds.

(3) you should take the TV out of a child's bedroom and have a back-up activity ready.

(4) a child will play with a spatula and cereal box for a time.

(5) a toddler should be allowed 2 to 3 hours of TV a day.

Answers

1. **(4)** Answer (1) is incorrect; it's not a detail in the passage. Answer (2) is not a correct detail in the passage. The passage does not recommend rewarding screaming with a treat. Answer (3) is not logical. Screaming children are not likely to learn a new game. Answer (5) is not a detail mentioned as an option.

2. **(5)** Answers (1) and (3) are incorrect. The writer's tone is the opposite of dramatic or theatrical. Answer (4) is incorrect; the author is the opposite of agitated, or frantic and stressed. Answer (2) is incorrect. The author does not criticize, but does offer helpful information.

3. **(3)** Answer (1) is incorrect. The author specifically states that children may watch a small amount of television each day. Answer (2) is incorrect since the author mentions the program as an alternative at special times. Answer (4) is a correct detail, not a main idea. Answer (5) is incorrect; it's opposite to the author's recommendations.

Reading Contracts

We do some of our reading to protect ourselves. For example, if you buy a car from someone, you will surely want a contract to protect you as well as the seller. The contract should provide a clear idea of the responsibilities of both the buyer and the seller. Read the following contract. What responsibilities do seller and buyer have in this transaction?

Contract for Purchase of a Car

Buyer's Name _____

Address _____

Phone _____

Seller's Name _____

Address _____

Phone _____

The Seller hereby conveys to the Buyer full ownership and title to the motor vehicle described below:

Description of Motor Vehicle Sold:

Year _____ Make _____ Model _____

VIN: _____

The Buyer hereby agrees to pay the Seller $X on MM/DD/YY, and $Y on the Nth day of each month beginning MM/DD/YY, until all payments made to the Seller total $X.

If Buyer fails to make a payment on or before its due date, a late fee of $X shall be added to the balance due and shall be payable immediately.

Both parties hereby agree that this is an "as-is" sale, with no warranties of any kind expressed or implied.

This agreement shall be governed by the laws of the State of _____ and the County of _____ and any applicable U.S. laws.

The parties hereby signify their agreement to the terms above by their signatures affixed below:

Buyer's signature, date _____

Seller's signature, date _____

Practice

1. Which statement summarizes the content or main idea of this contract?

   (1) A buyer and seller are still discussing the price of the car.

   (2) The buyer will fill out the contract because all the responsibility is with him or her.

   (3) The buyer and seller agree to terms of the sale and promise to abide by them.

   (4) The agreement is governed by the state in which the sale is made.

   (5) A buyer agrees to buy and a seller agrees to sell a car for a stated amount of money to be paid in a certain amount of time.

2. You can conclude from this contract that the buyer

   (1) needs to decide if the color is really right for him or her.

   (2) is the only one governed by the state's laws.

   (3) needs to check the car carefully because it is an "as-is" sale.

   (4) does not need anything more than a check to pick up the car.

   (5) has fewer responsibilities than the seller.

3. If you compare the buyer and seller responsibilities in this contract, you see that the

   (1) buyer only has to say he or she wants the car, while the seller has to deliver it in good shape.

   (2) seller only has to agree to sell the car at some date in the future.

   (3) seller promises to fix all dents, bring a car in perfect condition to the sale, and offer later dates for payments.

   (4) seller gives ownership to the buyer, while the buyer makes payments on a schedule, is penalized for late payment, and agrees that it is an "as-is" sale.

   (5) buyer has no reason not to sign the contract.

Answers

1. **(5)** This is the only answer that includes all the main idea elements. Answer (1) is incorrect because you sign a contract only after the details (including price) have been decided. Answer (2) is incorrect because both parties have responsibilities in the contract. Answer (3) is correct as far as it goes, but it is not the complete main idea. Answer (4) is one detail of the contract, not the main idea.

2. **(3)** The other answers are incorrect details.

3. **(4)** The other answers are incorrect details.

Reading Warranties

Here is another example of nonfiction reading that is meant to protect you: the product warranty. Following is a warranty you might expect to receive with your new coffeemaker.

Bright Mornings Coffeemaker

1-Year Limited Warranty

(Applies only in the United States and Canada)

What does it cover?

This warranty covers any defect in material or workmanship provided; however, Bright Mornings, Inc.'s, liability will not exceed the price of the coffeemaker.

For how long?

The coffeemaker is covered for 1 year after the date of purchase.

How will we help you?

We will provide you with a reasonably similar product as a replacement. The replacement will be either new or factory refurbished.

How do you get service?

Save your receipt as proof of date of sale.

Check our online service site for general warranty service and information (www.Brightmorningsproductprotect.com), or call our toll-free number, 1-555-555-5555, for general warranty service.

If you want to order parts or accessories, call 1-555-555-5555.

What does your warranty not cover?

Damage from misuse, abuse, or neglect.

Damage incurred through commercial use.

Products that have been changed in any way.

Products used or serviced outside the country of service.

Glass parts and other accessories packed with the coffeemaker.

Shipping and handling costs associated with the replacement.

How does state law apply to this warranty?

You have specific legal rights under this warranty. You may also have other rights that vary from state to state or province to province.

Practice

1. You can conclude that the purpose of this warranty statement is to

   (1) explain that a broken coffeemaker must be repaired at your expense.

   (2) ensure you that the product was inspected before you bought it.

   (3) describe the circumstances under which Bright Mornings will repair or replace the unit.

   (4) explain that a repair is the only alternative.

   (5) explain that Bright Mornings never assumes responsibility for a coffeemaker that doesn't work.

2. The main idea of the paragraph on state law is that

(1) only coffeemakers purchased in the state of Illinois are covered by this warranty.

(2) you should check the laws in your state because laws regarding warranties vary from state to state.

(3) you have only the legal rights mentioned in the warranty.

(4) products damaged from commercial use will be replaced.

(5) purchasers must use the coffeemaker only two to three times a week.

3. In order to have this coffeemaker repaired or replaced, the purchaser will have to

(1) send it back with a proof of purchase no older than 1 year.

(2) try to fix it before sending it back.

(3) live in Canada or the United Kingdom.

(4) accept a new or factory refurbished coffeemaker.

(5) answers (1) and (4) above.

Answers

1. **(3)** Answers (1), (4), and (5) are incorrect details. Answer (2) is incorrect; the warranty never mentions inspections.

2. **(2)** Answer (1) is incorrect. Illinois is never mentioned in the warranty. Answers (3) and (4) are opposite to the information in the warranty. Answer (5) is an incorrect detail.

3. **(5)** Answers (2) and (3) are incorrect details.

Reading Workplace Documents

Finally, workplace documents contain important information for employees. It is essential that you understand what any workplace document contains and how it applies to you. Following is a portion of a federal law.

What Does the FMLA (Family Medical Leave Act) Entitle Employees To?

The XYZ Clothing Company follows FMLA provisions with its employees. Please read this document carefully and refer to it whenever you face a family medical emergency. If you have questions related to this policy, please visit the personnel department and we will make every effort to clarify the following.

Basic Provisions/Requirements

The FMLA, a federal law passed in 1993, entitles eligible employees of covered employers to take job-protected, unpaid leave for specified family and medical reasons. Eligible employees are entitled to the following.

Twelve workweeks of leave in any 12-month period for:

Birth and care of the employee's child, within 1 year of birth

Placement with the employee of a child for adoption or foster care, within 1 year of the placement

Care of an immediate family member (spouse, child, parent) who has a serious health condition

For the employee's own serious health condition that makes the employee unable to perform the essential functions of his or her job

Any qualifying *exigency* [a need or emergency] arising out of the fact that the employee's spouse, son, daughter, or parent is on active duty or has been notified of an impending call or order to active duty in the U.S. National Guard or Reserves in support of a contingency operation

Twenty-six workweeks of leave during a single 12-month period to care for a covered service member with a serious injury or illness if the employee is the spouse, son, daughter, parent, or next of kin of the service member (Military Caregiver Leave)

If an employee was receiving group health benefits when leave began, an employer must maintain them at the same level and in the same manner during periods of FMLA leave as if the employee had continued to work. An employee may elect (or the employer may require) the substitution of any accrued paid leave (vacation, sick, personal, etc.) for periods of unpaid FMLA leave ....

Employees may take FMLA leave intermittently or on a reduced leave schedule (that is, in blocks of time less than the full amount of the entitlement) when medically necessary or when the leave is due to a qualifying exigency ….

When the need for leave is foreseeable, an employee must give the employer at least 30 days' notice, or as much notice as is practicable. When the leave is not foreseeable, the employee must provide notice as soon as practicable in the particular circumstances. An employee must comply with the employer's usual and customary notice and procedural requirements ….

An employee who returns from FMLA leave is entitled to be restored to the same or an equivalent job with equivalent pay, benefits, and other terms and conditions of employment ….

Practice

1. The main idea of this statement is that

   (1) employees may take leave of 12 unpaid workweeks in any 2-year period for family and medical reasons.

   (2) employees may take job-protected leave for the care of a child but not for a spouse.

   (3) employees are entitled to take unpaid leave for specified family and medical reasons.

   (4) employees are not entitled to take unpaid leave for medical care of family or spouse until the employee has worked for the company for 3 years.

   (5) medical care does not apply to the care of your parents.

2. Since the XYZ Clothing Company provides group health benefits, you can conclude that

   (1) on medical leave, employees will lose benefits until they return to work.

   (2) the employee on leave will maintain health benefits for 12 weeks.

   (3) the employee on leave will regain health benefits 1 year after returning to work.

   (4) the employee will maintain health benefits during and after the leave.

   (5) the employee will maintain only half the usual benefits during the leave.

3. Based on the information in this passage, which of the following statements is true?

(1) It is never necessary to give notice of a leave.

(2) An employee may take leave when a spouse returns to active military duty.

(3) Intermittent leave is never an option.

(4) An employee may not expect paid leave for the adoption of a child.

(5) Eligible employees are entitled to 4 weeks of leave in a 12-month period.

Answers

1. **(3)** All other answers contain incorrect facts.

2. **(4)** All other answers contain incorrect facts.

3. **(2)** Answers (1), (3), and (4) are opposite to what is stated. Answer (5) is an incorrect fact.

Fiction Reveals the Story

In This Chapter

- Overview of fiction: plot, setting, characters, conflict, and point of view in the short story and the novel
- GED-like questions to practice the skills you'll be tested on
- Answers and explanations for all the questions

Most people love to read short stories. Why? First of all, they're short. More than that, however, they can be very satisfying to read. If the story is well written, you'll be involved in the plot in no time. You'll ask yourself, "What's going to happen next?" and you'll search for the answers. You'll like or dislike the characters and put yourself in their places to solve problems. In this chapter, you'll learn about all the elements of a story. In addition to the plot and characters, you'll learn about the setting, the conflicts, and the point of view from which the story was written. All of these comprise the important foundation upon which a great story is built.

What about reading skills? Simply put, everything you've learned about main ideas, details, and vocabulary applies here as well. You see, the type of reading you do may change, but the basic skills do not. In this chapter you'll add to your treasury of reading skills. You'll learn to get meaning from context, draw conclusions, make judgments and inferences, and analyze the tone and more.

On the Language Arts: Reading Test, you'll read selections from novels and short stories. *Fiction* is defined as stories that are made up by the author and often based on imaginary events.

Uncover the Plot

Think of the plot of the story as a series of events that provide an opportunity for conflict. Plot holds the story together, just as your spine holds you upright. Plot gets and keeps our interest, but plot cannot stand alone. When you add the characters' emotions, plot becomes a story.

Another way of thinking of plot is that the author arranges a sequence of events to develop his or her basic idea (we're searching for main idea again!). The plot, then, becomes a logical series of events that allow for a beginning, middle, and end. Because short stories are exactly that—short—the author usually has time for only one plot.

IN THE KNOW

Have you ever had an idea for a short story? What were the important elements of the story? You began, if only in your mind, with a great idea—one in which you could envision the beginning, middle, and end. Here are all the elements you'd have to keep in mind as you constructed your story:

- **Plot.** The sequence of events that captures our attention and keeps us interested.
- **Setting.** Where does the story take place?
- **Characters.** You provide a summary of characters through what they do, say, think.
- **Conflict.** What goes wrong?
- **Point of view.** Who tells the story?

You met Edgar Allan Poe in Chapter 22 when you read the poem "The Raven." Edgar Allan Poe was not the first short story writer in American literature. Washington Irving has that honor, having written "Rip Van Winkle" and "The Legend of Sleepy Hollow." However, Poe is considered one of the best short story writers in American literature—and you'll soon see why. He draws you into the plot immediately. Someone once said that the plot of a short story involves a main character who wants something very badly. The character pursues what he wants despite opposition and struggles. In the end, he either wins or loses.

How does this definition of plot apply to Poe's story, "The Cask of Amontillado"? In the very first sentence you know that this plot is built upon something the narrator wants badly—*retribution*. This is simply another way to say he wants revenge, vengeance, or payback. In the second paragraph, the narrator smiles at the thought of Fortunato's *immolation*. The word means killing someone as a ritual sacrifice. This is a scary thought—perfect for a scary story.

Read this small portion of the story and find the lines that push the plot forward. What happens first, second, third …? What grievous deed does the narrator have planned?

"The Cask of Amontillado"

THE thousand injuries of Fortunato I had borne as I best could, but when he ventured upon insult, I vowed revenge. You, who so well know the nature of my soul, will not suppose, however, that I gave utterance to a threat. AT LENGTH I would be avenged; this was a point definitively settled—but the very definitiveness with which it was resolved precluded the idea of risk. I must not only punish, but punish with impunity. A wrong is unredressed when retribution overtakes its redresser. It is equally unredressed when the avenger fails to make himself felt as such to him who has done the wrong.

It must be understood that neither by word nor deed had I given Fortunato cause to doubt my good will. I continued as was my wont, to smile in his face, and he did not perceive that my smile NOW was at the thought of his immolation.

He had a weak point—this Fortunato—although in other regards he was a man to be respected and even feared. He prided himself on his connoisseurship in wine. Few Italians have the true virtuoso spirit. For the most part their enthusiasm is adopted to suit the time and opportunity to practise imposture upon the British and Austrian MILLIONAIRES. In painting and gemmary, Fortunato, like his countrymen, was a quack, but in the matter of old wines he was sincere. In this respect I did not differ from him materially; I was skillful in the Italian vintages myself, and bought largely whenever I could.

It was about dusk, one evening during the supreme madness of the carnival season, that I encountered my friend. He accosted me with excessive warmth, for he had been drinking much. The man wore motley. He had on a tight-fitting parti-striped dress and his head was surmounted by the conical cap and bells. I was so pleased to see him that I thought I should never have done wringing his hand.

I said to him—"My dear Fortunato, you are luckily met. How remarkably well you are looking to-day! But I have received a pipe of what passes for Amontillado, and I have my doubts."

"How?" said he, "Amontillado? A pipe? Impossible? And in the middle of the carnival?"

"I have my doubts," I replied; "and I was silly enough to pay the full Amontillado price without consulting you in the matter. You were not to be found, and I was fearful of losing a bargain."

"Amontillado!"

"I have my doubts."

"Amontillado!"

"And I must satisfy them."

"Amontillado!"

"As you are engaged, I am on my way to Luchesi. If any one has a critical turn, it is he. He will tell me"—

"Luchesi cannot tell Amontillado from Sherry."

"And yet some fools will have it that his taste is a match for your own."

"Come let us go."

"Whither?"

"To your vaults."

Practice

1. Poe immediately engages you in the plot by declaring,

    (1) "I have my doubts."

    (2) "… this was a point not definitively settled."

    (3) "… neither by word nor deed had I given Fortunato cause to doubt my good will."

    (4) "I vowed revenge."

    (5) "He had a weak point—this Fortunato."

2. In a short story, the plot needs a main or central character—called the pro-tagonist (the narrator here), but the protagonist needs someone to oppose, the antagonist. Who or what is the antagonist in this story?

   (1) Fortunato

   (2) motley

   (3) Luchesi

   (4) Amontillado

   (5) a pipe

Answers

1. **(4)** Poe has a plan for the plot, and that is revenge. Plot means the action you can expect. None of the other answers engage you in the plot. Answers (3) and (5) describe Fortunato, not the plot. Answer (2) is an incorrect version of the sentence. Answer (1) is a word play the narrator uses to entice Fortunato.

2. **(1)** Whom does the narrator oppose: the antagonist? The answer is clearly Fortunato, who is responsible for the "thousand injuries" the narrator has borne. None of the other answers is an antagonist. (2) is simply a description of his brightly colored outfit. (3) is a harmless character whose name is used to infuriate Fortunato. (4) Amontillado is important to the action, but it's still just the wine. (5), a pipe, is simply a wine container.

Imagine the Setting

As you would guess, the setting of a story has to do with the time, place, and condi-tions of the story's location. In the story you just read, the setting is clear—but also contradictory. The main characters meet at a carnival filled with fun and brightly dressed people. But Poe's story develops into a dark plot. Poe's theme or main idea for the story is that the narrator seeks revenge. This gives a very dark and mysterious feel to the setting. Early on you learn that the narrator wants revenge and you have the distinct feeling that it will take place in the vaults—a very dark thought. What contradiction between dark and light does Poe set up early in the story in order to set the scene?

Practice

1. Poe sets the scene by contrasting

   (1) happy people in motley with dark thoughts of revenge.

   (2) good wine with Amontillado.

   (3) sunny weather with the storms the revelers are experiencing.

   (4) the perfectly quiet Fortunato with the narrator.

   (5) good weather with bad.

Answer

1. **(1)** The other answers are either opposite to the truth or inaccurate.

Use Context Clues

No matter what the setting is or how the plot develops, as readers, we're always faced with vocabulary we may not be familiar with. Do we always get out dictionaries to look up unknown words? Of course we don't. For most people, that would ruin the progress of the story. It would be inconvenient as well. So what can we do? The answer is that we unlock meaning by using the clues around the unknown word. We call these context clues because we draw a conclusion about the meaning of a word by considering the *context* in which it's used. There may even be a synonym for the word. For example, look at this sentence: The Mann Building is the tallest *edifice* in a city of many tall buildings. The context tells you that *edifice* is a synonym for *building*. There are many opportunities to use this skill in "The Cask of Amontillado."

You make *inferences* when you take clues or a set of facts from the text and add your own knowledge and experience to figure out what the author means.

DEFINITION

Context includes all the words and sentences around the unknown word. In these sentences, you'll find hints to the meaning of the unknown word. Making **inferences** means making a judgment or drawing a conclusion based on events or hints in the story.

In the following quoted sentences, use what you already know to infer the meaning of an unknown word—*impunity*. In the following sentence, what does the narrator want?

> AT LENGTH I would be avenged; this was a point definitively settled—but the very definitiveness with which it was resolved precluded the idea of risk.

The narrator wants revenge. It must be definite and it must include no risk to himself. Now, with this explanation or context in mind, define the word *impunity* in the following sentence:

> I must not only punish, but punish with impunity.

The first thing you see is the similarity of one part of the word to the word *punish*. Adding *–im* to the beginning (a common negative prefix) simply makes the word negative. Add the idea that the narrator would not allow risk to himself and you realize that impunity means that he has set up his scheme to avoid punishment. Now you've actually used two techniques to unlock the meaning of an unknown word: You've used the content of the word itself (im+punity) and the ideas and words around it.

Let's try this again. Look at the third paragraph in the story, "The Cask of Amontillado." What does *connoisseurship* mean? Look at the entire paragraph for clues to its meaning.

Practice

1. As used in the third paragraph of "The Cask of Amontillado," *connoisseurship* means

   (1) tricking someone.

   (2) owning a wine shop.

   (3) expert opinion.

   (4) being a good friend.

   (5) winning a contest.

Answer

1. **(3)**. The narrator says Fortunato is not an expert (a synonym for *connoisseurship*) in art, but he is in wine. There is no mention of tricking (1), owning a wine shop (2), being a friend (4), or winning a contest (5).

Get to Know the Characters

As you've learned, the protagonist in a story is a central character, a leading figure who has a problem to solve. That is certainly true of Della in the story you are about to read. However, in this story, who is the antagonist—the person or thing who opposes Della? Is it Della's husband, or is it someone or something else entirely that Della must oppose?

The American writer O. Henry (1862–1910) published "The Gift of the Magi" in 1906. Here are some things to think about as you read the story:

- What is the setting of the story? Is it set in modern times?

- Who are the main characters?

- What is the main problem to be solved in the course of the plot?

- Which words didn't you know? How did the context help you to figure them out? What makes this young wife cry?

"The Gift of the Magi"

One dollar and eighty-seven cents. That was all. And sixty cents of it was in pennies. Pennies saved one and two at a time by bulldozing the grocer and the vegetable man and the butcher until one's cheeks burned with the silent imputation of parsimony that such close dealing implied. Three times Della counted it. One dollar and eighty-seven cents. And the next day would be Christmas.

There was clearly nothing left to do but flop down on the shabby little couch and howl. So Della did it. Which instigates the moral reflection that life is made up of sobs, sniffles, and smiles, with sniffles predominating.

While the mistress of the home is gradually subsiding from the first stage to the second, take a look at the home. A furnished flat at $8 per week. It did not exactly beggar description, but it certainly had that word on the look-out for the mendicancy squad.

Della finished her cry and attended to her cheeks with the powder rag. She stood by the window and looked out dully at a grey cat walking a grey fence in a grey backyard. Tomorrow would be Christmas Day, and she had only

$1.87 with which to buy Jim a present. She had been saving every penny she could for months, with this result. Twenty dollars a week doesn't go far. Expenses had been greater than she had calculated. They always are. Only $1.87 to buy a present for Jim. Her Jim. Many a happy hour she had spent planning for something nice for him. Something fine and rare and sterling—something just a little bit near to being worthy of the honour of being owned by Jim ….

Suddenly she whirled from the window and stood before the glass. Her eyes were shining brilliantly, but her face had lost its colour within twenty seconds. Rapidly she pulled down her hair and let it fall to its full length.

Now, there were two possessions of the James Dillingham Youngs in which they both took a mighty pride. One was Jim's gold watch that had been his father's and his grandfather's. The other was Della's hair. Had the Queen of Sheba lived in the flat across the airshaft, Della would have let her hair hang out of the window some day to dry just to depreciate Her Majesty's jewels and gifts. Had King Solomon been the janitor, with all his treasures piled up in the basement, Jim would have pulled out his watch every time he passed, just to see him pluck at his beard from envy.

So now Della's beautiful hair fell about her, rippling and shining like a cascade of brown waters. It reached below her knee and made itself almost a garment for her. And then she did it up again nervously and quickly. Once she faltered for a minute and stood still while a tear or two splashed on the worn red carpet.

On went her old brown jacket; on went her old brown hat. With a whirl of skirts and with the brilliant sparkle still in her eyes, she cluttered out of the door and down the stairs to the street.

Where she stopped the sign read: "Mme Sofronie. Hair Goods of All Kinds." Della ran up the steps to the shop and collected herself, panting.

"Will you buy my hair?" asked Della.

Practice

1. You can tell that Della and Jim's relationship is

    (1) caring and loving.

    (2) good when they give each other presents.

    (3) thoughtless.

    (4) lacking consideration.

    (5) one of protagonist and antagonist.

2. What is the meaning of *parsimony* in paragraph 1?

    (1) generosity

    (2) thriftiness

    (3) happiness

    (4) emotional

    (5) straitlaced

3. In terms of the plot, how do you think O. Henry will have Della solve the problem of having no money for gifts?

    (1) O. Henry will see that Della inherits a lot of money.

    (2) Jim will forbid Della from spending any money on him for Christmas.

    (3) O. Henry will have Della and Jim evicted from their apartment.

    (4) Della will get a well-paying full-time job.

    (5) Della will sell her hair to Mme Sofronie.

Answers

1. **(1)** The other answers are not true of the couple. The couple are not protagonist and antagonist (5), since we see that they care deeply for each other. If anything, the only protagonist—or force—in the story is the fact that they are poor.

2. **(2)** Della has to be thrifty to make her small amount of money last. *Parsimony* makes her cheeks burn. She's not happy (3) about it but neither does she show the tradesmen that she's overly emotional (4). You can't substitute the word generosity (1) for parsimony: You can't be broke and generous, at least not with money. Nothing in the story says that Della is straitlaced (5).

3. **(5)** There is no mention of people from whom they might inherit money (1). (2) is incorrect; Della and Jim don't have the sort of relationship in which Jim would forbid Della anything. Answers (3) and (4) are unlikely; there are no clues to either happening.

Reveal the Conflict

There may be no outright fighting in a story and still there is conflict. A good short story always has conflict. It's for you the reader to figure out what the main characters want or yearn for and what is standing in the way of their achieving it. The conflict may be literally one person against another, a person against himself, or a person against outside forces. In the story you just read, Della is clearly struggling against forces outside her marriage. She loves her husband and wants so badly to give him a Christmas gift. But circumstances didn't allow her to. As it says in the story, "Twenty dollars a week doesn't go far. Expenses had been greater than she had calculated. They always are. Only $1.87 to buy a present for Jim. Her Jim …." Try, if you can, to read the entire story. You'll see why O. Henry was considered the master of surprise endings.

Determine Point of View

Writers think very hard before deciding on point of view. For example, in some stories, one person's perspective (the "I" character) may be the most effective in describing the main character's feelings and reactions. If the point of view is from someone else's view, the narrator has the power to create a more complicated story line with many characters. The narrator knows all and can tell all!

IN THE KNOW

You may be asking, "What about longer works of fiction, such as novels? Do the same rules apply?" The answer is yes, a novel, although longer, still has a plot, setting, characters, conflict, and point of view.

Understand How Foreshadowing Works

Do you remember this paragraph in "The Gift of the Magi"?

> Now, there were two possessions of the James Dillingham Youngs in which they both took a mighty pride. One was Jim's gold watch that had been his father's and his grandfather's. The other was Della's hair.

You knew from this paragraph that these were things of value both monetarily and emotionally. The minute you read the next two sentences, you knew what was about to happen. The author uses a technique called *foreshadowing* to give the reader clues about what will happen later in the story:

> On went her old brown jacket; on went her old brown hat. With a whirl of skirts and with the brilliant sparkle still in her eyes, she cluttered out of the door and down the stairs to the street.

> Where she stopped the sign read: "Mme Sofronie. Hair Goods of All Kinds."

Now read the opening of a novel entitled *Buried*, written in 2005 by Michael Diamond (1939–). The main character is Gabriela Leone. Her innocent father was murdered by order of Gen. Augusto Pinochet in the aftermath of the military coup against the Chilean government of President Salvadore Allende in 1973. Gabriela is chosen to accomplish a mission on behalf of her people.

As you read, think about the technique of foreshadowing used by both short story and novel writers. Do you see evidence of that technique in *Buried*? What spiritual event takes place?

> *Buried*

> There is neither up nor down, nor width nor breadth in the realm of the spirit, and spirit moves through all matter and all manner of things, circling infinitely past our imagined beginnings and endings. But never, never is the world of spirit unmindful of us. We are its children.

> Occasionally, if we are disposed, it shows us some small part of itself, the hem of a garment or a shaft of light. By doing so, the spirit world reminds us that we are not alone and that we ought to be mindful. We may have stumbled upon a truth that we should not forget. We may have embarked on a path from which the spirits don't want us to stray.

So it was, in Calama, Chile, in the year one thousand nine hundred and sixty-eight, that Gabriela Leone, when she was fifteen years old, saw the statue of the Virgin Mary cry.

© 2005 by Michael Diamond

Practice

1. Which words foreshadow the way the plot will develop?

    (1) "neither up nor down"

    (2) "nor width nor breadth"

    (3) "saw the statue of the Virgin Mary cry"

    (4) "truth that we should not forget"

    (5) "We are its children."

2. In the second paragraph, the author talks about our "embark[ing] on a path from which the spirits don't want us to stray." This idea is meaningful for Gabriela because

    (1) no one will disbelieve her, so she'll never have to stray from the truth.

    (2) she doesn't believe that she has seen anything unusual.

    (3) she probably didn't choose to discuss her vision with anyone.

    (4) she will encounter people who will not believe in her experience, yet she can't stray from the truth.

    (5) she clearly does not believe that "the spirit moves through all matter …."

3. You can conclude that this introduction to the story is meant to

    (1) call to mind another warrior, St. Joan.

    (2) scare you with stories of the spirit world.

    (3) help you become a warrior.

    (4) give you absolutely no clue to plot development.

    (5) describe the afterlife.

4. You can infer that the following might happen as the plot develops:

(1) Gabriela seeks justice for her father's murder.

(2) Gabriela moves from Calama to Santiago.

(3) Gabriela meets and marries the man of her dreams.

(4) Gabriela loses all connection to the world of spirit.

(5) Gabriela becomes the mayor of Calama.

Answers

1. **(3)** The question asks about how the plot will develop. All of the other answers talk about or describe spirit, while answer (3) tells of something that happened. That happening will lead to actions and reactions in the plot.

2. **(4)** Answer (1) is not logical. Certainly many people will not believe her story. We have no proof that answers (2), (3), or (5) are true.

3. **(1)** There are great similarities to the hero, St. Joan. There is no proof that the author wants to scare you (2) and certainly no proof that he wants to help you become a warrior (3). Answer (4) is incorrect because the introduction does give clues to the plot. Answer (5) is incorrect; there are no descriptions of the afterlife.

4. **(1)** Answers (2), (3), (4), and (5) are incorrect. None of these answers point to details that are discussed or inferred in the opening to the novel.

Poetry Is Meant to Be Read

In This Chapter

- Overview of the meaning, figurative language, rhythm and rhyme, and imagery of poetry
- GED-like questions to practice the skills you'll be tested on
- Answers and explanations for all the questions

Perhaps you, like many people, have always thought that poems were puzzles to be solved. The meaning was not always apparent. The word choice was puzzling and even the form was strange. Well, you're about to solve the puzzle as you read through this chapter. You will figure out what the poet wants you to understand. You will encounter a better way to read poetry and easier ways to understand the words, the thoughts, and the forms.

There are as many topics—or themes—in poetry as there are in any other form of literature. Take your choice: love, war, nature, death, religion, happiness, sadness, new love, lost love, and more. One question to ask is, "How does the poet express thoughts on these subjects in a way that is significantly different from everything else I've read?"

How Poetry Compares to Prose

As you learned in Chapter 23, prose is a writing style that is straightforward. Poetry, however, uses figurative language and descriptive language that often appeals to our senses.

The following makes comparison of poetry to prose clear and dramatic. The descriptive poetry is from a poem called "Daffodils" by William Wordsworth (1770–1850):

> I wandered lonely as a cloud
> That floats on high o'er vales and hills,
> When all at once I saw a crowd,
> A host of golden daffodils;
> Beside the lake, beneath the trees,
> Fluttering and dancing in the breeze …

Here is the same thought in straightforward prose:

> I was walking one day when I saw a large number of yellow daffodils swaying in the breeze.

A poem is simply an idea the writer communicates by representing one thing in terms of another. In the previous example, the poet uses language in a special way to compare himself to a cloud ("I wandered lonely as a cloud"). This representation (man/cloud) allows you to experience, to see everything—as a cloud would from above. Sound mysterious? It really isn't. You may think of this as a puzzle—an idea inside an idea. But you can solve that puzzle by observing the important aspects of poetry writing. What can you specifically do to unlock the meaning?

Poets have many techniques for making a poem meaningful to the reader. How a poet accomplishes this and how you get meaning from poems are the main subjects of this chapter.

Getting Meaning from a Poem

What can you, the reader, do to start the process of deriving meaning from a poem? The answer is so simple, yet few people do it: read the title! Relate the title to what you already know so that you begin your reading thoughtfully and, possibly, with a picture in your mind's eye. When you read the title of Wordsworth's poem, did you see yellow flowers in your mind's eye? Undoubtedly you did.

Secondly, read the poem out loud. This is not an earth-shattering idea, and yet few people think to include this valuable step when they want to get meaning from a poem. When you read out loud, you pay attention to the flow of ideas. You are also more likely to pay attention to the poem's punctuation, and that is crucial for meaning. Remember to pause at a comma, stop briefly at a semicolon, and make a full stop at a period. Carefully observing the punctuation will make a big difference in how well and how quickly you understand the poem.

Figurative Language in Poetry

Have you ever said something that you didn't mean literally, or factually? However, what you said expressed an idea perfectly because it created a picture. For example, after being outside with the children in the snow, Amelia said, "My feet feel like blocks of ice!" We know that Amelia's feet have not turned to blocks of ice, but, if she wants sympathy, the picture is perfect. Blocks of ice represent her feet—and that is figurative language.

One of the great American poets, Carl Sandburg (1878–1967) was a genius with figurative language. Read his poem, "Fog." Ask yourself how the poet represents fog in the poem:

> The fog comes
> on little cat feet.
>
> It sits looking
> over harbor and city
> on silent haunches
> and then moves on.

This poem is more than a comparison: The fog becomes a cat. By bringing these two figures together, Sandburg painted a perfect picture of fog creeping in, sitting a while, and then moving on. Six lines say it all, and that is the power of figurative language.

Different figures of speech are used to accomplish different effects. In "Fog," the poet uses a figure of speech called a metaphor in which two unlike things—living cat and inanimate, or nonliving, fog—are shown to have something in common. The poem is a powerful example of a technique called *personification*. The poet gives living qualities to something that is not alive—such as the fog.

 DEFINITION

Personification attributes a human quality to an object.

There are many kinds of figurative language:

- *Metaphor:* Two unlike things are brought together. Examples:

  In August the streets were a furnace through which we had to walk.

  Her lips were perfect rosebuds.

- *Simile:* A comparison is formed using *like* or *as.* Examples:

  Her lips were like perfect rosebuds.

  Life is like an onion: you peel it off one layer at a time, and sometimes you weep.

- *Hyperbole:* An exaggerated statement. Example:

  "I think this is the most extraordinary collection of human talent, of human knowledge, that has ever been gathered at the White House—with the possible exception of when Thomas Jefferson dined alone."

  —President John F. Kennedy at a White House dinner honoring 49 Nobel Prize winners, April 29, 1962

- *Onomatopoeia:* Words that sound like the object or actions referred to. Examples:

  The bees buzzed around us, menacing our every move.

  If you hear the hiss of a snake, jump away!

Read the first three lines of "The Taxi" by Amy Lowell (1874–1925). What figure of speech does she use? What two things are compared?

> When I go away from you
> The world beats dead
> Like a slackened drum.

You probably realized that the unlikely—but effective—comparison was between the world and a slackened drum. You know that this is a simile because the comparison is joined by the word *like.*

Ralph Waldo Emerson (1803–1882) wrote "The Concord Hymn" in 1836 for the dedication of the *Obelisk,* a monument built in Concord, Massachusetts. The monument commemorates the men who died in the Battle of Lexington and Concord (April 19, 1775), the first battle of the American Revolution.

Following is the first *stanza* of the hymn. Can you identify an example of hyperbole in this stanza?

> By the rude bridge that arched the flood,
> Their flag to April's breeze unfurled,
> Here once the embattled farmers stood,
> And fired the shot heard round the world.

Although the sounds of war are loud, "the shot heard round the world" is obviously an exaggeration.

DEFINITION

A **stanza** is a number of lines of verse that form a unit within the poem. In many poems, each stanza has the same number of lines and the same rhythm and rhyme scheme.

And finally, read the very moving language of poet Linda Eve Diamond (1968–). How does she use figurative language in the following poem to enhance the image? Which form of figurative language appears in the first stanza?

TWO POETS

> Their lives were poetry
> elegant, metered and rhymed.
> Then she entered his poem
> and into her verse he climbed.

> Meter's graceful logic lost
> rhyme giving way to abyss
> to the free verse of love,
> the chaos and charm
> the epoch poem
> of two lives entwined.

Linda Eve Diamond, *The Human Experience* (ASJA Press, 2007)

In an extended metaphor, the poet compares two people's lives as they come together to poetry. Their lives were, as they intertwined, *elegant, metered,* and *rhymed*, all aspects of poetry.

Read the following poem, "The Road Not Taken," by Robert Frost (1874–1963). How does the term *metaphor* apply to the entire poem? As you read the poem, look for the answer to the question, what do you do at a fork in the road?

> Two roads diverged in a yellow wood,
> And sorry I could not travel both
> And be one traveler, long I stood
> And looked down one as far as I could
> To where it bent in the undergrowth.
>
> Then took the other, as just as fair,
> And having perhaps the better claim,
> Because it was grassy and wanted wear;
> Though as for that the passing there
> Had worn them really about the same.
>
> And both that morning equally lay
> In leaves no step had trodden black.
> Oh, I kept the first for another day!
> Yet knowing how way leads on to way,
> I doubted if I should ever come back.
>
> I shall be telling this with a sigh
> Somewhere ages and ages hence:
> Two roads diverged in a wood, and I—
> I took the one less traveled by,
> And that has made all the difference.

You'll recall that a metaphor employs two unlike things or ideas and brings them together to express what they have in common. The facts are easy to explain: The poet is out for a walk; he comes to a fork in the road; he has to choose a path. The question is, is that all the poem has to say? Of course, the answer is no.

What other meaning might the two roads have? Why are the diverging roads a figure of speech? One explanation is that the poem describes the difficult choices people make all along the road of life. The words *sorry* and *sigh*, however, make the tone of the poem somewhat gloomy. In the future, the traveler may regret not having chosen the other road. He realizes he probably won't pass that road again.

Robert Frost offered another explanation:

> "One stanza of 'The Road Not Taken' was written while I was sitting on a sofa in the middle of England: was found three or four years later, and I couldn't bear not to finish it. I wasn't thinking about myself there, but about a friend who had gone off to war, a person who, whichever road he went, would be sorry he didn't go the other. He was hard on himself that way."
>
> —Bread Loaf Writers' Conference, August 1953

Earlier in the chapter you read the first three lines of "The Taxi" by Amy Lowell. Now read the entire poem with an eye out for figurative language. As you read, ask yourself, what human qualities does the taxi ride have?

> When I go away from you
> The world beats dead
> Like a slackened drum.
> I call out for you against the jutted stars
> And shout into the ridges of the wind.
> Streets coming fast,
> One after the other,
> Wedge you away from me,
> And the lamps of the city prick my eyes
> So that I can no longer see your face.
> Why should I leave you,
> To wound myself upon the sharp edges of the night?

Practice

1. The main idea of "The Taxi" is that

    (1) the poet and her friend do not get along.

    (2) the poet has been wounded by glass.

    (3) this is going to be the shortest taxi ride she's ever taken.

    (4) leaving the one she loves is as painful as if she had been wounded.

    (5) the taxi driver is driving too slowly.

2. Which one of these phrases is an example of personification?

    (1) One after the other

    (2) I call out for you

    (3) Streets coming fast

    (4) Why should I leave you?

    (5) When I go away from you

Answers

1. **(4)** The entire poem talks about the pain of leaving someone and likens the pain to being wounded. Answer (1) is the opposite of the truth. Answers (2), (3), and (5) are facts not found in the poem.

2. **(3)** This is the only answer that assigns a living quality—the ability to move fast—to a nonliving thing—streets. Answers (1), (2), (4), and (5) are all details in the poem.

Rhythm and Rhyme in Poetry

If you read poetry aloud, you can hear the rhythm and rhyme. An excellent way to practice hearing rhythm and rhyme is to start by reading *limericks*. You may remember reading limericks as a child. Because they are simple and short, limericks were often used to introduce children to poetry (think back to Mother Goose rhymes). Limericks are only five lines. Lines 1, 2, and 5 have 7 to 10 syllables, (i.e., one or more letters that correspond to a unit of spoken language) and rhyme with each other. Lines 3 and 4 may have 5 to 7 syllables and also rhyme with each other. In limericks you can easily hear the stressed syllables and rhyming ends of lines. You need to know about rhythm and rhyme in order to get the full impact of poetry.

DEFINITION

A **limerick** is a humorous verse of five lines in which the first, second, and fifth lines rhyme with each other, and the third and fourth lines, which are shorter, form a rhymed couplet (a pair of rhyming lines).

As you may already know, limericks are an old form of poetry. A variety of limericks can be traced back to the fourteenth century. Start by reading this limerick by Edward Lear (1812–1888):

> There was an Old Man with a beard,
> Who said, "It is just as I feared!
> Two Owls and a Hen,
> Four Larks and a Wren,
> Have all built their nests in my beard!"

Does this limerick follow the limerick pattern? Count the syllables in the first line.

> 1   2 3 4 5 6 7 8
>
> There was an Old Man with a beard

The limerick has the correct number of syllables in lines 1, 2, and 5. All have eight syllables.

Which words are accented in lines 1, 2, and 5? In other words, which words do you hear emphasized when you read the limerick aloud? It's important to hear the accented words, because in the repeated accents you find the rhythm of the limerick. The accented words in lines 1, 2, and 5 are italicized below:

> There *was* an Old *Man* with a *beard*

> Who *said*, "It is *just* as I *feared*!

> Have *all* built their *nests* in my *beard*!"

Listening for Rhythm and Rhyme

Now when you return to Wordsworth's poem "Daffodils," you can read it with more understanding of the way it sounds. Read "Daffodils" out loud. Listen for accents (rhythm) and rhymes in each stanza:

> I wandered lonely as a cloud
> That floats on high o'er vales and hills,
> When all at once I saw a crowd,
> A host, of golden daffodils;
> Beside the lake, beneath the trees,
> Fluttering and dancing in the breeze.

Continuous as the stars that shine
And twinkle on the milky way,
They stretched in never-ending line
Along the margin of a bay:
Ten thousand saw I at a glance,
Tossing their heads in sprightly dance.

The waves beside them danced, but they
Out-did the sparkling leaves in glee;
A poet could not be but gay,
In such a jocund company!
I gazed—and gazed—but little thought
What wealth the show to me had brought:

For oft, when on my couch I lie
In vacant or in pensive mood,
They flash upon that inward eye
Which is the bliss of solitude;
And then my heart with pleasure fills,
And dances with the daffodils.

Practice

1. In the first stanza, daffodils

    (1) take a human form as a crowd.

    (2) stand perfectly still.

    (3) are not able to take the poet's attention.

    (4) is an example of onomatopoeia.

    (5) wander lonely as a cloud.

2. In the second stanza, you can conclude that these words are meant to enforce the idea of many, many daffodils.

    (1) Margin of a bay

    (2) Tossing their heads

    (3) Heads in a sprightly dance

    (4) Continuous, never-ending, ten thousand

    (5) On the milky way

3. The poet's mood is

   (1) one of yearning for a lost love.

   (2) dreamy and content.

   (3) anxious and fearful.

   (4) giddy.

   (5) fearful.

4. The theme of the poem

   (1) shows human emotion inspired by nature.

   (2) is that human beings are not inspired by beautiful nature.

   (3) the daffodils stand for the death of living things.

   (4) is that we should stop working every spring.

   (5) is that the poet wants to live in solitude at all times.

Answers

1. **(1)** The poet says, "at once I saw a crowd," as if he were talking about people. Answers (2), (3), (4), and (5) are all incorrect details.

2. **(4)** All of these words contribute to the idea of "many." Answers (1), (2), (3), and (5) are all incorrect details.

3. **(2)** In the first stanza, the poet floats. In the second stanza the poet says he couldn't be anything but gay. In the fourth stanza he says, "my heart with pleasure fills." Answers (1), (3), (4), and (5) are all incorrect details.

4. **(1)** Answers (2), (3), and (5) are the opposite of information in the poem. Answer (4) is an incorrect detail.

Blank Verse

Did you know that poetry does not have to rhyme? In fact, there is an enormous amount of unrhymed poetry called *blank verse*. While blank verse is unrhymed, it has rhythm. You will also read about free verse that has neither rhyme nor rhythm.

> **DEFINITION**
>
> **Blank verse** is unrhymed verse that has a regular meter, or beat. The beat in blank verse is called iambic pentameter. This simply means each line usually consists of 10 syllables, although 9 to 11 syllables are possible. There are five stresses per line. *Iamb-* means two syllables, unstressed-stressed, as in "today." The first syllable is unstressed and the second is stressed.

Here is an example of blank verse from William Shakespeare. The stressed syllables are italicized:

> How *do* I *count* the *clock* that *tells* the *time*?

As you read this line aloud, listen for the stress pattern:

> da DUM da DUM da DUM da DUM da DUM

Let's look at some other examples. From John Milton's poem "Paradise Lost," we have this line:

> Of *that* for*bid*den *tree*, whose *mor*tal *taste*.

From Shakespeare's "Romeo and Juliet," Juliet explains how much she does not want to marry Paris. What are the stress patterns?

> ... bid me leap, rather than marry Paris,
> From off the battlements of yonder tower;
> Or walk in thievish ways; or bid me lurk
> Where serpents are; chain me with roaring bears;
> Or shut me nightly in a charnel-house,
> O'er covered quite with dead men's rattling bones,
> With reeky shanks and yellow chapless skulls;
> Or bid me go into a new-made grave,
> And hide me with a dead man and his shroud ...

Practice

Answer these questions based on the three quotations you just read.

1. Which syllables are stressed in the first quotation?

   (1) In each two word combination, the first syllable is stressed.

   (2) Only the final syllable in the line is stressed.

   (3) Only the first syllable in each line is stressed.

   (4) In each two word combination, the second syllable is stressed.

   (5) Blank verse contains no stressed syllables.

2. The third quotation (from "Romeo and Juliet") has examples of hyperbole, such as:

   (1) bid me lurk where serpents are.

   (2) bid me leap off the battlements.

   (3) chain me with roaring bears.

   (4) or bid me go into a new-made grave.

   (5) all of the above.

3. Generally, the lines in the third quotation contain

   (1) fewer than 10 syllables.

   (2) a lot of words but no syllables.

   (3) a lot of syllables but no vowels.

   (4) 10 syllables.

   (5) strong rhymes.

Answers

1. **(4)** All other answers are incorrect details.

2. **(5)** All of the answers are exaggerations.

3. **(4)** All other answers are incorrect details.

Free Verse

Some readers are under the wrong impression that the word *free* in *free verse* means no rules apply. Some think that free verse is a new way of writing poetry. Both assumptions are incorrect.

> **DEFINITION**
>
> **Free verse** is verse that does not follow a fixed metrical, or rhyming, pattern.

It is true that free verse is mostly free of rhymes and may be free of the strong rhythms that you've seen so far. However, free verse is probably one of the most difficult forms of poetry to write. Why? Despite it's being "free," it is poetry, and that still requires precisely chosen words arranged artfully into verses. In free verse, there is no pattern to follow unless the poet constructs one. The American poet T.S. Eliot said it best: "No verse is free for the man who wants to do a good job."

Free verse goes all the way back to the Bible in such verses as Song of Solomon. As you read, you can imagine King Solomon arriving on the day of his wedding:

> Somebody is coming from the desert.
> And men are coming with clouds of smoke.
> They come with myrrh and incense.
> They have a wonderful smell.
> Look! It is Solomon's carriage!
> Sixty soldiers guard it.
> They are the best soldiers in Israel.
> All of them are skilful with the sword.
> People have trained them to fight.
> Their swords are at their sides.
> They are ready for any danger during the night.
> King Solomon made the carriage for himself.
> The wood came from Lebanon.
> He made the poles from silver.
> And it has a gold base.
> A purple cloth covers the seat.
> The women of Jerusalem made the beautiful inside of the carriage.
> They made it with grace.
> Women of Zion, come out and see King Solomon.

Look at the crown that his mother put on him.
This is the crown for his wedding.
And he is so happy because of his wedding.

Practice

Answer this question based on Song of Solomon.

1. The fact that Song of Solomon was written in free verse is evidenced in that

   (1) every other line rhymes.

   (2) there are no fixed rhymes.

   (3) there are no descriptive words.

   (4) the poem has no real meaning.

   (5) it has strict rhythms.

Answer

1. **(2)** As in free verse, generally, this poem has no rhyme scheme.

Imagery

Imagery in poetry is what the words of the poem make the readers "see" in their imagination. Imagery consists of the colors, sounds, and sometimes feelings evoked by the poem. Readers are drawn into the poem because it speaks of images the reader already knows. If you have had the same experience—seen, smelled, touched, felt— that experience always intensifies your reading.

IN THE KNOW

Imagery provides the mental pictures that open our minds to the meaning of poems. Similes and metaphors are two techniques that add imagery to poetry— and prose as well.

The poem "Daffodils" contains great examples of imagery. For example, the poet's open mind is touched by the picture of a thousand yellow daffodils swaying in the breeze (visual) against the background of waves breaking on the rocks (auditory). He conveys that vivid image to the reader. He gives us a word of caution as well. We should slow down enough, seek solitude (internal state), in order to see something very, very special in our wanderings. We can easily relate to what the poet sees, hears, and feels.

The Imagery of War

Finally, in one of the most moving poems to come out of World War I, you will find imagery that is the legacy of a battle at Ypres, Belgium. A Canadian doctor, Colonel John McCrae (1872–1918), wrote "In Flanders Fields" in May 1915. He had just spent more than 2 weeks treating severely wounded and dying soldiers and, exhausted, he sat down near a field and wrote this poem.

Can you answer the question so many readers have asked? Why did McCrae choose to use the poppy as an important image in the poem? What other images do you see?

> In Flanders fields the poppies blow
> Between the crosses, row on row,
> That mark our place; and in the sky
> The larks, still bravely singing, fly
> Scarce heard amid the guns below.
>
> We are the Dead. Short days ago
> We lived, felt dawn, saw sunset glow,
> Loved, and were loved, and now we lie
> In Flanders fields.
>
> Take up our quarrel with the foe:
> To you from failing hands we throw
> The torch; be yours to hold it high.
> If ye break faith with us who die
> We shall not sleep, though poppies grow
> In Flanders fields.

Practice

1. The poem is written through the voice of

   (1) the poet, John McCrae.

   (2) the dead soldiers.

   (3) Colonel McCrae's staff.

   (4) the priest.

   (5) the gardener in Flanders.

2. The main idea of the poem is that

   (1) these dead soldiers who "lived, felt dawn … loved, and were loved" should never be forgotten.

   (2) everyone knows the war will soon be forgotten.

   (3) the doctor was about to take up arms.

   (4) the fight took place in Flanders Field.

   (5) the war ended the day after the fight described here.

3. You can infer from this poem that poppies were the poet's choice of flowers because

   (1) poppies are red, the color of blood on the battlefield.

   (2) poppies grow in broken or uprooted soil, such as a battlefield.

   (3) poppies are a sign that this troop of men wanted to retreat.

   (4) they were a favorite of his troops.

   (5) Answers (1) and (2) above.

Answers

1. **(2)** The second and third verses both say the soldiers are dead, yet they speak to the living. Answers (1), (3), (4), and (5) all contradict the evidence that the dead soldiers are speaking.

2. **(1)** The soldiers ask to be remembered and ask the reader to take up the fight. There is no proof that answers (2), (3), and (5) are true. Answer (4) is a correct detail, not a main idea.

3. **(5)** If you know anything about growing flowers, you know that poppies' seeds can lie in the ground for years. They sprout only when someone uproots the soil. Also, poppies are red, the color associated with blood and war. Answers (3) and (4) are incorrect details.

Drama

In This Chapter

- Overview of a play's plot, characters, conflicts, and theme
- GED-like questions to practice the skills you'll be tested on
- Answers and explanations for all the questions

In Chapter 24 you read about short stories. The plays you are about to read are similar to the stories in some important ways. A play tells a story, too, but it does so on a stage. However, in a story, the author can simply fill in the important information. In a play, the characters perform that job with *dialogue* (a character's words). The plot develops as the characters talk to each other, or sometimes to themselves. In a play this is called the *exposition* (the information revealed about the story).

Every play has a conflict upon which the playwright builds. Stories and plays have this in common: major and minor characters meet, protagonists and antagonists reveal themselves, conflicts arise, the action comes to a climax, and the problem is resolved either happily or sadly.

The Developing Plot and Its Conflict

One very well-known play reveals a plot filled with conflict. The play "Romeo and Juliet" has an everlasting theme: young love, conflict, and tragedy.

The play opens with a device called a *prologue.* As you read the prologue (written in the rhymed verse you learned about in Chapter 25), think about what the writer accomplishes by using this device. You'll quickly realize how different English was at the time. Still, you will definitely be able to follow the story. Think about this as you read: what terrible situation exists between these two families—the Montagues and the Capulets? Keep this main theme in mind as you read. In addition, as you read, you will realize that even though this play was written a very long time ago, Romeo and Juliet has an everlasting theme of conflict that ends in tragedy.

DEFINITION

A **prologue** is an introductory statement by an actor or chorus to explain the coming action.

PROLOGUE

Two households, both alike in dignity,
In fair Verona, where we lay our scene,
From ancient grudge break to new mutiny,
Where civil blood makes civil hands unclean.
From forth the fatal loins of these two foes
A pair of star-cross'd lovers take their life;
Whose misadventured piteous overthrows
Do with their death bury their parents' strife.
The fearful passage of their death-mark'd love,
And the continuance of their parents' rage,
Which, but their children's end, nought could remove,
Is now the two hours' traffic of our stage;
The which if you with patient ears attend,
What here shall miss, our toil shall strive to mend.

Practice

1. Answer the question posed in the introduction to this reading: what terrible situation drives the plot?

(1) The two families are so poor they cannot even feed their families.

(2) The two families hold a grudge that ends in tragedy.

(3) A young man and woman fall madly in love.

(4) The parents have just died and were buried.

(5) There is a terrible traffic jam on stage.

2. You can conclude that the words *From forth the fatal loins of these two foes* refer to whom?

   (1) The Montagues and the Capulets

   (2) Romeo and Juliet

   (3) Romeo and Juliet's best friends

   (4) The reader

   (5) The playwright

3. You can conclude that a tragedy will occur when you read the words

   (1) both alike in dignity.

   (2) In fair Verona.

   (3) now the two hours' traffic.

   (4) if you with patient ears attend.

   (5) civil blood makes civil hands unclean.

Answers

1. **(2)** There is an "ancient grudge" that exists between the two families until the "star-cross'd lovers" end it with their death. Answer (1) is an incorrect detail. Nothing in the verse talks about the families being poor. Answer (3) doesn't answer the question. The couple being madly in love would not, on its own, be a bad thing. Answers (4) and (5) are incorrect details.

2. **(1)** Romeo and Juliet are the children of—*come from the loins of*—the Capulets and the Montagues. All other answers are incorrect details since they do not name Romeo and Juliet's parents.

3. **(5)** All other answers are incorrect because none of the other answers have to do with tragedy.

The Main Characters Reveal the Plot and Complications

In order to follow the plot, you need to identify the characters in the play—at least the main ones. The following lists identifies two families, the Montagues and Capulets, and some of their friends.

Montagues

- Romeo—the only heir to the Montague fortune
- Lord Montague—Romeo's father
- Lady Montague—Romeo's mother
- Benvolio—Romeo's cousin
- Balthasar—Romeo's faithful servant
- Abraham—Montague servant

Capulets

- Juliet—only heir to the Capulet fortune
- Lord Capulet—Juliet's father
- Lady Capulet—Juliet's mother
- Tybalt—Juliet's cousin
- The Nurse—Juliet's faithful nurse

Other Characters

- Rosaline—Romeo's first love, who never actually appears in the play
- Friar Lawrence—friend and advisor to Romeo and Juliet
- Mercutio—Romeo's best friend; prince's relative
- Paris—loves Juliet

The Plot and Its Protagonist and Antagonists

At the beginning of the play, a fight breaks out between the Montagues and the Capulets. Even the heads of the households, Lord Montague and Lord Capulet are involved. When Prince Escalus arrives, outraged at what he sees, he breaks up the fight. He warns that any more fighting will result in the execution of anyone who participates. Immediately after that, Romeo's (the *protagonist*) mother speaks to Benvolio, Romeo's friend. You can infer something about her state of mind having come upon this scene of *antagonists* fighting. Read to find out how she feels at this moment.

DEFINITION

The **protagonist** is the central character or a leading role in a play. The **antagonist** is a character in conflict with the protagonist.

LADY MONTAGUE

O, where is Romeo? saw you him to-day?
Right glad I am he was not at this fray.

BENVOLIO

Madam, an hour before the worshipp'd sun
Peer'd forth the golden window of the east,
A troubled mind drave me to walk abroad;
Where, underneath the grove of sycamore
That westward rooteth from the city's side,
So early walking did I see your son:
Towards him I made, but he was ware of me
And stole into the covert of the wood:
I, measuring his affections by my own,
That most are busied when they're most alone,
Pursued my humour not pursuing his,
And gladly shunn'd who gladly fled from me.

Practice

1. What do you learn about Romeo from his friend, Benvolio?

   (1) Romeo is unhappy and doesn't want company.

   (2) Benvolio feels he can invade Romeo's privacy.

   (3) Benvolio gives Romeo all the answers he wants.

   (4) Benvolio walks away from Romeo's mother, telling her nothing.

   (5) Romeo's mother walks away before she learns anything about Romeo.

2. Use context clues to explain the meaning of *covert* in line 8 of the second paragraph. It means

   (1) coping.

   (2) open.

   (3) undergrowth providing cover.

   (4) silent.

   (5) sneaky.

Answers

1. **(1)** Benvolio went to find Romeo, but Romeo didn't want to be found. Answers (2), (3), (4), and (5) are all opposite to the truth.

2. **(3)** Romeo doesn't want to be seen. It makes sense that he would seek cover. A covert—or undergrowth—would give him privacy. None of the other choices are synonyms for cover.

The Play's Theme

Get ready for a swift ride into more current drama. We'll jump from the sixteenth century to the twentieth and turn to a modern American playwright.

Following is a play, "The Wave," by Michael Diamond (1939–). Michael Diamond is an attorney and a writer of poetry, novels, and plays. His own statement clarifies the theme (the idea or point of view) of the play: "On occasion, the dominant American commercial culture is stilled by a feeling that there are realms of existence beyond what appears on the surface." "The Wave" has only two characters: husband and wife, Harold and Mary. Think about their relationship as you read. What words would you use to describe how they relate to each other?

What is the wave that Harold experiences?

(Harold and Mary, a married couple who appear to be in their 60s, have just exited an office building and are walking through a small park that is dotted with shade trees and benches.)

HAROLD

You know, you're supposed to feel better after you sign one of those things.

MARY

The living will?

HAROLD

The living will. (He pauses.) I don't feel better.

MARY

Forget about it. We go on with our lives. Believe me, in a week or two you won't even remember what you signed or what you said in that office.

HAROLD

I'll remember. I said not to bother too much keeping me alive. If it looks like I'm cooked ....

MARY

Cooked? That's funny. (Mary laughs and kisses Harold on the cheek. She holds his arm as they walk.)

HAROLD

... Then, pull the plug. Rip out the tubes. Nothing to eat or drink. In a couple of days, I'm on my way to a refrigerator with a tag on my big toe that says "Harold Macy was here." But he's not here any more.

MARY

Harold, that's awful. Why are you making such a big deal now?

HAROLD

Because I never really thought about it before. If I'm not here—and that's that it's gonna say on my big toe—then, where the hell am I?

MARY

Harold, you're sixty-seven years old. Don't tell me you never thought about death before. I heard you myself say it, many times, that you'll meet your father and your brother, Eddie, when you die. Oh, yeah and you'll meet your first wife, too. You weren't going to talk to her up there. And you always said that you looked forward to pulling up a cloud and sitting down for a long talk with your father, the kind of talk he didn't have time for when he was alive. You said all that, didn't you?

HAROLD

(Pauses to think.) I said it.

MARY

So, I'm not making this up, right? You remember?

HAROLD

Yes.

MARY

Okay. That's what happens. Nice. You'll like seeing Eddie again. You'll snub Vivian. Your pop will be glad to see you. You'll tell him that the Red Sox won the World Series. He'll say, "Why the hell did I have to die so soon?" And then you'll tell him which of those men hit home runs and …

HAROLD

Quit it, Mary. I never meant any of that. I never imagined an end. It was talk—talk to take up time.

(Harold sits on a bench. Mary sits next to him.)

HAROLD

You know how we sometimes say that we're doing things to take up the time? You know, so that life doesn't drag on too much? We do the crossword puzzle. You talk to your sister. We take a walk, and all of a sudden, it's time for lunch. And that's how we took the time up. Well, that's what my talking about death was about. A little noise to fill the time. And it made me feel smart. But I never imagined ….

MARY

So, now that you see an actual ending to the life of Harold A. Macy, where do you think what's left of him might go after the refrigerator door closes on his torso that's covered by a sheet?

HAROLD

He goes …

MARY

He goes …

HAROLD

Jesus, Mary, all I have him doing is looking at the top of the inside of a refrigerator. It's a stainless-steel drawer. And he's saying get me the hell out of here.

MARY

Okay. So death is the end. There is nothing else. Done. Gone. Harold used to be, and then he wasn't any more.

HAROLD

That's why you put down for them to use every means? No tubes are too many. "Keep me alive for as long as there are trees." That's exactly what you said. The lawyer laughed. He asked you to add that sentence at the end of the will in your own handwriting.

MARY

Well, I know there's nothing else. Once the door is closed on life, that's it. Candle out. Done. And we're all yesterday's sushi that gets thrown out with the trash.

HAROLD

But what if there's more?

MARY

Time to go. I didn't call my sister yet today.

HAROLD

Really. What if there's more? And what if the people on the other side know all about us? Mary, at the end, I don't think they'll ask you whether you thought to call your sister, that day.

MARY

Cut it out, Harold. You don't understand what you're talking about. For all you know, it could be that there's a spirit up there, and he'll tell me to get right back into my life so that I can call Helen.

HAROLD

I can't imagine an angel giving you a special pass to call her. All she does is gossip. And when she's not gossiping, she's telling you how much she weighs and whether her ass looks fat that day.

MARY

All of a sudden, you're on some high horse? Better than Helen? And what the hell made you so superior? The fact that you can see the inside of a refrigerator. Go ahead, shoot for sainthood. Picture what it must look like inside a box that's deep in the ground. (She gets up.) Are you coming?

HAROLD

Wait a minute … a wave. Did you feel it? I just felt it. Eddie and Pop must have moved, like in a pool, and I felt the ripple. Mary.

MARY

Harold, this is ridiculous. That was me standing up. What you felt was …

HAROLD

Please. Something happened. I don't know what to say or how to say it. Something … (long pause) … like what we live for.

MARY

Children feel things that go bump in the night.

HAROLD

Yes. They can feel God, but they don't have the words to talk about it. And if they say something that doesn't sound real, we tell them they're wrong. We tell them they imagined their bumps in the night.

MARY

I never heard you talk like this.

HAROLD

And I never … (Looks into the distance. Begins to talk. Says nothing.)

MARY

Harold.

HAROLD

I made the right choice. There's nothing to be afraid about. Only …

MARY

Only?

HAROLD

They'll ask us what we've done.

MARY

You mean? …

HAROLD

Not if we rooted for the Red Sox.

MARY

Shit. What the hell do you know? Here I am, taking your junky talk seriously. You said yourself that you only jabbered on to fill the time. This is no different. It's just a new patter, a new little dance routine, as you say, to while away the time.

(He rises. They walk a little, arm-in-arm.)

HAROLD

I don't think I'll ever use those words again: "filling up the time."

MARY

Harold, when we get older, we sometimes begin to get a little strange. Those around us are supposed to tolerate us, even though we're strange. That's what I'm doing now.

HAROLD

One day, Mary, you'll feel a presence. Like nothing you've ever experienced.

And everything will …

MARY

There's a game on tonight. I'll make corned beef, the way you like it. (Pause.) You know, sometimes I call my sister, and I hold the phone up so she can hear the noises that come out of you when you watch the game: yips and atta-boys and a lot of goddamnits. She laughs and I laugh. I never told you.

HAROLD

… everything will sort of go through you, like a wave. Mary, I never …

MARY

I'll turn the game on.

HAROLD

I don't think so. Maybe some other night.

(They walk off the stage together.)

© 2005 by Michael Diamond

Practice

1. What is the meaning of *wave* in the title?

   (1) We ride the wave of sadness.

   (2) Mary and Harold are happier living near the water.

   (3) A felt experience that goes beyond our everyday lives.

   (4) We make our own happiness.

   (5) The problems and concerns that surround us at all times.

2. In the play, Harold, the protagonist, seems disturbed by the experience with the living will, while Mary

   (1) is even more upset than Harold and spends the time crying.

   (2) accepts that signing the living will is just another event in her life.

   (3) only wants to go home and plan their funerals.

   (4) is more concerned about her sister than she is about Harold.

   (5) shows no concern for Harold at all.

3. You can conclude from the dialogue that regardless of their very different reactions to the living will, Harold and Mary are obviously

   (1) a well-suited, happily married couple.

   (2) a recently divorced couple.

   (3) a severely depressed couple.

   (4) at odds over every aspect of their lives.

   (5) still mourning Harold's father's death.

Answers

1. **(3)** The wave is never identified as happy or sad. Answers (1), (2), (4), and (5) are not correct since they do not deal with what appears beyond the surface of our lives.

2. **(2)** Answers (1), (3), (4), and (5) are all incorrect details.

3. **(1)** Answers (2), (3), (4), and (5) are incorrect details.

Language Arts: Reading Practice Test

The actual Language Arts: Reading Test is comprised of 40 multiple-choice questions that you will have 65 minutes to answer. There will be seven passages presented for you to use when answering the questions. For purposes of this book, the practice test is one-half the number of questions, or 20 multiple-choice questions. Therefore, you should allow yourself one-half of the 65-minute time allowance reserved for the full test, taking about 32½ minutes to complete this practice test.

If, after taking the test provided here, you feel you need more practice and want to take another simulated test, there are several online sites that offer free GED practice tests. One site we recommend is PBS Literacy Link (http:litlink.ket.org). Keep in mind, though, that the actual GED Tests are paper-and-pencil tests like those in this book and cannot be taken on a computer.

Instructions

The Language Arts: Reading Test is designed to measure your understanding of general reading skills and concepts. Each question is based on a short passage. Use the information provided to answer the question(s) that follow. You can refer to the passage as often as you want in answering the question(s).

You will have about 32½ minutes to complete the 20 questions on this practice test. Work carefully, but don't spend too much time on any one question. If you are having trouble with a question, make the best guess you can and move on. Your score is based on the number of correct answers; there is no penalty for guessing.

When taking the practice test, try to simulate actual test conditions. Get a timing device of some sort and a couple of No. 2 pencils with good erasers. Go to a place where you won't be interrupted and follow test instructions. Start the timer after you've read the instructions and are ready to begin the first question.

Once you check your answers, you may want to go back to the chapters in Part 4 to review the material on any questions that were answered incorrectly. This way you are focusing your attention only on the areas you need to.

Go on to the next page when you are ready to begin.

Question 1 refers to the following passage.

From *The Scarlet Letter* by Nathaniel Hawthorne, 1850

> After her return to the prison, Hester Prynne was found to be in a state of nervous excitement that demanded constant watchfulness, lest she should perpetrate violence on herself, or do some half-frenzied mischief to the poor babe. As night approached, it proving impossible to quell her insubordination by rebuke or threats of punishment, Master Brackett, the jailer, thought fit to introduce a physician. He described him as a man of skill in all Christian modes of physical science, and likewise familiar with whatever the savage people could teach, in respect to medicinal herbs and roots that grew in the forest. To say the truth, there was much need of professional assistance, not merely for Hester herself, but still more urgently for the child; who, drawing its sustenance from the maternal bosom, seemed to have drank in with it all the turmoil, the anguish, and despair, which pervaded the mother's system. It now writhed in convulsions of pain, and was a forcible type, in its little frame, of the moral agony which Hester Prynne had borne throughout the day.

1. Based on the passage, one could assume that Hester and her child needed medical attention because

    (1) They were having trouble sleeping.

    (2) Hester might hurt herself and the child.

    (3) The jailer had a friend who was a physician.

    (4) The child was suffering due to its mother's immorality.

    (5) Hester was filled with nervous excitement.

Question 2 refers to the following passage.

From *The Big Town* by Ring W. Lardner, 1921

> If the old codger had of only been half as fast a salesman as his two daughters this clipping would of been right when it called me a wealthy Hoosier. It wasn't two weeks after we seen the will when the gals had disposed of the odor factory and the old home in Niles, Michigan. Katie, it seemed, had to come over to South Bend and live with us. That was agreeable to me, as I figured that if two could live on eighteen hundred dollars a year three could struggle along some way on the income off one hundred and fifty thousand dollars.

2. The main subject of this passage is

   (1) Salesmen.

   (2) A wealthy Hoosier.

   (3) An inheritance.

   (4) Two daughters.

   (5) An odor factory.

Question 3 refers to the following passage.

From *Emma Goldman—Biographical Sketch* by Charles A. Madison, 1960 (Project Gutenberg)

> In the meantime, discouraged and lonely, she had welcomed a fellow worker's show of affection. She felt no love for him and, as a result of an attempted rape at the age of fifteen, she still experienced a "violent repulsion" in the presence of men, but she had not the strength to refuse his urgent proposal of marriage. She soon learned to her dismay that her husband was impotent and not at all as congenial as she had thought. However, the very suggestion of a separation enraged her father, who had recently come to Rochester. After months of aggravation she did go through the then rare and reprehensible rite of Orthodox divorce, but she had to leave town to avoid social ostracism. When she returned some months later, her former husband again pursued her, and his threat of suicide frightened her into remarrying him.

3. When Emma discovered her husband's impotence, she

   (1) Developed a revulsion toward men.

   (2) Called her father to come to Rochester.

   (3) Sought and was granted an orthodox divorce.

   (4) Threatened suicide.

   (5) Suggested a separation.

Questions 4–8 refer to the following passage.

From "The Raven" by Edgar Allen Poe, 1845

> Once upon a midnight dreary, while I pondered, weak and weary,
> Over many a quaint and curious volume of forgotten lore,
> While I nodded, nearly napping, suddenly there came a tapping,
> As of some one gently rapping, rapping at my chamber door.
> " 'Tis some visitor," I muttered, "tapping at my chamber door—
>
> Only this, and nothing more."
>
> Ah, distinctly I remember it was in the bleak December,
> And each separate dying ember wrought its ghost upon the floor.
> Eagerly I wished the morrow;—vainly I had tried to borrow
> From my books surcease of sorrow—sorrow for the lost Lenore—
> For the rare and radiant maiden whom the angels name Lenore—
>
> Nameless here for evermore.
>
> And the silken sad uncertain rustling of each purple curtain
> Thrilled me—filled me with fantastic terrors never felt before;
> So that now, to still the beating of my heart, I stood repeating
> " 'Tis some visitor entreating entrance at my chamber door—
> Some late visitor entreating entrance at my chamber door;—
>
> This it is, and nothing more."
>
> Presently my soul grew stronger; hesitating then no longer,
> "Sir," said I, "or Madam, truly your forgiveness I implore;
> But the fact is I was napping, and so gently you came rapping,
> And so faintly you came tapping, tapping at my chamber door,
> That I scarce was sure I heard you"—here I opened wide the door;—
>
> Darkness there, and nothing more.
>
> Deep into that darkness peering, long I stood there wondering, fearing,
> Doubting, dreaming dreams no mortal ever dared to dream before;
> But the silence was unbroken, and the darkness gave no token,
> And the only word there spoken was the whispered word, "Lenore!"
> This *I* whispered, and an echo murmured back the word, "Lenore!"

Merely this, and nothing more.

Back into the chamber turning, all my soul within me burning,
Soon again I heard a tapping, somewhat louder than before.
"Surely," said I, "surely that is something at my window lattice;
Let me see, then, what thereat is, and this mystery explore—
Let my heart be still a moment and this mystery explore—

'Tis the wind and nothing more!" Open here I flung the shutter, when, with many a flirt and flutter,
In there stepped a stately Raven of the saintly days of yore.
Not the least obeisance made he; not a minute stopped or stayed he;
But, with mien of lord or lady, perched above my chamber door—
Perched upon a bust of Pallas just above my chamber door—

Perched, and sat, and nothing more.

4. In the second stanza, the line "And each separate dying ember wrought its ghost upon the floor" refers to

   (1) A ghost in the room.

   (2) An ember falling to the floor.

   (3) A fire in a fireplace.

   (4) A shadow from the fire seen on the floor.

   (5) A memory of a fire long gone.

5. The author portrays the main character in the poem as

   (1) Afraid of his/her shadow.

   (2) Patiently waiting for a visitor.

   (3) Frightened by the visitor.

   (4) Half asleep.

   (5) Someone who is hearing things.

6. What was the main character doing before the knock came to the door?

   (1) Reading

   (2) Sleeping

   (3) Reading and sleeping

   (4) Falling asleep while reading

   (5) Waiting for a visitor

7. The reference to Lenore in this passage

   (1) Is explained at the end.

   (2) Tells how she is important to the main character.

   (3) Shows how the main character is related to her.

   (4) Leaves the reader wondering who she is.

   (5) Means nothing of consequence.

8. The visitor

   (1) Never showed up at the door.

   (2) Just kept tapping and rapping at the door.

   (3) Finally leaves without going into the house.

   (4) Is the Raven.

   (5) Was very rude.

Questions 9–14 refer to the following passage.

From "Romeo and Juliet" by William Shakespeare, believed written between 1591 and 1595

> *Romeo:* But soft! What light through yonder window breaks?
> It is the East, and Juliet is the sun!
> Arise, fair sun, and kill the envious moon,
> Who is already sick and pale with grief
> That thou her maid art far more fair than she.
> Be not her maid, since she is envious.
> Her vestal livery is but sick and green, And none but fools do wear it. Cast it off.

It is my lady; O, it is my love! O that she knew she were!
She speaks, yet she says nothing. What of that?
Her eye discourses; I will answer it.
I am too bold; 'tis not to me she speaks.
Two of the fairest stars in all the heaven,
Having some business, do entreat her eyes
To twinkle in their spheres till they return.
What if her eyes were there, they in her head?
The brightness of her cheek would shame those stars as daylight doth a lamp;
her eyes in heaven
would through the airy region stream so bright
that birds would sing and think it were not night.
See how she leans her cheek upon her hand! O that I were a glove upon that hand,
that I might touch that cheek!

Juliet: Ay me!

Romeo: She speaks.
O, speak again, bright angel! for thou art
As glorious to this night, being o'er my head,
As is a winged messenger of heaven
Unto the white-upturned wond'ring eyes
Of mortals that fall back to gaze on him
When he bestrides the lazy-pacing clouds
And sails upon the bosom of the air.

Juliet: O Romeo, Romeo! Wherefore art thou Romeo?
Deny thy father and refuse thy name!
Or, if thou wilt not, be but sworn my love,
and I'll no longer be a Capulet.

Romeo: [aside] Shall I hear more, or shall I speak at this?

Juliet: 'Tis but thy name that is my enemy.
Thou art thyself, though not a Montague.
What's Montague? It is nor hand, nor foot,
nor arm, nor face, nor any other part belonging to a man. O, be some other name!
What's in a name? That which we call a rose
by any other name would smell as sweet. So Romeo would, were he not

Romeo call'd,
retain that dear perfection which he owes
without that title. Romeo, doff thy name;
And for that name, which is no part of thee, take all myself.

Romeo: I take thee at thy word.
Call me but love, and I'll be new baptiz'd;
Henceforth, I never will be Romeo.

9. In the first passage spoken by Romeo, the author uses the words *light, sun, bright,* and *daylight* to describe Juliet. The author uses these terms to show

   (1) Romeo feels Juliet radiates a light like the sun with her presence.

   (2) Romeo is speaking during the daylight hours.

   (3) Romeo doesn't care for the nighttime.

   (4) Juliet has very fair skin.

   (5) Romeo is partial to bright light.

10. When Juliet proclaims, "What's in a name? That which we call a rose by any other name would smell as sweet," she means

    (1) A rose is always called a rose.

    (2) A name has no purpose.

    (3) Even if a rose were called cow dung, it would still smell sweet.

    (4) Things should not have names.

    (5) She is wondering what else she could call a rose.

11. From what Romeo says to Juliet, the reader can infer

    (1) Romeo is in love with Juliet.

    (2) Romeo has a fondness for all things bright.

    (3) Romeo has a keen interest in astrology.

    (4) Romeo has feelings for Juliet's maid.

    (5) Romeo is very shy.

12. When Juliet speaks to Romeo, her main concern is

    (1) Romeo's name.

    (2) A rose.

    (3) Romeo is her enemy.

    (4) Romeo doesn't love her.

    (5) Her name should be Montague.

13. When you read the exchange between Romeo and Juliet, you feel they

    (1) Are worried about something.

    (2) Haven't a care in the world.

    (3) Enjoy being outside together.

    (4) Have just met.

    (5) Despise each other.

14. In the last paragraph, when Romeo states, "Call me but love, and I'll be new baptiz'd; Henceforth I will never be Romeo," he means

    (1) He's willing to be baptized for Juliet.

    (2) He wants to change his name.

    (3) For Juliet's love, he would be whoever she wants him to be.

    (4) He's never been baptized before.

    (5) He doesn't want to be Romeo anymore.

Questions 15–17 refer to the following passage.

Workplace Smoking Policy

Introduction

Secondhand smoke—breathing in other people's tobacco smoke—has now been shown to cause lung cancer, heart disease, and many other illnesses in nonsmokers.

Section 2 (2) (e) of the **Health and Safety at Work Etc. Act 1974** places a duty on employers to provide a working environment for employees that is: safe, without risk to health, and adequate as regards facilities and arrangements for their welfare at work.

The **Health Act 2006** requires workplaces to be smoke-free by the end of May 2007. Smoking rooms will no longer be allowed. The employer acknowledges that breathing other people's tobacco smoke is both a public hazard and a welfare issue. Therefore the following policy has been adopted concerning smoking in **this organization.**

General Principles

This smoking policy seeks to guarantee nonsmokers the right to work in air free of tobacco smoke, while taking account of the health needs of those who smoke.

All premises will be designated smoke-free from this day forward. Smoking will only be permitted at designated smoking areas outside the buildings.

Smoking while on duty will only be allowed during official break periods.

15. The main concern of this policy is

    (1) Secondhand smoke is harmful to all.

    (2) Smoking will still be allowed outside.

    (3) Smoking is allowed only on breaks.

    (4) Employers need to provide smoking rooms.

    (5) Smoking is a matter of personal preference.

16. The policy appears to be

    (1) Complied on a voluntary basis only.

    (2) Punishment for smokers.

    (3) Harmful to those who choose to smoke inside.

    (4) Meant to keep all workers safe and healthy.

    (5) Discriminatory.

17. For employees, the organization is showing they are

    (1) Concerned about their well-being and health.

    (2) Afraid of getting sued.

    (3) Worried about hurting smokers' feelings.

    (4) Overreacting to research on smoking.

    (5) Trying to save money by getting rid of smoking rooms.

Questions 18–20 refer to the following passage.

U.S. Department of Labor's Disability Employment Policy

I. ADA BASICS

What is the ADA?

The ADA is a federal civil rights law that was passed in 1990 and went into effect beginning in 1992. Its purpose is to protect people with disabilities from discrimination in employment, in the programs and activities offered by state and local governments, and in accessing the goods and services offered in places like stores, hotels, restaurants, football stadiums, doctors' offices, beauty parlors, and so on. The focus of this guide is Title I of the ADA, which prohibits discrimination in employment and requires employers to provide reasonable accommodations for employees with disabilities.

Who must comply with Title I of the ADA?

Only "covered entities" must comply with Title I of the ADA. The term "covered entities" includes employers with 15 or more employees, employment agencies, labor organizations, and joint labor-management committees. For simplicity, this guide will refer to covered entities as "employers."

For more information about covered entities, see www.eeoc.gov/policy/docs/threshold.html#2-III-B.

Who is protected by Title I of the ADA?

Title I protects "qualified employees with disabilities." The term "qualified" means that the individual satisfies the skill, experience, education, and other job-related requirements of the position sought or held, and can perform the essential job functions of the position, with or without reasonable accommodation.

For additional information about the definition of qualified, see http://askjan.org/links/ADAtam1.html#II.

The term "employee" means "an individual employed by an employer." The question of whether an employer-employee relationship exists is fact-specific and depends on whether the employer controls the means and manner of the worker's work performance.

18. This policy is meant to protect

    (1) All workers in the organization.

    (2) Employers who employ the disabled.

    (3) Workers with disabilities.

    (4) The government from lawsuits.

    (5) Employees.

19. The policy contains information on

    (1) Who can be sued for noncompliance.

    (2) The reasons for hiring workers with disabilities.

    (3) What the ADA is.

    (4) Who must comply and who is protected.

    (5) Both 3 and 4.

20. The ADA's purpose is to

    (1) Make sure disabled workers can get high-paying jobs.

    (2) Allow disabled people to gain access to football games, hotels, and restaurants.

    (3) Get jobs for workers with disabilities.

    (4) Protect workers with disabilities from discrimination on the job.

    (5) Allow employers to hire whoever they want to.

Answers and Explanations

1. **(2)** Hester might hurt herself and the child is the best answer because of the passage, "lest she should perpetrate violence on herself, or do some half-frenzied mischief to the poor babe."

2. **(3)** The reference to the will and the fact that he now had $150,000 makes this answer most appropriate.

3. **(3)** This is the only answer that is supported in the passage.

4. **(4)** The line "And each separate dying ember wrought its ghost upon the floor" refers to a shadow from the fire seen on the floor.

5. **(5)** This is the only answer supported by the passage. He doesn't know it's a visitor until he opens the window.

6. **(4)** The reference to books in "Over many a quaint and curious volume of forgotten lore" and "While I nodded, nearly napping …" combine to make this the correct answer.

7. **(4)** The name is called out but no other explanation is provided, leaving the reader to wonder who she is.

8. **(4)** "In there stepped a stately Raven" reveals the Raven as the visitor.

9. **(1)** Romeo uses these terms to describe Juliet, making this the only correct answer.

10. **(3)** Juliet is saying that a name doesn't make the object or person what or who they are; their characteristics do.

11. **(1)** Romeo speaks in terms of beauty and passion for Juliet, displaying his love for her.

12. **(1)** One entire passage is devoted to her discussion of Romeo's name.

13. **(1)** Both Romeo and Juliet speak as if they are concerned with something.

14. **(3)** Romeo shows he is willing to give up his name and be someone new for Juliet.

15. **(1)** This passage provides the foundation for the smoking policy, making 1 the correct answer; "The employer acknowledges that breathing other people's tobacco smoke is both a public hazard and a welfare issue. Therefore the following policy has been adopted …."

16. **(4)** The passage "This smoking policy seeks to guarantee nonsmokers the right to work in air free of tobacco smoke, while taking account of the health needs of those who smoke" makes 4 the correct answer.

17. **(1)** The policy refers to health concerns of both smokers and nonsmokers, making 1 the correct answer.

18. **(3)** This sentence clearly states the intent of the policy: "Title I protects 'qualified employees with disabilities.'"

19. **(5)** Information about the ADA as well as who must comply and who is protected is provided in the policy.

20. **(4)** The sentence "Its purpose is to protect people with disabilities from discrimination in employment …" makes 4 correct.

Math

Part 5 consists of four review chapters: numbers, arithmetic, and number sense (Chapter 28); measurement and geometry (Chapter 29); data analysis, statistics, and probability (Chapter 30); and algebra, functions, and patterns (Chapter 31). Chapter 32 contains a description of the Math Test. Each chapter concludes with practice questions, most in multiple-choice format. However, the Math Test includes two other answer formats for student-constructed answers: the standard grid and the coordinate plane grid. You can practice gridding in those types of answers in Chapter 33's practice test.

Most of the problems on the Math Test ask you to apply math to everyday situations, such as finding percentages, determining measurements, reading charts or graphs, or recognizing patterns. Only rarely will you be asked to do a "straight math" problem, such as adding two fractions or multiplying two decimals. You may, however, have to know how to do these things in order to solve the problem you are asked.

Numbers, Arithmetic, and Number Sense

In This Chapter

- Overviews of numbers, arithmetic, and number concepts
- GED-like questions to practice the skills you'll be tested on
- Answers and explanations for all the questions

This chapter describes the categories of numbers you should be familiar with for the Math Test. You will read about counting numbers, whole numbers, integers, decimals, and fractions.

There are many words used in math that you may not ordinarily talk or read about. Math terminology is needed to describe mathematical ideas and methods. Without these special words, describing or explaining how to "do" math would be difficult, if not impossible. Look for definitions of math terms in sidebars throughout the chapters in this part of the book.

This chapter reviews how to recognize the various categories of numbers and how to do arithmetic (add, subtract, multiply, and divide) with them. The chapter also talks about percentages, ratios, and proportions. Percentages and ratios are special ways of looking at fractions. Proportions are used to scale quantities up or down while preserving their relative size.

The chapter concludes by reviewing the meaning of the symbols < (less than), > (greater than), ≤ (less than or equal to), and ≥ (greater than or equal to) that indicate the relative size of two numbers. All of the numbers discussed are brought together in a "picture" called the number line. Distances between two numbers on the number line can then be measured using a concept called absolute value.

Counting Numbers, Whole Numbers, and Integers

The numbers that you learned as a small child are called *counting numbers* (also called natural numbers). You use counting numbers to count things: 5 apples, 10 fingers, and so forth. You learned your number facts for addition, subtraction, multiplication, and division for counting numbers in elementary school. This book assumes that you've mastered these facts for the first 10 counting numbers.

To be able to tell someone that you don't have any apples, you need 0 (zero). Zero is also a number, and it means *none*. The counting numbers together with zero make up what are called the *whole numbers*.

DEFINITION

Counting numbers consist of 1, 2, 3, …. The … means "and so on, forever."
Whole numbers consist of 0, 1, 2, 3, ….

Numbers that are less than zero also play an important role in real life. Temperatures below zero come to mind. If it's 10 degrees colder than 0, you say it's 10 below zero, or −10 degrees. Locations such as Death Valley, California, that are below sea level have altitudes that are negative numbers. The altitude of Death Valley is −262 feet.

Numbers that are less than zero are called negative numbers. If you put the negative counting numbers and the whole numbers together, you have what are called *integers*. The integers consist of …, −3, −2, −1, 0, 1, 2, 3, …. The positive integers and counting numbers are different names for the same set of numbers. Pairs of integers that differ only in sign, such as 1 and −1, are called *opposites*. Opposite pairs are extremely important because when you add them, you always get 0.

DEFINITION

Integers are positive and negative whole numbers, including zero. **Opposites** are pairs of integers, such as 2 and -2, that add to make 0.

You have now seen three categories of numbers: counting numbers, whole numbers, and integers. Each category was built from its predecessor by attaching more numbers. First, the whole numbers were built from the counting numbers by attaching zero, and the integers were built by attaching negative counting numbers to the whole numbers. Before the chapter is concluded, you will see how fractions are built from integers and how decimal numbers are a convenient way of writing all these numbers.

When you add, subtract, multiply, or divide numbers, you do arithmetic. Here are some terms you need to know:

- The result of adding numbers is called a *sum*.

- When you subtract one number from another, the result is called a *difference*.

- Multiplying two numbers results in a *product*.

- The numbers being multiplied are called *factors*.

- Dividing one number by another results in a *quotient*.

- The number being divided is called the *dividend*, while the number doing the dividing is called the *divisor*.

If two integers have the same sign, add them without regard to sign and put the common sign on the sum. For example, 8 + 7 = 15, and −7 + (−8) = −15. The −8 is in parentheses because mathematicians don't like to see two signs right next to each other.

If two integers have opposite signs, ignore the signs and subtract the smaller from the larger. Then attach the sign of the larger number to this difference. For example, −8 + 10 = 2 because 10 − 8 = 2 and the larger number 10 is positive, so the answer 2 is positive. But −8 + 6 = −2 because 8 − 6 = 2, but the larger number 8 is negative, so the answer −2 is negative.

To subtract integers, just add the opposite. Let's look at some examples:

- 6 − 9 = 6 + (−9) = −3

- −2 − 7 = −2 + (−7) = −5

- 5 − (−4) = 5 + 4 = 9

- −7 − (−9) = −7 + 9 = 2

Subtraction is a good example of a technique that is used often in math. Instead of creating a new method to do a new problem, change the new problem to a problem that already has a method. Instead of having a new set of rules for subtraction, change the subtraction problem to an addition problem and use the addition rules we already have.

Multiplying integers is easier than adding them. If two integers have the same sign, their product is positive. If they have different signs, the product and quotient are negative. If either integer is 0, the product is 0. Thus, $4 \times 5 = 20$ and $(-4) \times (-5) = 20$, but $4 \times (-5) = -20$ and $(-4) \times 5 = -20$.

IN THE KNOW

When parentheses are used to enclose numbers, a multiplication sign isn't necessary. For example, $(-4) \times (-5) = 20$ has the same meaning as $(-4)(-5) = 20$.

The rule is the same for division. If two integers have the same sign and you divide, the quotient is positive. If they have different signs, the quotient is negative. So $20 \div 2 = 10$ and $(-20) \div (-2) = 10$, but $20 \div (-2) = -10$ and $-20 \div 2 = -10$.

You probably used the division symbol ($\div$) when you learned to divide in elementary school. The horizontal bar in this symbol indicates division, while the two dots represent the numbers. For example, $20 \div 10$ can also be written as $\frac{20}{10}$. The division bar, rather than the division symbol, is used almost all the time in high school math.

Decimals, Scientific Notation, and Rounding

Our number system uses 10 digits: 0, 1, 2, 3, 4, 5, 6, 7, 8, and 9. The prefix *deci-* means 10 in Latin (think of the word *decade*). A decimal number is a decimal point (.) with a bunch of digits around it, like 29.365. Each of the digits occupies a place value. The names of the place values to the left and right of the decimal point are shown in the next figure.

Whole Numbers												Decimals				
Billions			Millions			Thousands			Units							
10^{11}	10^{10}	10^9	10^8	10^7	10^6	10^5	10^4	10^3	10^2	10^1	10^0	10^{-1}	10^{-2}	10^{-3}	10^{-4}	10^{-5}
Hundred Billions	Ten Billions	Billions	Hundred Millions	Ten Millions	Millions	Hundred Thousands	Ten Thousands	Thousands	Hundreds	Tens	Units	Tenths	Hundredths	Thousands	Ten Thousandths	Hundred Thousandths

Place values.

Whichever column you start with in this table, each digit is 10 times the amount of the digit to its right. For example, a digit in the thousands column is 10 times what the value of that digit would have been in the hundreds column.

Because decimals are based on the number 10, it's easy to multiply or divide a decimal number by 10. To multiply by 10, move the decimal point one space to the right. To divide by 10, move the decimal point one space to the left. To multiply by 100, move the decimal point two spaces to the right. To divide by 100, move the decimal point two spaces to the left, and so forth.

For example, look at the decimal number 29.365. Start with the right most digit, 5. It is in the thousandths place. This number would read "twenty-nine and three hundred sixty-five thousandths." To multiply this number by 100, move the decimal two places to the right, yielding 2936.5, read "two thousand nine hundred thirty-six and five tenths." To divide 29.365 by 10, move the decimal point one place to the left, yielding 2.9365, read "two and nine thousand three hundred sixty-five ten thousandths."

Any integer can be written as a decimal. Just place a decimal point after the integer. The integer –14 and the decimal –14.00 have the same value. So do the integer 7 and the decimal 7.00. Therefore, even if you see an integer written without a decimal point, you can think of it as a decimal number.

You can attach zeros at the front and back of a decimal without changing its value. The number 0029.365000 is the same as the number 29.365. This is true because each zero multiplies its place value and zero times any number is zero. As you will see, this makes it easier to add and subtract decimals. Zeros attached to the front of a decimal number are called *leading zeros*, while those attached to the back are called *trailing zeros*.

The term *scientific notation* comes from science's use of very large numbers and numbers very close to zero. The distance (in miles) to the nearest star other than the sun is about 25.2 trillion miles. Scientific notation is used to compare astronomical distances because they are so large. At the other extreme, some physical constants in science are numbers very close to zero. Planck's constant—the energy of a photon divided by its frequency—would be written in decimal form as 33 zeros to the right of the decimal, followed by 626. Scientific notation is the only reasonable way to write a number this small!

The numbers 1, 10, 100, 1,000, and so forth are called "powers of 10." The number 10 is convenient because the powers of 10 can be determined by counting the number of zeros following the 1. For example, 10^3 (10 to the power 3) is $10 \times 10 \times 10$, which is 1,000, a 1 followed by three zeros.

The numbers $\frac{1}{10}, \frac{1}{100}, \frac{1}{1000}$, and so forth are also powers of 10. Since these numbers are smaller than 1, however, we use negative integers as powers of 10: $\frac{1}{10} = 10^{-1}$, $\frac{1}{100} = 10^{-2}$, $\frac{1}{1000} = 10^{-3}$, and so forth.

A number is said to be written in scientific notation if it is a number between 1 and 10 (including 1 but not including 10) times a power of 10. A method for changing a number in decimal form to its scientific notation is best illustrated by examples.

Suppose you start with the decimal number 145.23. Move the decimal point two places to the left to create the number 1.4523, which is between 1 and 10. Since the number you started with is larger than 10, you have to raise 10 to the power 2. Therefore, the scientific notation of 145.23 is 1.4523×10^2.

Suppose now that you start with the decimal number .0014523. This time you must move the decimal point three places to the right to get 1.4523, a number between 1 and 10. Since the number you started with is smaller than 1, you have to raise 10 to the power −3. Therefore the scientific notation for .0014523 is 1.4523×10^{-3}.

What about numbers larger than 1 and smaller than 10? What, for example, is the scientific notation for the number 4.61? Since this number is already between 1 and 10, there is no need to move the decimal point. In other words, you move the decimal point 0 places. Therefore, the scientific notation for 4.61 is 4.61×10^0.

IN THE KNOW

A decimal number is larger than 10, between 1 and 10, or smaller than 1. In these three cases, the powers of 10 are positive, zero, and negative when the number is written in scientific notation.

The method for changing a number written in scientific notation to a decimal number reverses the procedure just described.

Suppose you start with the number 5.6038×10^4. Since the exponent is positive, the decimal number will be bigger than 10, so move the decimal point four places to the right, resulting in the decimal number 56,038.

Suppose you start with the number 9.582×10^{-2}. Since the exponent is negative, the decimal number will be less than 1, so move the decimal two places to the left. You will have to attach a leading zero to the original scientific form, making it $.09582 \times 10^{-2}$. Then when you move the decimal point two places to the left, you get the decimal number .09582.

The difference in *order of magnitude* of two numbers is the difference in the powers of 10 when the numbers are written in scientific notation.

> **DEFINITION**
>
> The **order of magnitude** of a number is the power of 10 when the number is written in scientific notation. Basically, the order of magnitude tells you whether a number is in the hundreds, thousands, tenths, hundredths, etc.

To find a difference in the order of magnitude of two numbers, just write the numbers in scientific notation and subtract the powers of 10. Suppose you wanted to compare the orders of magnitude of 105 and 100,750. In scientific notation, $105 = 1.05 \times 10^2$ and $100{,}750 = 1.00750 \times 10^5$. The number 100,750 is 3 (5 – 2) orders of magnitude larger than the number 105. Or you could say that the number 105 is 3 orders of magnitude smaller than the number 100,750.

The power of an earthquake is measured on the Richter scale. Richter scale numbers represent orders of magnitude. An earthquake of Richter number 8 is 100 times more powerful than one of Richter number 6 because they are 2 (8 – 6) orders of magnitude apart.

Add or subtract decimals the same way you would add and subtract whole numbers, but be careful to add or subtract digits of the same place value. The safest way to add decimals is to arrange them vertically and line up the decimal points. To add the decimal numbers 6.2, 8.03, and 35.49, arrange them vertically, attach trailing zeros, and add:

$$
\begin{array}{r}
6.20 \\
8.03 \\
+\,35.49 \\
\hline
49.72
\end{array}
$$

After elementary school, few if any math textbooks use a vertical form for problems because it is an inefficient use of space. You would be more likely to see this problem stated: Find the sum of 6.2 + 8.03 + 35.49, and you would have to mentally line up the decimal point and corresponding place values.

When you subtract decimal numbers, you also need to line up the decimal point and attach trailing zeros. Then subtract just as you would if they were integers, but keep the decimal point where it is. For instance, find the difference of 48.5 – 29.72. First attach a trailing zero to get 48.50 – 29.72. Then subtract as though you were subtracting 4,850 – 2,972, but retain the decimal point to get 18.78 as the difference.

To multiply decimals, multiply as though the numbers were whole numbers. Then count the total number of places to the right of the decimal in both factors. Place the decimal point that total number of places in from the right of the product.

Suppose you are asked to multiply 5.1 × 2.36. Multiply 51 times 236 as whole numbers, getting 12,036. The factors have a total of three digits to the right of the decimal point, so place the decimal point three places in from the right. The product is 12.036.

To divide decimals, move the decimal point of both the divisor and dividend the same number of places to the right until both are whole numbers. Attach trailing zeros as necessary. Then divide as you would the whole numbers.

Suppose you need to find the quotient $\frac{9.45}{2.1}$. Attach a trailing zero on 2.1 to make it 2.10. Now you can move both decimal points two places to the right. Then use long division to divide 945 by 210 to get 4.5 as the quotient.

Rounding numbers and doing mental arithmetic with these rounded numbers will really help you develop your numbers sense. For example, if you want to know how much you spent in cash during the past week, you could round your expenditures to the nearest 10 dollars and add the rounded numbers mentally.

There is a rule for rounding to a particular place value. Call the digit in the place value you are rounding to the *rounding digit*. Look at the digit just to the right of the rounding digit. If this digit is less than 5, leave the rounding digit as it is and drop all remaining digits. If this digit is 5 or more, increase the rounding digit by 1 and drop the remaining digits. If the rounding digit is 9, and the digit to its right is 5 or larger, change the rounding digit to 0 and add 1 to the digit to its left.

The following examples illustrate this rule:

- **Round 4,746 to the nearest hundred.** The rounding digit is the 7 (hundreds place). The digit to its right is 4, which is less than 5. Therefore, 4,746 rounds to 4,700.

- **Round .2653 to the nearest hundredth.** The rounding digit is 6, and the digit to its right is 5, so round the 6 up to 7: .2653 rounded to the nearest hundredth is .27.

- **Round 8.98 to the nearest tenth.** The rounding digit is 9, and the digit to its right is 8, so round 9 to 0 and 8 to 9: 8.98 rounded to the nearest tenth is 9.0. You need the .0 even though 9.0 and 9 are the same value because 9 is 8.98 rounded to the nearest unit.

Fractions

Fractions are numbers such as $\frac{1}{2}$, $\frac{3}{7}$, and $\frac{10}{3}$. The top number is called the *numerator* and the bottom number is the *denominator*. A fraction cannot have a 0 in the denominator. The first two fractions are examples of proper fractions because the numerator is smaller than the denominator. The third number is an example of an improper fraction because the numerator is larger than the denominator.

Fractions are most often used to represent part of a whole with the numerator measuring the part and the denominator measuring the whole. If you eat three pieces of an eight-piece pizza, you have eaten $\frac{3}{8}$ (three-eighths) of the whole pizza.

A fraction can also be thought of as the result of a division. One-half is the result of dividing one by two. Three-sevenths is the result of dividing three by seven. Ten-thirds is the result of dividing ten by three. In this last case (the improper fraction), the result of dividing is three and one-third. So an improper fraction is an integer plus a proper fraction.

If you divide a number by 1, the result is the same as the number. This means that an integer can be regarded as a special type of fraction—namely, one whose denominator is 1. For example, 17 is the same number as $\frac{17}{1}$. Fortunately, the rules of arithmetic work the same whether a number is regarded as an integer or a fraction.

Fractions have opposites (negatives), and they can be added and subtracted just like integers. Remember that when you add opposite number pairs, the answer is zero. For instance, $6+(-6)=0$ and $\frac{2}{3}+\left(-\frac{2}{3}\right)=0$.

A fraction is also paired with another number called its *reciprocal*. The reciprocal of a fraction is obtained by switching the numerator and denominator. The reciprocal of $\frac{5}{8}$ is $\frac{8}{5}$. The reciprocal of an integer such as –17 is $\frac{1}{-17}$ because –17 is the same number as $\frac{-17}{1}$. A number times its reciprocal is 1. The number 0 doesn't have a reciprocal because no number times 0 equals 1. This is why division by zero is impossible.

DEFINITION

Reciprocals are pairs of numbers that have a product of 1.

A fraction is in reduced form if no number divides evenly into both its numerator and denominator. For example, $\frac{2}{3}$ is in reduced form while $\frac{4}{6}$ isn't, because 2 divides evenly into both 4 and 6. Reducing fractions is easy: just find a number that divides evenly into both the numerator and denominator of the fraction. The fraction $\frac{12}{28}$ reduces to $\frac{6}{14}$ because 2 divides evenly into both 12 and 28. But you can reduce $\frac{6}{14}$ further to $\frac{3}{7}$ if you divide by 2 again. This is as far as you can go because there is no other number that divides evenly into both 3 and 7. If your number facts are good, you may realize at the beginning that you could divide both by 4, and you would get to the answer faster.

Multiplying two fractions is the easiest arithmetic with fractions because all you do to get the product is multiply the numerators to get the numerator of the answer and multiply the denominators to get the denominator of the answer. For example, in $\frac{3}{8} \cdot \frac{1}{5} = \frac{3 \cdot 1}{8 \cdot 5} = \frac{3}{40}$, the answer $\frac{3}{40}$ can't be reduced.

Now look at this multiplication problem: $\frac{2}{3} \cdot \frac{9}{14} = \frac{18}{42}$. You can then reduce $\frac{18}{42}$ by dividing numerator and denominator by 6: $\frac{18 \div 6}{42 \div 6} = \frac{3}{7}$. Notice that in the original problem, there is a 3 in the denominator of the first fraction and a 9 in the numerator of the second fraction. Since 3 divides evenly into both of these numbers, you could divide both by 3. Similarly, 2 divides evenly into both 2 (the numerator of the first fraction) and 14 (the denominator of the second fraction). This procedure can be set up as follows:

$$\frac{\cancel{2}^1}{\cancel{3}^1} \cdot \frac{\cancel{9}^3}{\cancel{14}^7} = \frac{1 \cdot 3}{1 \cdot 7} = \frac{3}{7}$$

When it's possible, dividing ahead of time like this makes it unnecessary to reduce as a second step.

The word *of* usually means *multiply* in math. Suppose, for example, that you and your friends order 3 pizzas and you eat $\frac{3}{8}$ of the total. There are 24 slices in 3 pizzas, so you eat $\frac{3}{8}$ of 24 slices. Multiply $\frac{3}{8}$ times 24, to get 9 slices you eat altogether.

To divide one fraction by another, just multiply the first fraction by the reciprocal of the second. For instance, $\frac{2}{3} \div \frac{7}{8}$ is the same as $\frac{2}{3} \cdot \frac{8}{7}$, and both are equal to $\frac{16}{21}$. This is another example of doing a new problem by changing the form of the problem and using a method we already know.

Adding and subtracting fractions can be more involved, depending on whether the denominators of the two numbers are the same. If the denominators are the same, you just add or subtract the numerators. For example, $\frac{2}{7} + \frac{3}{7} = \frac{5}{7}$ or $\frac{8}{9} - \frac{3}{9} = \frac{5}{9}$. If

necessary, answers can be reduced: for example, $\frac{7}{8} - \frac{3}{8} = \frac{\cancel{4}^{1}}{\cancel{8}_{2}} = \frac{1}{2}$.

When you add or subtract fractions that have different denominators, you must first find the *least common denominator*.

DEFINITION

The **least common denominator** of two fractions is the least common multiple of the two denominators. This is the smallest number that is a multiple of both denominators.

Here are some examples of adding and subtracting two fractions with different denominators:

- $\frac{1}{4} + \frac{2}{3}$. The denominators are 4 and 3, and 12 is the smallest multiple of both. Since 12 is 3 times 4, multiply both numerator and denominator of $\frac{1}{4}$ by 3 to get $\frac{3}{12}$. Since 12 is 4 times 3, multiply both numerator and denominator of $\frac{2}{3}$ by 4 to get $\frac{8}{12}$. Add $\frac{3}{12}$ and $\frac{8}{12}$ to get the sum, $\frac{11}{12}$.

- $\frac{2}{5} + \frac{2}{15}$. The denominators are 5 and 15, and 15 is a multiple of both. Since 15 is 3 times 5, multiply both numerator and denominator of $\frac{2}{5}$ by 3 to get $\frac{6}{15}$. Since 15 equals 1 times 15, multiply both numerator and denominator of $\frac{2}{15}$ by 1 to get $\frac{2}{15}$. Add $\frac{6}{15}$ and $\frac{2}{15}$ to get $\frac{8}{15}$.

- $\frac{3}{4} - \frac{7}{10}$. The two denominators are 4 and 10. Look at multiples of the larger denominator and see if they are multiples of the smaller one. The larger denominator is 10. The smallest multiple of 10 is 1 times 10, which is 10, but

10 isn't a multiple of 4. The next multiple of 10 is 2 times 10, which is 20. Since 4 goes into 20 (5 times), 20 is the least common denominator. Finish the problem as in the two previous examples to get the difference, $\dfrac{1}{20}$:

$$\frac{3}{4} - \frac{7}{10} = \frac{5 \cdot 3}{5 \cdot 4} - \frac{2 \cdot 7}{2 \cdot 10} = \frac{15}{20} - \frac{14}{20} = \frac{1}{20}$$

Ratios

Ratios provide a method of comparing two numbers. For example, if I am 50 years old and you are 25 years old, the ratio of our ages is 50 to 25. You could write this as the fraction $\dfrac{50}{25}$, which reduces to $\dfrac{2}{1}$. Therefore you could say that I've lived 2 years for each year you've lived.

Unit pricing at the supermarket is another example of using ratios to make comparisons. The brand-name cereal may cost $4.25 for 15 ounces while the generic brand costs $2.50 for 11.5 ounces. By comparing the ratio $\dfrac{4.25}{15} = .28$ and $\dfrac{2.5}{11.5} = .22$, you know that you save about 6 cents an ounce by buying the generic brand.

Sometimes it's convenient to compare the numerators of two fractions as a ratio. Suppose, for example, there are 42 people at a dance, 24 boys and 18 girls. You could say that $\dfrac{18}{42}$ of those at the dance are girls and $\dfrac{24}{42}$ are boys. If you're interested in comparing the number of girls to boys, you could look at the ratio $\dfrac{18}{24}$. By reducing $\dfrac{18}{24}$ to $\dfrac{3}{4}$, you could say that there are three girls to every four boys at the dance.

Percentages are fractions or ratios that have denominators of 100. Using 100 as a standard denominator makes comparison of numbers easier since you only have to look at the numerators to determine which number is larger. We encounter percentages all the time in our daily lives. Sales tax is 6% of the price of an item; the electronics store is offering 30% off of high-definition TVs; a professional quarterback completes 60% of his passes. The word *percent* means "out of every 100." So 6% sales tax means the tax is 6 cents out of every 100 cents (1 dollar); 30% off means 30 cents off for every dollar; and 60% completion rate means 60 complete passes for every 100 passes thrown.

Because percentages are so useful for making comparisons, you should know a simple way of changing a fraction to a percentage. The method is simple. Do the division that is implied in the fraction. This gives you a decimal number, which you then multiply by 100. For example, to change the fraction $\frac{3}{5}$ to a percentage, first divide 3 by 5 and get .6. Then multiply .6 by 100 by attaching a trailing zero to .6 and moving the decimal point 2 places to the right. The answer is 60%.

Percentages are often used to described discounts or mark-ups on prices. If an item you want to buy is 15% off, this means you only pay 85% (100 – 15)% of the cost. Therefore, you would only pay .85 times the price of the item.

GOOD IDEA

If a discount is described as a percentage off, subtract that percentage off from 100 and multiply the result by the original value.

You cannot add percentages taken off a single item. If a store offers 25% off and once you get there you get another 10% off, your final price isn't 35% off. Suppose, for example, you buy a $100 item. With a 25% discount, your item now costs $75. The extra 10% off is off $75, not $100. Therefore you only get $7.50 more off instead of $10. Your item's final cost would be $67.50, and not $65.

A *proportion* is simply a statement that says two ratios are equal. In the previous dance example, the ratio of 18 girls to 24 boys was equal to the ratio of 3 girls to 4 boys: $\frac{18}{24} = \frac{3}{4}$. This statement is a proportion. We could also say that 18 girls to 24 boys is proportional to 3 girls to 4 boys.

Proportions are important in geometry because they preserve shape. When you blow up a photograph of a person's face, the whole face is larger but the parts of the face are proportional to the face in the original photo. The mirrors in the funhouse of an amusement park compress the face to look fat or stretch it to look long. Neither of these reflections is proportional to the actual face.

There are four numbers in a proportion: the numerators and denominators of the two fractions. In the dance example, $\frac{18}{24} = \frac{3}{4}$. You can also write a proportion using colons, which look like division symbols without the horizontal line. In this case, 18:24 = 3:4. The outside numbers (18 and 4) are called the *extremes* of the proportion. The two inside numbers (24 and 3) are called the *means* of the proportion. In a proportion, the product of the means is equal to the product of the extremes. In this case, 18 × 4 = 3 × 24. Both products are 72. Applying this fact is often called *cross-multiplying*.

DEFINITION

If you write a proportion as *a:b = c:d*, *a* and *d* are called **extremes,** and *b* and *c* are called **means.**

If you know any three of the numbers in a proportion, you can determine the fourth. Suppose, for example, that a basketball player typically makes 8 of 10 free throws. How many free throws would you expect this player to make if he takes 20 free throws? If you let x stand for the number of free throws the player makes out of 20, you have the proportion: $\frac{8}{10} = \frac{x}{20}$. Cross-multiply to get 10 × x = 8 × 20, or 10 × x = 160. To get the value of *x*, divide 160 by 10, getting 16. A player who makes 8 of 10 free throws can expect to make 16 of 20.

This method can always be applied to solve a proportion if you know three of the numbers. Call the missing number *x;* cross-multiply; then divide by the number that multiplies *x*.

The Number Line and Absolute Value

Given two numbers, call them *a* and *b*, there are three possibilities:

- The two numbers are equal (*a = b*).

- The first number is smaller than the second (*a < b*).

- The first number is larger than the second (*a > b*).

The symbols < and > are used to compare the sizes of numbers. For example, 3 < 6 and 12 > 4.

A *number line* provides a way of picturing the location of the numbers according to their size.

Start with the number 0 at the "center" of the number line. Positive numbers get larger as you move to the right, while negative numbers get smaller (but larger in magnitude) as you move to the left. The following number line illustrates these ideas and points out a few number locations.

Since a number line is only a visual aid, there is no attempt to show the exact locations of numbers.

Notice that on the number line, 5 and –5 are the same distance from 0 (namely, 5 units). The concept of distance is a positive number. The distance between a number and zero is called the *absolute value* of the number. The absolute value of a positive number is just the number itself, while the absolute value of a negative number is its opposite (the positive number).

The symbol for absolute value is | |. Using this notation, you would write the absolute value of 5 as $|5|$ and the absolute value of –5 as $|-5|$. In math notation, $|5| = 5$ reads "the absolute value of 5 equals 5," and $|-5| = 5$ reads "the absolute value of –5 is 5."

The absolute value symbol is a grouping symbol, like parentheses. For example, $|8 - 12|$ is equal to $|-4|$, which is 4. Don't make the mistake of taking the absolute value of 8, which is 8, and then subtracting the absolute value of 12, which is 12, to get –4.

More generally, the distance between any two numbers on the number line is the absolute value of the difference between the two numbers. The distance between 7 and 12 is 5 because the absolute value of 7 – 12 is 5 ($|7 - 12| = 5$).

Practice

You may use a calculator for some of the practice questions that are in this chapter, Chapters 29, 30, and 31, and on the practice test in Chapter 33. GED test centers provide Casio *fx*–260 calculators, which are described in Chapter 32.

 1. Jackson leased a new car for 3 years. He agreed to pay $1,900 down and a $269 payment each month. He also agreed to pay $0.125 per mile over 30,000 miles. During the 3-year period, Jackson drove the car 32,458 miles. Excluding taxes, what was the cost of leasing this car for 3 years?

(1) $5,435.25

(2) $9,991.25

(3) $11,891.25

(4) $13,741.25

(5) $15,641.25

2. Susan drove to her mother's house at an average speed of 36 miles per hour. The trip there took a half hour. If it took her 20 minutes to return, what was her average speed coming home?

(1) 32 mph

(2) 40 mph

(3) 46 mph

(4) 50 mph

(5) 54 mph

 3. A $1,200 computer is on sale at 20% off. How much would you save by purchasing this computer on sale?

(1) $20

(2) $24

(3) $96

(4) $240

(5) $960

 4. A pancake recipe calls for $\frac{3}{4}$ cup of flour for each batch. You have 3 cups of flour and enough of the other ingredients to make six batches of pancakes. How many batches of pancakes can you make? Mark your answer on the standard grid below.

5. Jack and Jill were picking weeds in the garden. Jack picked $\frac{1}{3}$ of the weeds, and Jill picked $\frac{1}{5}$ of them. What fraction of the weeds did they pick together?

(1) $\frac{1}{4}$

(2) $\frac{1}{2}$

(3) $\frac{8}{15}$

(4) $\frac{4}{5}$

(5) $\frac{7}{8}$

Answers

1. **(3)** Add the three costs: down payment ($1,900), total monthly payments (36 × $269 = $9,684), and mileage over 30,000 (2,458 × $.125 = $307.25) to get $11,891.25. In answer choice (1) only 12 monthly payments were included. In answer choice (2), the $1,900 was left out. In answer choice (4), the per-mile charge of $.125 was applied to the total mileage instead of the mileage over 30,000, and the $1,900 was left out. Answer choice (5) is answer choice (4) with the $1,900 included.

2. **(5)** If it took Susan a half hour to get to her mother's house with an average speed of 36 miles per hour, her mother must live 18 (distance = speed × time) miles away. It took 20 minutes, or one third of an hour, to return, so $\text{time} = \dfrac{\text{distance}}{\text{speed}} = \dfrac{18}{1/3} = 54$. The only unreasonable answer choice is (1) because she could not return home in less time (20 minutes instead of 30) if she were moving more slowly. Answer choice (3) adds the 10 fewer minutes for the return trip from the original speed of 36 miles per hour. The other answer choices are guesses.

3. **(4)** Twenty percent of $1,200 is .20 × 1,200 = 240. Answer choice (1) represents a misreading that the discount is $20 instead of 20%. In answer choice (2), the decimal is misplaced. Answer choices (3) and (5) use 8% and 80% instead of 20%.

4. To determine the number of batches of pancakes you can make with 3 cups of flour, divide 3 by $\frac{3}{4}$ to get four batches. Although you have enough of the other ingredients to make six batches, the amount of flour limits your total yield to four batches. Grid in the number 4 in any of the columns (or 4.0 in any 3 columns).

5. **(3)** This problem requires you to add two fractions without a calculator. The common denominator is 15, the smallest number that both denominators divide into. The fraction $\frac{1}{5} = \frac{3}{15}$, and $\frac{1}{3} = \frac{5}{15}$. Add 3 and 5 to get $\frac{8}{15}$. Answer choice (1) results from adding the numerators (1 + 1) and the denominators (5 + 3) to get $\frac{2}{8}$, which equals $\frac{1}{4}$. Answer choices (2), (4), and (5) are guesses that are greater than either fraction.

Measurement and Geometry

In This Chapter

- Overviews of measurement and geometry
- GED-like questions to practice the skills you'll be tested on
- Answers and explanations for all the questions

This chapter opens with tables that summarize units of length, liquid volume, weight, and temperature, in both the customary (English) system and the metric system. Test-takers are expected to be familiar with these measurements and their relationships. This is followed by definitions of geometric concepts and objects, organized around lines, angles, polygons, triangles, quadrilaterals, circles, and solid figures. Most readers will be familiar with many of these definitions. Again, test-takers are expected to know these definitions. Important facts about triangles, including the famous Pythagorean Theorem, are reviewed next. You may have to use these facts to answer certain questions on the Math Test. This is followed by an explanation of how to use formulas for determining the area, perimeter, and volume of geometric objects. These formulas are described in Chapter 32 and are included in the Math Test. The chapter ends with a general discussion of lines on a coordinate grid. A fuller discussion of lines can be found in Chapter 31.

Common Measurements

There are certain measurements involving length, weight, volume, and temperature that you should know when you take the Math Test. These are summarized in the following tables of customary and metric measurements. Sample problems for each group of units are given.

Units of Length

Customary	Metric
foot is the basic unit	meter is the basic unit
12 inches make 1 foot	100 centimeters make 1 meter
3 feet make 1 yard	1,000 millimeters make 1 meter
5,280 feet make 1 mile	1,000 meters make 1 kilometer

When converting to smaller units, you should multiply. When converting to larger units, you should divide.

Sample Problems

• Doreen wants to fence in her flower garden, which has a perimeter of 60 feet. Fencing comes in 2-yard sections. How many sections of fencing will Doreen need? Since there are 3 feet to a yard, 60 feet is 60 ÷ 3 = 20 yards. Since each section is 2 yards, Doreen will need 10 sections of fence.

• Gary trained for a track meet by running 250 meters, 175 meters, 300 meters, and 275 meters on four consecutive days. How many kilometers did he run altogether? Add these four numbers to get 1,000 meters, or 1 kilometer.

• Guy is reading a map that has a scale of 1 centimeter equals 5 kilometers. The map distance to his destination is 8 centimeters. How far away is his destination? Since each centimeter on the map represents 5 kilometers, a map distance of 8 centimeters represents 8 × 5 = 40 kilometers.

Units of Liquid Volume

Customary	Metric
gallon is the basic unit	liter is the basic unit
4 quarts make 1 gallon	100 centiliters make 1 liter
2 pints make 1 quart	1,000 milliliters make 1 liter

Sample Problems

• Chris makes 10 quarts of lemonade from concentrate. How many gallons of lemonade is this? Since there are 4 quarts to a gallon, divide 10 by 4 to get 2.5 gallons of lemonade.

- Bob and Jack's ice cream costs $3 a pint, and Chicken Farm ice cream costs $5.75 a half gallon. Which ice cream is less expensive? Let's change a half gallon to pints so we can compare pints to pints. A gallon is 4 quarts, so a half-gallon is 2 quarts. A quart is 2 pints, so 2 quarts is 4 pints. Four pints of Bob and Jack's ice cream costs $12, compared to $5.75 for Chicken Farm, so Chicken Farm is less expensive.

- Marge needs to take 3 milliliters of medication every other day. How many centiliters of her medication will she take in 30 days? Since she takes her medication every other day, Marge will take 15 × 3 = 45 milliliters of medication in 30 days. Since there are 10 milliliters to a centiliter, this amounts to 4.5 centiliters over 30 days.

Units of Weight

Customary	Metric
pound is the basic unit	gram is the basic unit
16 ounces make 1 pound	1,000 milligrams make 1 gram
2,000 pounds make 1 ton	1,000 grams make 1 kilogram

Sample Problems

- A drug enforcement agent seizes 12 pounds of marijuana, which sells on the street for $175 per ounce. What is the street value of the 12 pounds seized? There are 16 ounces to a pound, so 16 × 12 = 192 ounces are seized. At $175 per ounce, the street value is $33,600.

- The Chins want to buy stone to landscape their front yard. They will need to buy 3 tons altogether. Their pickup track will carry 750 pounds per trip. How many trips will they have to make in their pickup to carry all the stone home? Since there are 2,000 pounds per ton, 3 tons is 6,000 pounds. Divide 6,000 by 750 to get 8 trips.

Units of Temperature

Customary	Metric
degrees Fahrenheit	degrees Celsius
water freezes at 32°	water freezes at 0°
water boils at 212°	water boils at 100°

- The formula for changing Celsius temperature to Fahrenheit is $F = \dfrac{9}{5}C + 32$. If it is 20° Celsius in Paris, what is the Fahrenheit temperature? Substitute 20 for C in the formula: $\dfrac{9}{\cancel{5}_1}\left(\cancel{20}^{\,4}\right) + 32 = 36 + 32 = 68°\text{F}$.

Geometry Definitions

Geometry is the study of shapes. The geometry of flat surfaces, such as triangles, rectangles, and circles, is called *plane geometry. Solid geometry* is the study of three-dimensional figures, such as rectangular prisms or solids, spheres, cylinders, cones, and pyramids.

DEFINITION

Plane geometry is the study of two-dimensional figures. **Solid geometry** is the study of three-dimensional figures.

You see geometry all around you. A yield sign is a triangle. A stop sign is an octagon. The U.S. Department of Defense building in Washington has the shape of a pentagon. Common three-dimensional objects are cereal boxes, water glasses, and ice-cream cones. The great pyramids of Egypt are probably the best known examples of that shape.

Congruence is a central concept in geometry. The math symbol for congruence is ≅. Two line segments are congruent if they have the same length. Two angles are congruent if they have the same degree measure. A polygon is a closed figure whose boundary consists of segments connected end to end. Two polygons are congruent if they have the same size and shape. A pair of congruent polygons is shown in the following figure.

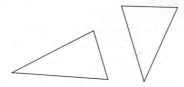

Congruence between two triangles can be established in several ways. In the abbreviations that follow each, S stands for side and A stands for angle.

- If the lengths of the three sides are equal in the triangle (SSS)
- If the lengths of two sides and the measure of the angle they form are equal in the triangles (SAS)
- If the measures of two angles and the length of the side between them are equal in the triangles (ASA)
- If the measures of two angles and the length of the side opposite one of the angles are equal in the two triangles (AAS)

The concept of triangle congruence will be illustrated further in the practice questions at the end of this chapter and in the practice test in Chapter 33.

Two polygons can have the same shape but different sizes. In this case, they are called *similar* (∼).

In similar figures, the angles have the same measure, but the side lengths are proportional instead of equal. In other words, the side lengths of one polygon are all the same multiple of the side lengths of the other. For example, two triangles are similar if they have three equal angle measures and the side lengths of one are all two times the side lengths of the other. The next figure shows a pair of similar polygons.

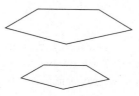

In the following table, each definition consists of a name, a math symbol or symbols, and a figure for the named object.

Item	Symbol/Definition	Figure
Lines		
Line	$\overleftrightarrow{AB}$	
Segment	$\overline{AB}$	
Ray	$\overrightarrow{AB}$	
Parallel lines	$\overleftrightarrow{AB} \parallel \overleftrightarrow{CD}$	
Perpendicular lines	$\overleftrightarrow{AB} \perp \overleftrightarrow{CD}$	
Transversal	t	
Angles		
Angle	$\angle A$	
Degree measure	45°	
Right angle	90°	
Acute angle	less than 90°	

Item	Symbol/Definition	Figure
Obtuse angle	more than 90° (but less than 180°)	
Supplements	sum is 180°	
Complements	sum is 90°	

Polygons

Triangle	3 sides	
Quadrilateral	4 sides	
Pentagon	5 sides	
Hexagon	6 sides	
Octagon	8 sides	

Triangles

Isosceles	2 ≅ sides	
Equilateral	3 ≅ sides	
Scalene	no ≅ sides	

continues

continued

Item	Symbol/Definition	Figure
Acute	3 acute angles	
Obtuse	1 obtuse angle	
Right	1 right angle	

Quadrilaterals

Parallelogram	2 pairs $\parallel$ sides	
Rectangle	4 right angles	
Square	rectangle w/4 $\cong$ sides	
Rhombus	4 $\cong$ sides	
Trapezoid	only 1 pair of pararllel sides	

Circles

Center	O	

Circumference	distance around
Radius	length r
Chord	$\overline{AB}$
Diameter	$\overline{CD}$

Item	Symbol/Definition	Figure
Solids		
Rectangular prism	shaped like a box	
Pyramid	sides come to a point	
Cylinder	shaped like a can	
Cone	shaped like a funnel	

Important Triangle Facts

There are several important facts about triangles that you need to know for the GED.

- The measures of the angles of any triangle sum to 180°. Suppose you know that two angles of a triangle have measures 28° and 63°. These two measures sum to 91°, so the measure of the third angle is (180 − 91)° = 89°.

- The base angles of an isosceles triangle are congruent. Suppose that one of the base angles is 38°. Then the other base angle is also 38°, so the vertex angle must be 104° because 180° − 2 × 38° = 180° − 76° = 104°.

- If you know that the vertex angle of an isosceles triangle has measure 50°, you can find the measure of a base angle by subtracting 50° from 180° (130°) and dividing by 2 to get 65°.

- An equilateral triangle is also *equiangular*. Since the sum of the three angle measures is 180, each angle measure is 60° (180° ÷ 3).

  DEFINITION

A triangle is **equiangular** if all three of its angles have equal measure.

Recall that the square (second power) of a number is the number times itself. This fact underlies the *Pythagorean Theorem*, which only applies to right triangles. It states that the square of the hypotenuse of a right triangle is equal to the sum of the squares of the legs. Angle C in the right triangle $\triangle ABC$ in the figure is the right angle. If a, b, and c are the side lengths, then the Pythagorean Theorem says $a^2 + b^2 = c^2$.

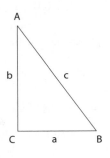

$$c^2 = a^2 + b^2$$

If the legs of a right triangle have lengths 3 and 4, then the hypotenuse has length 5, because $3^2 = 9$, $4^2 = 16$, $9 + 16 = 25$, and $5^2 = 25$. If the legs have lengths 5 and 12, then the hypotenuse has length 13. (Work it out!)

Suppose both legs of a right triangle are 1 unit long. The Pythagorean Theorem says that the square of the length of the hypotenuse is 2 ($1^2 + 1^2$). This means the length of the hypotenuse is a number that equals 2 when you multiply it by itself. No whole number times itself equals 2. Nor is any decimal number times itself, although 1.414^2 = $(1.414)(1.414) = 1.999396$ is very close to 2. This is why *square root* numbers were created. The symbol $\sqrt{2}$ represents a number whose square is 2: $\left(\sqrt{2}\right)^2 = 2$.

> **DEFINITION**
>
> The **square root** of the number a is b if $b^2 = a$. For example, the square root of 16 is 4 because $4^2 = 16$.

Unless a number is a perfect square, such as 25 or 16, you need a calculator to get a decimal value for its approximate square root. Key SHIFT/x^2 on the Casio *fx–260* calculator to find a square root. The following problem can be solved using the Pythagorean Theorem.

A sliding board is 8 feet long and the ladder from the ground to the top of the slide is 6 feet. If the ladder is perpendicular to the ground, how far is the bottom of the slide from the bottom of the ladder?

The slide is the hypotenuse of the right triangle formed by the ladder, the slide, and the ground. Let x stand for the desired distance. Then $8^2 = 6^2 + x^2$, or $64 = 36 + x^2$. So $x^2 = 64 - 36 = 28$ and $x = \sqrt{28} \approx 5.3$. The desired distance is about 5.3 feet.

It is also true that if the square of the length of the longest side of a triangle is equal to the sum of the squares of the lengths of the other two sides, then the triangle is a right triangle. You might be asked, for example, whether a triangle with side lengths 4, 5, and 6 is a right triangle. Square the two smaller numbers and add them: $4^2 + 5^2 = 16 + 25 = 41$. Then square the largest number, $6^2 = 36$. Since $41 \neq 36$, this triangle is not a right triangle.

Perimeter, Area, and Volume

Perimeter, area, and volume are measures of the size of geometrical objects. You measure perimeter when you determine how much fencing you need around your yard. The amount of wall you have to paint is an area. Finally, the amount of mulch you need to cover the garden to a 3-inch depth is a volume.

Perimeter is a one-dimensional measure. It is measured in feet, miles, centimeters, or other measure of length. Area is a two-dimensional measure. It is measured in square feet (ft^2), square centimeters (cm^2), and so forth. Volume is a three-dimensional measure. It is measured in cubic feet (ft^3), cubic centimeters (cm^3 or cc), and so forth.

The number π is the ratio of the circumference to the diameter of a circle. On the GED, the approximate decimal value of π, 3.14, is used to calculate the circumference (perimeter), area, or volume of a circle. The area of a circle of radius 5 inches is approximately $(3.14)(5^2) = (3.14)(25) = 78.5 \text{ in}^2$.

The Math Test includes a formula sheet for finding, among other things, the perimeter, area, and volume of most of the shapes in the table shown earlier in this chapter. This portion of the formula sheet is shown below.

Formulas

Area of *a*:

Square	area = side²
Rectangle	area = length × width
Parallelogram	area = base × height
Triangle	area = ½ × base × height

| Trapezoid | area = $\frac{1}{2}$ × (base$_1$ + base$_2$) × height |
| Circle | area = π × radius^2 (π is approx. 3.14) |

Perimeter of *a:*

Square	perimeter = 4 × side
Rectangle	perimeter = 2 × length + 2 × width
Triangle	perimeter = side$_1$ + side$_2$ + side$_3$

Circumference of *a:*

| Circumference = π × diameter of circle |

Volume of *a:*

Cube	volume = side^3
Rectangular solid	volume = length × width × height
Square pyramid	volume = ($\frac{1}{3}$) × base edge^2 × height
Cylinder	volume = π × radius^2 × height
Cone	volume = ($\frac{1}{3}$) × π × radius^2 × height

The entire formula sheet is shown in Chapter 32.

Examples of how to apply these formulas can be found in the practice questions at the end of this chapter and in the practice test in Chapter 33.

Coordinate Geometry

A *coordinate plane* is formed by two perpendicular number lines that cross at the zero points, called the *origin*. The horizontal number line is called the *x axis*, and numbers get larger as you move from left to right. The vertical number line is called the *y axis*, and numbers get larger as you move from bottom to top.

A point is located on a coordinate grid using an *ordered pair* of numbers. The first number, or *x coordinate*, is measured along the *x* axis. The second number, or *y coordinate*, is measured along the *y* axis.

The following figure shows a coordinate grid with the following points:

- point A (1,4)
- point B (–2,3)
- point C (4,–1)
- point D (–4,–2)
- point E (3,0)
- point F (0,–3)

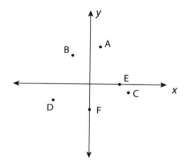

IN THE KNOW

Any point with a *y* coordinate of 0 is on the *x* axis, while any point with an *x* coordinate of 0 is on the *y* axis.

There are two things you need to be able to find about a line on a coordinate grid:

- The distance between two points on the line
- The *slope* of the line (the amount of "tilt" from the horizontal)

Formulas for finding these are on the formula sheet in Chapter 32. For horizontal and vertical lines, it's better (and easier) not to use the formulas. Look at the two points (–3,2) and (5,2) on the grid in the figure. The distance between these two points is 8 units (count horizontally from –3 to 5). Since a horizontal line has no tilt, its slope is 0.

Now let's look at the vertical line through the points (1,–7) and (1,5), also shown in the next figure. Count vertically from –7 to 5 to find the distance 12. A vertical line is completely tilted, so its slope is undefined.

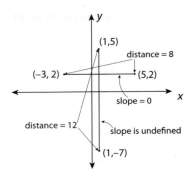

Finding distance and slope of a diagonal line (neither horizontal nor vertical) takes more work. Suppose you want to find the distance between the point (–5,2) and the point (7,–3) shown in the next figure.

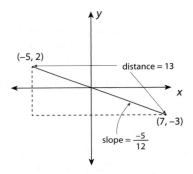

Use the distance formula on the formula sheet with $x_1 = -5$, $y_1 = 2$, $x_2 = 7$, and $y_2 = -3$:

$$\text{distance} = \sqrt{(x_2 - x_1)^2 + (y_2 - y_1)^2}$$
$$= \sqrt{(7 - (-5))^2 + (-3 - 2)^2}$$
$$= \sqrt{12^2 + (-5)^2}$$
$$= \sqrt{144 + 25}$$
$$= \sqrt{169}$$
$$= 13$$

Now use the formula for slope from the formula sheet with the same two points:

$$\text{slope} = \frac{y_2 - y_1}{x_2 - x_1}$$

$$= \frac{-3 - 2}{7 - (-5)}$$

$$= \frac{-5}{12}$$

One interpretation of slope is how far you go up (or down) for each unit you move right. In this case, you go down 5 (because the numerator is –5) for every 12 steps right. If the slope had been positive $\frac{5}{12}$, you would have gone up 5 for every 12 steps right.

IN THE KNOW

A line with a positive slope goes up as you move left to right while a line with a negative slope goes down as you move left to right.

There will be more on coordinate planes and line graphs in Chapter 31.

Practice

 1. A base angle of an isosceles triangle measures 34°. What is the degree measure of the vertex angle? Mark your answer on the standard grid below.

2. The profile of a sliding board has the shape of a right triangle. As shown in the figure, the bottom of the board and the bottom of the slide are 4 feet apart and the slide is 7 feet long.

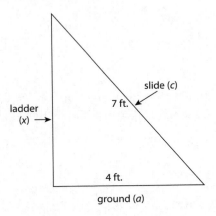

How high is the ladder?

(1) 2.5 ft

(2) 5.4 ft

(3) 5.8 ft

(4) 6.1 ft

(5) 8.3 ft

3. In addition to the information given in the figure, which fact or facts would allow you to conclude that triangle *PQR* is congruent to triangle *XYZ*?

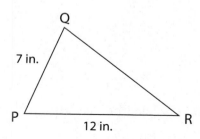

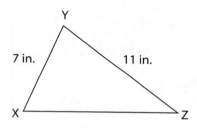

(A) $\angle R \cong \angle Z$

(B) $XY=12$

(C) $\angle P \cong \angle X$

(1) (A)

(2) (B)

(3) (C)

(4) (A) and (C)

(5) (B) and (C)

4. As shown in the figure, the roof of a house has the shape of an isosceles triangle.

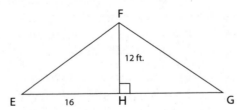

The 12-foot perpendicular line from the peak divides the base of this triangle in half. The sides of the roof have slopes of $\dfrac{3}{4}$ and $-\dfrac{3}{4}$. Find the length of $\overline{EG}$.

(1) 16 ft

(2) 24 ft

(3) 30 ft

(4) 32 ft

(5) 48 ft

 5. As shown in the figure, the Robinsons' dining room has 12-foot ceilings and is in the shape of a rectangle 20 feet by 25 feet. Ignoring space taken up by doors and openings, find the amount of wall space to the nearest square foot.

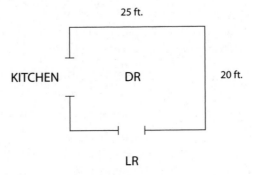

(1) 500 ft²

(2) 540 ft²

(3) 1,080 ft²

(4) 1,200 ft²

(5) 6,000 ft²

Answers

1. The correct answer is 112°. An isosceles triangle has two base angles that have the same measure and a vertex angle. Since one base angle has measure of 34°, so does the other one, and the sum of these measures is 68°. The sum of the measures of all three angles is 180°, so subtract 68° from 180°, to get 112°.

2. **(2)** Since the slide, ladder, and ground between the bottoms of the slide and the ladder form a right triangle, use the Pythagorean Theorem to find x, the length of the missing leg (the ladder):

   $a^2 + x^2 = c^2$

   $(4.5)^2 + x^2 = 7^2$

   $20.25 + x^2 = 49$

   $x^2 = 49 - 20.25$

   $x^2 = 28.75$

   $x = \sqrt{28.75}$

   $x \approx 5.4$

   In answer choice (1), 4.5 was subtracted from 7, based on the belief that $a + b = c$. Answer choice (3) is the average of the lengths of the hypotenuse and one leg. Answer choice (4) is an incorrect guess, while answer choice (5) is the result of using x as the hypotenuse instead of a leg in the Pythagorean Theorem.

3. **(5)** This answer choice will make a pair of sides and the included angle congruent (SAS). None of the other answer choices results in enough information to conclude that the triangles are congruent.

4. **(4)** The slope of a line is the vertical change *(FH)* divided by the horizontal change *(EH)*. The vertical change is 12 feet, and the horizontal change is *EH*. Therefore, $\frac{12}{EH} = \frac{3}{4}$. Solve this proportion by cross-multiplying: $3 \times EH = 48$, so $EH = 16$. *EG* is twice as much as *EH*, so *EG* = 32. Answer choice (1) is for people who forget to multiply by 2 to answer the question, or people who take *EG* as the horizontal change. Answer choice (2) doubles the vertical change. Answer choice (3) results from an arithmetical error, and answer choice (5) is double the correct answer.

5. **(3)** Each of the four walls has an area of 12 × the length of the wall. Two walls have areas of 12 × 25 = 300, for 600 ft². The other two walls have areas of 12 × 20 = 240, for 480 ft². The four walls have a total of 600 + 480 = 1,080 ft². Answer choice (1) is the area of the floor, while answer choice (5) is the volume of the room. Answer choice (2) is half the correct answer, and answer choice (4) is the result of an arithmetic error.

Data Analysis, Statistics, and Probability

In This Chapter

- Overviews of charts, tables, graphs, statistics, and probability
- GED-like questions to practice the skills you'll be tested on
- Answers and explanations for all the questions

Data analysis, statistics, and probability play a larger role in today's digital world than they did before. The advent of computers makes it possible to tabulate information into statistical summaries that one could only dream about 50 years ago. The twenty-first century has been deemed the "Information Age," where being able to extract knowledge from sometimes "uncertain" information is a useful skill.

Data Analysis

For the Math Test, data analysis means answering questions by studying a chart, graph, or table. The following examples illustrate these types of visual presentations.

Bar charts are best for showing frequency counts in various categories. A bar chart consists of rectangles sitting on a horizontal axis.

The heights of the rectangles are proportional to the counts in the categories. The vertical scale could also show the percentage of the total in each category. The following figure shows the number of first-, second-, and third-class passengers and crew on the maiden voyage of the *Titanic*.

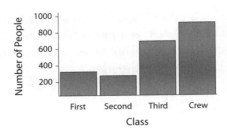

A glance at this visual tells you that the largest group was the crew, followed by third class, then first-class passengers. Second-class passengers were the smallest group.

Pie charts are another type of visual representation of data. These are most useful in showing how a total is divided into parts. A pie chart is a circle that is cut up into pie-shaped pieces that are proportional to the number or percentage in each category. The following pie chart shows the percentage breakdown of the *Titanic* passengers and crew.

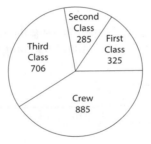

Note how it's easy to see that first- and second-class passengers together make up about a quarter of the total count.

Line graphs provide a third way of illustrating data. Line graphs are a good way of showing change over time. The following line graph shows the monthly natural gas usage for a year in a home where natural gas provides heat and hot water.

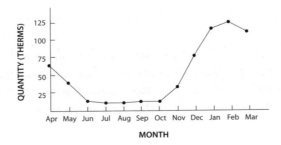

A coordinate plane can be used to graph a function. Such a graph provides a visual image of how one variable depends on another. For example, the following coordinate plane shows the distance a person is from home as a function of the length of time the person has been walking in one direction.

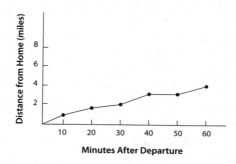

You can tell whether the person is walking faster or more slowly by just looking at the slopes of the segments.

Tables provide the simplest way of summarizing data. The following table shows a household budget broken into various spending categories.

Household Budget Categories

Category	Monthly Budget
Rent	$1,200
Food	$ 600
Clothing	$ 150
Utilities	$ 300
Insurance	$ 250
Auto	$ 400
Entertainment	$ 300
Miscellaneous	$ 250

There is no single "method" for answering questions about a chart, graph, or table. As a general rule, these problems are quite easy, but you must be sure to read these problems carefully and answer the question asked. The practice questions at the end of the chapter give several examples of this type of question.

Statistics

Statistics are numbers that are used to summarize a body of data. Statistics can also mean the broader discipline involving the study of data. Statistics you need to know for the Math Test are limited to a few ways of describing a data set. It is useful to think concretely about data sets, such as a group of test scores.

Any set of numbers has a largest (maximum) value and smallest (minimum) value. The difference between the maximum and minimum (maximum – minimum) is called the *range*. Put the numbers in order from largest to smallest. If the number of numbers is odd, there is a middle one, called the *median*. If the number of numbers is even, there are two "middle" numbers, and the median is their average. In either case, half the numbers are smaller than or as small as the median, and half are as large or larger. The median is one way of representing the "center" of a data set.

DEFINITION

The **range** of a set of numbers is the largest number minus the smallest number. The **median** of a set of numbers is the middle number when the numbers are in order from largest to smallest.

Consider the following 15 test scores:

95, 93, 93, 89, 86, 82, 82, 82, 79, 74, 74, 62, 61, 55, 52

The range is 43 (95 – 52) and the median is 82, the eighth number in from the maximum. Now suppose the highest score, 95, were not in the list. Then the two middle numbers would be 82 (the seventh) and 79 (the eighth). The median in this case would be 80.5, the average of 82 and 79.

A second way of measuring the center of a data set is with the *mean*. This is what most people think of as the average. Add all the numbers and divide by the number of numbers. Adding the 15 test scores above gives a total of 1,161. Dividing by 15 gives a mean of 77.3 rounded to the nearest tenth.

DEFINITION

The **mean** of a data set is the sum of the numbers divided by the number of numbers.

The median and mean represent two ways of representing a data set with a single number. Since such a number should be "centered" within the data set, median and mean are called "measures of central tendency." The question of when it's best to use which of these measures is beyond the scope of the GED. In any question on the test, you may be asked to find the median, mean, or both.

Another measure of central tendency is the *mode*. This is the value that occurs with the greatest frequency. For example, suppose a die is rolled 50 times: 4 ones, 6 twos, 5 threes, 12 fours, 15 fives, and 8 sixes. The mode would be 5 because that number was rolled more frequently than the other numbers.

Probability

Probability is a way of measuring uncertainty. The subject has its origin in games of chance such as cards, dice, and coins and spinners. Loosely speaking, the probability of an event is the number of ways that event can occur divided by the total possible number of outcomes.

For example, the probability of tossing heads when tossing a fair coin is $\frac{1}{2}$ because there are two possible outcomes of a coin toss (heads or tails), and one is heads. The probability of tossing a number less than three spots in the roll of a fair die is $\frac{1}{3}$ because a die has six sides, and two of them show less than three spots. If you draw a card from a well-shuffled standard deck of cards, the probability of drawing a picture card (king, queen, or jack) is $\frac{12}{52} = \frac{3}{13}$ because there are 52 cards altogether and 12 of them are picture cards. If a spinner has eight equal-size sectors named 1 through 8, the probability of the needle pointing to 3 is $\frac{1}{8}$.

Here are some facts about probability that you should know and examples illustrating them:

- The probability of an event is a number between 0 and 1. The probability of the impossible event is 0, while the probability of the certain event is 1. What is the probability of rolling seven spots on a die? A die doesn't have seven spots on a side, so the probability is 0.

- If you are asked about the probability of one event *or* another event occurring, add probabilities of the individual events. If a die is rolled, what is the probability that the outcome is a 1 *or* 2? The probability of each outcome is $\frac{1}{6}$ so add: $\frac{1}{6} + \frac{1}{6} = \frac{2}{6} = \frac{1}{3}$.

- If you are asked about the probability of more than one event occurring, multiply the probabilities of the individual events. If you draw two cards from a standard deck, what is the probability that both are spades? Since 13 of the 52 cards are spades, the probability that the first card is a spade is $\frac{13}{52} = \frac{1}{4}$. Now there are 51 cards left, and 12 are spades, so the probability that the second card is also a spade is $\frac{12}{51}$. The probability that both are spades is $\frac{1}{4} \cdot \frac{12}{51} = \frac{1}{17}$.

- The probability of an event *not* occurring is 1 minus the probability that the event does occur. What is the probability that on a toss of a die, the number of spots turning up is not one or two? This means the number of spots is three, four, five, or six. Therefore the probability is $\frac{4}{6} = \frac{2}{3}$. We saw from the first example that the probability of seeing one or two spots is $\frac{1}{3}$ and $1 - \frac{1}{3} = \frac{2}{3}$.

Practice

 1. What is the median of the following data set?

Value	Frequency
1	7
2	3
3	8
4	5
5	8

 2. If a family has two children, what is the probability that both are boys? (Assume that boy or girl births are equally likely.)

    (1) $\frac{1}{8}$

    (2) $\frac{1}{4}$

    (3) $\frac{1}{2}$

    (4) $\frac{2}{3}$

    (5) $\frac{3}{4}$

3. What percent of the Johnson family budget is used for housing, food, and clothing?

Johnson Family Budget (Percent of Income)

Housing	31%
Food	18%
Transportation	12%
Clothing	9%
Utilities	8%
Entertainment	6%
Insurance	4%
Miscellaneous	12%

 4. The following table shows the number of people who survived and died when the *Titanic* sank. What percent of those who died were first-class passengers?

	First	Second	Class Third	Crew	Total
Survived	202	118	178	212	710
Died	123	167	528	673	1,491
Total	325	285	706	885	2,201

(1) 5.59%

(2) 8.25%

(3) 14.8%

(4) 38.7%

(5) 62.2%

5. Which of the answer choices could not be determined from the following graph?

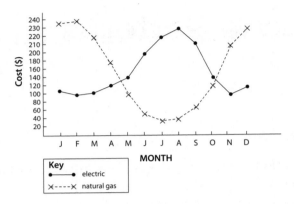

(1) Electric costs are highest in the summer months.

(2) Natural gas costs are lowest in the winter months.

(3) The total monthly costs (both natural gas and electric).

(4) The amount of natural gas used in August.

(5) The monthly differences in costs between natural gas and electric.

Answers

1. The median of a data set is the middle value when the values are ordered from smallest to largest. There are seven 1s, three 2s, eight 3s, five 4s, and eight 5s, for a total of 31 values. The middle value is the 16th one, which, counting up, is a 3.

2. **(2)** There are four ways a family can have two children: BB, BG, GB, and GG. One of the four ($\frac{1}{4}$) consists of two boys.

3. Add the three percentages: 31%, 18%, and 9%, to get 58%.

4. **(2)** Of the 1,491 who died, 123 were first-class passengers, or 8.25%. The other choices result from calculating other incorrect percentages from the table.

5. **(4)** The amount of natural gas used cannot be calculated because the problem does not tell the cost per unit volume.

Algebra, Functions, and Patterns

In This Chapter

- Overviews of variables, order of operations, exponents, equations, functions, and word problems
- GED-like questions to practice the skills you'll be tested on
- Answers and explanations for all the questions

This chapter highlights some of the main ideas in algebra. These ideas have been selected because they are most likely to be in problems on the Math Test. No attempt is made here to cover everything that would be covered in a first- or second-year algebra course you would take in school.

Variables, Notation, and Order of Operations

Algebra gives us a general way of analyzing numbers and their relationships. Suppose, for example, you wanted to multiply a number by 2 and add 3 to the result. You could express this idea for a single number, say 5. If you multiply 5 by 2, and add 3 to the result, you get 13. All this does is give you an answer to a computation. It does not express the idea of multiplying by 2, then adding 3.

One way of expressing this idea for any number is to start by calling the number x. A letter that you use to stand for a number is called a *variable*. To show that you multiply x by 2, write $2x$. When multiplying a number and a variable, no dot or times sign is necessary. The number 2 is called a *coefficient*.

To show that you add 3 to the result, write $2x + 3$. This is called an *expression*. Other examples of expressions are $y^2 + 5$, $3 - \frac{2}{5}w$, $2x - 1$, and $6x^2 - x + 2$.

> **DEFINITION**
>
> A **variable** is a letter that stands for a number. When a number and variable are multiplied, the number is called the **coefficient.** An **expression** is a number, a variable, or the result of adding, subtracting, multiplying, dividing, or applying exponents to numbers and variables.

How do we know that $2x + 3$ means multiply a number by 2, then add 3, instead of add 3 to number, then multiply the result by 2? Mathematicians agreed long ago to a convention called *order of operations*. This convention established a set order in which addition, subtraction, multiplication, division, and applying exponents are done.

The convention for ordering math operations has the acronym PEMDAS. Let's first look at the MDAS part. These four letters stand for multiplication, division, addition, and subtraction. Of these four, M and D have the same status and are done first, from left to right. The A and S also have the same status and are done next, left to right. The following examples will help clarify these ideas:

- $5 \times 4 \div 10 = 20 \div 10 = 2$

  (Multiply 5 times 4 to get 20; then divide 20 by 10 to get 2.)

- $12 \div 2 \times 6 = 6 \times 6 = 36$

- $5 + 4 - 6 = 9 - 6 = 3$

- $2 - 6 + 4 - 12 = -4 + 4 - 12 = 0 - 12 = -12$

The MD combination precedes the AS combination in PEMDAS because all multiplication and division must take place before any addition and subtraction. The following examples illustrate this:

- $3 \times 5 + 2 = 15 + 2 = 17$

  (Multiply 3 times 5 to get 15; then add 2 to get 17. <u>Do not</u> add 5 and 2 first to get 7, then multiply by 3 to get 21.)

- $8 + 3 \times 5 - 10 \div 2 = 8 + 15 - 5 = 23 - 5 = 18$

- $3 - 2 \times 8 \div 4 + 6 = 3 - 16 \div 4 + 6 = 3 - 4 + 6 = -1 + 6 = 5$

The E in PEMDAS stands for exponents. Recall that an exponent is a raised number that means the number just to its left is multiplied by itself that many times. For example, $2^3 = 2 \times 2 \times 2$, which equals 8. The expression 2^3 is read "two to the third power." E precedes MDAS because all exponents should be calculated before multiplication, division, addition, or subtraction. Again, some examples:

- $2 \times 3^2 = 2 \times 9 = 18$

  (Raise 3 to the second power first to get 9; then multiply 9 by 2 to get 18. <u>Do not</u> multiply 2 times 3 to get 6, then raise 6 to the power 2.)

- $5 - 6 \times 2^3 = 5 - 6 \times 8 = 5 - 48 = -43$

HEADS UP!

When a variable is raised to the first power, don't write the power 1 (for example, $x^1 = x$).

Finally, P in PEMDAS stands for parentheses. Perform all operations within parentheses first. More examples illustrate this convention:

- $3 \times (1 + 4)^2 = 3 \times 5^2 = 3 \times 25 = 75$

  (Add the 1 and 4 in parentheses first to get 5. Then raise 5 to the second power to get 25. Then multiply 25 by 3 to get 75.)

- $6 + (3 \times 4)^2 = 6 + 12^2 = 6 + 144 = 150$

Let's look at the meaning of a few more expressions with PEMDAS in mind, this time with variables:

- $(x + 3)^2$. Add 3 to the number that x stands for, then square the result. This is not the same as squaring x, squaring 3, and adding the results. See why not by trying it for $x = 1$! This is probably the most common mistake made in all of algebra—all because the PEMDAS convention was not followed.

- $5 - 2x$. This is not equal to $3x$ because you have to multiply the number x by 2 before subtracting the result from 5.

- $7x^2$. Because exponents come before multiplication, the exponent 2 means square the number x first, then multiply the result by 7. If x were the number 2, then $7x^2 = 7 \times 2^2 = 7 \times 4 = 28$ and not $(7 \times 2)^2 = 14^2 = 196$.

Evaluating and Simplifying Expressions

An expression is any arrangement of numbers and variables. It's important to realize that an expression is not an equation because there is no equal sign. We'll get to equations in the next section.

When you *evaluate an expression*, you are given a number to substitute for the variable. Then you do the calculations following the order of operations just described. Here are a few examples:

- Evaluate $6x - 5$ if $x = 2$.

$$6x - 5$$
$$= 6(2) - 5$$
$$= 12 - 5$$
$$= 7$$

- Evaluate $x^2 - 3x + 4$ if $x = -1$.

$$x^2 - 3x + 4$$
$$= (-1)^2 - 3(-1) + 4$$
$$= 1 + 3 + 4$$
$$= 8$$

You may be asked to simplify an expression—literally, make an expression look "simpler." One way of simplifying is by adding or subtracting like terms. The following examples illustrate this idea:

- Simplify $2x + 3x$. The expression $2x + 3x$ consists of the like terms $2x$ and $3x$. They are like terms because they consist of the same variable x (raised to the same power 1).

- Simplify $6y - y$. You have to be careful here because you can't just subtract $y - y$ if you follow the order of operations (because you have to multiply the first y by 6 first). Think of y as $1 \times y$, so $6y - 1y = 5y$.

- Simplify $3x^2 + 5x$. This can't be simplified because x is raised to two different powers (2 and 1).

A second way of simplifying an expression is to combine exponents. Remember, an exponent is simply a raised number that counts the number of times another number is multiplied, such as $3^3 = 3 \times 3 \times 3 = 27$. If you multiply 3^3 by 3^2, you are multiplying 3 five times because $(3 \times 3 \times 3) \times (3 \times 3) = 3 \times 3 \times 3 \times 3 \times 3$. When you multiply two expressions that have the same base raised to powers, add the powers. This general property can be written as $a^m \times a^n = a^{m+n}$. In the problem just discussed, $a = 3$, $m = 3$, and $n = 2$.

Another way exponents can be combined is if you have a "power to a power," such as $(x^3)^2$. This means $x^3 \times x^3$ (x^3 multiplied twice) which, by the previous property, is x^6. Multiply the powers ($3 \times 2 = 6$) when you have a power to a power. Stated in general, this property is $(a^m)^n = a^{mn}$. In the example just discussed, $a = x$, $m = 3$, and $n = 2$.

The final property of exponents is for division. Suppose you are asked to simplify $\dfrac{x^6}{x^3}$.

In this case, you subtract the exponents to get x^3. This is because three of the six factors of x in the numerator cancel with the three factors of x in the denominator, leaving three factors of x in the numerator divided by 1, or x^3.

Solving Linear Equations and Inequalities

An *equation* is a statement that says one quantity equals another. Equations can be true or false. The equation $2 + 2 = 4$ is a true equation, while $2 + 3 = 4$ is a false equation. An equation with a variable in it is neither true nor false: $2x - 7 = 11$ is neither true nor false. If $x = 9$, the equation is true because $2(9) - 7 = 18 - 7 = 11$, but if x is any other number, the equation is false.

A *solution* is a number that makes an equation true (satisfies the equation) when you substitute it for the variable. Figuring out what number makes an equation true is called *solving* an equation. An equation is called *linear* if the variable is raised to the first power (has no exponent).

Some equations can be easily solved by inspection. For example, when you look at the equation $6x = 30$, think what number multiplied by 6 makes 30. The answer is 5, so $x = 5$. When you have to solve an equation in a multiple-choice format, you can substitute each answer choice until you find the one that works (called *backsolving*). Backsolving doesn't help, however, if the solution to the equation doesn't answer the question, or if the question is not in multiple-choice format.

Fortunately, there is a more structured method for solving any linear equation. Let's look at a specific example to illustrate the method. Solve the equation $5x + 2 = 17$.

Think of the two sides of the equation as scales and the = sign as a balance point. Take 2 away from both sides, and you still have balance, so the second equation reads $5x = 15$. The equations $5x + 2 = 17$ and $5x = 15$ are called equivalent equations because they have the same solutions. Divide both sides of this equation by 5. This maintains the balance, and the new equivalent equation reads $x = 3$, the solution. This process *transforms* the original equation to one whose solution is evident. While not necessary, it's best to always isolate the variable on the left side when you solve an equation.

DEFINITION

An equation is **transformed** if you add a number to both sides, subtract a number from both sides, multiply both sides by a number, or divide both sides by a number. When you transform an equation, you get an equivalent equation.

We already learned about proportions as a special type of equation in Chapter 28. A proportion is an equation that says two ratios are equal, such as $\frac{3}{8} = \frac{6}{16}$. When you are asked to solve a proportion, one of the four numbers is unknown and represented as x. For example, solve $\frac{2}{7} = \frac{x}{21}$. Cross-multiply to get $7x = 42$ and divide both sides by 7 to get $x = 6$.

Look at a few more examples:

- $2x - 3 = 7$. Add 3 to both sides to get $2x = 10$. Divide both sides by 2 to get $x = 5$.

- $8 - 3x = -1$. Subtract 8 from both sides to get $-3x = -9$. Divide both sides by -3 to get $x = 3$.

An inequality is a statement that says one expression is smaller or larger than another. An example of simple inequality is $x < 3$ (a number is less than 3). Just as with equations, an inequality may be true or it may be false. A solution to an inequality is a number that when substituted for x makes the inequality true. The inequality $x < 3$ has an infinite number of solutions: 2, 1, 0, −15, and 2.9, to name a few. This is different from equations because all the equations we have seen so far only have one solution.

There are three other inequalities besides <. These are ≤ (less than or equal to), > (greater than), and ≥ (greater than or equal to). The difference between $x < 3$ and $x ≤ 3$ is that 3 is not a solution to the first inequality, but it is a solution to the second one: 3 is less than or equal to 3 because it equals 3.

The inequality $x < 3$ is already solved because the solutions are evident (all numbers less than 3). Suppose instead that you had the task of solving the inequality $4x - 5 < 7$. You could solve this just as you would solve the corresponding equation $4x - 5 = 7$. First add 5 to both sides, with the result $4x < 12$. Then divide both sides by 4 to get $x < 3$.

Solving inequalities is just like solving equations, with one important difference. When you multiply or divide both sides of an inequality by a negative number, you must change the direction of the inequality. This is because $3 < 4$, but when you multiply or divide both sides by -1, $-3 > -4$. For example, suppose you want to solve the inequality $-5x < 20$. To get x by itself on the left side, divide both sides by -5. The result is the inequality $x > -4$.

GOOD IDEA

As with equations, it's best to isolate the variable on the left side of the inequality. For example, $7 < 3x + 2$ should be changed to $3x + 2 > 7$.

The following examples illustrate solving inequalities:

- $6x + 1 > 13$. Subtract 1 from both sides to get $6x > 12$. Then divide both sides by 6 to get $x > 2$.

- $8 - 5x \geq -2$. Subtract 8 from both sides to get $-5x \geq -10$. Then divide both sides by -5 to get $x \leq 2$.

- $x - 5 < 3x - 5$. Add 5 to both sides to get $x < 3x$. Subtract $3x$ from both sides to get $-2x < 0$. Divide both sides by -2 to get $x > 0$.

HEADS UP!

Zero divided by any number except 0 is 0. You can't divide any number by 0.

You may be asked to graph the solutions to an inequality on a number line. Again, consider $x < 3$. Recall that the values increase as you move from left to right on a number line. Since the solutions are all numbers less than 3, you want to show all numbers to the left of 3 on the graph. The open circle on the following graph shows that 3 is *not* on the graph. The arrowhead pointing to the left shows that the graph continues indefinitely in that direction.

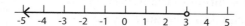

Functions

A *function* is an equation that relates two variables. The equation tells you how to get the value of one variable (the output) if you know the value of the other variable (the input). The output variable is usually called y and the input variable x.

> **DEFINITION**
>
> A **function** is an equation that tells you how to calculate the value of one variable if you know the value of another. Such an equation will always begin with $y =$.

An example of a function is $y = 2x - 6$. When $x = 1$, substitute 1 into the equation for x to get $y = -4$, and when $x = 2$, $y = -2$. A table of values for the function is a list of x values together with the y values calculated using the function equation. Which, or how many, x values doesn't matter. We just want enough values to detect a pattern that illustrates the relationship between x and y. Here is a table of values for the function $y = 2x - 6$:

x	y
−2	−10
−1	−8
0	−6
1	−4
2	−2
3	0

This table of values exhibits a definite pattern: each time x goes up by 1, y goes up by 2.

A function can be graphed on the coordinate plane like those discussed in Chapter 29. Plot each ordered pair: (−2,−10), (−1,−8), etc. Note that these five points seem to line up. If you plotted points in between these (by using fraction values for x), they too would fall right in line. The reason why this happens is because $y = 2x - 6$ is an example of a *linear function*—its graph is a line. Other examples of linear functions are $y = -2x + 5$ and $y = \dfrac{2}{3}x + 5$.

DEFINITION

If x is raised to the power 1 and not to any higher power, a function is called **linear**.

It is useful to be able to talk about linear functions as a group, rather than specific linear functions. For example, we could talk about the function $y = 5x - 4$ or about the function $y = -2x + 1$ by talking about the function $y = mx + b$. In the first case, $m = 5$ and $b = -4$, while in the second case, $m = -2$ and $b = 1$. The two numbers in each of the linear functions are the number that multiplies x and the number added or subtracted. Mathematicians agreed to use the letters m and b. They are variables because they are letters that stand for numbers, but they are different from x and y because they don't change for a given function. They are called *parameters* instead of variables. Thus, $y = mx + b$ is the equation of any linear function.

DEFINITION

A **parameter** is a letter that stands for a value that defines a specific function.

The parameter m is called the *slope*, which was discussed in Chapter 29. The slope of the function $y = 2x - 6$ is 2. The slope tells you how y changes when x increases by 1. In this equation y goes up by 2 when x goes up by 1. If the slope were -2, y would go down by 2 when x increases by 1. If the slope were a fraction such as $\frac{2}{3}$, y would increase by 2 when x increases by 3.

Besides the slope, two other aspects of a line that are of interest are the points where the line crosses the two axes. Since $y = b$ when $x = 0$ in $y = mx + b$, $(0,b)$ is on both the line and the y axis. Therefore the point $(0,b)$ is the point where the line crosses the y axis, called the *y-intercept*. In the equation $y = 2x - 6$, the y-intercept is -6 ($b = -6$).

The x-intercept—the point where the line crosses the x axis—is the value of x when $y = 0$. For the function $y = 2x - 6$, the equation is $0 = 2x - 6$. Solve this equation for x and conclude that the x-intercept is 3.

The intercepts are shown for the equation $y = 2x - 6$ in the following figure.

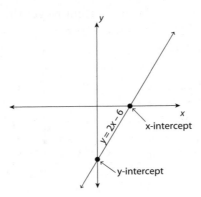

Let's look at some sample linear functions:

- $y = -2x + 3$. The slope is -2 and the y-intercept is 3. We can graph this line by first plotting the y-intercept at $(0,3)$. Since the slope is -2, you can get a second point by starting at $(0,3)$ and moving 2 units down and 1 unit right to the point $(1,1)$. Since you know the graph is going to be a line, you only need to plot two points to draw the line. Here is the graph of $y = -2x + 3$:

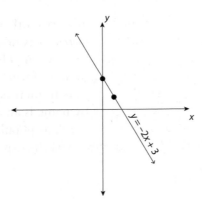

$y = \dfrac{3}{4}x - 1$. Plot the point $(0,-1)$, the y-intercept. From that point, move three spaces up and four spaces to the right to get the second point $(4,2)$. The graph of this line is shown in the next figure.

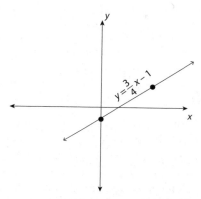

Functions can be used to represent real life behavior. For example, if you sell pencils for 10 cents each, the amount of money you make is a function of the number of pencils you sell. The formula in this case is $y = .1x$, where x is the number of pencils you sell and y is the amount of money (in $) you make. We'll see more real-life functions in the practice test (see Chapter 33).

For the GED, you need to be able to recognize two other types of functions by looking at their equations. In a *quadratic function*, x is raised to the second power. An example of a quadratic function is $y = 2x^2 - 5x + 6$. The distance an object falls to the ground is a quadratic function of the amount of time it falls. This is not a linear function, because gravity causes falling objects to increase their speed as they fall. A third type of function you should know by name is an *exponential function*. Such functions are used to represent phenomena such as population growth and the decay of nuclear waste. In an exponential function, x is the exponent. An example of an exponential function is $y = 2^x$.

DEFINITION

A **quadratic function** is an equation with y on one side and x^2 as part of the other side. An **exponential function** is an equation with y on one side and an expression with x in an exponent on the other.

Solving Word Problems

We can define a word problem as a math problem that contains words beyond those that tell you what to do, such as add, multiply, simplify, or solve. These problems either contain additional math terminology, such as "consecutive integers" or "stories" that have to be interpreted mathematically.

This section examines a variety of word problems that might be encountered on the GED.

Consecutive Integers

Consecutive integers are, loosely speaking, whole integers "in a row." You have a starting number, and you count up one number at a time until it's time to stop. Examples: 3, 4, 5, and 6 are four consecutive integers starting with the number 3; and –4, –3, and –2 are three consecutive integers starting with –4.

Suppose you were asked to find three consecutive integers with a sum of 45. You could guess and check: 10 + 11 + 12 = 33, which is too small. This method might take many tries to get the correct three numbers. Eventually you would see that 14 + 15 + 16 = 45. A more reliable method for solving this problem is to let the variable n stand for the starting number. The next number is one more than n, or $n + 1$, and the third number is one more than that, or $n + 2$. The three numbers n, $n + 1$, and $n + 2$ add up to 45, so $n + n + 1 + n + 2 = 45$. The solution n to this equation and the next two numbers provide an answer to the original question.

To solve this equation, you should first simplify the left side. The new equation would be $3n + 3 = 45$. You can then subtract 3 from both sides, getting $3n = 42$ and then divide both sides by 3 to get $n = 14$. The three consecutive integers that add to 45 are 14, 15, and 16.

In other examples of this section the emphasis will be on setting up, and not on solving, an equation whose solution will lead to an answer to the question.

Geometry Problems

Geometry word problems usually require you to use a formula for length, area, or volume, but in reverse. For example, instead of being given a length and a width and being asked to find the area, you are told what the area is and asked to find the length and width. The following illustrate this idea:

- The area of a circle is 400 in². To the nearest tenth of an inch, what is the diameter of this circle?

  Use the formula sheet (see Chapter 32) to find the formula for the area of a circle with radius is area = π r^2, where r stands for the radius.

  Substitute 400 for area and 3.14 for π. The resulting equation is 400 = 3.14 · r^2. To get the value of r, divide 400 by 3.14 and round the answer to the nearest tenth: 127.4 inches. But wait a minute! This is the radius, not the diameter, which is double the radius of 11.3. The diameter is two times that or 22.6 inches.

HEADS UP!

Don't assume that the solution to an equation is always the answer to the problem.

- A rectangle is 4 feet longer than it is wide. The perimeter of the rectangle is 36 feet. What are the dimensions of the rectangle?

  Let x stand for the length of the shorter side. Then $x + 4$ is the length of the longer side. Use the formula sheet to find the formula for the perimeter of a rectangle as twice the length of the shorter side plus twice the length of the longer side. This gives you the equation: 36 = 2x + 2 (x + 4).

  In this equation, 2 (x + 4) = 2x + 8, so 36 = 2x + 2x + 8. Combine 2x + 2x = 4x and subtract 8 from both sides to get 28 = 4x. Then divide both sides by 4 to get x = 7. The dimensions of the rectangle are 7 by 11 (7 + 4).

Motion Problems

A motion problem is one that relates distance, speed, and time. The primary formula is $d = rt$, where d = distance, r = speed, and t = time. The two related formulas are $r = \dfrac{d}{t}$ and $t = \dfrac{d}{r}$. These formulas express familiar ideas if you drive an automobile. If you travel for 3 hours at an average speed of 50 miles per hour, you will drive 150 miles (150 = 50 × 3). If you drive 60 miles in 2 hours, your average speed is 30 miles per hour ($\dfrac{60}{2}$). And finally, if you travel 90 miles at an average speed of 45 miles per hour, it will take you 2 hours ($\dfrac{90}{45}$).

- A train leaves the station at 10 A.M. traveling at an average speed of 50 miles per hour. Two hours later, another train leaves the same station on the same track traveling at an average speed of 70 miles per hour. At what time will the second train catch up with the first?

When the second train catches up with the first, the two trains will have gone the same distance, but the second train's time of travel is 2 hours less. The distance traveled by the first train is $50t$, and the distance traveled by the second train is $70 (t - 2)$. Since these distances are equal, we have the equation $50t = 70 (t - 2)$. This is equivalent to $50t = 70t - 140$. Subtract $70t$ from both sides to get $-20t = -140$, then divide both sides by -20 to get $t = 7$. The second train will catch up with the first one 7 hours after the first one leaves the station, or at 5 P.M.

- A husband and wife have an argument and walk away from each other in opposite directions. The husband walks at an average speed of 4 miles per hour, while his wife walks at an average speed of 3 miles per hour. How far apart will they be in 30 minutes?

Thirty minutes is one half of an hour, so $t = .5$. The distance the husband walks is $4 \times .5 = 2$ miles, and the distance his wife walks is $3 \times .5 = 1.5$ miles. Since they're walking in *opposite* directions, they will be 3.5 (2 + 1.5) miles apart in 30 minutes.

These examples are all solved using algebra, and they illustrate the sequence of steps one should follow when trying to solve any word problem:

1. Be absolutely clear about what the problem wants you to find.

2. Think about what kinds of things you need to know to answer the question in the problem. Sometimes this requires looking up or knowing a formula.

3. Match what you need to know with the information the problem gives you. If something is missing, it's probably the variable that stands for what the problem is asking you to find (usually called x).

4. Write an equation that relates the quantity you are to find with other quantities in the problem.

5. Solve the equation.

6. Reread what the problem asks you to find, and make sure you've answered the question.

Unfortunately, word problems are not like equations. There is no specific sequence of steps that can be used to solve every word problem the same way. The more experience you have translating words to math symbols, the better you'll be doing word problems.

Practice

 1. What is the product of $x^5 \times x^3$?

    (1) x^2

    (2) x^8

    (3) x^{15}

    (4) $2x^8$

    (5) $2x^{15}$

 2. Which inequality is graphed on the number line?

    (1) $x = 2$

    (2) $x < 2$

    (3) $x \leq 2$

    (4) $x > 2$

    (5) $x \geq 2$

 3. Ten less than three times a number equals one more than two times the same number. What is the number?

    (1) 2

    (2) 2.2

    (3) 5.5

    (4) 9

    (5) 11

4. Solve for x: $3x - 1 = 4(5 - x)$

    (1) 1

    (2) $\dfrac{10}{7}$

    (3) 3

    (4) 5.25

    (5) –21

 5. What is the next number in the sequence 3, –6, 12, –24, …?

    (1) 12

    (2) 21

    (3) 36

    (4) 48

    (5) 52

Answers

1. **(2)** When multiplying expressions with the same base, add the exponents. In this case, 5 + 3 = 8. Answer choice (1) subtracts exponents (the rule for division), while answer choice (3) multiplies exponents. Answer choices (4) and (5) would appeal to those who believe that the presence of x in both factors means the product involves $2x$.

2. **(5)** The circle over 2 is filled in ($x = 2$) and the arrow is pointing to the right ($x > 2$), so $x \geq 2$. The graph of answer choice (1) would be a filled in circle over the 2. Answer choices (2) and (4) would have open circles because 2 would not be included in these graphs. Answer choice (3) would show the heavy arrow pointing to the left.

3. **(5)** Ten less than three times a number is written as $3x - 10$. One more than two times the same number is $2x + 1$. You must solve the equation $3x - 10 = 2x + 1$. First add 10 to both sides to get $3x = 2x + 11$. Then subtract $2x$ from both sides to get $1x = 11$, or $x = 11$. The other answer choices result from incorrect translations from words to symbols or errors solving the equation.

4. **(3)** First distribute the 4 on the right side of the equation: $3x - 1 = 20 - 4x$. Then add $4x$ to both sides: $7x - 1 = 20$. Add 1 to both sides: $7x = 21$. Finally, divide both sides by 7: $x = 3$. Answer choices (1), (2), and (4) result from distributing incorrectly. Answer choice (5) is the result if you subtract $4x$ from $3x$ instead of adding.

5. **(4)** The pattern in this sequence is to multiply each number by -2 to get the next number. Other answer choices are based on patterns that don't work for all numbers in the given sequence.

Taking the Math Test

In This Chapter

- Overview of the Math Test
- Description of the answer sheet
- Description of the formula sheet
- Use of the Casio *fx*-260 calculator

The Math Test has 50 questions to be completed in 90 minutes. It consists of two 45-minute parts, each with 25 questions. You may use a calculator—a Casio *fx*-260 supplied by the testing center—on Part I only.

Each part of the test is preceded by front material consisting of the following:

- An answer sheet
- Directions for that part
- Directions for using the Casio *fx*-260 calculator (Part I only)
- Directions and an example for filling out the standard grid
- Directions and an example for filling out a coordinate plane grid
- A formula sheet

The Answer Sheet

There is an answer sheet for each 25 question part of the Math Test. An answer sheet consists of the numbers 1 through 25, each followed by five circles (multiple choice), a blank standard grid (for a student-constructed single-number answer), or a blank coordinate plane grid (for a student-constructed ordered pair answer).

Forty of the fifty questions are in multiple-choice format. Each question in this format has five answer choices. You are asked to choose the best of the five answer choices and use a No. 2 pencil to fill in the corresponding circle.

Answers to the remaining 10 questions must be constructed by test-takers. Answers that consist of a single number are entered on a standard grid, as explained in this chapter. The other type of constructed answer is an ordered pair which is entered on a coordinate plane grid, also explained in this chapter.

Directions

The directions for both Parts I and II are identical, except that Part I allows the use of a calculator and Part II does not. These directions tell you not to write in the test booklet and state that the test administrator will give you scrap paper for hand calculations. The directions also tell you not to make stray marks on or fold/crease the answer sheet, as the answer sheet is scored by machine.

Calculator Directions

Even if you have experience using calculators, you will benefit on the Math Test by familiarizing yourself with the Casio *fx*-260. Directions for using this calculator are included on a page following the directions for Part I of the Math Test. The directions explain how to turn the calculator on and off and how to use the AC (all clear) key. It also explains how to use parentheses, find square roots, and enter negative numbers. You can go online to view an instructional video on how to use this calculator. The following paragraphs give a more detailed description of how to operate the Casio *fx*-260 calculator.

The *fx*-260 is a scientific calculator. As such, it has many more keys than you would ever need to use on the GED. As you can see in the following photo of the keyboard, the lower left consists of the number keypad, while the lower right has the arithmetic keys and = sign. There are only a few keys in the top three rows that you may need to use.

The Casio fx-260 calculator.

The left-most key in the third row (+/-) changes the sign of a number that has been entered. For example, if you want to enter the number –6, first key 6, then key +/-, and –6 will appear on the keyboard.

The left-most key in the second row is used to enter fractions and mixed numbers. For example, to enter the mixed number $3\frac{1}{2}$, key 3, then $a\frac{b}{c}$, followed by 1, then $a\frac{b}{c}$, and finally 2 $a\frac{b}{c}$. This will show on the screen as a 3 followed by a backwards capital L, followed by a 1, followed by a backwards L, followed by a 2.

You can add, subtract, multiply, or divide two numbers entered as fractions, decimals, or whole numbers. The answer will only display as a fraction if both numbers are entered as fractions. Otherwise, it will display as a decimal.

The left-most key in the first row is the SHIFT key. This key activates the gold-colored command that appears above any key. You will need this key to calculate the decimal approximation to a square root ($\sqrt{\ }$). For example, to get the decimal approximation to $\sqrt{6}$, key 6, then SHIFT followed by x^2 (thereby activating the $\sqrt{\ }$ command rather than the x^2 command).

The SHIFT key used in conjunction with the $a\frac{b}{c}$ key changes a mixed number to an improper fraction. You may need to use this feature if your answer to a grid-in question is a mixed number, since you can only grid in a decimal or improper fraction.

The Standard Grid

The standard grid appears on the answer sheet when a single number is constructed by a test-taker. If your constructed answer is a single number, it must be positive, and it may be gridded as a decimal or fraction but *not* as a mixed number. There can be more than one acceptable way to grid in a correct answer. For example, equivalent answers $\frac{3}{5}$ and .6 are gridded in several different correct ways in the following figure. Answers do not have to be left- or right-justified, and trailing zeros may or may not be included.

Test-takers may also have to construct answers that are ordered pairs. Both numbers in an ordered pair must be integers. Ordered pairs are graphed by bubbling in the appropriate circle on a coordinate plane grid. An example showing an unmarked coordinate plane grid (a) and a coordinate plane grid with the point (3,–4) gridded in (b) is shown on the next page.

(a)   (b)

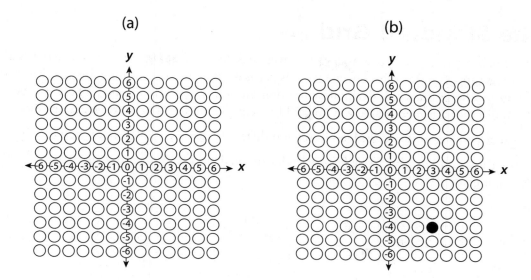

Explanations of how to grid answers of both types are provided in the pages preceding each part of the Math Test.

Formula Sheet

As mentioned previously, each part of the Math Test includes a formula sheet, shown on the next page. This sheet includes the following formulas:

- Area, perimeter, circumference, and volume of geometric shapes
- The distance between two points on the coordinate plane
- The slope of a line containing two points on the coordinate plane
- The mean and median of a data set
- Simple interest
- Distance as a function of speed and time
- Total cost as a function of number of units and price per unit

FORMULA SHEET

Formulas

Area of *a*:

Square	area = side^2
Rectangle	area = length × width
Parallelogram	area = base × height
Triangle	area = $\frac{1}{2}$ × base × height
Trapezoid	area = $\frac{1}{2}$ × (base$_1$ + base$_2$) × height
Circle	area = π × radius^2 (π is approx. 3.14)

Perimeter of *a*:

Square	perimeter = 4 × side
Rectangle	perimeter = 2 × length + 2 × width
Triangle	perimeter = side$_1$ + side$_2$ + side$_3$

Circumference of *a*:

Circumference = π × diameter circle

Volume of *a*:

Cube	volume = side^3
Rectangular solid	volume = length × width × height
Square pyramid	volume = (1/3) × base edge^2 × height
Cylinder	volume = π × radius^2 × height
Cone	volume = (1/3) × π × radius^2 × height

Coordinate Geometry

distance between points = $\sqrt{(x_2 - x_1)^2 + (y_2 - y_1)^2}$; (x_1, y_1) and

(x_2, y_2) are two points on a plane slope of a line = $\dfrac{y_2 - y_1}{x_2 - x_1}$; (x_1, y_1)

and (x_2, y_2) are two points on the line

Pythagorean Relationship	$c^2 = a^2 + b^2$; a and b are the legs and c the hypotenuse of a right triangle
Measures of Central Tendency	$mean = \dfrac{x_1 + x_2 + \cdots + x_n}{n}$, where the x's are the values for which a mean is desired, and n is the number of values
	median = the middle value of an odd number of scores or the average of the two middle values of an even number of scores
Simple Interest	interest = principal × rate × time
Distance	distance = rate × time
Total Cost	total cost = # of units × cost per unit

Problems that require the use of formulas from the formula sheet are most likely to be in Part I of the Math Test (which allows the use of a calculator). Examples of substituting of numbers into a formula and performing the computation on a calculator are illustrated in the solutions to the problems on the practice test in the next chapter.

Math Practice Test

This chapter provides a 25-question, half-length practice test. The various ways that the questions are broken down reflect roughly the same percentages as the actual Math Test. Calculators may be used on 13 of the questions only. This practice test does not separate problems into Part I (calculator allowed) and Part II (calculator not allowed) as they are on the actual Math Test. Problems in which a calculator is allowed are marked with a calculator icon.

Six questions belong to each of three of the topical categories, while seven questions belong to the fourth. Nineteen of the questions are multiple choice; four go on a standard grid; and two go on a coordinate plane grid.

You should allow yourself 45 minutes for the practice test, and you should not use a calculator unless the question is marked with a calculator icon. Read the explanations of all the problems you got wrong. If you are still uncertain about how to get the correct answer, go back to the chapter covering that topic and reread the appropriate material.

There are many online resources that you can check as well. These provide instruction, practice questions, or both. Just enter "math ged" in your search engine. One site we recommend is PBS Literacy Link (http:litlink.ket.org). Keep in mind, though, that the actual GED Tests are paper-and-pencil tests like those in this book and cannot be taken on a computer.

Instructions

The Math Test is designed to measure your understanding of general math skills and concepts. You will have 45 minutes to complete the 25 questions on this practice test. Work carefully, but don't spend too much time on any one question. If you are having trouble with a question, make the best guess you can and move on. Your score is based on the number of correct answers; there is no penalty for guessing.

When taking the practice test, try to simulate actual test conditions. Get a timing device of some sort and a couple of No. 2 pencils with good erasers. Go to a place where you won't be interrupted and follow test instructions. Start the timer after you've read the instructions and are ready to begin the first question.

Go on to the next page when you are ready to begin.

1. A map has a scale of 2 inches equals 10 miles. If the map distance between Center City and Sun City is 5 inches, approximately how far apart are the cities? Mark your answer on the standard grid.

  2. The shadow of a woman standing next to a tree is 3 feet long, and the shadow of the tree is 12 feet long. If the woman is 5 feet, 6 inches tall, how tall is the tree?

(1) 15 ft

(2) 22 ft

(3) 25 ft

(4) 28 ft

(5) 32 ft

3. A number cube is rolled. What is the probability that the side facing up is less than 3?

(1) $\frac{1}{6}$

(2) $\frac{1}{4}$

(3) $\frac{1}{3}$

(4) $\frac{1}{2}$

(5) $\frac{2}{3}$

4. Simplify x^3x^3.

   (1) x^3

   (2) x^6

   (3) $2x^6$

   (4) x^9

   (5) $2x^9$

 5. A pile of solid waste at the local landfill is cone shaped. It is 10 meters high, and the base has a diameter of 40 meters. To the nearest 10 cubic meters, what is the volume of this solid waste?

   (1) 630

   (2) 1,250

   (3) 12,560

   (4) 50,260

   (5) 150,790

 6. Paul is in the market for a new car. The sticker price for the car Paul is interested in is $22,500. One dealer offers him 15% off the sticker price. Another dealer offers him 20% off. How much money will Paul save if he buys the car from the second dealer?

   (1) $225

   (2) $450

   (3) $1,125

   (4) $3,375

   (5) $4,500

7. The heights of the five starters on the basketball team are 67 inches, 71 inches, 79 inches, 70 inches, and 79 inches. What is their median height?

(1) 67 in

(2) 71 in

(3) 79 in

(4) 70 in

(5) 72 in

 8. What is the next number in the list? 1, 1, 2, 3, 5, 8, 13, ...? Mark your answer on the standard grid.

 9. Matt's Electronics advertises big-screen TVs at 20% off. Jack's Gadgets advertises the same sets at 30% off. After you buy a discounted TV at Matt's, the cashier takes an additional 10% off at the register. Which store offers the better deal?

(1) Matt's

(2) Jack's

(3) They are the same.

(4) It depends on the original cost of the TV.

(5) You can't tell.

10. A square is to be drawn on a coordinate plane. The corners are at (–2,3), (4,3), and (4,9). Mark the fourth corner on the coordinate plane grid.

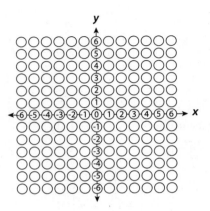

Problems 11 and 12 are based on the following table, which shows favorite colors of boys and girls.

Color	Boys	Girls	Total
Red	12	18	30
Green	7	5	12
Blue	6	8	14
White	2	4	6
Black	5	3	8
Total	32	38	70

 11. What percent of the girls chose blue as their favorite color?

(1) 11%

(2) 21%

(3) 47%

(4) 57%

(5) Can't be determined

12. What percent of those choosing green were girls?

(1) 7%

(2) 13%

(3) 17%

(4) 27%

(5) 42%

 13. Show the location of the *y*-intercept of the graph of $3x + y = 7$. Mark your answer on the coordinate plane grid.

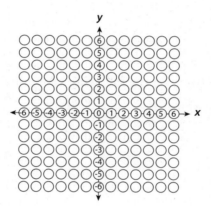

 14. Alex and his girlfriend Alana went shopping at the mall, which is 20 miles from their house. If it took them 40 minutes to get there, what was their average speed in miles per hour?

(1) 24 mph

(2) 30 mph

(3) 32 mph

(4) 38 mph

(5) 40 mph

15. Mr. Rotundo left a large piece of property with a creek running through it to his sons. The property is rectangular in shape and the creek runs diagonally from one corner of the property to one of the long sides, as shown in the diagram below. The elder son gets the larger piece of land, while the younger son gets the smaller piece. Using the dimensions shown in this figure, determine how much more land the older son got than the younger.

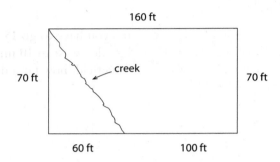

(1) 2,450 sq ft

(2) 4,500 sq ft

(3) 6,000 sq ft

(4) 7,000 sq ft

(5) 8,000 sq ft

16. Otis bought a table that was discounted by 33%. If t represents the original price of the table, what was Otis's cost?

(1) .67t

(2) t + .33

(3) t − .33

(4) t + .33t

(5) .33t

17. The ratio of Chris's age to Michelle's age is 5:3. In 10 years, this ratio will

(1) be 50:30.

(2) be 15:13.

(3) remain at 5:3.

(4) get smaller.

(5) get larger.

 18. To drive from Silver City to Urbana, you have to go 15 miles due north to Wakefield. Then you turn left and go due west to 10 miles. If there were a road directly from Silver City to Wakefield, how far a drive would this be (to the nearest mile)?

(1) 15 mi

(2) 16 mi

(3) 17 mi

(4) 18 mi

(5) 19 mi

 19. The following table shows the percentage of those in each class who would recommend the class to a friend. Which conclusion *cannot* be drawn from the information?

Class	% Recommending
Biology	88%
British Literature	46%
Calculus	38%
Chemistry	72%
Economics	61%
Psychology	71%

(1) Psychology is the third-highest recommended course.

(2) Chemistry and Economics are recommended at about equal percentages.

(3) Less than half those who took Calculus would recommend it to a friend.

(4) More people would recommend British Literature than Economics.

(5) A higher percentage recommended Biology than any other course.

20. Lucy is an American traveling to Paris. She learns that the exchange rate is 0.75 euros per dollar. When she returns, she has 203 euros in her wallet. About how much money is that, to the nearest dollar?

(1) $95

(2) $102

(3) $203

(4) $271

(5) $432

 21. Sharon wants to paint the study in her house. This room is rectangular, 12 feet by 14 feet, with a 7-foot ceiling. A gallon of paint covers 300 square feet, and she will need two coats. How many gallons of paint will Sharon need to buy? Mark your answer on the standard grid.

	⊘	⊘	⊘	
⊙	⊙	⊙	⊙	⊙
⓪	⓪	⓪	⓪	⓪
①	①	①	①	①
②	②	②	②	②
③	③	③	③	③
④	④	④	④	④
⑤	⑤	⑤	⑤	⑤
⑥	⑥	⑥	⑥	⑥
⑦	⑦	⑦	⑦	⑦
⑧	⑧	⑧	⑧	⑧
⑨	⑨	⑨	⑨	⑨

22. Eight cards are dealt face down on a table: two spades, three hearts, one diamond, and two clubs. A card is drawn, and it is a spade. A second card is drawn. What is the probability that it is a heart?

(1) $\frac{1}{7}$

(2) $\frac{1}{4}$

(3) $\frac{3}{8}$

(4) $\frac{3}{7}$

(5) $\frac{1}{2}$

23. If the population of a city increases by an average of 2% per year, which word describes this type of growth?

(1) Linear

(2) Quadratic

(3) Cubic

(4) Exponential

(5) Constant

 24. The half-life of radioactive material is the length of time it takes the level of radioactivity to be halved. If the half-life of a radioactive substance is 50 years, what fraction of the original amount will remain after 150 years? Mark your answer on the standard grid.

	⊘	⊘	⊘	
◯	◯	◯	◯	◯
⓪	⓪	⓪	⓪	⓪
①	①	①	①	①
②	②	②	②	②
③	③	③	③	③
④	④	④	④	④
⑤	⑤	⑤	⑤	⑤
⑥	⑥	⑥	⑥	⑥
⑦	⑦	⑦	⑦	⑦
⑧	⑧	⑧	⑧	⑧
⑨	⑨	⑨	⑨	⑨

25. Solve the equation $5x + 3 = 2x - 6$.

(1) $x = -3$

(2) $x = -1$

(3) $x = 1$

(4) $x = 3$

(5) No solution

Answers and Explanations

1. A map distance of 5 inches is 2.5 times greater than 2 inches. Therefore the actual distance is 2.5 times 10 miles, or 25 miles.

2. **(2)** Because the lengths of objects and their shadows are proportional, the easiest way to do this problem is to observe that the shadow of the tree is four times longer than the shadow of the woman, so the tree is four times taller than the woman. Four times 5 feet, 6 inches is 22 feet.

3. **(3)** A number cube has six faces, and two of them are less than 3. The probability is therefore $\frac{2}{6} = \frac{1}{3}$.

4. **(2)** $x^3 = x \times x \times x$, so $x^3 x^3 = x \times x \times x \times x \times x \times x = x^6$. Other answer choices will appeal to those who misunderstand the properties of exponents.

5. **(3)** Use the formula for the volume of a cone from the formula sheet. Since the diameter is 40 meters, the radius is 20 meters. Using 3.14 for π gives $V = \frac{1}{3}\pi r^2 h = \frac{1}{3}(3.14)(20)^2(30)$. On the Casio *fx*-260 calculator, multiply 30 times 20 times 20 again times 3.14; then hit = and divide by 3. Other answer choices will appeal to those who substitute incorrectly into the formula.

6. **(3)** The second dealer offers Paul the car for 5% less. Five percent of $22,500 is $(.05)(22,500) = \$1,125$.

7. **(2)** The median of a list of numbers is the middle number if the numbers are in order from largest to smallest (or vice versa). Ordered from largest to smallest, the numbers are 79, 79, 71, 70, 69, so 71 inches is the median height.

8. Starting with the 2, each number is the sum of the two numbers that come before it. Therefore the next number is 21.

9. **(2)** Jack's gives 30% off the original price of the TV. Matt's gives 20% off the original price and then takes 10% off the already discounted price of the TV. This latter amount is less than the 10% more that Jack's takes off the original price. Suppose, for example, that the TV costs $1,000. The discount at Jack's is $300 $(.30 \times 1,000)$. The first discount at Matt's is $200 $(.20 \times 1,000)$, reducing the price to $800. The additional 10% is off the $800. This amounts to $80 $(.10 \times 800)$, making the total discount at Matt's $280 instead of $300. Therefore, Jack's has the better deal.

10. The second point is 6 units to the right of the first, and the third point is 6 units above the second. Therefore, the fourth point should be 6 units above the first point, or at (–2,9).

11. **(2)** There were 38 girls in the survey. Of those 38, 8 chose blue as their favorite color, and 8 of 38 is 21%. Other answer choices will appeal to those who calculated other percentages from the table.

12. **(5)** Green was the favorite color of 12 of those surveyed. Of those 12, 5 were girls, and 5 of 12 is 42%. Other answer choices will appeal to those who calculated other percentages from the table.

13. The y-intercept is the value of y when x is equal to zero. If $x = 0$, the equation would read: 3 (0) + y = 7, or y = 7. The point (0,7) should be marked.

14. **(2)** Forty minutes is $\frac{40}{60}$ or $\frac{2}{3}$ of an hour. Since average speed is distance divided by time, divide 20 by $\frac{2}{3}$. To do this, multiply 20 by $\frac{3}{2}$, getting $\frac{60}{2} = 30$. It is worthwhile noting that 60 mph is a mile a minute. In this case, it took 40 minutes to go 20 miles, and this is a half mile a minute, so their average speed is 30 mph.

15. **(4)** The creek divides the property into a triangle and a trapezoid. According to the formula sheet (see Chapter 32), the area of the triangle is $\frac{1}{2}$ × (base) × (altitude) and the area of the trapezoid is $\frac{1}{2}$ × (base₁ + base₂) × (height). The figure shows that the base of the triangle is 60 feet and the altitude is 70 feet, so the area of the triangle is $\frac{1}{2}$ × (60) × (70) = 2,100. The height of the trapezoid is also 70 feet, and its two bases have lengths of 160 feet and 100 feet, so its area is $\frac{1}{2}$ × (160 + 100) × (70) = 9,100. Subtract to get 9,100 – 2,100 = 7,000 square feet.

16. **(1)** Since the table was discounted by 33%, Otis paid 100% – 33% = 67% of the original price. This is .67t.

17. **(5)** Test-takers may be tempted to choose answer (2), but this is only correct if Chris is 5 and Michelle is 3. Suppose Chris is 50 and Michelle is 30 (ratio is 5:3). Then in 10 years, Chris will be 60 and Michelle will be 40, for a ratio of 60:40, which is 3:2. If you add a positive number to both the numerator and denominator of a fraction, the value of the fraction is decreased. So even though we don't know either Chris or Michelle's age, we know that when you add a positive number to both, the ratio will get smaller.

18. **(4)** Since due north and due west form a right angle, the three cities form a right triangle. The distance from Silver City to Wakefield is the hypotenuse of this right triangle. The legs of this right triangle are 15 and 10 miles. According to the Pythagorean Theorem, hypotenuse^2 = 15^2 + 10^2, which equals 325. Therefore, the length of the direct route is $\sqrt{325} = 18$ to the nearest mile.

19. **(4)** This conclusion cannot be drawn because the table doesn't provide any information about *numbers* of people.

20. **(4)** Since each dollar is 0.75 euros, she will have more than $203. She should divide 203 by 0.75, which equals $271 to the nearest dollar.

21. Two of the walls of the study are 12 feet long and 7 feet high, and two are 14 feet long by 7 feet high. Therefore, the total area to be painted is 2 × 12 × 7 + 2 × 14 × 7, or 364 square feet. Since she's doing two coats, she will need to cover 728 square feet. Since a gallon of paint covers 300 square feet, she will need 2.3 gallons, rounded to 3 gallons of paint.

22. **(4)** After the first card is drawn, there are seven cards left: one spade, three hearts, one diamond, and two clubs. Three of these seven are hearts, so the probability of a heart is $\dfrac{3}{7}$.

23. **(4)** Two percent growth each year means each year's population is 1.02 times the previous year's population. Since you multiply to get the next year's population, the growth is called exponential.

24. Since the half-life is 50 years, the original amount will be cut in half three times in 150 years: to half in 50 years; one-quarter in 100 years; and one-eighth in 150 years. The answer is $\left(\dfrac{1}{2}\right)\left(\dfrac{1}{2}\right)\left(\dfrac{1}{2}\right) = \dfrac{1}{8}$.

25. **(1)** A quick way to solve an equation in a multiple-choice problem is to backsolve—try each answer choice in the equation to see which one makes the equation true. In this case, you get the solution right away since both 5 (–3) + 3 and 2 (–3) – 6 equal –12.

Index

I

imagery, poetry, 365-368
immigrants, 125
immune system, 245
imperialism, 175-176
inclined planes, 269-271
incomplete sentences, 12-13
indefinite pronouns, 52-53
inferences, 342
infiltration, 229
inflation, 154
integers, 400-402
   consecutive, 456
integumentary system, 245
interactions, matter, 258-260
interest groups, 148-150
interjections, 20, 31-32
interrogative pronouns, 52
interruptors, 74-76
intransitive verbs, 37-38
introductory words,
  commas, 75
inverted sentences, 45
ionic bonds, 256
irregular verbs, 38-40

J–K–L

James, Henry, 66
Jefferson, Thomas, 354
judicial branch, 140-142

Kennedy, John F., 354
kinetic energy, 268
King Jr., Martin Luther, 129

Language Arts
  Reading Test, practice,
   383-396
  Writing Test, practice,
   103-115

law of gravity, 218
law of supply and demand,
  154
layers of earth, 282-283
leading zeros, 403
least common denominators,
  409
legislative branch, 141
levers, 269
limericks, 358
limited government, 140
Lincoln, Abraham, 131
linear equations, solving,
  449-451
linking verbs, 25-26
Linnaeus, Carolus, 224
liquid volume, units of, 418
lithosphere, 277-278
Louisiana Purchase, 124
Lowell, Amy, 357
lymphatic system, 245
lysosomes, 242

M

Madison, Charles A., 386
mantle, 282
market economies, 158
mass, 253
  conservation, 274-275
Math Test, 463
  answer sheet, 464
  calculators, 464-467
  formula sheets, 467-469
  practice, 471-484
matter, 253
  interactions, 258-260
  properties, 262-264
Mayan civilization, 171
McCrae, John, 366
means, 440
means of the proportion,
  411-412

measurements, 417
  customary, 417
  metric, 417
  units of liquid volume,
   418
  units of temperature,
   419-420
  units of weight, 419
medians, 440
meiosis, 246-249
membranes, cells, 242
Mendel, Gregor, 219, 246
Mendeleev, Dmitri, 219, 254
metaphase (mitosis), 248
metaphors, 354-356
meteorology, 277, 283-284
metric measurements,
  417-418
mitochondrion, 242
mitosis, 246-249
mixtures, 259-260
modes, 441
modifiers, 68-70
molecules, 254
momentum, 265
monetary policy, 162
money economies, 154
motion, 265-266
motion problems, 457-461
multicelled organisms, 241
multiple adjectives, commas,
  75
multiplication, decimals, 405
muscular system, 245

N

natural selection, 250
nervous system, 245
neutral substances, 258
neutrons, 253-254